W.B.
YEATS

W.B. YEATS

THE MAN
AND THE MILIEU

KEITH ALLDRITT

CLARKSON POTTER / PUBLISHERS
NEW YORK

Published by Clarkson N. Potter/Publishers, 201 East 50th Street, New York, New York 10022. Member of the Crown Publishing Group.

Random House, Inc. New York, Toronto, London, Sydney, Auckland

http://randomhouse.com/

CLARKSON N. POTTER, POTTER, and colophon are trademarks of Clarkson N. Potter, Inc.

Printed in the United States of America

Design by 2b Group, Inc., N.Y.

Library of Congress Cataloging-in-Publication Data is available upon request.

ISBN 0-517-79989-8

10 9 8 7 6 5 4 3 2 1

First American Edition

For Joan once more with love

[*Contents*]

[*Illustrations*]

22. Margaret Ruddock
23. Ethel Mannin
24. Yeats with Edmund Dulac and Edith Shackleton Heald

The author and publishers would like to thank the following for permission to reproduce illustrations: Plates 1, 2, 3, 4, 5, 6, 9, 10, 11, 18, 19 and 22, The National Library of Ireland; 7, The Ulster Museum; 8, The National Gallery of Ireland; 12, 13 and 17, Anna MacBride White; 14, Anne Yeats; 15, Omar Pound; 20, The Harry Ransome Humanities Research Centre, Austin, Texas; and 24, The Huntington Library.

WILLIAM BUTLER YEATS WAS A MASTER CRAFTSMAN AND ONE OF HIS most skilful constructs was his own image. Through his autobiographies in particular, Yeats has succeeded for many years in determining how biographers have perceived him. He has been presented as he wished to be remembered, as, above all, an Irishman and a poet; a man whose nature had been determined by the almost magical qualities of his childhood in Sligo and whose character had been shaped by the influence of admirable men, one of whom was his father. John Yeats in his son's writing emerges as a witty, unusually well-read and well-connected man with a wonderful eye for a painting and an excellent ear for poetry. Just as there is a truth in Yeats's portrait of his father so there is in his depiction of himself. But in both cases it is a partial truth only. In my biography I have attempted to place William Butler Yeats in a much larger context than has been done previously and to look closely at the many aspects of his life and personality which he chose either to ignore or to reduce in importance.

In the accounts supplied by Yeats's previous biographers, notably Richard Ellman and Norman Jeffares, to both of whom I owe a debt of gratitude, we see Yeats's life as primarily a psychological journey, a spiritual, philosophical and literary progress. The individuals around him, colleagues, contemporaries, family, are subordinated to the story of Yeats's inner development. Certainly throughout his life his consciousness was singularly rich, intricate, contradictory, and as volatile as was his physical health. But his consciousness went far beyond the interior struggles and subjective feelings he so much emphasized. Yeats was, I believe, a man unusually susceptible to his surroundings and to the people in them and his life unfolded as a result of formative interaction with the personal, social, political and literary forces that confronted him.

In this biography I attempt to go beyond his interior world and to evoke and do justice to those individuals and external forces which in their turn made up part of the dialectic of Yeats's life. Yeats lived through a period of profound and unceasing change for the Western world. I have tried to place him firmly in his generation and to show how his times and the important people and places in his life affected him.

Not only Ireland but London, Paris and Mussolini's Italy contributed significantly to Yeats's development and to his art. Some of the persons who are given a new but proper prominence in this biography are the young men of the *Dublin University Review* who gave him his literary start, members of the first government of the Irish Free State headed by W.T. Cosgrave, the innovative writers who made up the Rapallo Group in the early 1930s, and the four young women who became his mistresses at the end of his life.

Looked at in these terms, a less familiar Yeats begins to appear. No longer essentially the sensitive introvert who began as the mooning dreamer and who, after a lifetime seeking philosophial and hermetic wisdom, ended as the learned sage, Yeats now shows himself to be a dedicated careerist, a man of determined self-interest, a man preoccupied with money, a seeker after social standing and a combative man with a violent temper that sustained him in many nasty quarrels. Earlier accounts, particularly Yeats's own, have down-played these characteristics. In his *Autobiographies* he wrote little or nothing about himself as a brawler and scrapper. To take just one example, he says nothing of his lifelong quarrel with his younger sister Lolly whose earnings helped to keep him as a young man and who was one of his publishers for some thirty-five years.

The arrogant, bullying, aggressive Yeats that Lolly, and some others, provoked was, to be sure, not the only Yeats. He could be extremely impressionable, deferential, malleable. As was the case with Goethe, another singular multiform consciousness, part of Yeats's genius was his ability to attract to himself, and open himself to those who had creative influences to bring him. In young manhood, for instance, it was the Fenian, John O'Leary; in middle age it was the dynamic young American, Ezra Pound.

At times Yeats would seek energetically, even aggressively, to impose his will on others; at times he permitted others to compel him. He was very much what he was because of these 'others'. They primarily constitute what I mean by the word 'milieu' in my subtitle.

My interest in and admiration for Yeats go back a long way. I was first introduced to his work at my Midlands grammar school by my English master, the Irish poet R.N.D. Wilson, who had known Yeats and who had been an associate of Yeats's murdered friend Kevin O'Higgins. At Cambridge I was at St Catharine's College and my tutor was the Yeats scholar T.R. Henn. The college was full of talk of Yeats criticism and research.

Later, as a critic writing on T.S. Eilot's *Four Quartets* and Ezra Pound's *Pisan Cantos* Yeats was brought to mind in different ways. Eliot presents him in terms that Yeats himself would have endorsed. Alluded to as the figure of the 'dead master' in *Little Gidding*, Yeats is the poet of wisdom and redemptive vision. He is portrayed much less reverentially, comically even, in the *Pisan Cantos* where he appears as 'old Billyum'. Pound, unlike Eliot, is entertained rather than awed by Yeats's incantatory chanting; he views him as a man as well as a poet. He offers a strong sense of Yeats's social and historical context. This kind of perspective is what I have attempted to establish. For an important part of Yeats's genius was his keen and often manipulative relationships with the turbulent life around him as well as with the turbulent life within.

K.A.
October, 1996

[*Acknowledgements*]

ALL QUOTATIONS FROM THE POETRY OF W.B. YEATS ARE TAKEN FROM *Yeats's Poems*, Gill Macmillan edition, 1989. All quotations from Yeats's drama and prose writings are from the Macmillan edition. There are also quotations from the *Gonne-Yeats Letters* published by Hutchinson. It has not been possible to quote from any Yeats materials published after 1939. The authorized biographer Professor Roy Foster has been granted a *UIP* monopoly on such quotations until the completion of his work some years in the future. This embargo means that others writing about Yeats's life can only offer evidence in paraphrase. However my footnotes will help direct the interested reader to the relevant sources.

I must also acknowledge the kind assistance of Anna MacBride White, Omar Pound, Peter Busby, Kathleen Kinsella and the following libraries: the Library of the City of Lichfield, the London Library, the Library of the University of British Columbia, the Library of the City of Birmingham. I have spent many hours in the National Library of Ireland and the Manuscript Library there and I would like to thank the librarians for their kindness.

I should like to thank Lord Hemphill for allowing me to visit him at his home in the west of Ireland and for talking to me about his ancestor Edward Martyn and his relationship with Yeats. That period in Yeats's life came vividly alive when Mr and Mrs Jack Darian, the present owners of Tillyra Castle in County Galway, gave my wife and me a tour of their home and shared their extensive knowledge with us.

I also learned a good deal about Ireland past and present from Ted, Maura and Maírin MacSweeney of Blackrock, County Dublin. I thank all three for their hospitality, insights and information. It was a great help and pleasure for me to meet and talk with Hilary Pyle, the biographer of Jack Yeats and Curator of the Yeats Collection in the National Gallery of Ireland. Another Yeats scholar with whom I have had stimulating conversation over the years is my friend and former colleague, Professor Andrew Parkin.

Especially important to me have been my conversations with the poet's daughter, Anne B. Yeats. It was a privilege to visit her in her house at Dalkey, to see Yeats's library intact, and to enjoy her down-to-earth, humane, feminist and witty perspectives.

My greatest debt is to the dedicatee of this book, my wife Joan Hardwick. She most generously took time from the book she herself was writing and assisted me substantially at every stage of my work.

I dined with Goethe today, and the conversation soon turning again on the Daemonic . . .

'The Daemonic,' said he, 'is that which cannot be explained by Reason or Understanding; it lies not in my nature, but I am subject to it.' . . .

'Is not the Daemonic,' said I, 'perceptible in events also?'

'Particularly,' said Goethe . . . 'It manifests itself in the most varied manner throughout all nature – in the invisible as in the visible. Many creatures are of a purely daemonic kind.' . . .

'Has not Mephistopheles', said I, 'daemonic traits too?'

'No,' said Goethe, 'Mephistopheles is much too negative a being. The Daemonic manifests itself in a thoroughly positive power.'

GOETHE, *Conversations with Eckermann, 2 March 1831*

I

An Irish Childhood, An English Education

*His childhood, boyhood and young manhood were passed among painters, writers
and clever talkers. His father, the painter, linked by temper and training to the
protesting paintings schools of France and England, was one of the wittiest
talkers of his time. His sisters and brother all practised the arts. He, too, trained
for a time as a painter, spoke always of painting as a painter speaks, and from
time to time worked for his amusement with paints and pastels . . . From an early
age he was deeply moved by the beauty and mystery of the Sligo coast.*

John Masefield, *Some Memories of W.B. Yeats*

$[1865-1880]$

WILLIAM BUTLER YEATS WAS BORN IN THE SAME YEAR AS Rudyard Kipling, who early in life was acclaimed poet of the British Empire. Jean Sibelius was also born that year, but in contrast spent much of his life expressing the cultural claims of a small people against those of the vast empire of Czarist Russia. Another composer, Richard Strauss, was born a year earlier and H.G. Wells a year later. Henry Ford and David Lloyd George were two years older and Arnold Bennett and Frank Lloyd Wright two years younger. In 1865 a unified Britain and Ireland were ruled by a government headed by the 73-year-old Whig, Lord John Russell; William Gladstone was his Chancellor of the Exchequer and would himself become Prime Minister when Willie Yeats was three. The year of Yeats's birth saw the publication of Dickens's *Our Mutual Friend*, Lewis Carroll's *Alice in Wonderland*, Matthew Arnold's *Essays in Criticism* and also the first performance of an opera that was to influence greatly European literature, Wagner's *Tristan und Isolde*. The Pre-Raphaelite poet and painter Dante Gabriel Rossetti, whom Yeats was greatly to admire, was working on a picture inspired by his namesake to which he gave the title *Beata Beatrix*. The year was 1865 and the elaborate monument to Queen Victoria's dead husband, in Hyde Park, had been completed some twelve months earlier.

Yeats was born on 13 June in a far more modest piece of Victorian design. It was a small redbrick semi-detached house, consisting of one storey and a basement, on the south side of Dublin: George's Ville No. 1, now 5 Sandymount Avenue. It was an undistinguished house, with a long flight of stone steps going up to the shallow front porch. For the poet who in later life would gain entry into some of the great mansions of Ireland and England this rented semi in a then rather raw suburb was a humble beginning, but his father John Yeats still had his way to make. He was in his mid-twenties at the time of the arrival of his first-born, and had not yet completed his studies to become a lawyer. His prospects, however, looked good. He was intelligent, an entertaining and persuasive talker, and he possessed great charm. He also had financial assets; his inheritance included a house in Dorset Street in Dublin and more than five hundred acres of land in County Kildare. And he came of a good family.

Of Yorkshire origins, the Yeatses appear to have established themselves in Dublin by the end of the seventeenth century.[1] Jervis Yeats, the first of the family to settle in Dublin, where he died in 1712, was a merchant in the linen trade. His business was successful and the family prospered so that in 1773 his grandson Benjamin Yeats was able to marry up in the world. His wife was Mary Butler, a member of the family headed by the Dukes of Ormonde, leading figures in the Anglo-Irish aristocracy. Mary Butler brought to the family not just a famous name but also, as a dowry, a substantial amount of land in County Kildare which yielded a good revenue in the form of rents. In subsequent generations members of the Yeats family used Butler as a middle name in order to commemorate this connection with their prestigious ancestor. By the beginning of the nineteenth century the family had abandoned the textile business for more genteel pursuits. After graduating from Trinity College Dublin, just before the Union of Ireland with Britain in 1801, John Yeats, the son of Benjamin Yeats and Mary Butler, became a clergyman, serving as rector in the ancient little settlement of Drumcliffe, a few miles west of the port of Sligo on Ireland's west coast. He too made a good marriage: his wife was Jane Taylor, the sister of a well-placed official in the headquarters of British rule in Ireland, Dublin Castle, and she too had a considerable dowry. This couple sent their son, William Butler Yeats, to Dublin to complete his education at Trinity College and, like his father, he was ordained in the Protestant Church of Ireland and began his ministry as a curate in a parish in Ulster.

This grandfather and namesake of the poet was a skilled horseman and not greatly concerned with matters of theology. In 1835 he was promoted to the rectorship of Tullylish near Portadown, south-west of Belfast, and in that same year he married Jane Grace Corbet who, like her mother-in-law, was well connected. The couple had a family of nine children and as the family grew, William's stipend was insufficient to support them all in the style he considered appropriate. Fortunately he also had an income from the properties he had inherited from his grandmother Mary Butler. His eldest son, the poet's father John Butler Yeats, was born in 1839. In the 1840s John Yeats was still a child but the distress of the adults in his comfortable home as they spoke despairingly of the potato famine that had brought starvation to the poor people of Ireland made a lasting impression on him.

John Yeats's education began when he became a pupil in a boarding school at Seaforth in Lancashire; he was then sent to Atholl Academy on the Isle of Man where discipline was maintained by a good deal of heavy flogging. Here John Yeats was very much drawn to a couple of his school-mates, Charles and George Pollexfen, two rather gauche, unmannerly boys whose father had built a spectacularly successful shipping business in Sligo. John Yeats, witty and socially adroit, already interested in the arts and literature, had little in common with the Pollexfen brothers except that all three had connections with Sligo. He was intrigued by the boys' tales of the region of Ireland where his grandfather had ministered and where some of the family still lived.

When the Pollexfen boys finished at the Academy they went straight into the family business. But John Yeats continued his family's tradition and in 1857 became an undergraduate at Trinity College. A few years earlier, his father had retired from his parish in unhappy circumstances. Never a very dedicated churchman, he had not even maintained the parish register properly. Years later John Yeats discovered as a result of his youngest daughter Lolly's visit to Tullylish that William had failed to register a single christening. The result had been that many of his parishioners had difficulty in collecting their pensions when the time came to do so because they were unable to prove their birth dates.[2] When William left Tullylish he had no income apart from his rents and so he went to live under the auspices of Robert Corbet, his wife's apparently prosperous brother. Sandymount Castle, Robert Corbet's home on the southern edge of Dublin, was an eighteenth-century house to which turreted towers had been added early in the Gothic Revival. While he was a student John Yeats regarded Sandymount Castle, spacious and well furnished, as his home. He admired and respected his Uncle Robert who was a man of culture and expensive tastes and at whose table there was always good conversation.

At Trinity College John Yeats was attracted to the rationalism of John Stuart Mill and the evolutionism of Charles Darwin, and he became a member of an informal 'brotherhood', a group of lively young men with intellectual interests. The 'brotherhood' included Edward Dowden, a future professor of English at the College, and John Todhunter, who became a doctor and later made a name as a poet, essayist and dramatist. In 1862 John Yeats obtained his degree and also won a prize in an essay competition on the subject of John Stuart Mill. He decided to use the prize money to visit his former schoolmates Charles and George Pollexfen in Sligo. The Pollexfen family were holidaying just outside Sligo town on Rosses Point. Here John Yeats met for the first time Susan Mary Pollexfen, the oldest daughter of the family. She was twenty-one years old, slimly built and pretty. She had full lips and her eyes were beguiling, perhaps disconcerting, for one eye was blue and the other brown. John Yeats saw Susan Pollexfen at her best for she loved Rosses Point and she was happy to take long walks along the strand and to listen quietly while he talked. Before he returned to Dublin John Yeats was engaged to marry her.

Had he first seen the Pollexfen family in Sligo town and not on a seaside holiday John Yeats might have been less ready to commit himself to Susan Mary. There he would have seen how much more important money-making was to the Pollexfen family than to the Yeats family. He would have seen how cushioned from the realities of managing a home and family were all the Pollexfen girls and he would have seen how dour and withdrawn Susan could be. As it was, back in Dublin, he had second thoughts about his engagement. In a draft of an autobiographical novel written many years later, he suggested that once away from Sligo he had realized that he did not love Susan. He did think, however, that her quiet personality would ground and balance his own happy-go-lucky nature. The death of his father in November strengthened his commitment to marry. He was now the head of the family and had inherited the let property in Dublin and tenanted land in County Kildare. The time was ripe to take a wife. John Yeats married Susan Pollexfen in St John's Church in Sligo in the second week of September 1863.

At first the wealthy Pollexfen parents approved of this marriage, seeing the gentlemanly and well-connected lawyer-to-be as a good prospect for their daughter. But their expectations were misplaced. John Yeats may have inherited land and property but he had also inherited mortgages and family responsibilities. Furthermore he showed no ability to manage his assets; he immediately put them into the hands of his uncle Robert Corbet. Within three years, however, the relative in whom he had placed such trust had committed suicide rather than be declared a bankrupt.

Even John Yeats's career in the law was not quite so secure as the Pollexfens assumed. Although he was called to the Bar and devilled for Isaac Butt, the prominent Dublin lawyer and leader of the Irish Party in Westminster, he preferred to draw caricatures of his legal colleagues rather than listen to their arguments. In the cheap rented house near Sandymount Castle Susan Yeats began to worry about her husband's cavalier attitude to the law. The couple soon had two children, Willie, born in 1865, and Susan Mary (Lily), born a year later. But these two additions to the family had not made John Yeats any more dedicated to the notion of making money. Little over a year after being called to the Dublin Bar, John Yeats decided to abandon his career as a lawyer in order to train as an artist. His wife was dismayed and angry, but, regardless, early in 1867 he set off to London and enrolled as a student at Heatherley's Art School. This was a private institution in Newman Street formerly known as Leighs, where the Pre-Raphaelite painter Edward Burne-Jones, six years older than John Yeats, had studied drawing. Whilst John Yeats used his family income to pay his art school fees and to support himself in London, Susan took her two babies and returned to her family in Sligo.

In the England to which John Yeats removed himself Ireland was a subject of passionate, often bitter, controversy. That year public attention was focused on the dramatic events leading up to the murder trial in Manchester of three Fenians, violent agitators for the independence of

Ireland. An English policeman had been shot dead when some other Fenians had escaped from a police van. None of the three on trial had fired the fatal shot, but to placate strong anti-Irish public opinion they were convicted and hanged. This harsh retribution outraged even those who were opposed to the violent tactics of the Fenians. A song composed in their memory, 'God Save Ireland', became one of the best known of all republican anthems.

In July 1867 John Yeats managed to persuade Susan Yeats to leave her beloved Sligo and to join him with the children in London. The family leased a reasonably substantial three-storeyed Victorian terraced house at 23 Fitzroy Road, just north of Regent's Park. Though he had undoubted gifts as an artist, John Yeats had so far had no success in his new profession of portrait painter. He found it difficult to complete canvases and to obtain commissions. He often did portraits of people whose faces interested him, knowing full well his sitter could not afford to buy the finished painting. Engaging in extended conversation with his subjects, he worked painfully slowly. Sometimes he was simply unlucky. On one occasion a man commissioned a portrait of his wife but by the time John Yeats had finally completed it, the couple were divorced and the husband refused to pay for the painting. He was also a bad manager of money and the income from the properties in Dublin and Kildare dwindled alarmingly as they were repeatedly remortgaged. Yet as money became less plentiful, the family increased. The year after the Yeats moved to London, Elizabeth Corbet Yeats, always called Lolly, was born. A year later Susan found herself pregnant yet again, the fourth time in five years. This child, born in 1870, was christened Robert Corbet Yeats in memory of John Yeats's uncle.

For Susan Yeats marriage had now come to mean endless childbearing and a miserable and humiliating comedown in the world. Her witty, intellectual and charming husband had taken her from a life of affluence and comfort in Sligo to one of lonely exile and depressing poverty in suburban London. Her family could not make the claims of ancestry that John Yeats so often did for his; the Pollexfens were *nouveaux riches* in Sligo. Nevertheless Susan had been brought up to think of herself as a lady. She had grown up in a substantial house in Union Street (an address that suited the family's politics). Her parents now lived in a mansion called Merville on the edge of town. It had an imposing classical façade, a coach house and extensive stables; it was the centrepiece of an estate of some sixty acres. Surrounded by servants, Susan never had to worry about housekeeping. Like her family she had assumed that her marriage would mean a continuation of this life of leisured ease.

Susan came from a large family; she had six brothers and was the eldest of five sisters. Her father, William Pollexfen, was not Irish, but <u>Cornish</u>. He began life as a sailor and, when still a very young man, he managed to buy a boat for himself. In his early twenties, a few years before Victoria became Queen, he left England and sailed *The Dasher* up the west coast of Ireland to Sligo to offer his recently widowed cousin, Elizabeth Pollexfen Middleton, assistance in running her shipping business. Her husband had died in a cholera epidemic in Sligo. In 1837, the year of Victoria's coronation, he married her daughter, another Elizabeth, having already gone into partnership in a grain business with his brother-in-law William Middleton. The partners exploited William Pollexfen's seagoing skills by founding the Sligo Steam Navigation Company; their steamers sailed to various ports in the west of Ireland and as far away as Liverpool. The William Pollexfen who had first appeared in Sligo as a young adventurer lived to become one of the most distinguished and wealthy citizens of the place.

Grandfather Pollexfen was physically strong and courageous. Once, when his workers were afraid to examine a damaged rudder below the waterline on one of his ships in Sligo harbour, he unhesitatingly dived in and attended to it himself. Very much the Victorian self-made man, he had little tolerance for those, like his son-in-law John Yeats, who failed to advance themselves. He was gruff, irritable and difficult to deal with. A die-hard Unionist, he often carried a gun with which to confront any Fenians or Home Rulers who might try to disturb the peace in Sligo. As Joan Hardwick has observed in her recent account of the lives of Lily and Lolly, 'William Pollexfen's position in Sligo was aptly symbolized by the tower room he had had built for himself over the company's headquarters at the corner of Adelaide Street and Wine Street. From this high eminence with its windows all around he could look out over the whole town and over the quays to the ships approaching Sligo from the estuary of the Gavarogue

River.'[3] In later years William Butler Yeats would write about the terror his grandfather inspired in him and how he saw him as a King Lear figure. And Lily, when she wrote about him in her Scrapbook, recalled: 'Grandpapa Pollexfen, we liked, admired, and avoided . . . He never talked to anyone . . . The past and the future had no interest for him at all. He was in such a state of irritation with the present moment that he could think of nothing else . . . He was quite unsuspicious so it was only what he saw that irritated, so there was everything to be said for "keeping out of the master's way".'[4] Only one person could quieten this irascible man and that was his wife Elizabeth, a lady with an equable temperament. She enjoyed her luxurious life at Merville and was gratified by the family's ever higher station in Sligo society. The widely respected mother of eleven children, she was, Lily remembered, always the impeccably dressed Victorian lady wearing a 'black silk dress, real lace cap, collar and cuffs, quilted black satin petticoat, thin cream-coloured stockings, and thin black shoes'.[5] She painted delicate watercolours on rice paper, and enjoyed driving about Sligo in her carriage and presenting gifts to the deserving poor.

John Yeats had a view of the Pollexfens which he passed on to his son Willie. They were not of gentlemanly stock; they lacked manners; they were obsessed with money-making and with social status. Also there was mental instability in the family. John Yeats did grant that they had certain qualities, the ones that had attracted him to Charles and George when they had all been at boarding school together on the Isle of Man. To his friend and fellow student at Trinity College, Edward Dowden, John Yeats remarked that the Pollexfens had 'all the marks of imagination', but not of an intellectual kind, rather 'of the affections and desires and the senses'. This he thought gave them 'magnetism'. But these qualities were hidden by their crass preoccupation with money.

As his own career failed to prosper John Yeats found the attitude of his numerous in-laws hard to take. However, it is doubtful that they were all as committed to the harsh middle-class attitudes and the Samuel Smiles ethic of self-help as the struggling portrait painter sometimes made out when he generalized about 'the Pollexfens'. His sister-in-law Isabella Pollexfen had artistic gifts, practised as a painter and married an artist, John Varley. She was also a dedicated student of the occult. Aunt Isabella

Pollexfen it was who sent her nephew Willie Yeats, in his late teens, a copy of A.P. Sinnett's *Esoteric Buddhism* and thus helped him begin that lifelong study of the supernatural and the spiritual which constituted such an important part of his development as a man and a poet. Isabella's brother George also interested himself in the occult. Willie, in his poverty-stricken early manhood, spent a good deal of time housed and fed by Uncle George, who eagerly participated in his nephew's study of the horoscope and spiritualism.

For all John Yeats's often repeated depreciation of his in-laws, there can be little doubt that the Pollexfens had a powerful effect on the early development of his oldest son. Above all they gave him his richly memorable childhood years in Sligo. The small harbour city in its beautiful surroundings – the table mountains of Ben Bulben to the north and Knocknarea to the south – was the great formative influence on his imagination. At Merville the Yeats children enjoyed the company of their grandparents' servants who were always ready to tell them stories about the ghosts and fairies of the locality. They heard of mysterious lights moving at night on Knocknarea and of the white door on the side of Ben Bulben which opened up straight into the land of fairy. Just a few miles outside the city was the ancient burial-ground of Carrowmore with its mysterious stone circles and ruined tomb structures that gave a sense of the proximity of the dead. There were more ghost stories at Rosses Point when the Yeats children visited their Middleton cousins who spent the summer at a seaside house there called Elsinore. This house, with views from the Point out to the Atlantic ocean, had been built by a Sligo smuggler, John Black. He had chosen the site because it overlooked the fishing harbour and the Sound between Rosses Point and Coney Island. He was said to haunt his house, and Lily, whose psychic gifts always interested her older brother, reported that when staying with the Middletons she had heard the smuggler tapping on the window at night.

There were some members of the Yeats family in the area as well as large numbers of Pollexfens and Middletons. John Yeats was always eager for his children to visit their relatives from his side of the family. They went to play with their cousins at the home of Matthew Yeats, a land agent who lived in a long low house beside a ruined mill and a fast-flowing stream in the village of Rathbroughan. Uncle Matthew had none of John Yeats's wit and entertaining talk; he was a solemn, devoutly religious man. More fun for the children were their visits to their youngest great-aunt, Mary Yeats, always known as Micky, who lived in a house called Seaview covered in creepers and surrounded by box hedges standing on the hilltop above Ballincar on the road between Rosses Point and Sligo. Just north of the house began the steep slope of Ben Bulben. Aunt Micky determined to make the children aware of their Yeats ancestry. She showed them a Jacobean cream jug which had been handed down in the family and also a gold cup which had the date 1534 engraved on it and which had belonged to their great-great-grandfather, Jervis Yeats. Aunt Micky reminded them frequently of the Butler connections with the grand Ormonde family. But for all her stories of the family's distinguished past the children could not but be aware of the straitened circumstances of Aunt Micky's present life. She ran Seaview as a smallholding with the aid of just one servant. She made little money out of it and at harvest time was dependent upon the help of her neighbours. There can be little doubt that, to John Yeats's frequent distress, it was the Pollexfens, the numerous aunts and uncles, the servants and the great Georgian house of Merville that constituted by far the greater part of the background of Willie Yeats's Sligo childhood.

Willie's first extended experience of Sligo began a month after his seventh birthday in July 1872, when Susan and her children left Fitzroy Road and returned to Ireland to live with her parents. There were now five children under the age of eight. Willie, Lily, Lolly and Bobbie now had a baby brother John Butler Yeats, always known in the family as Jack, who had been born a year earlier. The older children were always excited to set off for Sligo, even Willie, who was frequently sea-sick on the 30-hour crossing. They felt their lives begin to change when they arrived in Liverpool where they embarked on one of their grandfather's ships, the *Sligo* or the *Liverpool*. They were transformed from children of no particular account to important passengers with special privileges because they were the grandchildren of the owner. On board they immediately felt their grandfather's power and his attitude towards their father. The crews of the Pollexfen ships were never happy to carry John Yeats; they had been led to regard him as unlucky.

Susan and her children came back to Sligo in 1872 as virtual paupers and dependants of the Pollexfens. Susan's mortification was intensified by the wedding of her younger sister Elizabeth to a prosperous Anglican clergyman, the Reverend Barrington Orr, shortly after their arrival. The Pollexfen grandparents spared no expense arranging a lavish wedding. The shabby Yeats children all had new clothes: Lily and Lolly were bought white muslin dresses with blue sashes and Willie and Bobbie had blue knickerbocker sailor suits. The wedding day was a colourful occasion both for Merville and for Sligo.

Willie remained at Merville for almost two and a half years of his impressionable childhood. Though fearful of his grandfather, he was not unhappy. The immense garden had interesting ships' figureheads. There was a pony to ride and dogs to play with. Johnny Healey, the stable boy, gave him his first experience of Irish poetry by reciting Unionist ballads to him. When there was talk of a Fenian rebellion, Willie imagined himself dying a hero's death fighting the Fenians. At Merville at this time, Yeats later remembered, he saw his first 'fay' or fairy; it descended down a moonbeam towards him. This was an experience that caused no great stir in the family. Second sight, such as his cousin Lucy Middleton had, was an accepted part of life in those days in the west of Ireland. Another Middleton relative gave Willie experience of spirits of a different kind. He took him sailing and, when the sea became stormy off Rosses, had the pilot give him neat whisky. Back on land, Willie stumbled through Sligo shouting to everybody that he was drunk. Only when Grandmother Pollexfen put him to bed in Merville did he quieten down.

During those Sligo years Willie only saw his father during the summer, when the luckless painter came over from London to combine a visit to his family with painting commissions which he obtained from well-to-do people in such nearby mansions as Muckross Abbey and Stradbally Hall. John Yeats worried a great deal about his older son, seeing in him some of the excessive sensitivities of his sister-in-law Elizabeth. 'From his resemblance to Elizabeth he derives a nervous sensitiveness,' observed John Yeats to his wife, contrasting Willie with the more robust Bobbie. However, this physically stronger child developed croup and died in Sligo shortly before his third birthday.

On his brief visits John Yeats did his utmost to moderate the Pollexfen influence. Still an admirer of Darwin and of Mill and a sceptic in religious matters, he demonstrated his independence by refusing to go to church with the family on Sundays. He took his son on walks out towards Rosses Point and, once clear of the Pollexfens, would read aloud to him from works he considered to be of some literary quality: *Ivanhoe*, *The Lays of Ancient Rome* and *The Lay of the Last Minstrel*. He told him the story of Shakespeare's *The Merchant of Venice* and of Balzac's *La Peau de Chagrin*. This was his way of trying to offer a supplement to the Sligo dame school which Willie's Pollexfen aunts had chosen for him.

A few months after Willie's ninth birthday John Yeats prevailed upon his reluctant wife to bring the children over from Sligo to London and in late October 1874 the family established a new home in a small, artisan house at 14 Edith Villas, North End Road, in West Kensington, a dwelling since destroyed by bombing in the Second World War. This was the first of a series of west London houses in which Yeats lived until he was thirty. An Irishman and born Dubliner, he thus became for many years of his life a Londoner. It was not only beautiful, slow, magical Sligo that helped form him; there was also the vast, animated, often ugly metropolis and imperial capital. Sligo encouraged the dreamer in him; London developed the quick, sharp worldliness that was also part of his character. It was in London that he would make his name as a writer.

The first year back in London did not begin well. Four months after their return Susan was distressed to find herself pregnant for the sixth time. But John Yeats's hopes for better success with his portraits had not materialized and the family was painfully aware of the shortage of money. The sixth child that Susan Yeats had delivered in ten years was born in August 1875, a couple of months after Willie's tenth birthday. She was christened Jane Grace Yeats. Just a week before Willie's eleventh birthday the baby died of bronchial pneumonia. The bereaved family left Edith Villas and its unhappy memories to spend some of the summer in Sligo. But John Yeats, always uncomfortable with his in-laws at Merville, soon returned alone to London. He had decided that his future lay not just as a portraitist but also as a painter of landscape. He took lodgings at Burnham Beeches in Buckinghamshire where he set himself to paint the beautiful wooded scenery. John Yeats still worried about Willie back in Sligo, remembering all too well the effect on his son of the harsh bullying criticisms of the Pollexfens and his seeming backwardness in previous years. He had been especially irritated by his sister-in-law Agnes Pollexfen, an outspoken girl in her late teens, who had made it her business to try to educate Willie. Like other Pollexfen aunts, Agnes was scandalized that Willie had been so slow in mastering his alphabet and learning to read. Convinced that his son was a highly strung, imaginative child who would not benefit from the relentless rote learning insisted on by the exasperated Agnes and her sisters, John Yeats demanded that Willie come and stay with him in his lodgings at Beech Villa in Farnham Royal, a guest house for artists run by Mr and Mrs Earle. This was the first of a succession of occasions in his life in which Willie lived within a community of artists.

A few months later, in January 1877, Susan Yeats reluctantly agreed to return to England and the family reassembled in the shabby lower-middle-class house at Edith Villas. Willie's formal education could now begin. He was sent to nearby Godolphin School (subsequently Godolphin and Latymer, now a girls' school) on Iffley Road, a dull thoroughfare in the west London borough of Hammersmith. Years later when he wrote the first of his autobiographies, Yeats looked back on Godolphin with distaste, but it was the best his father could scrounge and borrow the money for. It was 'a cheap school' and the other boys had rough manners. It was 'an obscene, bullying place, where a big boy would hit a small boy in the wind to see him double up, and where certain boys, too young for any emotion of sex, would sing the dirty songs of the street'. Though he did make one friend, Cyril Vesey, who shared his enthusiasm for collecting butterflies and moths and who taught him how to resist the school bullies, Yeats felt himself set apart. As the son of a well-read and highly intelligent artist he could not share his schoolfellows' confident lower-middle-class assumptions and aspirations. And as an Irish boy he was often the butt of their crude imperialist and Unionist prejudices which were aggravated by the disturbances presently going on in Ireland. For this was the time of the Land War when the tenant farmers of rural Ireland were locked in an often bloody struggle with tyrannical landlords who used force to evict those peasants who could not afford to pay their rent.

One day in the schoolyard at Godolphin, around the time Michael Davitt was founding the Land League to organize the oppressed tenantry of Ireland, Yeats was crudely insulted. Another boy called him 'Mad Irishman'; Yeats felt he had no choice but to fight. He won, but his feeling of alienation in that suburban school did not abate, and the nearly four years he spent there entrenched his deep and combative sense of himself as an Irishman. Godolphin, with its coarseness and vulgarities, confirmed in him the view that things Irish were finer than anything the English had to offer. Nevertheless in his early teens his life was that of a London school-boy at a fee-paying school. And his growing maturity was marked by a very English ritual. On his fifteenth birthday Willie was confirmed as a member of the Church of England by the Bishop of London, a ceremony which would have pleased Susan and the Pollexfens more than the sceptical John Yeats. In any event the future devotee of spiritualism and the occult began his formal religious career as a communicant Anglican.

A little over a year before Willie's confirmation the Yeatses had moved to a more attractive but inexpensive house at 8 Woodstock Road in Bedford Park. Just north of old Chiswick, this was a suburban estate planned for artists and for those with artistic tastes. During their first summer in this new house the family had a modest seaside holiday at Branscombe in Devon, where they stayed in an old farmhouse. All the children did draw-ings of various sights in the area. In his picture of a boat putting out to sea Jack gave an early indication of his future career as an artist; Willie did a detailed drawing of the medieval church at Branscombe. Willie was also intrigued by the Devonshire accent. Once, one of the local boys with whom he went looking for smugglers' caves said to him, 'I saw thee and the little maids and little brother in church yesterday'; for days after, Willie went about repeating this item of west country English. On the weekends when he came down from London John Yeats read aloud to his children Dickens's *David Copperfield* and Scott's *Old Mortality* and *The Antiquary*. The chil-dren looked back on this time in Devon as a very happy period, but it proved to be the last time the family lived together for a long time. A humiliated John Yeats finally agreed that the Pollexfen grandparents should take over the rearing of seven-year-old Jack. For the next eight years he grew up in Sligo, which provided him with so many subjects for his future paintings.

In the year and a half following their Devon holiday Willie had successes at Godolphin. He became proficient as a swimmer, learned to dive
and won a cup for running. A tough side to him was beginning to show.
But for his father there was little success to report, and he finally concluded
that coming to London had been a mistake. In the summer of 1881 he took
the decision to return to Ireland to re-start his career there, ending the
tenancy of the Bedford Park house, and renting a studio in central Dublin.
He then reassembled what was left of his family in a rented cottage to the
north of the city.

II

THE YOUNG NATIONALIST

There is no doubt that the number of nationalist movements increased consider-
ably in Europe from the 1870s . . . There were now 'national movements' not only
among peoples hitherto considered 'unhistorical' (i.e. who had never previously
possessed an independent state, ruling class or cultural élite), such as Finns and
Slovaks, but among peoples about whom hardly anybody except folklore enthusi-
asts had previously thought at all, such as Estonians and Macedonians. And
within long-established nation-states regional populations now began to mobil-
ise politically as 'nations'; this happened in Wales where a Young Wales move-
ment was organised in the 1890s under the leadership of a local lawyer of whom
much was to be heard in the future, David Lloyd George, and in Spain where a
Basque National Party was founded in 1894. And about the same time Theodor
Herzl launched Zionism among the Jews, to whom the sort of nationalism it
represented had hitherto been unknown and meaningless.

E.J. HOBSBAWM, *The Age of Empire 1875–1914*

$[1880 - 1885]$

THE DECADE OF THE 1880s AT THE BEGINNING OF WHICH JOHN Butler Yeats removed his family from London back to Ireland was one of the most distinctive, dramatic and colourful decades in Irish history in the nineteenth century. And the decade so stands out chiefly because it was increasingly dominated by one very forceful, charismatic leader, Charles Stewart Parnell. As John Kennedy introduced an entirely new mood and sense of possibility in American politics in the decade beginning in 1960 and as Franklin Roosevelt had done with his 'New Deal' at the start of the 1930s, so did Parnell bring a quickening to the political life of his country throughout the 1880s. Then at the end of those ten years his career was suddenly, shockingly ended, swept away in scandal and high drama.

Another political meteor in the House of Commons during the same ten years was Lord Randolph Churchill, the exponent of a new kind of Toryism for an electorate that had recently come to include part of the working class. One of Lord Randolph's Irish admirers was Standish O'Grady, the author of *Toryism and Tory Democracy* and of a two-volume history of Ireland and its legends and myths which had a great influence on Yeats on his return to Dublin. Lord Randolph's spectacular career burned out a little before Parnell's. Lord Randolph's son, Winston, who grew into his teens during these years, took a great interest in his father's almost exact contemporary, Parnell. Winston Churchill's very earliest

childhood memories were of growing up in the ambience of Dublin Castle
to which his father had been virtually exiled after the Prince of Wales had
banned him from London high society following a disagreement about a
lady. And as a schoolboy Winston Churchill 'heard many tales and received
many vivid pictures of Parnell' from an Irish lady who paid him visits whilst
he was recovering from a serious accident.[1] This was Mrs T.P. O'Connor,
wife of 'Tay Pay', one of the most famous Irish journalists of the day who
went on to publish the highly successful *T.P's Weekly*. From the talkative
and always entertaining Mrs O'Connor young Winston Churchill heard
how 'an air of mystery and legend had hung about Parnell from his
Cambridge days . . . Indeed, the paradoxes of his earnest and sincere life
were astonishing: a Protestant leading Catholics; a landlord inspiring a "No
Rent" campaign; a man of law and order exciting revolt; a humanitarian
and anti-terrorist controlling and yet arousing hopes of the Invincibles and
Terrorists . . . His Irish Nationalism, which persisted and grew upon this
unusual background has been traced to his mother and her admiration for
the idealistic Fenians.'[2]

What especially fascinated the young Winston Churchill was Parnell's
immense confidence and presence. Parnell was 'a man, stern, grave,
reserved . . . no spinner of words and phrases; but a being who seemed to
exercise unconsciously an indefinable sense of power in repose – of
command awaiting the hour.'[3] As leader of the Irish MPs in the House of
Commons Parnell was aloof and preoccupied. The Irish members who followed him unquestioningly hardly dared to address him. A cold nod in the
lobby or a few curt directions given in an undertone along the Benches –
stern, clear guidance in the secret conclaves – these were the only contacts
of the Irish political party with their leader. 'Can't you go and see him, and
find out what he thinks about it?' inquired an English politician in the
1880s to an Irish member. 'Would I dare to inthrude upon Misther Parnell?'
was the answer.[4]

In the late autumn of 1881, as the Yeats family was setting up house
again in Ireland, there came the startling news that Parnell had been
arrested and imprisoned without trial in Kilmainham Jail in Dublin. The
government in London was jittery about the growing unrest in rural
Ireland. Parnell's colleague from the Land League, Michael Davitt, was

continuing to give leadership to the oppressed tenant farmers by helping them to fight evictions. He encouraged the delaying of rent payments and the withdrawal of services. In this decade the Land League gave the English language a new word when it helped to organize the total ostracism of harsh land agents such as Captain Boycott in County Mayo. In London, Parnell, as the new leader of the Irish Party, organized an effective programme of parliamentary obstructionism which greatly annoyed the English Members. Frustrated, the Liberal Prime Minister, William Ewart Gladstone, using emergency powers, engineered Parnell's imprisonment. He would remain in Kilmainham Jail for some seven months as a martyr to the Irish cause until May 1882, just before Willie's seventeenth birthday, when Gladstone, under continuing pressure, decided to try to work with Parnell and had him released under the agreement known as the 'Kilmainham Treaty'.

John Butler Yeats did not care for Parnell, whom he saw as implicated with the men of violence. He much preferred the leader of the Irish Party whom Parnell had helped to oust, the gentlemanly, accommodating and finally ineffective Isaac Butt for whom he had worked during his brief career as a lawyer. Years later John Yeats wrote, 'The Irish took to hatred when they deserted the statesman Isaac Butt for the politician Parnell . . . Parnell was not a great man.'[5] But for Willie, Lily and Lolly, these new times in the Ireland to which they had returned were exciting, and never more so than when, shortly after Parnell's release from Kilmainham, the Invincibles – the radical, armed wing of the Fenians – stabbed to death in Phoenix Park the newly appointed Chief Secretary for Ireland, Lord Frederick Cavendish and his Under-Secretary Thomas Burke. In a notebook dated some sixty years later Lily would still remember, and write about, travelling through Dublin at that dramatic, tense time. John Butler Yeats suspected that his studio landlord was involved in the plot. As the police searched nearby premises his landlady grew increasingly anxious. Finally she brought a package to John Yeats and asked him to hide it. He had little doubt that it contained a gun. The parcel was taken back when the police left the area but Willie and his sister were thrilled by their father's story.

The Yeats family first lived at Howth, the hilly promontory on the northern end of the long, beautiful semi-circular curve of Dublin Bay. From one of his former associates in the law John Butler Yeats had managed to rent Balscadden Cottage, a long thatched house which stands high on the cliffs of the north side of Howth Head looking down immediately on the Irish Sea. Some six months later, just before the Phoenix Park murders, the family moved the short distance into the fishing village of Howth itself where they rented a cottage called Island View with an outlook over the harbour to the rocky island known as Ireland's Eye. The months the family lived in 'this ancient village with its crooked lanes, its old abbey church-yard full of long grass, its green background of small fir-trees, and its quay, where lie a few tarry fishing-luggers'[6] were the happiest they had known or were to know. Mrs Yeats especially enjoyed living there. In Yeats's *Reveries*, his account of the time at Howth contains one of the very rare passages in which his mother, Susan Yeats, emerges from the shadows. His writings generally give little sense of his mother's effect on his growing up, particularly when compared with the massive and complex influences that he would remember coming from his father. But now, when he was sixteen and seventeen, she, who took no interest in books and paintings, would come out of herself and talk about 'the only themes outside our house that seemed of interest – the fishing people of Howth or the pilots and fishing people of Rosses Point – she and the fisherman's wife would tell each other stories that Homer might have told, pleased with any moment of sudden intensity and laughing together over any point of satire.'[7]

While his mother and two sisters spent their days at Howth (Jack was still living with his Pollexfen grandparents), sixteen-year-old Willie, along with his father, took the early morning steam train that ran into Dublin. These times when they travelled and breakfasted together were a high point in the relationship between father and son that was so important in making Yeats a poet. In the near future Willie's views on Parnell and religious and artistic matters would begin to diverge from those of his father. But now, in these first years back in Ireland, his father was his tutor and he the pupil, one to one, especially on the subject of literature. 'We went to Dublin by train every morning, breakfasting in his studio. He had taken a large room with a beautiful eighteenth-century mantelpiece in a York

Street tenement house, and at breakfast he read passages from the poets, and always from the play or poem at its most passionate moment.' John Yeats's readings aloud and his subsequent comments came to constitute a theory of what literature should be and one that anticipated the modernist theory of the first two or three decades of this century: 'He never read me a passage because of its speculative interest, and indeed did not care at all for poetry where there was generalisation or abstraction however impassioned . . . He thought Keats a greater poet than Shelley, because less abstract . . . He disliked the Victorian poetry of ideas.' John Yeats shared the characteristic emphasis in modernist poetics upon 'things' rather than abstractions, on *res* rather than *verba*, on images rather than ideas. He liked the particularities of Pre-Raphaelite writing and painting. In the fine arts he disliked the grand rhetorical configurations then taught in the great academies such as the Académie des Beaux-Arts and the Royal Academy, and deriving from the Renaissance: 'He despised the formal beauty of Raphael, that calm which is not an ordered passion but an hypocrisy . . . In literature he was always Pre-Raphaelite, and carried into literature principles that, while the Academy was still unbroken, had made the first attack upon academic form.'[8] Such Pre-Raphaelite taste was his son's point of departure, as it was for his son's friend of thirty years on (who would also be the elderly John Yeats's friend and admirer), the great iconoclast and destroyer of 'academic form' in literature, the modernist innovator Ezra Pound.

Yeats would later declare of this period, quite simply, 'My father's influence upon my thought was at its height.' To his breakfasts which were also poetry readings and tutorials there would come, from time to time, John Yeats's friends, eminent figures from the buoyant intellectual and artistic life of Dublin in the early 1880s. One regular visitor was the painter Sarah Purser, far shrewder and more pushy than he in the Dublin art world. A confirmed spinster of thirty-four, she was already making a good living from her portraits and two years earlier had been invited to exhibit at the Royal Hibernian Academy. Though basically kind-hearted she was forthright with a considerable, if sometimes destructive, wit. Another visitor was Edward Dowden, John Yeats's near contemporary and college friend who had been elected to the Chair of English at Trinity College at the age of twenty-four. He had published several books on literature and was presently working on his *Life of Shelley* which would appear in 1886. Dowden's manner was ironic, non-committal; he had none of John Yeats's ready enthusiasm. At these breakfast meetings Willie listened to him respectfully. But a day would come when he would feel it necessary to distance himself from the Unionist sensibility which his father's friend exemplified in such a brilliant yet cool fashion.

After the breakfasts, with the sophisticated conversation of his father's friends still occupying his mind, Willie would walk a few minutes along Stephen's Green, to the Erasmus Smith High School in Harcourt Street. On his first day there he had found 'a bleak eighteenth-century house, a small playing field full of mud and pebbles, fenced by an iron railing',[9] yet he was certainly happier here than he had been at his English school. There was not the same brutality and crassness that there had been at Godolphin, though he found it something of an intellectual comedown after his early morning discussions with his father and his father's friends. He considered the teaching to be pedestrian and demoralizing. He wondered, 'What could I, who never worked when I was not interested, do with a history lesson that was but a column of dates?' The future poet was even more depressed by his English lessons: 'I was worst of all at literature, for we read Shakespeare for his grammar exclusively.'[10] The general atmosphere of the school too was distasteful to him. 'Here, as I soon found, nobody gave a thought to decorum. We worked in a din of voices.'[11]

Willie's discomfort at the High School was made worse by his father's attitude. For while Willie struggled to do the dull homework he had been given, his father, with his strong convictions about an education befitting a gentleman, 'often interfered, and always with disaster, to teach me my Latin lesson. "But I have also my geography," I would say. "Geography," he would reply, "should never be taught. It is not a training for the mind. You will pick up all that you need in your general reading." And if it was history, he would say just the same, and "Euclid," he would say, "is far too easy. It comes naturally to the literary imagination."'[12]

Yeats thought in retrospect that his father's lofty, dismissive views concerning his son's education were justified. But he also blamed his father for not acting on them. 'All he said was, I now believe, right, but he should have taken me away from school. He would have taught me nothing but Greek and Latin, and I would now be a properly educated man, and would not have to look in useless longing at books that have been, through the poor mechanism of translation, the builders of my soul, nor face authority with the timidity born of excuse and evasion.'[13] But at the time when he first felt his calling, his vocation to be a poet, he also felt a terrible tension in his life between the insistencies of his father and those of his schoolmasters. Once, when the headmaster, Mr Wilkins, learned of one more piece of interference by John Yeats in Willie's homework, he angrily punished Willie, saying, 'I am going to give you an imposition because I cannot get at your father to give him one.' One of Yeats's contemporaries at the High School remembered that Mr Wilkins 'had neither then or subsequently a very high opinion of Yeats: "the flighty poet" he used to call him.'

In the unpublished essay 'How I Began to Write' Yeats recalls this period as one of failure, misery and humiliation. But it is also the case that he made important and sustaining friendships at the school, among them those with Charles Johnston from an Ulster loyalist family who shared his developing interest in the supernatural, with W.K. Magee who as 'John Eglinton' would also become a writer, and with Frederick Gregg who would become a poet and then a journalist in New York. When they looked back, these and other contemporaries at school showed no awareness of Yeats's intense unhappiness; rather they were impressed by him. As so often in his career there was a sharp contrast between the torment, misery and lack of self-esteem within and the bold, confident figure he cut externally. Magee remembered him as 'a kind of super-boy who enjoyed an enviable immunity from the various ignominies of school discipline'. He was impressed by Yeats's knowledge and his settled ambition to become a writer, remembering him as 'an unusually well-read young man . . . with a conscious literary ambition'. Magee also felt himself a little condescended to by this schoolmate who already had a 'philosophy': 'I used to feel flattered when he would mention Huxley or Herbert Spencer, names which had hardly come within my ken, and announce himself a complete "evolutionist".' Magee also surmised that John Yeats, far from being an embarrassment to his son at school, was the reason for Willie's intellectual eminence in the schoolyard. 'His privileged standing among the boys was due, no doubt, to some arrangement with his father, who had applied certain educational principles to his children's upbringing of which spontaneous development was the essential.'[14] Parents can sometimes appear more intriguing and admirable to their children's schoolfriends than to their children themselves.

Another of Yeats's schoolmates, who went on to become a Doctor of Divinity, also held him in high esteem. Years later he wrote of Yeats, 'He was a gentlemanly dreamy fellow, lackadaisical too, didn't go in for games . . . was a good talker. He would argue and discuss matters with the master . . . He was a favourite I should say, everyone liked him and he used to spout reams of poetry to us, which none of us could comprehend as his delivery was so fast. And when we were ordered to write English verse, his was always astounding to us . . . He was really a charming fellow, rather fond of attitudinising . . . His father was an artist and the boy was not properly looked after.'[15]

Another classmate in an anonymous article remembered Yeats as an attitudinizer and poseur. He described him as a 'queer chap' and went on to say that 'there was something quietly repellent in his manner which affected even his relations with his masters'.[16] In the memoir of his youth written at the end of his life, Yeats acknowledged that people were put off by his posing and by his artificial manner. He attributed this affectation to an occasion in his youth when he had been overwhelmingly stagestruck. In an age when the theatre in its several forms was the chief medium of public entertainment, such experiences were had by many, but by none more intensely than the highly susceptible Willie Yeats. It was passionate admiration at first sight, focused on the great star of the day, Henry Irving, who would become the first actor ever to be knighted. George Bernard Shaw, then still an unknown earning his living as a theatre critic in London, thought that Irving's great achievement was to have ended the ranting school of acting that had dominated the mid-Victorian stage, 'the old domineering, self-assertive, ambitious, thundering, superb school'. 'Irving's vision', wrote Shaw, 'was to re-establish on the stage the touching, appealing nobility of sentiment and affection – the dignity which only asserts itself when it is wounded.'[17]

Yeats's infatuation began when his father took him to see the great actor play Hamlet. In the essay written at the end of his life Yeats still remembered the power of this role model. 'Years afterwards I walked the Dublin streets when nobody was looking, or nobody that I knew, with that strut Gordon Craig has compared to a movement in dance, and made the character I created speak with his brooding, broken wildness.' In the same essay he recalled that only a few months earlier, around the time of his seventy-third birthday, he had written a couplet which recalled the lofty dignity of the artist he had so looked up to in youth: 'What brushes fly and gnat aside?/ Irving and his plume of pride.'

The theatrical in Yeats, the 'attitudinising' and the role-playing which were so important a part of his evolving personality, combined to develop and provoke both liking and dislike among his school contemporaries. But at Howth he could relax his pose; here his activities and concerns were less precious. He continued to collect insects and moths, in which he took a serious scientific interest, and he became a keen chess player. He would go rowing with his school friend Charles Johnston. Once they rowed out to Ireland's Eye and were stranded there for many hours by the tide. John Yeats became increasingly worried and set out in search, only to find them utterly calm and involved in 'never-failing conversation'. John Yeats was impressed by their indifference to danger and their intellectual seriousness. Here, he began to think, were the marks of genius.[18] Doubtless one of the subjects the two young men talked about was evolution, that theory which was so controversial in late nineteenth-century life and which Willie, after a struggle, had now come to accept. He read the works of all the major theorists, 'Darwin and Wallace, Huxley and Haeckel'. As a very knowledgeable young man in this field he 'would spend hours on a holiday plaguing a pious geologist, who, when not at some job in Guinness's brewery, came with a hammer to look for fossils in the Howth cliffs'. The devout geologist who took a creationist view of the universe was scandalized by Willie's view of the fossils and declared, 'If I believed what you do, I could not live a moral life.'[19]

Willie also took an intense pleasure in being alone in the then unspoiled hill country around Howth. In his solitary wanderings about this beautiful place with its woods and seascapes he one day found 'a cave some hundred and fifty feet below the cliff path and a couple of hundred above the sea'.[20] Here he would pass the hours and eat and sleep in total isolation, 'on the excuse of catching moths'.[21] And sometimes, to his father's dismay, he would go and sleep at night 'among the rhododendrons and rocks in the wilder part of the grounds of Howth Castle'.[22] During these extended periods of solitude he gradually stopped seeing himself as a scientist and began to assume a new role. Growing tired of collecting butterflies and other specimens he roamed Howth still carrying his green net, but beginning 'to play at being a sage, a magician, or a poet'.[23] He also imagined himself as some of the heroes in the works of Romantic poets such as Byron and Shelley. 'I was now Manfred on his glacier, and now Prince Athanase with his solitary lamp, but I soon chose Alastor for my chief of men and longed to share his melancholy, and maybe at last to disappear from everybody's sight as he disappeared drifting in a boat along some slow-moving river between great trees.'[24] Out of such empathizings and identification in the solitudes of late adolescence came his first poems. It was then that he began 'to write poetry in imitation of Shelley and of Edmund Spenser, play after play – for my father exalted dramatic poetry above all other kinds – and I invented fantastic and incoherent plots.'[25]

Another reason for the young man's cultivation of solitude was the chance it gave him to dwell on his erotic feelings as well as on questions of selfhood and literature. His first important sexual experience had occurred when he was fifteen and holidaying in Sligo. He had been swimming off Rosses Point and then, naked in the sunlight, lay down on the beach and covered his body with sand. The weight of the sand roused him to erection and then brought him off. He did not understand what was happening to him and later remembered that it was some time before he discovered how to repeat the sensation. From then on he had a struggle against an experience that left him nervously exhausted.[26] But the erotic sensations which he cultivated during the Howth years were less limited and mechanical. He later wrote of this time that when he looked back he seemed to discover that his passions and despairs, far from being his enemies, became sufficiently beautiful that he had to give them his whole attention. To enjoy them he needed to be alone.[27] Some of the images of passion that so consumed him were literary ones, deriving from Shelley and other Romantic poets. 'When I thought of women they were modelled on those in my favourite poets and loved in brief tragedy, or like the girl in *The Revolt of Islam*, accompanied their lovers through all manner of wild places, lawless women without homes and without children.'[28]

But then, suddenly, real life intruded on these exotic literary reveries. One bright autumn day he was walking alone up one of the green hills of Howth. He heard the sound of hoofs and wheels behind him but paid no attention. Then a pony carriage drew up beside him. The driver was a pretty red-haired girl all on her own. Unconventionally for those times she was not wearing a hat. With breezy confidence, and without any preliminaries, she introduced herself to him as Laura Armstrong. She was staying just up the lane from Balscadden Cottage at Kilrock House, the small mansion which was the home of Judge Wright, the landlord of the Yeatses. Laura invited Willie to join her in the carriage, so he climbed up and sat beside her. She had a small, fine face; a large brow with red curls nodding over it; a delicate, sensitive mouth and intense, expectant eyes. She loved to talk and was intrigued to discover that Willie wrote poetry. They arranged to meet again, and in no time Willie was completely in love with her.

But from the outset there were difficulties. It turned out that Laura, who was some three years older than Willie, was engaged. She often quarrelled with her intended, a young solicitor, Henry Morgan Byrne, and several times the engagement had been broken off. Willie had to listen to her long accounts of the ups and downs of her relationship with Henry, all the time inwardly burning with jealousy. He had, he later remembered, 'more than one sleepless night through anger with her betrothed'.[29] Older and far more experienced in relations with the opposite sex than Willie, Laura Armstrong was a flirt and a tease. She was also emotionally volatile 'and given to bursts of religion'. When Willie escorted her to the Protestant church in Howth, her responses would oscillate wildly. 'I had known her to weep at a sermon, call herself a sinful woman, and mimic after.' Laura was 'a fine mimic and very self-dramatising'. Some years later, when himself treating his friend Katharine Tynan somewhat provocatively and flirtatiously, Yeats in a letter remembered 'Laura's wild dash of half insane genius', and he went on in one of his unpunctuated sentences to credit Laura with motivating him to turn from science to art and to write his first dramatic poem: 'Laura is to me always a pleasant memory she woke me from the metallic sleep of science and set me writing my first play.' She was the actress; he was her playwright. He said that he wrote *Time and the Witch Vivien* for her to perform before her family and friends. He began *The Island of Statues* with the same idea, but it soon developed into something larger than a piece for drawing-room acting.[30]

The title of the first named of these two early pieces, *Time and the Witch Vivien*, refers to the two characters who confront each other, throw dice and then play chess. Finally the overweening confidence of Vivien, Merlin's enchantress, is shown to be misplaced as Time defeats and claims her. Laura, in her actual relationship with Willie, and when writing to him, came to call herself Vivien. She was indeed an enchantress and a witch in Willie's life, serving, as John Yeats later observed, as the original for the 'wicked heroine in Willie's only novel', *John Sherman*.[31] But for a young man who was so much a product of Romantic reading, if a Belle Dame Sans Merci had not appeared and bewitched him, perhaps he would have needed to invent her. In their literary games and role-playing he adopted the name Clarin, remembering the sad pastoral figure in *As You Like It*. But the relationship between Willie and Laura Armstrong was more than just the self-dramatization of two self-centred young people. Something was created. Yeats began his career as a theatrical impresario, the play was written, the lines learned and a production took place. W.K. Magee remembered travelling out to Howth to see that piece of 'drawing-room acting', *Vivien and Time*, performed in Judge Wright's fine house by the ocean.[32]

At about this time the Yeats family had a painful setback. John Yeats was required to repay a debt to Sarah Purser's brother Louis and the family was forced to move to cheaper, rented accommodation. In the autumn of 1883 they had to leave Howth with its wooded green hills and its wide seascapes and take a tenancy in the lower-middle-class suburb of Terenure on the south side of Dublin. Their new home at 10 Ashfield Terrace had a bay window and was built of raw red bricks which, Willie remarked disgustedly, 'were made pretentious and vulgar with streaks of slate colour'.[33] And he hated the neighbours: 'there seemed to be enemies everywhere'. The move to Terenure was one of several drastic social displacements during his youth and adolescence that had a profound effect upon Willie, greatly heightening his sensibilities on matters of class. It was a terrible come-down in the world. Pastoral Howth, peopled for him by spirits, fishermen and a few wealthy and friendly lawyers, was now lost to him and he must live at close quarters with the lower classes. When Grandfather Pollexfen came to Dublin to see a doctor Willie and his sisters were embarrassed to view Ashfield Terrace and the contrast with Merville through his eyes.

Another cause of emotional malaise for the eighteen-year-old Willie was his entire lack of any idea as to what further education or employment he might pursue. These were the uneasy, uncomfortable months full of 'the uncertainty of his setting forth'. He had left Erasmus Smith High School the previous Christmas and his father thought he should enrol at Trinity College as he, and Willie's grandfather before him, had done. But Willie's academic record at Erasmus Smith had not been impressive. He felt that neither his mathematics nor his classics were good enough to pass the examinations for entry into the intellectual centre of the Ascendancy. His conspicuous inability to spell and punctuate, which continued throughout his life, must have strengthened such doubts. And, of course, his father's persistent intervention in his homework and his reading meant that his general education had been far from orthodox.

For months they hesitated about what he should do. Blunt, energetic Sarah Purser was shocked to see Willie looking so directionless and idle. 'You can make the boy a doctor for fifteen shillings a week,' she forcefully reminded his father.[34] But medicine was of no interest to Willie. In his shabby dark clothes with a flamboyant bow at his neck, Willie roamed the streets of Dublin, sometimes being Henry Irving, sometimes flapping his arms about as he recited or composed poems aloud. The city was full of talk of Parnell and Gladstone and the possibilities for Home Rule. But Willie was chiefly concerned at this moment with poetry and love. As often as was seemly he would pay calls on prettily dressed Laura Armstrong in the drawing-room of the grand house on the south-east corner of fashionable Stephen's Green where she lived with her mother. But he still had no idea of a career.

He was more acutely aware of this because Lily and Lolly had made up their minds what to do. Though John Yeats had not been able to afford any formal education for either of them (except for Lily's brief attendance at Notting Hill High School in London), the two sisters had decided to become art students. In the autumn of 1883 they had both enrolled at the Metropolitan School of Art on Kildare Street, then, as now, one of Dublin's most imposing thoroughfares and a long tram ride from suburban Terenure. Exactly a year later, and for lack of a better idea, Willie followed suit and became a student there also. But his commitment was always half-hearted. He later confessed that he was at the Art Schools because painting was the family occupation, and because he did not believe that he could pass the matriculation examination to enter Trinity.[35]

The teaching policies of the Metropolican School of Art were controlled from the South Kensington Art School in London. This did not help to promote originality or initiative among the instructors. Entrance requirements were minimal and attendance was casual and sporadic. Willie soon wished that he had gone to the other art school in Dublin, the Royal Hibernian Academy, and after a while he did spend some time there. In his first year at the Metropolitan he won a prize for his freehand work which was considered 'excellent'. But he found the instruction there uninspiring, even stifling. More than twenty years later when he had achieved eminence in his true calling as a writer, he was invited to give evidence to a committee of inquiry reporting to the Council of the City of Dublin on 'the work carried on' by the two art schools. Recalling his experiences as an art student, Yeats commented harshly on the Metropolitan, which he said was 'boring and destructive of enthusiasm, and of all kinds of individuality. That primarily arose from one cause . . . you went through a routine; you were in your fourth year before you got into the Life Class. You kept working at geometry; you kept drawing eyes and noses; you were kept working from the antique and then when you came to the Life Class, you came to it with whatever individuality you had largely crushed out.' The middle-aged witness clearly was remembering his own unsatisfactory experiences when he continued, 'If a very young boy joined the school, he did not, I think, suffer so much; but any young man of seventeen or eighteen, in whom individual life was working, suffered very greatly. The occupation of every student was simply to evade the system.'[36]

For nearly two years the young Yeats studied in this sterile system. But he admitted that he was not a good student, for his true creative energies were occupied elsewhere. 'I do not believe that I worked well, for I wrote a good deal and that tired me.' He admired a couple of the sculpture students in the senior class but otherwise found the student body as ignorant aesthetically as he was himself. 'We had no scholarship, no critical knowledge of the history of painting and no settled standards.' Weakly and without discrimination they would look to the world's art capital, Paris. 'A student would show his fellows some French illustrated paper that we might all admire some statue by Rodin or Dalou and now some declamatory Parisian monument, and if I did not happen to have discussed the matter with my father I would admire with no more discrimination than the rest.' Left to himself Willie looked to English Romantic painting as he looked to English Romantic poetry; he returned 'again and again . . . to gaze at Turner's "Golden Bough"' and he 'longed for pattern, for pre-Raphaelitism, for an art allied to poetry'.[37]

But for all his sense of isolation in this uninspired provincial art school his years there were by no means entirely barren. In fact they brought him an important, sometimes problematic but long-enduring friendship. One day he found himself in a class with a shy lanky student who could not draw from the model. He simply could not. Always some other image rose up in front of his eyes and he would feel obliged to paint this. Once, Yeats remembered, it was 'a St John in the Desert'. This young Ulsterman was the socially awkward and spiritually intense George Russell. Already a mystic and a regular seer of visions, he would later become a writer and poet who would publish under the pseudonym AE. He was a gentle, good-hearted young man whose unfailing kindness led Lily and Lolly to refer to him as 'the strayed angel'. Katharine Tynan also came to like him after some initial awkwardness due to his shyness. After their first meeting she wrote that the young man came out wonderfully when a kindly interest was shown in him.[38] George Russell was pale and bespectacled and had a full beard and thick dark hair. James Joyce in later years, with surely a de-aspirated pun intended, called him 'the hairy fairy'.

Russell quickly joined Charles Johnston among Yeats's companions in studying and exploring the occult. Russell's consciousness was even more tremulous than Yeats's. One day he abruptly announced that he was giving up the art school 'because his will was weak and the arts and any other emotional pursuit could but weaken it further'.[39] Instead he became a cashier and bookkeeper in a draper's shop. He had a considerable gift for business organization and management, which in future years he dedicated to the service of his country. But the spiritual was his chief concern, and his bond ⌐ with Yeats. The relationship grew closer as the two young men, against the opposition of their fathers, increasingly devoted themselves to the investigation of the supernatural.

For all his growing involvement with Russell, the chief and most compelling relationship for Yeats in the months after he entered the art school continued to be with Laura Armstrong. His emotional turmoil was a stimulus to the strenuous practice of the art of poetry to which, he now knew, he was going to commit his life. He was already planning a poetic drama of much greater complexity than his piece about Vivien. Again it was designed as a play for Laura to act in, and Laura was encouraging. A letter from her in the second week of August 1884 told him that she liked his poems, and wanted to hear him read them, but she frankly confessed that she had not finished reading them.[40] And if this last statement suggests a lack of dedication on Laura's part, the letter as a whole must have been provoking to him. It is for the most part a belated apology (the sincerity of which is not entirely conviving) for standing him up the last time he had accepted her invitation to come to the Stephen's Green house to read his poetry to her. 'My dear Clarin,' she begins, going on to apologise to him. Then, after a succession of hasty sentences, she concludes perfunctorily that she should have written sooner but had been away from home. Signing off archly, she wrote, 'Trusting to see "the poet"! and with kind regards – Believe me Ever yrs "Vivien".'

Such games between 'the poet' and his first muse were not to last much longer. Just five weeks after she sent that invitation Laura Armstrong at last married her intermittent fiancé, the solicitor Henry Byrne. So the relationship which had in great part set Yeats to writing was now at an end. But he continued to write, and worked hard at it. In their depressing home at Terenure the family of five would sit at night around a solitary lamp. Susan, as she darned and mended clothes, silently made plain her discontent that her husband was an artist and all three children were art students. The girls

and John Yeats were oppressed by her steady disapproval but Willie, oblivious of everyone else, would start to murmur, developing lines of poetry.
Then he would speak them louder. And louder. Then, still utterly preoccupied, he would chant and declaim. Finally, as John Yeats remembered,
'his sisters would call out to him, "Now, Willie, stop composing!" And he
would meekly lower his voice. After a while such composition would begin
again and Lily and Lolly would object once more.' Sometimes Willie
would finally retreat to the kitchen and 'murmur verses in any voice he liked
to his heart's content'.[41] Less than six months after his relationship with
Laura was so abruptly terminated in the autumn of 1884, he had his first
public recognition as a poet. For in the following year, and in a way he could
not have expected, he had the pleasure of seeing his poems in print for the
first time. It was a decisive year in Yeats's life. It was the same year in which
Parnell decided to bring down Gladstone's government in London; the
Irish Party held the balance of power in the new Parliament. Yeats first saw
his poems printed in a year that seemed full of possibilities and hope for
Ireland.

$[1885 - 1887]$

I N THE THIRD WEEK OF 1885, THE YEAR IN WHICH YEATS BEGAN HIS career as a published writer, there occurred in Dublin the inaugural meeting of a new Young Ireland Society, held in the grand eighteenth-century Round Room of the Rotunda at the end of Sackville Street beside Rutland Square or, as the location would become in less than forty years, the end of O'Connell Street beside Parnell Square.

As the first speaker rose to deliver the opening address, there came excited cheering from the audience. For this strikingly handsome 55-year-old man with the full grey beard, strong characterful nose and piercing eyes was John O'Leary, who from this time on would virtually replace John Butler Yeats as Willie's chief elder and mentor. The editor of the *Irish People*, the newspaper of the Irish Republican Brotherhood, John O'Leary along with other Fenians had been arrested in 1865 on suspicion of organizing a revolution. O'Leary, who had studied both law and medicine, was treated like a common criminal rather than a political prisoner and was given a twenty-year prison sentence which meant he had to labour for long hours hauling and splitting rocks in the stone quarries in Portland Prison on the south coast of England. After serving six years of such 'penal servitude' he was released on condition that he stay away from Ireland for the duration of his sentence. The remaining fourteen years of exile he spent mostly in Paris, where he came to know some of the leading writers and artists of the time. But in January 1885, the moment his sentence was completed, he was back in Dublin, acknowledging the admiring, affectionate applause of this large audience consisting in great part of young people who had been but small children at the time of his arrest.

O'Leary began with a ringing declaration: 'I have come back from exile with the same opinions and feelings I carried with me into prison.'[1] This brought loud and extended cheering; it was just what the crowd wished to hear. Tears came into the eyes of the speaker's sister Ellen O'Leary, sitting in the front row. Herself a nationalist and a poet, she would serve as her brother's hostess as people with nationalist sympathies, including the nineteen-year-old Willie Yeats, sought out the returned exile.

When the cheers at last subsided, John O'Leary went on to emphasize the importance of the literary tradition which the new society inherited from the Young Ireland movement of the 1840s and which he urged them to perpetuate. 'The name of your society . . . is before all things associated with that great wave of literary activity which spread all over Ireland some forty years ago.' With slow, passionate deliberation he declared, 'I am here to call upon you, young men of the rising and risen generation, and to urge you now, with all the earnestness I can command, and with the blessing of God, to keep on urging you, to imitate and emulate that body whose name you have taken.' He continued, 'Shortly speaking, we have as much need as ever for such aid and inspiration as is to be got from ballad and song, from story, essay or history.'[2] The practical consequences of his demands, he went on, were the creation of a new kind of literature for today, the publishing and circulation of Irish books, and the creation of Irish libraries. Quoting of one of the famous and colourful figures of the previous Young Ireland movement, Charles Gavan Duffy, now in his seventieth year, O'Leary repeated to the new generation sitting before him, 'Educate that you may be free.'[3]

When O'Leary's speech was published a little later that year by the Young Ireland Society, the author presented a copy to C.H. Oldham, a young man who was very much in sympathy with the ideas expressed in the address.[4] Some five years older than Willie Yeats at this time and a recent graduate of Trinity College, Charles Hubert Oldham responded to the new nationalist mood and to O'Leary's urgings by undertaking to found a new literary periodical for Ireland. Called the *Dublin University Review*, 'a monthly magazine of Literature, Art and University Intelligence', its first issue appeared in February 1885. The second, which appeared the following month, contained two slight, short poems by another young O'Leary sympathizer, W.B. Yeats. The two lyrics, full of melancholy, were entitled 'Song of the Faeries' and 'Voices'. This was the first time his poetry had appeared in print.

A future professor of political economy, Oldham was twenty-four years old when he founded the *Review*, which announced its editorial office as being at his address, 29 Trinity College, Dublin. He was very conscious of having gained his degree only shortly before and in the early issues he presented himself to the readership as C.H. Oldham, BA. A handsome and extremely energetic young man, he was also tactless and gauche. Years later Yeats remembered that Oldham was always rude, without ill-feeling or temper. Rather coarse in some ways, he was himself exceedingly sensitive. But Yeats added that when inspired by hot morality and his good heart, he could arouse people's emotions.[5]

Oldham's 'hot morality' was fuelled by his passionate belief in the righteousness of Ireland's cause. A Protestant nationalist, he was always sensitive about the good name and dignity of his country. Yeats recalled hearing of one occasion when Oldham was staying in a small country hotel on the west coast of Ireland. This was, of course, at a time long before indoor toilets were in use and when chamber pots were a necessary part of bedroom furnishing. Suddenly a large party of French visitors arrived at the hotel. Not long after, the landlady was amazed to see Oldham holding one end of a long rope, and a local lad the other, and the rope passing through the handles of what Yeats termed 'much crockery ware of a kind that are not usually carried through the streets in broad daylight'. As he led his little procession into the hotel Oldham was confronted by the outraged landlady. He replied that the sudden large influx of visitors must, he knew, find the hotel imperfectly provided. 'I must consider', he said, 'the reputation of my country.'

Oldham's introductory editorial in the *Dublin University Review* took a firm but not strident nationalistic tone:

It is true that, nowadays in the world of intellectual effort, all roads seem to lead to London; but if it is anywhere possible to resist successfully the centralising tendencies of the time, and to strive for local individuality, it is surely in a great national seat of learning, the home of much of the rising talent of the country. It is believed, therefore, that without sinking into mere provincialism, without discussing too exclusively Irish topics, without giving undue importance to the writings or achievements of Irishmen, The Review *can assume and maintain a distinctly national tone; and in its pages Irish writers can express to Irish readers their views on the social problems of the day, and on the phases and aspects of contemporary art and literature.*[6]

The *Review* was very much a product of Trinity College and there were numerous reports, in the early issues, on the activities of the various clubs and societies in the College. At the same time the main articles showed the broad intellectual range and cultural cosmopolitanism of the magazine. During 1885 the *Review* had translations from the German of Heinrich Heine by John Yeats's friend John Todhunter, a serialization of Turgenev's recently translated *On the Eve* and an article on Victor Hugo, who died that year. T.W. Lyster, a future head librarian of the National Library of Ireland (the Quaker librarian in the 'Scylla and Charybdis' section of Joyce's *Ulysses*), contributed an article on a new illustrated edition of the *Rubáiyát of Omar Khayyám*, Edward Dowden wrote on the contemporary French philosophical poet Sully-Prudhomme and there was an article on Lord Randolph Churchill, then approaching the zenith of his political career as the proponent of Tory Democracy, an alliance between the aristocracy and the working class.

Such articles were published alongside others dealing with the issues of the day. One of Lord Randolph Churchill's Irish admirers, the barrister, writer and defender of the Anglo-Irish Ascendancy, Standish O'Grady, contributed two articles on Irish Conservatism. After O'Leary, Standish O'Grady, who Yeats thought had recreated in strong Romantic English old heroic legends of Ireland,[7] was the most important new influence on Yeats at this time, both as political theorist and historian of Ireland. In a subsequent issue of the *Review* O'Grady's vision of aristocratic renewal in

Ireland provoked a critical retort entitled 'Irish Conservatism and Its Outlook' from Michael Davitt, the Fenian who had served fifteen years' imprisonment and emerged to found the Land League with Charles Stewart Parnell. To the exchanges on the subject of the future of Ireland Oldham himself contributed a forceful essay on the inspirational importance of the now neglected statue of Thomas Davis, a leader and a poet of the old Young Ireland and author of the rousing verses beginning 'A nation once again'. The *Review* also published articles on the role of the Irish language and on the value of the folk-songs and folk-tales of Ireland. In his essay 'The Irish Language and Literature', Justin Huntly McCarthy, the last of the Irish MPs to desert Parnell in the great political drama at the end of the decade, expressed a hope which Yeats, as well as Standish O'Grady, would seek to fulfil. 'What I should like to see come to pass . . . is that every Irishman should be as familiar with these varied legends, which are his own magnificent heritage, as with the stories which were told by Athenian fathers to their children.'8

The publication of his work in the *Dublin University Review* was not the only major event in Yeats's career in 1885. In its July issue the 'Notes and News' section of the *Review* reported his involvement in the creation of the Dublin Hermetic Society. As a child Willie had a keen sense of the spiritual, of religious and unseen realities, which was confirmed by the atmosphere of his beloved Sligo with its second-sighted people, its tales of a fairy world, its many superstitions and its great prehistoric burial grounds nearby. But his father, a confident, cheerful agnostic, had mocked religion – Catholicism and Protestantism alike – an attitude which caused a serious and painful conflict in the mind and feelings of the growing boy. He later wrote, 'My father's unbelief had set me thinking about the evidences of religion and I weighed the matter perpetually with great anxiety, for I did not think I could live without religion.'9 Now, just three days after his twentieth birthday, by helping to found the society he began an experiment in an alternative way of institutionalizing his religious quest.

The *Review* went on to report, 'The Society met for the first time on June 16th in Trinity College. Mr W.B. Yeats having given an address on the objects of the Society, a paper was read by Mr Smeeth . . . His remarks were illustrated by several experiments.' In that same issue of the *Review* there was printed a paper by Yeats's schoolfriend Charles Johnston entitled 'Esoteric Buddhism'. The title is the same as that of the book by A.P. Sinnett which Aunt Isabella Pollexfen, by now married to the painter John Varley, had recently sent William from London and which he had passed on to Johnston who had been profoundly affected by it. In what Lewis Mumford termed 'The Brown Decades' of the late nineteenth century, as industrialization in the Western world developed rapidly and often brutally, there were a number of movements, such as theosophy, which preached and promised spiritual renewal. The Society for Psychical Research was founded in Cambridge at about this time. There was much searching for something with which to confront the inexorable advance of secularism and to make up for the loss of faith in the wake of Darwin.

The Theosophical Society had been founded in New York in 1875 by Colonel Henry Olcott and Madame Blavatsky, a Russian-born woman who as an eighteen-year-old bride deserted her highly placed husband in order to travel the world in search of divine wisdom. She later spoke of the time she had spent in Tibet studying with mahatmas, spiritual leaders and adepts such as Koot Hoomi. Madame Blavatsky, whom a report for the Society for Psychical Research described as 'one of the most accomplished, ingenious, and interesting impostors in history', laid out the principles of theosophy in her book *Isis Unveiled* of 1877. The book is based on notions derived from both Buddhist and Hindu traditions and presents life as a series of reincarnations that may possibly lead to Nirvana. She also argued the unity of all religions and preached a world brotherhood of all faiths. In the near future Yeats would seek out Madame Blavatsky in London and hear of her spiritual quest, including her many dialogues with Koot Hoomi on secret and occult lore. Sinnett's book *Esoteric Buddhism* is in many respects a restatement of Madame Blavatsky's doctrine, and Charles Johnston's paper, which he read to an early meeting of the Dublin Hermetic Society, a summary of Sinnett. According to Johnston the leading assumption is that 'The embodiment of such a complex being as man is destined to become does not take place on the earth alone, but is extended through a chain of seven planets, each of which has a part to play in the development of humanity. Man it appears had to pass seven times round the complete planetary chain . . .'[10] With such basic ideas did Yeats, the lifelong cartographer of the supernatural, set off on his journey to an ever more complex and intricate understanding of the world of spirit.

Though hospitable to the ideas and writings of the young occultists, the *Dublin University Review* made a point of keeping its distance from them. If theosophy was widely fashionable at this time, so also were the comic operas of Gilbert and Sullivan. And the editors printed a piece of doggerel in the style of Gilbert, which they described as a 'satire on the young Buds'. It was entitled 'A.P. Sinnett (lines suggested by the late Theosophical Movement in T.C.D.)'. One stanza (perhaps one of the down-to-earth jests of C.H. Oldham, BA) ran:

> *I'm an Esoteric swell*
> *A boss of the Buddhists as well*
> *A Theosophistico*
> *Occulto-Mystico*
> *Koot Hoomi Lal Singhi swell.*[11]

The poems of Yeats which appeared in this and other issues of the *Review* in 1885 pre-date in their subject-matter his new, declared concern with theosophy. These early publications are distinguished chiefly by their literariness and none more so than his early and very ambitious long dramatic poem 'The Island of Statues'. When he was eighteen or nineteen he had written a pastoral play in the manner of Keats and Shelley, but also influenced by Ben Jonson's *Sad Shepherd*, Yeats later remembered.[12] After the first two lyrics published in the March issue which marked Yeats's début, the editors of the *Review* made a serious commitment to the young poet by undertaking to serialize this extended dramatic piece over four issues. Set in that long-established literary location, pastoral Arcadia, where nymphs and shepherds pursue their idylls, it concerns a characteristic Romantic quest, found in works as diverse as Beethoven's Ninth Symphony and Wordsworth's 'Intimations of Immortality' – the quest for joy.

Naschina, Yeats's heroine, is weary of the banality of the life around her; so Alminto, the hero, sets out to find and pluck for her 'the goblin flower of joy'. To do this he must go to the Island of the Enchantress where previous questers have been turned into stone statues. Alminto too is turned to stone. Naschina, earlier indifferent to him, now misses him and sets off for the island, leaving behind two shepherds fighting over her. Arriving on the island, Naschina proves to be the person 'long years ago foretold' who can end the power of the Enchantress. This she does. She is then able to wake Alminto and the other statues who prove to be figures from ancient stories, the Knights of the Round Table and characters from the *Iliad* and the *Aeneid*. Naschina has saved the questing but unsuccessful man and also liberated and revitalized the past so that it may speak. Possessing 'the goblin flower of joy' she now also embodies some of those important Romantic abstractions that signify the possibility of transcending the quotidien, for

> *To her that wears that bloom comes truth,*
> *And elvish wisdom, and long years of youth*
> *Beyond a mortal's year.*

It is possible to speculate on biographical elements in the poem. Alminto perhaps owes something to the experience of the young Yeats struggling to entertain and enrich the life of the sometimes interested, often indifferent Laura Armstrong. Like Yeats Alminto gets nowhere and, at the last, needs her more than she him. Naschina, like Laura, is a powerful force − by far the most potent character in the poem. The first of a succession of powerful, problematical female presences in Yeats's art, like Laura she is a beautiful young woman who can make for hurt and discord among men but also bring them intense happiness, the difficult muse who can rouse the living dead to life and speech.

'The Island of Statues' reveals a nineteen-year-old writer already steeped in the tradition of English poetry, especially that of the Romantic period. This long, ambitious piece is rarely more than derivative. But it does show two particular literary skills characteristic of the maturer Yeats. The thematic patterning is carefully worked out. And throughout the piece there is a highly finished verbal intricacy. From the outset Yeats put much effort into the craft of his writing.

Getting Oldham to publish such a lengthy piece as 'The Island of Statues' in the *Dublin University Review* constituted an early rite of passage for a poet still in his teens. Over fifty years later, little more than a year before his death, in a piece he prepared for the BBC entitled 'How I Began to Write', Yeats still remembered vividly his intense embarrassment and self-consciousness on that occasion. Oldham had looked at the poem and asked the young student from the Art School to come over to his rooms in Trinity College and read the poem aloud to some of his colleagues. Oldham was particularly concerned to have the opinion of J.B. Bury, a contemporary of his at Trinity and one of its intellectual stars who would later become a distinguished historian, an editor of Gibbon and, at the end of his career, Regius Professor of Modern History at Cambridge. The young poet who had not had sufficient confidence in his academic abilities to sit the Trinity entrance exams quailed at the prospect of reading to an audience that included such a figure. He was tormented by shyness. Left alone with Bury, his conversation was abrupt and brief. Outsiders at this time remarked on the young poet's affectation, his arrogant showing off, but Yeats himself spoke only of the terrible inner turmoil, the churning sense of inadequacy within. As he approached his twentieth birthday his sense of self was unformed, still volatile and a mass of contradictions. His later theories of selfhood derived from experiences such as that of proving himself on that day in Oldham's rooms overlooking the eighteenth-century courtyard of Trinity College.

In any event Bury made no objection to 'The Island of Statues'. Oldham went ahead and published it. With this substantial piece of writing, the unmotivated art student began to define himself, and to be recognized in Dublin as a poet. During that spring of 1885, while the poem was being serialized in the *Review*, C.H. Oldham also assisted Yeats's career in another way. For it was Oldham who introduced him to Katharine Tynan, a young woman four years older than Yeats and herself a published poet who had recently brought out her first volume of poems, *Louise de la Vallière*, the title of which alluded to the first mistress of Louis XIV. But Katharine Tynan's home environment was far removed from that of the Sun King. She lived with her parents at Clondalkin, then a pleasant rural place where the Tynans had a farm. Their cottage had immense overhanging eaves of thatch and a front door set within a green trellis. It stood in a picturesque spot on the Grand Canal on which the horse-drawn barges, brightly painted, made their way westward into quiet inland

Ireland. Katharine did not accept the orthodox ideas of a woman's role current in the Ireland of her day. Her father greatly admired and respected his daughter's literary achievements and her keen desire for personal independence and gave her her own sitting-room in which to receive and to entertain independently. Here C.H. Oldham came one day to discuss, among other things, Katharine's contributions to the *Dublin University Review*. Suddenly in his abrupt, awkward way he announced, 'I've got a queer youth named Yeats,' and asked if he might bring his new discovery to see her. Katharine Tynan agreed and a few days later the young man appeared at the farm. There then began a friendship, a literary comradeship, that was to be important and creative for both of them. Katharine's first impression of the lanky, gentle young man was that he was 'beautiful to look at, with his dark face, its touch of vivid colouring, the night black hair, the eager dark eyes'.[13]

Katharine Tynan herself was, in appearance, characterful rather than beautiful. She was acquainted with an English Jesuit poet, Gerard Manley Hopkins, who had recently come to Dublin to teach and preach and whose own great and innovative contributions to English poetry had to wait more than thirty years for posthumous publication and recognition. Hopkins liked Katharine; he described her as 'a simple brightlooking Biddy with glossy very pretty red hair'.[14] Her jaw was square, her lips full. By the standards of the time her red hair was cut short. She had an eye condition and wore a pince-nez. But in the painting that John Yeats later did of her, her eyes shine alertly bright.

Katharine and Willie took to each other immediately, a ready sympathy resulting from their being poets together, both to some degree social outsiders and both keen to discuss all possibilities of developing their literary careers. Willie returned often to the charming and comfortable farmhouse, and Katharine would drive him round the countryside in her pony and trap. Their youthful friendship was intensely literary and they talked and talked about books and writing. Only some years on would romantic possibilities develop. More conventional girls might have been put off by Willie's occasional eccentricities. On one occasion he tried to hypnotize the hens in the farmyard at Clondalkin. On another, in the pouring rain, he passionately recited Shelley's 'The Sensitive Plant', oblivious of everything but the poem, and certainly not noticing that he was holding the umbrella in such a way that Katharine's clothes were soaked through. On their long walks around Dublin he would flail his arms around in a violent way that, Katharine noticed, intrigued policemen. But she was not perturbed; she was taken with his sincerity and the passion he brought to his writing.

In time she visited the Yeats home, where she made friends with Lily and Lolly. She went with Willie to his father's studio in the centre of Dublin and they also encountered each other at the home of the charismatic John O'Leary. Here the pair of them were influenced ever more strongly to write on Irish themes. In the coming years some of Yeats's most important letters about his thoughts and feelings and practice as a writer were addressed to her who became 'My Dear Katey'. She was the first in that succession of women who were primarily Yeats's helpmates rather than his lovers, women to whom he would refer for all kinds of support – emotional, psychological, spiritual, social, financial – as his career went on.

In 1885 Yeats also joined the Contemporary Club, another initiative of C.H. Oldham and thus much involved with the aims of the *Dublin University Review*. The first meetings were held in Oldham's rooms at Trinity, but towards the end of 1885 the Club removed to premises over a bookshop on fashionable Grafton Street. Oldham called it the Contemporary Club because members were required to have nothing in common except being alive at the same time. He wished to be hospitable to all shades of opinion on current Irish political and cultural issues, though he never managed to attract Unionists of the extreme right such as the colourful and outspoken Sir John Pentland Mahaffy, Professor of Ancient History at Trinity College. Among the regulars at the Contemporary Club, which would continue as an institution in Dublin life for some sixty years, were Yeats, his father, John O'Leary, Michael Davitt the self-educated Fenian, and T.W. Rolleston, a gifted scholar in the field of Irish, Greek and German literature who had a prominent role in the editing of the *Review*. Rolleston was someone who would often reappear in Yeats's life. Some eight years older than Yeats, Rolleston was in 1885 also very much under the influence of John O'Leary. Yeats was impressed by Rolleston's excellent translations from the German and also by his physical attractiveness.[15]

Yeats expected great things of the handsome, gifted Rolleston but within just a few years felt betrayed by him. Later he wrote scathingly of him, 'His Nationalist convictions had never been more than the toys of a child, and were put away when the bell rang to meals.' Mocking his own naivety at the age of nineteen, Yeats added, he had once thought him a possible leader of the Irish.[16]

But there were others in the Contemporary Club and of that distinctive and lively generation in Dublin in the 1880s who did not default on the cause of Ireland's independence. One was the seemingly timid Douglas Hyde, who a few years later would found the Gaelic League 'to keep the language alive among the people', and more than half a century on would become Ireland's leader and serve as the first President of the Republic. Another of the strong personalities at the Club and a major challenge and threat to Yeats's precarious sense of himself was the 35-year-old John F. Taylor QC. Taylor was a journalist and an eloquent barrister, one of whose highly rhetorical speeches urging the defence of the Irish language would be remembered in the 'Aeolus' section of Joyce's *Ulysses*. In Taylor, with 'his coarse red hair, his gaunt ungainly body, his stiff movements as of a Dutch doll', Yeats encountered his harshest critic and most contemptuous opponent at the Club. Yeats, who for years reflected on their confrontations in forms of debate that were much rougher than those in England, was not sure whether it was Taylor's strong belief in scientific method or his strict Catholic orthodoxy which made him 'become enraged with my supernaturalism'.[17] Yeats saw in Taylor a pedantry created by his Irish Catholic education and furthered by an intense energy which made his mind like some noisy and powerful machine.[18] Remembering those bitterly antagonistic debates, Yeats wrote that Taylor's notorious temper only augmented the vigour of his mind, whilst Yeats, whose beliefs were not based upon logic but upon fine insights, became confused and spoiled his case by overstating it.[19] Yeats made an effort to see these very public quarrels from Taylor's point of view: he suggested that Taylor probably thought him effeminate. He added that a stone is always stronger, more masculine than something living.[20] Yeats also suspected that another reason for Taylor's hostility was that he was 'jealous of my favour in O'Leary's eyes'.[21]

Whatever his motives, Taylor's verbal assaults on the young man who was little more than half his age were ferocious, and brought out in Yeats a side entirely different from the dreamy, sensitive self that Katharine Tynan first knew. Along with all his many susceptibilities the young poet had determination and perseverance. At the Contemporary Club, defending himself against the sneers of the massively confident Taylor, Yeats showed that he could be forceful, even aggressive. He may not have won the debates, but neither was he defeated nor made to look a fool. His exchanges with the barrister were for him a hardening process. He later remembered, 'I made a good many speeches, more I believe as a training for self-possession than from desire of speech.'[22]

The Contemporary Club was always pleased to welcome visiting speakers from outside Ireland. One of these was the distinguished late-Victorian figure William Morris, poet, designer, father of the Arts and Crafts movement and socialist campaigner. He addressed the Club in 1885 on 'The Aims of Art' and whilst there was sketched by John Butler Yeats. The burly, bearded Morris with his mass of hair and strong presence had energetic opinions on dozens of subjects and took a kindly interest in the impressionable young Irish poet. Like his friend, the Pre-Raphaelite painter Edward Burne-Jones, Morris was a keen supporter of the Irish cause. Yeats, who under O'Leary's influence was about to become a member of the Irish Republican Brotherhood (though without taking the oath),[23] felt he should challenge the famous man for not having chosen to speak to the Club on an Irish topic. With genuine sadness William Morris replied that he would 'gladly lecture in Dublin on Irish literature but that the people knew too little about it'.[24] This was a remark which impressed Yeats and which he would quote some months later when, in the pages of the *Dublin University Review*, he made his début as a prose writer and a literary critic, arguing the Irishness of the poetry of Samuel Ferguson.[25] The relationship between Morris and Yeats was to be a creative one.

Another of the visitors to the Contemporary Club who became an enduring memory for Yeats was the Indian theosophist, Mohini Chatterji. The address which this young Brahmin figure delivered to the Club was printed in the *Dublin University Review* of May 1886 and entitled 'The Common Sense of Theosophy'. Yeats's meeting with this visitor stimulated his feeling for the occult and more than forty years later he would recall how this Indian associate of Madame Blavatsky spoke calmingly to him, in such a way 'That he might set at rest / A boy's turbulent days'. When the young and spiritually confused Yeats asked the visitor if he should try to pray, Chatterji replied that he should not. Instead he should recognize the infinite reincarnations in which his selfhood was and had been involved. Rather than praying, he should say every night in bed

> *I have been a king,*
> *I have been a slave,*
> *Nor is there anything,*
> *Fool, rascal, knave,*
> *That I have not been.*[26]

But for all the steadying reassurances of Mohini Chatterji, Yeats's progress in the occult was to continue to be tumultuous. In the year of Chatterji's visit, 1886, which was also the year Charles Johnston obtained a charter to set up a Dublin lodge of the Theosophical Society, Yeats attended his first séance. It was a shocking, unnerving experience. As the medium dozed in his chair and the lights were turned down, the half-dozen people present sat around a table in dim firelight, their hands linked. Suddenly Yeats's hands and shoulders began to twitch. His whole body shook ever more violently. Finally he was thrown backward against the wall behind him. Members of the group called to him that if he did not resist the force, some wonderful thing would happen. In spite of himself Yeats banged the knuckles of the woman whose hand he held down on the table. Yeats was terrified. He tried to pray but could not remember a prayer. Then he shouted out the first four lines of Milton's *Paradise Lost*. He could no longer see anything. Slowly he calmed down. But he was frightened and greatly confused by the experience of being so possessed. Not for several years would he feel able to attend another séance.

During 1886, the second year of his association with the *Dublin University Review*, Yeats's political consciousness evolved rapidly along with his exploration of the occult. He increasingly looked up to John and Ellen O'Leary. As he pondered the possibilities of epic poetry, they seemed to him like the noble Greeks and Romans: 'I found sister and brother alike were of Plutarch's people.'[27] O'Leary, Yeats later said, could move young people by the power of moral genius.[28] Yeats also saw O'Leary as a man of literary discrimination, remembering that when O'Leary lent him the poetry of Davis and the Young Irelanders, about whom Yeats knew nothing, O'Leary did not, despite his patriotism, claim that it was poetry of any distinction.[29] O'Leary's influence on Yeats's art first shows itself in a poem published by the *Review* called 'The Two Titans' and subtitled 'A Political Poem'. The two figures of the title are allegories of Ireland and the British Empire:

> *Two figures crouching on the black rock, bound*
> *To one another with a coiling chain;*
> *A grey-haired youth, whose cheeks had never found,*
> *Or long ere this had lost their ruddy stain;*
> *A sibyl, with fierce face as of a hound*
> *That dreams . . .*

The poem goes on to describe the devitalization and the grotesque distortions that the shackling together of the two has produced. The poem was shown to Gerard Manley Hopkins, then a lecturer at University College on Stephen's Green. Quick to see its obscurities and deficiencies, Hopkins wrote that 'It was a strained and unworkable allegory about a young man and a sphinx on a rock in the sea (how did they get there? what did they eat and so on). People think such criticisms very prosaic; but common sense is never out of place anywhere.'[30]

For all his 'political' intentions, Yeats in 'The Two Titans' is still awkwardly confined within the derivative literary allegory that he had employed in 'The Island of Statues'. Yeats contributed a more important and less inhibited piece of political writing to the *Review* towards the end of the year: an essay on the poet Samuel Ferguson, a neighbour of the Yeats family when they lived at Howth, who had recently died. The essay, which also marks the beginning of Yeats's long career as a literary critic, shows the young man writing in the service of John O'Leary's agenda. Mahaffy, the leading Unionist intellectual, had assured his readers in the prestigious London periodical the *Athenaeum* that Ferguson, knighted for his work as an antiquarian, was as a man and a writer loyal to the British crown. But Yeats would have none of this. Such misunderstandings and false definitions of Ferguson's achievement were, he claimed, a consequence of the weaknesses of Irish literary criticism. Criticism is a necessary part of a larger literary culture, he argues. 'If Ireland has produced no great poet, it is not that her poetic impulse has run dry, but because her critics have failed her, for every community is a solidarity, all depending upon each and each upon all.' Yeats then declares independence for himself, his generation and the new phase of national literary consciousness in Ireland. In so doing he impudently attacks that most prominent and successful figure of his father's generation and, of course, his father's friend, Professor Edward Dowden. Yeats writes:

> *It is a question whether the most distinguished of our critics, Professor Dowden, would not only have more consulted the interests of his country, but more also, in the long run, his own dignity and reputation, which are dear to all Irishmen, if he had devoted some of those elaborate pages which he has spent on the much bewritten George Eliot, to a man like the subject of this article . . . If Sir Samuel Ferguson had written to the glory of that, from a moral point of view, more than dubious achievement, British civilization, the critics, probably including Professor Dowden, would have taken care of his reputation.*[31]

Yeats had strong objection to George Eliot, who had published her last novel *Daniel Deronda* some nine years earlier. To his schoolfriend Frederick James Gregg he wrote a letter containing major criticisms of her work. Tito in *Romola*, he wrote, is without interest as a human being. In George Eliot there is lacking the beauty with which Hugo endowed everything he wrote. He goes on to say that she understands only human consciousness, intellectual and moral issues; she knows nothing of the instinctive and the unconscious, which Darwin regarded as the wisdom acquired by all living creatures. Becoming ever more scornful of that eminent Victorian who had died four years before, the young poet went on to say that all major works of literature are Homeric, but George Eliot was too much governed by reason: she had morals but no religion.[32]

Returning to his essay on Ferguson, Yeats's own strong commitment to Romantic feeling voices itself again as he characterizes and passionately commends his work, 'the greatest poet Ireland has produced, because the most central and most Celtic', an artist 'made by the purifying flame of National sentiment, the one man of his time who wrote heroic poetry . . . In these poems and the legends they contain lies the refutation of the calumnies of England and those amongst us who are false to their country.' In a final rousing and rhetorical paragraph appealing for attention to be paid to Ferguson and his work, O'Leary's young follower again sneers at Dowden and his like and calls to the young people of his own generation. 'I do not appeal to the professional classes, who, in Ireland, at least, appear at no time to have thought of the affairs of their country till they first feared for their emoluments – nor do I appeal to the shoddy society of "West Britonism" – but to those young men clustered here and there throughout our land, whom the emotion of Patriotism has lifted into that world of selfless passion in which heroic deeds are possible and heroic poetry credible.'[33] The young introvert and dreamer who brooded on the mystical works of Mohini Chatterji could also be the combative polemicist. Indeed in the next edition of the *Review* the editors felt it necessary to respond to an angry letter deploring 'the rather petulant intrusion of political polemics in almost every page of Mr Yeats's article'.[34]

In the November 1886 issue of the *Review* the editors again had done what they could to back their young poet by placing the following announcement in 'Notes of the Month': 'We are glad to note the publication by Messrs Sealy, Boyes and Walker of the powerful and pathetic poem "Mosada" contributed to a recent number of this review by Mr W.B. Yeats. The reprint contains a pen-and-ink portrait of the author by Mr J.B. Yeats – a very beautiful and characteristic piece of work, admirably reproduced on zinc by a Dublin engraver, Mr Lewis.' This was Yeats's first ever separate, independent publication. A ten-page pamphlet with a small print run and now very rare, 'Mosada' is another dramatized version of Yeats's quarrel with George Eliot. Mosada is a young Moorish girl who employs what are clearly narcotic herbs to stimulate more intense consciousness and feeling.

> *Thus do I burn these precious herbs whose smoke*
> *Pours up and floats in fragrance o'er my head.*

For her activities she is arrested or 'taken in magic' by the Roman Catholic authorities. The poem then proceeds as a confrontation and argument between her and the stern moralist who is the priest of the Inquisition.

The December issue of the magazine, the editors announced, 'terminates at once the second volume and the existence of the *Dublin University Review*'. Two months later there was a short-lived attempt to revive it after what was called 'a change in the Editorial Department'. But the few issues that appeared during the first half of 1877 had little in common with what had gone before. There was a new concern with the law and with military matters, and such poetry as was published was dreadful. Effectively the *Dublin University Review*, as a historic intellectual and cultural force in Irish life, ended in December 1886. Its two years of existence had been almost exactly contemporaneous with the first two years of Yeats's career as a published writer, and in its pages his writings had grown ever more prominent, confident and ambitious, but that first phase in his life as a writer was now at an end. The break was confirmed in a still more dramatic and painful way. For his father, now in advancing middle age and fearful that he could not find financial success in Dublin, decided to return to London to try there once again. Willie, now aged twenty-one, but still emotionally and financially dependent upon his family, would have to go along too. Just as he was establishing himself as a Dublin writer, he was forced to leave the city and start all over again in London.

$[1887 - 1889]$

FTER THE YEATS FAMILY'S RETURN TO LONDON IN THE SPRING of 1887, Willie's letters back to Dublin are full of homesickness and deep distaste for his new surroundings. Katharine Tynan, his principal correspondent, was made continually aware of his despondency and depression. Unnerved by the extremes of wealth and poverty all around him in London, he told her that he looked to letters from Ireland to give him pleasure.[1] Five weeks later his gloom continues unabated as he tells Katharine that he does not expect he will ever find London very tolerable and that he expects to gain nothing from the place.[2]

There was however one inspiring moment shortly after his arrival. This was when he went to the Visitors' Gallery of the House of Commons and heard a speech by T.M. Healy MP, an eloquent, emphatic Irish nationalist, a master of invective and one of Parnell's chief parliamentary lieutenants. *The Times* had published a series of articles entitled 'Parnellism and Crime' which implicated Parnell in the Phoenix Park murders and in the violence and unrest in rural Ireland. Healy mounted a powerful defence of one of the Irish members whom *The Times* had singled out for criticism. Looking down on the debate, Willie was excited by the speech. Here was Ireland and its cause come close again, and he saw in Healy that elemental quality which he so much missed in people in London. He told Katharine Tynan that he was greatly pleased with Healy; he saw in him a good earth power.[3]

But in these first months back in London such moments of exhilaration were few. A year after returning Willie still hated the place. He took a delight in imagining his letter leaving London and joining other letters in the basket going from Clondalkin to White Hall. He wished that he could join his letter, especially as he suspected that spring had arrived in Ireland while in London there was still snow.[4] Ten months later profound homesickness shows itself again in a first draft of a poem which he sent to her who was his closest and most trusted literary friend. After revision, this was to become one of his most famous poems, 'The Lake Isle of Innisfree'.

One reason for the unhappiness which affected Yeats and other members of his family during this time was their intense dissatisfaction with the house which John Yeats had rented. It was in Earl's Court, close to the underground station, at 58 Eardley Crescent. An end house in a stuccoed row in the debased classical style typical of mid-Victorian developments, their new home seemed to them even more squalid than the one at Terenure. John Yeats himself described it as 'old and dirty and dank and noisy', while Lily wrote that the house was 'horrible' and the garden just a bit of sooty ground dirtied by cats.[5] Like Terenure, this western edge of Kensington was a lower-middle-class suburb and clearly upsetting to the family of one who had once contemplated practising at the Dublin Bar. For the large Earl's Court Exhibition ground, which was very close to the house, gave to the area a funfair atmosphere and a noisy vulgarity. Steam organs blared out the music-hall songs of the day and at the time the Yeats family unenthusiastically moved in, Buffalo Bill and his Cowboy and Indian troupe were putting on shows that entailed whooping war cries and rattling gunfire. As the slender, bespectacled Willie went down into the underground station pondering his new project, a poem about Oisin, one of the noble heroes of ancient Ireland, he was met by crowds of working-class cockneys surging up from the steam-hauled trains, eager to cross the street to the Wild West show.

Less than a mile from this rackety, congested suburb there stood (and still stands) a beautiful eighteenth-century house beside the River Thames: Kelmscott House, a five-bay brick house of three storeys on Upper Mall, an extension of Chiswick Mall near Hammersmith. It looked out across the broad river to the lush and unspoiled countryside of the Surrey shore, and was the home of William Morris. He and his wife Janey, the famous Pre-Raphaelite beauty, and their two daughters May and Jenny, had lived in this quiet riverside place for nearly ten years. Morris the wealthy socialist used the stables of the house for political meetings; Morris the father of the Arts and Crafts Movement had a tapestry loom installed in his bedroom; and Morris the poet, publisher and propagandist had his Kelmscott Press set up in a riverside cottage just a little further down Lower Mall. The place was one of the great intellectual centres in the England of the day. Here came, for instance, the leaders of the burgeoning British socialist movement, R.M. Hyndman and Karl Marx's daughter Eleanor. Here came the fashionable painter and book illustrator Walter Crane and the left-wing journalist George Bernard Shaw. And here in the spring of 1887 came the 21-year-old Willie Yeats. With his fast developing career in Dublin abruptly halted, his first step in entering the literary life of London was to renew his acquaintance with Morris.

Yeats received a kindly welcome at Kelmscott House. It was a great pleasure for the unhappy and impoverished young Irishman to dine and converse in this house in which there were so many artefacts in the Pre-Raphaelite taste which his father had taught him to admire: 'We sat round a long unpolished and unpainted trestle table of new wood in a room where hung Rossetti's *Pomegranate*, a portrait of Mrs Morris, and where one wall and part of the ceiling were covered by a great Persian carpet.'[6] Short, burly William Morris, with so many projects of his own, made efforts to help the young man more than thirty years his junior. Morris invited him often and talked to him about heroic poetry and medieval art. He offered Yeats the opportunity to write on Irish subjects for his socialist magazine *Commonweal*. Gradually the young Irishman became an insider in the Morris set. He was greatly impressed by Morris's daughter May; he told Katharine Tynan that she was markedly beautiful and very intelligent.[7] Like most members of the Morris circle Willie found May's fiancé, Henry Sparling, much less satisfactory. He was effeminate and peculiar; Lily, on one of her first visits to Kelmscott House, described him as tall, thin and stooped, with great round eyes and small chin.[8] And the time would come when Willie would write irritably of Sparling as a little wretch spouting atheisms and negations.[9] But Sparling, like everyone else at Kelmscott House, sympathized strongly with the Irish cause and Willie, on those first visits to Hammersmith, appreciated Sparling's informed interest in current Irish writing. Sparling was in fact preparing a volume of songs entitled *Irish Minstrelsy* and on one of his first Sundays at Kelmscott House Willie heard him lecture pleasingly on Irish Rebel Songs.[10]

Another early contact at Kelmscott House enabled him to begin rebuilding his career as a writer. This was Ernest Rhys, a young man of Welsh extraction some six years older than Yeats. Born into a middle-class family, Rhys began as a mining engineer in the north of England but then gave this up and went to London to pursue a career as a writer. He lived in a garret in a house in Cheyne Walk, Chelsea, and quickly became acquainted with literary Bohemia. He did not prosper as a poet and began to work as the London editor and representative of a publishing house, the Walter Scott Company, which had its headquarters in Newcastle-upon-Tyne. Some years later Rhys, whom Yeats would remember as weak-willed and dreamy but kindly,[11] would have a famous success in publishing when he created the 'Everyman Library', a series of classic works for the house owned by the apoplectic and irascible J.M. Dent. On first meeting Rhys at Kelmscott House Yeats thought him a 'not brilliant but very earnest Welshman'. But Rhys, as he looked across William Morris's 'lavishly spread' table with 'cold meats, apple pasties, wine and fruit and lots of green branches', was greatly taken by his fellow guest. Rhys remembered him as 'a tall, pale, exceedingly thin young man, with a raven lock over his forehead; his face so thin indeed that there was hardly room in it for his luminous black eyes'.[12] The two young men walked some of the way home together, and when the time came to go their separate ways, the dark-clad figures continued talking under a gas-lamp in World's End Passage on the western edge of Chelsea. Rhys invited Yeats to come to supper a few days later and was amazed to see how much food he put away, and how quickly, whilst all the time he talked of Indian mysticism and Mohini Chatterji and Madame Blavatsky. Yeats later invited Rhys back to his home. Rhys was somewhat un-comfortable with John Yeats who, he wrote, was 'a vehement Irishman, hot on politics'.[13] Father and son argued strenuously about Parnell. As he averted his eyes from the quarrelling Rhys noticed that 'it was the mother, with her strange dark eyes all but blind, who seemed nearest to her black-eyed eldest son in mould.'[14]

One of the bonds between Yeats and Rhys was their passionate interest in Celtic culture. When they met, Rhys was involved in publishing the Camelot series of books for the Walter Scott Company. These were cheap reprints of prose classics. Rhys thought it might be possible to interest the company in a volume of Irish fairy-tales for the Camelot series. By the middle of the summer Yeats received a contract for such a book. Fairy-tales were fashionable; interest in them was a part of that concern with folklore that had become an item on the agenda of Romanticism. As Willie started putting together his anthology of Irish fairy-tales, Andrew Lang was working on his *Blue Fairy Book*, the first in what would be for him an immensely successful sequence of such collections.

The need to do some research into this aspect of Irish folklore gave Willie the excuse to visit Ireland in mid-August of 1887, after some five miserable months in London. His Pollexfen relatives offered him the opportunity to travel free on one of the vessels of the Sligo Steam Navigation Company, of which his grandfather was a director. He accepted eagerly and sailed from Clarence Basin in Liverpool past the Isle of Man and round the rocky coast of the north of Ireland, before arriving in some excitement, as he had done as a child, at the quays in Sligo.

He stayed first with his uncle, George Pollexfen, in his large house overlooking the ocean out on Rosses Point. From here he soon wrote a letter to Katharine Tynan that showed him to be much happier than he had been for a long time. 'It is a wonderfully beautiful day; the air is full of trembling light. The very feel of the familiar Sligo earth puts me in good spirits. I should like to live here always not out of liking for the people so much as for the earth and the sky here, though I like the people too.'[15] His first literary activities were related to the project he was trying to develop with Ernest Rhys. He went around Sligo and the surrounding area looking 'for people to tell me fairy stories'.[16] He revelled in the Irishness of the tales he was told, and he repeatedly urged Katharine to be true to her Irishness. His advice to her often sounds like advice to himself on the planning of a career in writing. He tells her, 'Remember by being as Irish as you can you will be the more original and true to yourself and in the long run more interesting to English readers.'[17]

His other major literary enterprise during this escape to Sligo showed him sticking to this advice. For by the time he left he had completed his long poem on an Irish subject, 'The Wanderings of Oisin'. The work showed both the literary ambition and the artistic staying power of Yeats at the age of twenty-two. The poem gave him a great deal of trouble and he badly wanted to finish it before he left the west of Ireland and the hospitality of his family there. To Katharine who was keen for him to come and stay at Clondalkin he apologized, asking her not to be angry with him for failing to write. He told her that he would rather be at White Hall than at any other place but that it was essential for him to finish Oisin first. The poem had proved very difficult and he had needed to rewrite the third part.[18]

As the summer turned into autumn he moved from his uncle's house at Rosses Point to his grandparents' new home, Charlemont, in Sligo. William and Elizabeth had given up Merville and moved to a smaller, though still imposing house overlooking the harbour. And here by mid-November Willie at last managed to complete 'The Wanderings of Oisin'. Next Tuesday it would be with her, he promised Katharine, before going on to tell his fellow poet that he was extremely relieved to have finished Oisin, a poem which had given him so much trouble that it had made sleep difficult and left him nervous and depressed. He told her that he liked the poem better now it was finished than when he had been writing it. He wondered whether his poor health had affected his view of his work. The poem had been like an illness raging in him but now he had gone from thinking it the worst thing he had ever written to viewing it as a success.[19]

Some thirty pages long, 'The Wanderings of Oisin' belongs in the tradition of European Romanticism that persisted until the last years of the nineteenth century. Wagner had been dead nearly four years, but Yeats's legendary hero has much in common with Siegfried and Tannhäuser. And though Yeats did not know it then, at the other end of Europe in another small and colonized nation, his exact contemporary Jean Sibelius was thinking along similar lines. This fervent believer in the cause of the Finnish people and the Finnish language, which then laboured under the domination of the Russian empire and language, pondered a work on a comparable hero taken from the Finnish national epic, the *Kalevala*. This hero was Lemminkäinen, the subject of an important early composition by Sibelius entitled *Four Legends* or the *Lemminkäinen Suite*.[20] As Sibelius in his hero celebrated Finnishness and Wagner in Siegfried and Tannhäuser celebrated Teutonism, so Yeats, yet another nationalist Romantic, celebrated Irishry in Oisin.

The hero of his poem, who is the son of the leader of the military order of the Fenians, is a figure drawn from Yeats's extensive reading in the stories and legends of ancient Ireland. Like Tannhäuser entering the Venusberg, Oisin is lured by the vision of a beautiful woman into worlds apart. Oisin surpasses Tannhäuser in that he spends time not in just one alternative world, but in three. First he travels with the beautiful Niamh to the Island of Dancing where they stay for a hundred years. Then they go on to the Island of Victories where for another century Oisin struggles with a demon. Then, after Oisin's efforts prove inconclusive, he and Niamh move on to the Island of Forgetfulness for another hundred years. Explaining the symbolism of the islands, Yeats wrote of them as the 'three incompatible things which man is always seeking – infinite feeling, infinite battle, infinite repose'.[21]

When Oisin returns to the real world after his three hundred years in these longed-for but impossible islands, he finds that the age of the Fenians is long gone. Ireland is now Christianized and it is to St Patrick that Oisin relates and justifies his journeyings. Again like Tannhäuser Yeats's hero finds himself set apart from the way of living as Christianity defines and urges it. Part of the emotional power of the conclusion comes from Oisin's defiance of Patrick, his rejection of future immortality among the blessed of Christendom and his adherence to an alternative notion of reality. After his burial he will go to the Fenians, pagans all, whether they be feasting or in hell fire. No longer iambic pentameters, these lines of sixteen and seventeen syllables are expansively, passionately rhetorical.

> *It were sad to gaze on the blessed and no man I loved of old there;*
> *I throw down the chain of small stones! when life in my body has*
> *ceased,*

> *I will go to Caoilte, and Conan, and Bran, Sceolan, Lomair,*
> *And dwell in the house of the Fenians, be they in flames or at feast.*

Yeats's own heterodox feelings for the spiritual infuse the poem, along
with his identification with Oisin and with ancient, heroic Ireland. He
wrote to Katharine Tynan about the secret lore and the esoteric in the
poem, saying that 'under disguise of symbolism I have said several things,
to which I only have the key.'[22] And in one respect the poem treats a subject
that is important to theosophy, the progress of a human soul between two
existences on earth. In *Esoteric Buddhism* A.P. Sinnett calls this interval
Devachan and maintains that 'Between each physical existence the individual unit passes through a period of existence in the corresponding spiritual world.'[23] Yeats's poem begins on earth and ends there; what intervenes
is a Devachan for Oisin and surely, in part at least, for Yeats. The three
aspirations realized in the three islands are, of course, negative definitions
of spiritual progress. (Devachan is not necessarily a progressive development.) The islands are what Yeats later called 'vain gaiety, vain battle, vain
repose'.[24] But Oisin, like a true theosophist, learns to recognize them as
delusions and allows himself to be drawn back to the human world with its
educative suffering which alone can produce the true development of the
spirit. The three etherial states so finely realized in the diction and verbal
texture of the poem are, at the last, rejected. Oisin the spiritual quester, like
Oisin the Irish hero, returns to his true home and his true mission.

The impression of a literary exercise given by 'The Island of Statues' is
replaced in 'Oisin' by a sense of urgent personal concern. The symbolism
at times may seem overwrought, there may be verbal lushness for its own
sake and there may be jarring rhymes, but there is also a strong feeling of
the poet's emotional involvement.[25] Especially for Irish readers, but even
for those not Irish, the 22-year-old writer here compellingly creates, in the
current idiom of English poetry deriving from Tennyson, Rossetti,
Swinburne and Morris, a new and pagan image of Ireland, its spirituality
and its ancient past.

The feeling for the Ireland of legend that so pervades 'Oisin' found ready
sympathizers after Yeats took the train across to the east coast and went to

stay with Katharine Tynan at the farm at Clondalkin. Here he could renew his friendship not only with her but with his other literary, nationalist and occultist friends in Dublin. These winter weeks at White Hall farm were a stimulating time. But it was not just the pleasure of being with old friends that detained him. One reason he stayed in Ireland for the winter and Christmas of 1887 was that the situation in the family home had become much worse. Lily was ill and Susan Yeats had suffered a stroke. In December mother and daughter went to recuperate in Yorkshire. They stayed at the home of Susan's sister Elizabeth who, at that colourful wedding in Sligo in 1873, had married the Reverend Barrington Orr. He was now the vicar of Denby in Yorkshire on the edge of the High Peak, south-west of Wakefield. It was a prosperous, well-tended village, much involved in the raising of horses. The rectory was a large, impressive residence in its own grounds. Elizabeth's well-appointed home must have been yet one more reminder to Susan Yeats of the harsh poverty of her own home in Earl's Court. But Denby was to bring a far worse experience, for it was here that Susan Yeats soon had a second stroke which rendered her an invalid for the rest of her life.

Christmas 1887 must also have been a lean time in Eardley Crescent for John Yeats, Lolly and Jack, who had now returned to the family from Sligo and was attending art school. But energetic Lolly made the best of things and supplied some entertainment by bringing out the first edition of a hand-produced magazine called 'Ye Pleiades', containing a fine comic story by herself and poems and sketches by six of her friends. Willie was a little pompous about the venture at first and slow to recognize that all his siblings had artistic gifts, but he did contribute a poem, 'The Priest of Colooney', to a later edition of the magazine.

Over in Dublin he himself had some exhilarating experiences during that Christmas period. He spent time not only with the Tynans at White Hall but also with the O'Learys in their new lodgings at 30 Grosvenor Road on the south side of Dublin. While in London Parnell continued to defend himself against the libels published in *The Times*, John O'Leary in Dublin also contributed to the war of words in which Ireland's cause was being fought. He was now the literary editor of *The Gael*, a magazine dedicated primarily to the promotion of Irish sports. That Christmas he spoke enthusiastically to Willie about another new project of his, which was to publish an anthology of poems by Irish writers. He would do it under the auspices of the new Young Ireland Society which he had addressed so memorably just two years before. The volume appeared the following spring. Entitled *Poems and Ballads of Young Ireland*, it had contributions from, among others, Yeats, Ellen O'Leary, Douglas Hyde, Katharine Tynan and Frederick James Gregg. Another of O'Leary's ideas that was especially exciting to Yeats was a subscription scheme that would enable 'The Wanderings of Oisin' together with other poems by Yeats to be brought out by a London publisher. As O'Leary turned up more and more subscribers, negotiations were begun with Charles Kegan Paul, an elderly publisher with Christian Socialist leanings.

When he finally felt it necessary to return to the family in London, Willie set off confident that his extended stay in Ireland had helped his career in several ways. Back in Earl's Court he worked hard to find sub-scribers for his Kegan Paul volume but always acknowledged that John O'Leary with his worldwide Fenian connections obtained most of the names and the money.[26] Willie did not enjoy having to negotiate with Kegan Paul: he did not like the publisher's 'particular compound of the superciliousness of the man of letters with the oiliness of a tradesman'.[27] But the determined careerist that was a part of Willie's nature made him persevere. He was fully aware of the importance of publishing a complete volume as the next step in making his name and establishing himself as a poet.

Willie returned to London in the New Year of 1888 and in early March there came another hopeful development. He and his father discovered a much better house to rent. Doubtless they were helped in finding it by John Todhunter, for it was on the Bedford Park estate where John Yeats's old friend from Trinity College days himself now lived. Willie wrote enthusi-astically to Katharine Tynan that it was 'a fine roomy house' in 'a silent tree-filled place where everything is idyllic except the cockroaches that abound there'.[28] Most important of all it was cheap; the rent for the Yeatses would be forty-five pounds a year. And they were returning to the famous garden suburb where they had first gone to live briefly when Willie was thirteen. Their new house at 3 Blenheim Road was further from the centre of this planned community, further from the Tabard Inn with its tile-hung gables, the bank, the church and the parish hall than their first house had been. The estate had grown during their ten years' absence but the new houses were consistent in style, either designed by Norman Shaw or imitations of his 'Queen Anne' manner. This, the chief innovation in English domestic architecture in the late nineteenth century, entailed much use of Dutch gables, white window casements, cosy porches, oriel windows and decorative tiles.

The character of Bedford Park's population had not changed very much. Still favoured by people with an interest in the arts, it was a place, noted a writer on the *St James's Gazette* in December 1881, 'where men may lead a chaste correct Aesthetical existence'. Not far from Todhunter there lived the family of the French impressionist painter Camille Pissaro. His son Lucien Pissaro, a future founder of the New English Art Club, operated a printing press in the house. The poetry publisher Elkin Matthews would later be a next-door neighbour of the Yeatses. A shy little man whom *Punch* once described as monkish and medieval, he was to have an important part to play in Yeats's career. So did another of his Bedford Park neighbours, Frederick York Powell, of whom young Willie was in some awe. A man in his late thirties, York Powell was a successful academic, a future Regius Professor of Modern History at Oxford and presently teaching at Christ Church. But he preferred his London home to his rooms in Oxford and spent as much time in Bedford Park as possible. Yeats described him as 'a broad-built, broad-headed, brown-bearded man clothed in heavy blue cloth and looking, but for his glasses and the dim sight of a student, like some captain in the Merchant Service'.[29]

When York Powell singled out Douglas Hyde's contributions to *Poems and Ballads of Young Ireland* for special commendation, Willie wrote to Hyde to tell him of the honour. Willie also became indebted to York Powell for occasional literary jobs which the older man kindly found for him. Although the Yeats family now had a far pleasanter house in Bedford Park, their poverty still oppressed them. One paying job York Powell obtained for Willie was the copying of Caxton's edition of Aesop in the Bodleian Library for a journalist friend. When Willie travelled up to Oxford to do the job, York Powell let him use his rooms in Christ Church's Meadow

Buildings, full of books and also of Japanese prints which were very fashionable in the late 1880s.

But such odd jobs could not do much to help alleviate the chronic poverty of the Yeatses. Pale and undernourished with neglected teeth, Willie, researching his volume of Irish fairy-tales, would often forgo the underground train and walk the several miles from Bedford Park to the British Museum in Bloomsbury in order 'to save pennies for a cup of coffee in the afternoon'. And he was reduced to 'blacking my stockings to hide the rents in my boots'. Always thinking about his image and his role, Willie made a cult of his 'poor look'. Like Verlaine and some of the *poètes maudits* in France, whose work he had still to read, he chose 'a deliberate poverty as a foppery of youth'.[30]

York Powell made another effort to help Willie earn some money. Having a contact on the *Manchester Courier*, he recommended the young poet to him as a contributor. Discovering that it was a Unionist newspaper, Willie felt obliged to turn down the opportunity. His father's response to this was, 'You have taken a great weight off my mind.' In fact Willie did contribute a few small items to the Manchester paper, but it went against the grain. Willie's sensibilities were again bruised by York Powell when the burly historian hosted a gathering at which he passed around 'caricatures of the night life of Paris by some famous French artist'. The virginal young poet was shocked and embarrassed and removed himself to the end of the room. At the age of twenty-two sex was for him problematically involved with the spiritual: 'I was a romantic, my head full of the mysterious women of Rossetti and those hesitating faces in the art of Burne-Jones.'

Another older man, about the same age as York Powell and likewise a Bedford Park neighbour, took a liking to Willie and helped him greatly, though he also shocked Willie by a certain coarseness in conversation. This was the famous journalist William Ernest Henley, a distinctive and well-known figure in and around Bedford Park. Having lost his left leg during his teens he clumped about the curved, tree-lined streets with the aid of a heavy crutch. He was the inspiration behind the one-legged Long John Silver, the character in *Treasure Island* written by his one-time close friend and exact contemporary, Robert Louis Stevenson. As a journalist and editor Henley knew many writers. He assisted the careers of Joseph

Conrad, Rudyard Kipling and H.G. Wells along with that of his young neighbour, Willie Yeats. Things Henley said often horrified him, and on occasion he determined to flee the older man's company, but he did not. For here was a new literary patron, a poet and an experienced editor who could help his career. Syphilitic, often foul-mouthed, coarse and yet at the same time highly sensitive, Henley had a considerable reputation as a poet and a literary journalist. If he is remembered at all nowadays it is probably for four lines from his poem declaiming his Victorian belief in self-reliance and individualism:

> It matters not how strait the gate,
>> How charged with punishments the scroll,
> I am the master of my fate:
>> I am the captain of my soul.

He had worked on the *Cornhill Magazine* in Edinburgh and at the early age of twenty-seven had become editor of a weekly called *London*. He went on to edit the *Magazine of Art* as well as doing a good deal of free-lance writing. When he was first getting to know the young Yeats, he was about to take over the editorship of the *Scots Observer* which, in hopes of increasing circulation, he retitled the *National Observer*. Henley liked to bring on talented young writers and Yeats became one of those called Henley's young men[31] or sometimes the 'Henley Regatta'. He was an unlikely protégé for he did not like Henley's poetry ('except those early gay verses in the measure of Villon') and he thought his prose 'violent and laboured'. He was, said Yeats, the founder of the 'declamatory school of imperialist journalism'. Henley was interested in the new Impressionist painting and had no time for Willie's beloved Pre-Raphaelites. As an editor he was cavalier with the work of his young men. Yeats long remembered that 'He rewrote my poems as he re-wrote the early verse of Kipling.' Henley was to draw close to that imperialist poet who was Yeats's exact contemporary. To Henley the British Empire was a 'great thing'. He urged Willie to tell his nationalist friends that the great Empire should be supported.[32]

But for all their many differences Yeats had a genuine affection for Henley, one of those replacement father figures who, like William Morris,

helped to advance his literary career. Obviously possibilities of being published also drew Yeats to Henley. But Henley's literary patronage was of a
special kind. For Henley took a fatherly interest and, indeed, a pride in his
'young men'. And with this bond of feeling he sustained Willie Yeats in the
same way (though to a much lesser extent) that John O'Leary continued to
do. In his middle age Yeats kept a lithograph of Henley by William
Rothenstein hanging over his mantelpiece 'among other friends'. When, in
his maturity, he asked himself what had appealed to him in Henley he concluded, 'I disagreed with him about everything, but I admired him beyond
words.'[33] He was drawn to Henley, he later confessed, by his aristocratic attitudes and his despising of the mob.[34] Despising the 'logical realism' of such
as George Eliot, Henley was an ultra-conservative visionary. 'He dreamed
of a tyranny, but it was that of Cosimo de Medici.'[35]

At least one of the 'young men' was sceptical about Henley; Rudyard
Kipling once remarked brutally, 'Henley is a great man . . . but he is not
going to come the bullying cripple over me.' Angus Wilson observed, 'He
must have seen how Henley's poor crippled body ached to be powerful in
the literary world and that, with all his bonhomie and Victorian-
Rabelaisian comradeliness, he was a poor thirsty man who needed able
young writers to be his disciples . . . Henley and his world meant the world
of journalism and Kipling had every intention of putting journalism behind
him.'[36] So, of course, had the poet Yeats, who retained no very clear
memory of Kipling from Henley's 'evenings'. But Yeats also wrote of
Henley that 'I began my education under him'.[37] Yeats was ready, like
Henley's other young men, to test himself against that man's sincerity.[38]
Henley was Yeats's first experience of a man who stood for exacting standards in the practice of writing: 'He terrified us also and certainly I did not
dare, and I think none of us dared, to speak our admiration for a book or
picture he condemned, but he made us feel always our importance and no
man among us could do good work, or show promise of it, and lack his
praise.'[39] Yeats also thought that the visionary, illiberal, vehement Henley
had a special, generational appeal to himself and to the other 'young men':
'I think we listened to him, and often obeyed him, partly because he was
quite plainly not upon the side of our parents.'[40]

It was at a Sunday night gathering at Henley's house that Yeats made the acquaintance of someone who would also become important to him – the elegant, dandified Oscar Wilde, a fellow Dubliner, some eleven years older than he and further advanced in his writing career, but not yet the spectacularly successful dramatist that he was to become. During the time he was drawing close to Henley, Yeats also continued to be a regular visitor to William Morris of Kelmscott House. Here Yeats came to know yet another brilliant young Dubliner who was about the same age as Oscar Wilde and who would soon have great success as a playwright. This was George Bernard Shaw, at this time making his living as a theatre critic. Like Morris he was a socialist, and preached his political creed in parks and on street corners. He was a striking figure with a large yellow beard, wearing 'rational dress' as advocated by the Austrian hygienist, Gustave Jaeger. This consisted of a reddish-brown woollen suit with a military-style double-breasted jacket, knee breeches and stockings instead of trousers. Shaw's Jaeger outfit proclaimed his radical rationalism just as Wilde's silks and laces proclaimed his aestheticism. Like young Willie Yeats these other two Irishmen dressed in a way that differentiated them from the conventionally and soberly dressed men of the Victorian middle class. But of course the three were very different from each other, though Willie's sympathies were far more easily engaged by that connoisseur of artifice, Oscar Wilde. On his first meeting with Bernard Shaw at Kelmscott House Yeats's response to him was ambivalent. He told Katharine Tynan that he found Shaw very witty but he suspected that his mind lacked depth.[41]

As the spring came on, some of the young socialists who met at Kelmscott House decided to undertake a tour through France. William Morris, always the organizer, decided that it would be appropriate for them to study French and he arranged for a class to be held in the coach house. Willie attended and for the first few classes prided himself on his progress in the language and on the compliments of the grey-haired French mistress. But then his father decided that Lily and Lolly should attend the classes too. This rather cramped Willie's carefully crafted style within the Morris set; he felt his sisters' presence in the class was an intrusion of his domestic life.[42] Lolly noted in her diary that Willie's pronunciation of French caused considerable mirth among some of the other students, especially May Morris's fiancé, Henry Sparling. The young poet whose writing would soon be so strongly affected by contemporary French poetry now spoke the language dramatically, intensely and, as Lolly remembered, with completely wrong pronunciation.[43]

William Morris planned to join the classes but, as it turned out, had far too many other things to attend to. One of his many projects during the spring of that year was the production and rehearsal of his play *The Tables Turned; or Nupkins Awakened; A Socialist Interlude*. Morris staged his comedy in a small auditorium in the East End of London just off Cable Street. He and his daughter May played parts (Morris was the Archbishop of Canterbury), and Willie who went along was impressed. He told Katharine Tynan that Morris 'really acts very well. Miss Morris does not act at all but remains herself most charmingly throughout her part.'[44] For all his enjoyment of the play, Morris's socialism was what interested Yeats least about him. Yeats was vastly more interested in Morris the devotee of the Middle Ages, the adherent of Pre-Raphaelitism, the apostle of the beautiful, the writer of epic poems, the believer in heroic possibility.

From his many visits to Kelmscott House and from witnessing the diversity of creative activities there, Yeats became aware of the importance of management and promotion in the development of the arts. Lily and Lolly, who went on to have their own business in the applied arts of needlework, printing, bookmaking and publishing, also learned a good deal from Kelmscott House; Lily especially, for she became an embroideress for May Morris and the Morris firm, working for them for six years. Willie, who went on to manage so carefully his career as a writer and then to take the major responsibility in founding and running a theatre company, had his first experience of such organizing skills from his membership of the Morris entourage.

Every week Yeats spent many hours in the Reading Room of the British Museum researching Irish folklore. His continuing interest in the psychic and the occult was developed and refined through visits to the house of Madame Blavatsky, a rather grand one in Lansdowne Road near Holland Park in west London which had been supplied and furnished for her by her theosophical disciples. Here Yeats encountered many people he found unimpressive, but he also met up again with his old schoolfriend and fellow occultist, Charles Johnston. As Yeats was striving to establish

himself as the anti-imperialist poet of Irish consciousness, his old friend
was preparing for a career in the civil service of the British Empire. Soon
he would go out to India. By now Charley had developed, Yeats thought,
a pose of clever insolence and efficiency. Despite himself, Yeats was
impressed by Charley's air of the man about town as he confidently spoke
French and smoked cigarettes with Madame Blavatsky's niece.[45] Charley
Johnston went on to disappoint his theosophical friends by falling in love
with Madame Blavatsky's niece. They had hoped that he would become an
adept in their movement, a Mahatma; such a calling required abstinences
that included chastity. But Charley pursued Madame's niece all the way
back to Russia, married her in Moscow, then took her with him when he
began his imperial career in Calcutta.

For Yeats, the occult and Ireland were inextricably related concerns.
On his visits to Madame Blavatsky's house he was intrigued to discover
that other theosophists expected Ireland to produce some great spiritual
teacher.[46] His own investigations into Ireland and the supernatural continued to focus on the traditions of the Irish fairy-tale. Another important and
long-enduring persona, that of Yeats the lecturer, first showed itself in June
1888 when he agreed to give a talk on this subject at the Irish Literary Club
in working-class Southwark on the south bank of the Thames. The invitation to the Club came from one of its leading members, David
O'Donoghue, an energetic self-educated young man of Yeats's own age
who sought to maintain a cultural contact with his Irish background. A
clerical worker, he was one of the subscribers to Yeats's forthcoming Oisin
volume. Yeats reported to Katharine Tynan that 'My lecture on Sligo fairies
at the Southwark Literary Club went off merrily.'

In the hot summer months of 1888, following his twenty-third birthday, Willie worked unceasingly, almost desperately, to meet the publisher's
deadline for his anthology of Irish fairy stories, for which his friend Ernest
Rhys had finally arranged the contract. Inexperienced as a systematic
folklorist, any command of the subject was very much a matter of on-the-
job training. His letters to friends appealing for assistance reveal an element
of panic. He turned first, of course, to Katharine Tynan, telling her of the
harsh delivery date stipulated by the Walter Scott publishing company in
Newcastle-upon-Tyne. He told her in mid-June that it had to be done by

the end of July. He was fearful that he did not have the time to make a really good book. He coaxed her to search up suggestions for him.[47] And he tells her that he has also written to T.W. Rolleston to borrow a recent book by Oscar Wilde's mother. Lady Wilde, under the pseudonym 'Speranza', had published nationalist poetry back in the days of Young Ireland but the book which Yeats wanted to see now was her *Ancient Legends, Mystic Charms and Superstitions of Ireland*, published the previous year. Katharine Tynan had met Lady Wilde and Yeats asked his old friend to supply him with a written introduction. Such were the formalities of the day. Katharine promptly supplied the letter and Yeats quickly became a regular visitor at Speranza's home in Oakley Street, not far from her son's household in Tite Street, Chelsea.

Douglas Hyde, the passionate student of Irish language and literature, was also a great help to Yeats in the hurried research and proofreading of the book. 'Can you help me in the matter of folklore?' begged Yeats in mid-July. 'Could you let me know about this and other matters shortly? I have so little time.' Hyde from his Ascendancy family's home in rural Roscommon straight away sent material. His generous assistance became ever more important when Yeats made the devastating discovery that what he thought was long enough for a book, in fact was not. Yeats wrote again, asking for as many more stories as possible to make up the 60 or 70 pages he was short.[48] The O'Learys were also called in to help, Willie under the pressure of the deadline writing them almost discourteously brief notes. But at last the book was done, in great part due to Douglas Hyde who along with other assistance sent him translations from the Irish. These greatly impressed Yeats. One of Hyde's translations, he declared, was one of the most impressive things in all Irish folklore and the best piece in the book.[49] The Walter Scott Company moved speedily, and little more than a month after Yeats had sent off the manuscript, the anthology with his introduction was published. The time was right for Irish subjects and for fairy-tales. The book was a success and Ernest Rhys was extremely pleased with the venture.

When he had time to relax and assess this rushed publication Yeats concluded in a letter to Katharine Tynan that all the hard work had been worth doing, if only because of all the material it gave him for his poetry.

He expressed his hope that they could both turn some of the stories into poems.[50] In November of that year he returned to this idea, saying that some of the stories he had found 'would do for ballads' and singling one out in particular: 'I shall some day try my hand at "Countess Kathleen O'Shea".' This was a story which Yeats, in a footnote to his anthology, claimed 'was quoted in a London-Irish newspaper. I am unable to find out the original source.'[51] A tale set 'in old Ireland', it tells of the Countess Kathleen O'Shea, 'an angel of beauty' and 'the idol of the people and the providence of the indigent'. Two 'traders in souls' working for the devil create a situation in which the people must either 'perish in the agonies of hunger' or sell their souls to the 'two emissaries of Satan'. Kathleen sells them her own soul, 'pure, spotless, virginal', a 'priceless acquisition'. The people are saved. The satanic traders do not win, however, because 'the sale of this soul, so adorable in its charity, was declared null by the Lord; for she had saved her fellow-citizens from death.'[52]

Yeats dedicated his collection of fairy and folk-tales to George Russell: 'my mystical friend G.R.'. The ever kindly and generous Russell had taken the trouble to go to the National Library of Ireland where he had copied out some folk-tales not to be found in England.[53] But in the Introduction, after mentioning the many students and scholars of Irish folklore to whom he is indebted, Yeats pays his highest tribute to Douglas Hyde, 'now preparing a volume of folk-tales in Gaelic, having taken them down for the most part, word for word among the Gaelic speakers of Roscommon and Galway. He is, perhaps, most to be trusted of all. He knows the people thoroughly. Others see a phase of Irish life; he understands all its elements . . . he is the last of our ballad writers . . . whose work seems fragrant with turf smoke.'[54]

The 'fairy book', Willie confided to Katharine Tynan, 'is not much liked by my father who does not wish me to do critical work. He wants me to write stories.' And this Willie, still to some extent the dutiful son, tried to do. During this busy year he worked away on his realistic novel of contemporary life which would finally be published some three years later in 1891 under the title *John Sherman*. When he had been staying with Uncle George at Rosses Point earlier in the year Willie had written a story called 'Dhoya', 'a fantastic tale of the heroic age' in Ireland. But a mythic story of 'a man of giant stature named Dhoya' was not what his father had in mind or thought saleable, so Willie had to set to work again, on *John Sherman*.

The main reason John Yeats urged his son to write realistic fiction was financial. The family now had a pleasing house and neighbours with similar tastes and interests, but the shortage of money continued to be painful. John Yeats's career still had not prospered as a result of the move back to London. Willie and Jack were only just beginning their careers and their earnings were sporadic. The most reliable income at this time was Lily's, from her work as an embroideress for May Morris at Kelmscott House. But the family's combined earnings were simply not enough: often they were uncertain where the money for the next meal would come from. Sometimes Willie has to tell his correspondents that he is ending his letter because the candle is burning down and cannot, so it would seem, be replaced. It may well have been the lack of supplies and comforts of home that led Willie in late December of that year to give the impression of being alone in London and to accept Oscar Wilde's invitation to eat Christmas dinner in Chelsea.

With an interior designed by Edward Godwin, one of the most advanced and flamboyant architects of the Aesthetic Movement, who had earlier built several of the houses in Bedford Park, Wilde's house was one of the most talked-about pieces of domestic design in late Victorian London. Nearby was the White House designed by Godwin for Whistler a few years before, though his bankruptcy meant Whistler only enjoyed it for a short time. Its front was entirely asymmetrical with no traditional architectural motifs or references; with its heavy horizontal emphases it looked rather like one of the houses Godwin's admirer, Frank Lloyd Wright, was about to design in Chicago. The interior of Wilde's house was also unusual; it owed more to Whistler's notions of concerted design than to those of the Pre-Raphaelites, and magazines of the time were full of photographs and descriptions of it. The dining-room was entirely white with white chairs, white cushions and white curtains embroidered with yellow silk. But the white table had a red cloth table centre with a red terracotta statue and above it a red hanging lamp.

The young Yeats was entranced by this ultra-fashionable elegance so different from his own shabbily furnished home. The 23-year-old, highly conscious of 'my own shapelessness, my lack of self-possession and of easy courtesy', was most impressed by his host 'who as a man of the world was so perfect'. Yeats greatly enjoyed his Christmas with Wilde and his wife and children.[55] After the dinner Wilde provided entertainment by reading aloud from the proofs of his new essay, 'The Decay of Lying'. This prose work of wit and masks and paradoxes very much interested the young poet, who continually pondered the masks he should wear and the roles he should play. But, except for the wit, he did not much care for the rest of Wilde's work; rather he admired the man who was later to show so much courage and to remain loyal to the intellect.[56] Yeats was here referring to Wilde's conduct during his sensational trial, imprisonment and disgrace.

In the second week of January 1889, *The Wanderings of Oisin and Other Poems* was at last, after several delays, published by Kegan Paul, Trench and Company. The collection of fairy-tales had been no more than an editing job; this small volume with its navy blue cover with gold lettering on the spine and front was really the first book written by W.B. Yeats. It contained one hundred and fifty pages and thirty-one poems. Twenty days after this important moment in his career there came another. In the early afternoon a horse-drawn hansom cab drew up outside 3 Blenheim Road and a tall and very beautiful young woman got out. She was a part of the far-flung network of sympathizers with the Irish cause and had been sent by Ellen O'Leary with a letter of introduction. The social proprieties of the time required that the letter be addressed to John Yeats as the head of the family, but it was of Willie that the O'Learys had chiefly spoken to this ardently nationalist young woman, and it was Willie she was intrigued to meet.

She carried herself well, almost haughtily. She wore a large-brimmed hat and a coat and skirt of modish French styling. Yet strangely she did not wear the formal shoes that went with such a grand outfit. This omission teasingly suggested a certain informality, a statement of independence even. When the door was opened to her she announced that she was Maud Gonne, recently come from Dublin. Once she had crossed the step into the hall, the life of W.B. Yeats was affected for ever. Later that

afternoon in the sitting-room she spoke about Ireland in her rich, melodious voice, with passion and even violence, and her beauty overwhelmed
him. One of the grand passions of the twentieth century had begun.
Ireland and mysticism were now joined by the third great theme of Yeats's
art: love.

MAUD WAS BORN IN ENGLAND, THE DAUGHTER OF A CAPTAIN IN the British Army, a year before Willie. When she was three her father's regiment was sent to Ireland as part of the military reinforcements against the Fenians. Maud lived there until she was ten. She lost her mother when she was small and her father rented a little house near the Bailey Lighthouse on Howth Head, where she and her younger sister Katharine were looked after by a nurse. When her father was posted back to England and then overseas, he left the two sisters in the charge of governesses. Maud loved her father but her experiences as a teenage girl in England were not the happiest. She was pleased to be put in the care of relatives in France and to continue her education there. A French governess with strong Republican sympathies was a powerful influence upon her.

When she was sixteen, already strikingly beautiful, her father, now a colonel, was again sent to Ireland. Maud went with him and served as his hostess. Though a conspicuous figure in Ascendancy society in Dublin, Maud was shocked by what she saw of the miseries of the peasantry during her travels in Ireland. The brutal eviction of poor tenant farmers who could not pay their rent particularly appalled her. She became a strong sympathizer with the Home Rule cause and more and more identified with Ireland and the Irish.

When she was twenty, Maud's father died and she inherited enough money to be financially independent. She travelled for a while and then returned to France. A boisterously high-spirited girl, she contemplated a career as an actress, and was billed in the title role in a play about Adrienne Lecouvreur, the eighteenth-century actress and courtesan. But again a political cause captured her energetic imagination. An important force in French politics at this moment was the populist movement led by General Georges Boulanger who had been an officer in the French colonial armies of Indo-China and Algeria. At the time Maud was preparing to settle in France, the General's popularity was immense, sometimes, indeed, infected with hysteria. He was violently hostile to the new, unified and increasingly prosperous Germany created eighteen years earlier, after the humiliating defeat of France by the Prussians in 1870. He preached a rabid nationalism that appealed to a large constituency in France. He also sneered at the inadequacies in France's republican system of government, believing the country needed a strong man, someone like Bismarck, to take power and save it. Boulanger projected himself as just such 'a man on a horse', a second Napoleon come to rescue *la patrie*. He and his disciples started to plan a *coup d'état*.

While staying at Royat in the Auvergne with her great-aunt Mary, Maud met one of Boulanger's most zealous followers. This was Lucien Millevoye, a lawyer and journalist. Older than she, sophisticated and separated from his wife, Millevoye excited Maud with the passion of his beliefs. He was happy to explain to her Boulanger's aspirations and Maud persuaded herself of an affinity between this kind of French nationalism and her own deep dedication to Ireland. Now began her ambition to become Ireland's Joan of Arc. Millevoye introduced her to General Boulanger and then helped her to write her first article in support of the Irish nationalist cause, about the horrific evictions of peasants that she had witnessed in Donegal. The article was entitled 'Un Peuple Opprimé' and was published in *La Nouvelle Revue Internationale*. Tutored and encouraged by Millevoye and his leader in nationalist thought and feeling, Maud left France to dedicate herself to the Irish cause. One of the great beauties of Anglo-Irish high society who had dined and danced at Dublin Castle now recreated herself as an activist in the Irish Nationalist movement. She presented herself first to Michael Davitt of the Land League, but he was uneasy with this flamboyant, outspoken woman. However, the stolid, hard-working nationalist C.H. Oldham was, beneath his gauche, bumbling exterior, absolutely entranced by her. He took her to the Contemporary Club in Grafton Street. As he led the beautiful, statuesque woman with the striking red-blonde hair through the door into the upstairs room where members were chatting, smoking and drinking tea Oldham boomed dramatically, 'Maud Gonne wants to meet John O'Leary; I thought you would all like to meet Maud Gonne.' Soon Maud was an established member of the circle around the O'Learys. When Douglas Hyde, the campaigner for the Irish language, was introduced to her, he declared her 'the most dazzling woman I have ever seen'.[1]

When Maud entered the Yeatses' house on Blenheim Road on that historic afternoon, some members of the family had, like Michael Davitt, reservations about the tall beauty. Lolly quickly decided that she disliked Maud's 'sort of royal smile', and John Yeats was shocked to hear her ready justification of the use of violence in Ireland's cause. But Willie, utterly captivated by her, stoutly agreed with her, upsetting his father even more. Years later Willie continued to maintain that his father ought to have understood that 'a man young as I could not have differed from a woman so beautiful and so young'.[2] Willie never forgot her first impact upon him: Virgil's line 'She walks like a goddess' was 'meant for her alone'. As she stood by the window in the suburban sitting-room on that January day the image that he would long associate with her first showed itself to him. 'Her complexion was luminous, like that of apple blossoms through which the light falls, and I remember her standing that first day by a great heap of such blossoms in the window.'[3]

Along with this beguiling image an affinity between them in thought, feeling and sensibility quickly became apparent to Yeats. They were Romantics together; neither was inspired by the mid-Victorian belief in scientific and material progress. Maud like Willie sought passionately for something other, for she was also a Romantic and out of sympathy with Victorian notions of a prosperous future.[4] Maud was, in fact, already a fervid admirer of the operas of Richard Wagner. She was interested in Willie, though by no means as much as he was in her. However, as she ended her visit, Maud quite unabashedly invited him to come and dine with her that evening in the house where she was staying in Ebury Street,

Belgravia. In fact, as he later remembered, he went on to dine with her every day of her nine-day stay in London.[5]

He found her exuberant and direct. She said she wanted power in order to do what she believed in. Yeats felt himself in the presence of someone possessing generosity and courage but not peace.[6] But her politics he admitted were 'a little sensational'. For instance, she mistakenly believed that Bismarck had poisoned or got murdered the Austrian prince[7] – Prince Rudolph who had committed suicide at Mayerling when he could no longer reconcile the claims of a love affair with his princely responsibilities. Maud's lifestyle was unconventional too: she had her pet monkey and two young pigeons in a cage in her rooms in Belgravia. As she moved from France to England and then to Ireland and then back to France she was surrounded by 'cages full of birds, canaries, finches of all kinds, dogs, a parrot, and once a full grown hawk from Donegal'.[8]

She reminded Willie of Laura Armstrong: she had the same indifference to proprieties and the same spiritedness, and both were interested in becoming actresses. Over these dinners in Ebury Street one of the things that Maud and Willie talked about was the possibility of creating a new Irish theatre. When Maud said that she would like to act in Dublin Willie suddenly thrilled to the idea of writing his play about the Irish heroine, the Countess Kathleen, and of Maud playing the leading role. Both greatly excited by the prospect, they spoke freely of themselves and their aspirations. In a letter to Ellen O'Leary he burst out, telling her how much he admired Miss Gonne. He said that he believed she would make many converts to her political belief. Even if she said the world was flat or the moon an old caubeen [a shabby hat] tossed up into the sky he would be proud to be of her party.[9] In the course of those nine days in London he became intoxicated with her. And then she was off, back to her apartment in Paris. For Willie her going meant a painful feeling of loss. He was miserably aware that as a young man still learning his craft, he could not hope to marry her. He realized that she was not cut out to be a wife sharing in the life of a student.[10] His love could never be declared. The weeks passed by and still his lovesickness continued; only 'as the months passed I grew master of myself again'.

During these difficult months in early 1889 Willie tried to ease his pain by writing his play *The Countess Kathleen* which he now regarded as *her* play. To write it was to pledge some future relationship between them. He worked at it through spring and summer. Another comfort and diversion during these months was to collect and study all the reviews of his first volume of poems. He made a book of critical notices and kept it until his death when it was found among his papers. Many of the reviews were friendly. The one in the *Dublin Evening Telegraph* in the first week in February made a valid distinction in saying that in the main and title poem Yeats 'oversteps the borders of verse and claims companionship in the larger domain of poetry'. But another Dublin publication, the *Freeman's Journal*, sneered: 'He hides a jumble of confused ideas in a mass of verbiage and calls it *The Wanderings of Oisin*.' The British newspapers were generally well disposed. In the *Pall Mall Gazette* Oscar Wilde wrote of his young friend's work in a way that in great part echoes Yeats's own notions of his agenda as a writer. 'Here', wrote Wilde, 'we find nobility of treatment and nobility of subject matter', and he goes on to say, 'If he has not the great simplicity of epic treatment, he has at least something of that largeness of vision that belongs to the epical temper. He does not rob of their stature the great heroes of Celtic mythology.'[11]

In the American publications that had welcomed contributions from Yeats as a result of his connection with John O'Leary, the reviews were mostly friendly – indeed were often by friends. Katharine Tynan was asked to do the review in the *Providence Journal* and wrote admiringly, as did Ernest Rhys in the *Boston Evening Transcript*. But the review in the *Boston Pilot* in early May was double-edged: Yeats's problematical 'friend' T.W. Rolleston wrote his piece as 'A Criticism in Dialogue', a Wildean conversation in which one speaker, Leonard, comments pleasantly on the book, whilst the other, Lucius, the more prominent speaker, stresses its deficiencies. Yeats, declares Lucius, 'needs patience – the patience of labour under strict discipline – before he uses the freedom of mastery. He needs a philosophy of art. He needs to interest himself in realities.'

Certainly some of the companion poems in *The Wanderings of Oisin* are about an unreal, highly literary world. The volume contains verses that go right back to Yeats's beginnings as a poet, including the final scene from 'The Island of Statues'. There are also poems with titles such as 'Song of the Last Arcadian' and 'A Lover's Quarrel Among the Fairies'. But Rolleston's last recommendation does not take into account the evolution in Yeats's poetic art shown by the volume as a whole. In 'The Ballad of Moll Magee', for instance, he deals with the realities of poverty and infanticide in rural Ireland. Here he also turns away from the received literary language of his early pieces and instead employs Irish speech. Other poems have a down-to-earth political agenda. The poem 'How Ferencz Renzi Kept Silent' is a 'rouser' for those who would resist the political and cultural oppression of small nations by large empires. Here the analogy for Ireland is Hungary seeking to oppose the tyranny of the Hapsburg Empire. Renzi, a Hungarian schoolmaster, fiddle player and dreamer, is involved in revolutionary activity. The Austrian General Haynau, a 'man of rules' and a 'man of system', demands that Renzi betray the whereabouts of his fellow freedom-fighters. But Renzi steadfastly refuses even when Haynau kills his family and his sweetheart. Finally the Hungarian hero frees himself and, crazed by horror, makes his escape. The poem is prefaced by a Kiplingesque epigraph in which Yeats establishes the similarity between the Irish and Hungarian predicaments. He concludes by saluting and toasting Ireland's comrades in oppression and struggle; for Ireland is 'The Hungary of the West'.

> *We, too, have seen our bravest and our best*
> *To prison go, and mossy ruin rest*
> *Where homes once whitened vale and mountain crest;*
> *Therefore, O nation of the bleeding breast,*
> *Libations, from the Hungary of the West.*

Such lines would doubtless have pleased John O'Leary and made him feel justified in his efforts to organize the subscription process which made publication of the book possible. The poem, first published in the *Boston Pilot*, a magazine for Irish Americans, had a political explicitness which Yeats as a poet would later renounce. He did not republish it in later collections of his work.

With the success of Yeats's first collection of Irish tales behind him Ernest Rhys felt able to arrange a contract for another collection of prose pieces no longer in copyright. This time Yeats put together for the Camelot series a collection of fiction by the nineteenth-century Irish novelist William Carleton, whose works had recently been reprinted by a Dublin publisher. W.E. Henley became interested and asked Yeats to do a piece for the *Scots Observer*. Yeats, short of money as usual, readily agreed and supplied a piece summarizing Carleton's career. The essay concluded by characterizing Carleton's achievement: 'The great thing about Carleton was that he always remained a peasant, hating and loving with his class. On one point he was ever consistent . . . that is the land question. Almost every story he wrote deals with it.'[12] In his Introduction to the collection he put together for Ernest Rhys, *Stories from Carleton*, Yeats makes much larger claims, declaring: 'He is the greatest novelist of Ireland, by right of the most Celtic eyes that ever gazed from under the brows of story-teller.' More particularly, 'Carleton was a great Irish historian. The history of a nation is not in parliaments and battlefields, but in what people say to each other on fair-days and high days, and how they farm, and quarrel, and go on pilgrimage. These things has Carleton recorded.'

As he worked on his selections from Carleton for the Camelot series Yeats also came into contact with an American publisher, G.P. Putnam's Sons of Boston. They, like the Walter Scott Company, did reprints and they contracted with Yeats for a two-volume collection of Irish fiction, *Representative Irish Tales*, to be brought out in their 'Knickerbocker Nuggets' series. This was Yeats's first book to be published in the United States. Early on in his career he looked to a readership in America as well as in Great Britain. As with his first two anthologies he undertook it with pleasure at the prospect of the fee he would receive but also with a clear realization of the extent of his ignorance of the subject. He confessed to Douglas Hyde, when negotiating with Putnams, that he knew little of the Irish prose writers. When he wanted to read up a subject he got a commission for a book and so wrote to read and never merely read to write.[13] As a writer Yeats was very much self-taught, an autodidact. And his 'reading up' for his early commissions for anthologies was an important part of his apprenticeship as an Irish writer.

His research for *Representative Irish Tales* was both intensive and purposeful. He told the editor of the magazine *Irish Monthly*, Father Matthew Russell, that he was trying to include stories illustrative of some phase of

Irish life so that the collection would be a kind of social history.[14] The two
volumes contained the work of ten Irish authors, beginning with Maria
Edgeworth's *Castle Rackrent* of 1800 and concluding with a story by a living
Irish writer, Rosa Mulholland, residing in Dublin, whose fiction had been
published by Dickens in *Household Words* and whose poetry had appeared
in H.H. Sparling's *Irish Minstrelsy*. In his Introduction, which is an assured
and well-managed piece of literary criticism, Yeats identifies two 'accents'
in the sequence of Irish stories he is offering: 'the accent of the gentry, and
the less polished accent of the peasantry and those near them'.[15] The
former was best exemplified by Maria Edgeworth; the latter by Carleton.
But for Yeats at this moment in his life, increasingly fascinated by the folk-
tales and culture of the Irish peasantry, Carleton is the greater of the two:

> *Beside Miss Edgeworth's well-finished four-square house of the*
> *intelligence, Carleton raised his rough clay 'rath' [a primitive fortified*
> *earthwork] of humour and passion. Miss Edgeworth has outdone writers*
> *like Lover and Lever because of her fine judgement, her serene culture, her*
> *well-balanced mind. Carleton, on the other hand, with no conscious art at*
> *all, and living a half-blind, groping sort of life, drinking and borrowing,*
> *has, I believe, outdone not only them but her also by the sheer force of his*
> *powerful nature. It was not for nothing that his ancestors had dug the*
> *ground. His great body, that could leap twenty-one feet on a level, was*
> *full of violent emotions and brooding melancholy.*[16]

The last two phrases show the strong personal empathy that Yeats, in his
mid-twenties, felt for Carleton. Then in words that prefigure important
attitudes of his later life Yeats goes on to speak of his reservations about
recent writers who derive from the Irish Catholic middle class. Theirs is a
'new accent', 'the accent of people who have not the recklessness of the
landowning class, nor the violent passions of the peasantry, nor the good
frankness of either . . . Their main hindrances are a limited and diluted
piety, a dread of nature and her abundance, a distrust of unsophisticated
life.'[17] Such people are of no assistance to Yeats in his urgent desire to dis-
pense with 'the stage Irishman' and to bring to the fore the dignity of Irish
experience as shown in its fiction and founded in what he terms 'the deep
earth song of the peasant's laughter'.[18] The robust campaigning side to

Yeats's Introduction is supported strongly and explicitly by the poem of 'Dedication' which heads the collection. Working now for a Boston publisher he speaks directly, as he had done in his poem in the *Boston Pilot*, to Irish Americans and indeed to Irish emigrants and their descendants throughout the world. He knows his readership and its feeling for Ireland and its cause and he appeals to that feeling. What he offers is metaphorized as a green branch with bell flowers, a branch of Irish willow with catkins:

> *Ah, Exiles, wandering over many lands,*
> *My bell branch murmurs: the gay bells bring laughter,*
> *A honied ringing! under the new skies*
> *They bring you memories of old village faces*
> *Cabins gone now, old well-sides, old dear places,*
> *And men who loved the cause that never dies.*

Yeats's intellectual history was always an interaction between the political and the spiritual, and in the months following Maud Gonne's departure, as he began work on *Representative Irish Tales*, he also started on another book which was to constitute a major episode in his exploration of the occult. The project was a commentary on the mystical system of William Blake as articulated in his Prophetic Books. This ambitious enterprise, so important to Yeats in his compulsive attempts to know a non-material world, came about unexpectedly. One of the visitors to the Yeats home early in 1889 was the painter Edwin Ellis, an old friend of John Yeats who had only recently returned to London after living for years in Italy. In his early forties now, balding and unworldly with a wealthy and dictatorial German wife, the painter Edwin Ellis had long cared for Blake, a passion he had picked up in Pre-Raphaelite studios.[19] That evening in the shabby sitting-room in Blenheim Road Willie's interest was captured as Ellis spoke of the relations between Blake's mystical works and the works of the late Renaissance precursor of theosophy, the German Jakob Boehme, and those of the eighteenth-century Swedish proponent of the New Jerusalem, Emanuel Swedenborg. The young man immediately and excitedly saw that some of the ideas that were being talked about by Ellis were similar to those in the Christian Cabbala and Ellis had never heard of this.[20]

A spark of intellectual sympathy flashed between the middle-aged painter, dreamy and socially maladroit, and the young poet avid for spiritual experience, seventeen years his junior. It fired a four-year collaboration from which finally emerged their three-volume edition of Blake. In this way Blake's vision became an important part of Yeats's mystical understanding. He found work on the edition exciting. Both he and Ellis took it as a sign of 'Blake's personal help' when they realized that the first published of the Prophetic Books, *The Book of Thel*, had come out in 1789, exactly a century before they decided to work together. Unhappy in love, Willie found consolation in exploring with Ellis the complex spirituality described by Blake. Willie grew increasingly impressed by his collaborator, describing him to Katharine Tynan as an elderly man with a kind of genius who had been for years in Italy, painting and studying Dante.[21]

Their research proceeded through the summer and autumn and led them to an exciting discovery. They traced the whereabouts of a long mystical poem by Blake, *Vala, or the Four Zoas*, which had never before been published. It was in the possession of the elderly descendants of Blake's friend and patron John Linnell. The manuscript was in a house of theirs at Redstone Wood, near Redhill in Surrey, where Yeats and Ellis would go in order to copy it. The pleasant countryside gave Willie a change from tramping the London streets to the British Museum and to one editor's office or another, and the two scholars of mysticism were well received. The grey-haired brothers and sisters who owned the manuscript were greatly pleased to see their heirloom so appreciated, serving their visitors thirty-year-old port. Yeats also told John O'Leary that all the time he was writing the oldest of the old men sat beside him with a penknife in his hand to sharpen his pencil when it grew blunt.[22]

But O'Leary was none too pleased to hear of these activities. He wanted Yeats to concentrate on being an Irish poet and he complained about this interest in mystical texts, as he also did about his protégé's involvement with Madame Blavatsky. Yeats sought to placate his mentor in Dublin, by maintaining, incorrectly, that Blake was Irish by descent.[23] And Madame Blavatsky he defended strongly; he regarded her as resembling Dr Johnson in her passionate nature.[24] To O'Leary he insisted on her humanity and her hard work: 'She is the most human person alive, is like an old peasant woman, and is wholly devoted, all her life is but sitting in a great chair with a pen in her hand. For years she has written twelve hours a day.'[25] When John O'Leary visited London in the summer, Willie invited him to come along with him to one of Madame Blavatsky's theosophist evenings. John O'Leary wrote of the sect's high priestess that at first she struck him as a terrific termagant, but she was at bottom, he thought, a good-natured old woman. But those around her he thought were not impressive. In his view most of the men were far more of women than Madame Blavatsky and the women just feeble echoes of her.[26]

John O'Leary was not the only visitor to Blenheim Road that summer of 1889. A month earlier in July, shortly after Willie's twenty-fourth birthday, Katharine Tynan, on a tour of England, had come to see the Yeatses. It was a happy reunion and she and Willie grew close to each other. Ever the shrewd, tireless planner of his own literary career, he also sought to organize hers. He tried to persuade her to write in literary forms longer than the lyric. He suggested that she attempt a miracle play, and indeed a few years later she did so.[27] Not long after her return Willie broached the possibility of addressing her by her first name, to which she agreed.

Nearing the end of her twenties now, Katharine Tynan had put on weight. But as Yeats told John O'Leary, he thought this suited her and that she looked better than when he had seen her in Dublin.[28] Willie's own appearance also changed during this year that began with such lovesickness. He experimented with a beard and a moustache. At Christmas he shaved them off but not before a Bedford Park neighbour, Henry Marriott Paget, a painter friend of John Yeats, had done a portrait of the young man bearded. With a floral buttonhole and without his spectacles the young poet is, some two months before his twenty-fourth birthday, very much the gentle, dreaming – perhaps pining – visionary. But what the letters of this year show, as the painting does not, is Yeats's steely determination in building his literary career and his near daemonic industriousness. Putting in long hours on his two books of Irish fiction and on the one dealing with the poetry of William Blake, he also did an increasing amount of occasional journalism.

Henley gave him this kind of work in London but Yeats also contributed to Irish American magazines published on the eastern seabord. For the *Providence Sunday Journal* he reviewed volumes of Irish poetry, including *The Banshee and Other Poems* by his neighbour and friend John Todhunter. He wrote further pieces for the *Boston Pilot*, the periodical to which John O'Leary had introduced him. In fact he contributed what amounted to a regular *causerie* or literary gossip column to it. Here he commented on matters as diverse as the death of Browning that year, a conversation with Lady Wilde, an auction of literary manuscripts at Sotheby's, yet one more subscription scheme (this time for publishing O'Leary's memoirs) to which Parnell was a subscriber, and the production in the following year of Todhunter's 'charming little pastoral drama' after Theocritus entitled *A Sicilian Idyll*. This play was performed at the small club theatre in Bedford Park, an attractive venue which 'with its black panels and gilt Cupids had been crowded with really distinguished audiences'. Willie the columnist then goes on to list the 'social and literary notables' who attended.[29] He always presents himself to his readers in Boston as the worldly, well-connected and experienced London hand. Here, for instance, is what the young journalist has to tell them about the imperial capital as 'the season' ends and the summer holiday begins:

> *London has been empty a long while now, all folk who could having fled to the continent or Brighton or elsewhither in search of green fields and sea winds. They will soon be on their way home, with much secret satisfaction, for your Londoner, in spite of all he may say, does not much care for the country. He is not used to being alone, and considers the joys of country solitude a fiction of the poets, all the pleasanter to read about because it is only a fiction and no reality questioning his own noisy, talkative existence.*[30]

In every one of these articles London and 'cosmopolitanism' are rejected in favour of what is Irish. He ends one column with the ringing declaration that 'there is no fine nationality without literature, and . . . no fine literature without nationality'.[31] This principle required that he send a patronizing rebuke to his 'sometime friend' and recent reviewer, T.W. Rolleston. Rolleston, he reports, 'who just translated Walt Whitman into German, is now busy on a life of Lessing for Mr Walter Scott'. Rolleston is also intending to settle in London. All this brings a sigh from Willie.

Rolleston 'is a fine Greek scholar and quite the handsomest man in Ireland, but I wish he would devote his imagination to some national purpose. Cosmopolitan literature is, at best, but a poor bubble but a big one. Creative work has always a fatherland.'[32]

During the summer Willie set off to Oxford for a few days to earn money as a copyist again, hurting his weak eyes by working for six and a half hours each day. One of his rare pleasures was a walk into the Cotswold countryside on a literary pilgrimage to see the Thames ford at Bablock Hythe, one of the places figuring in Matthew Arnold's poem 'The Scholar Gypsy'. Then it was back to the hard work in the Bodleian Library. As he laboured away on his many enterprises during that summer and autumn, being copyist, journalist, research scholar and dramatist, gradually the memory of Maud receded.

In late October he learned that she was back. She had in fact been in London for a while, nursing her younger sister Katharine who was seriously ill, but had not sought any contact with him. He rushed over to where she was staying only to find that she was at that very moment setting off back to Paris, so could only give him five minutes. Willie passed on the sad news he had just received, that Ellen O'Leary had died. Maud wished to send her condolences to John O'Leary and asked for his address. Willie gave it to her and she put it in a pocket-book which she then lost somewhere on the journey from Victoria to the Gare du Nord. After only a few minutes of conversation with him the beautiful Maud had, once again, vanished back to the city which Willie had never seen and in which General Boulanger's long meditated *coup d'état* had been attempted and thwarted. Lucien Millevoye was in a state of deep dejection, but Paris was in a gay holiday mood. There was an international exhibition to celebrate the centennial of the beginning of the French revolution, and its centrepiece was the newly opened Eiffel Tower.

The remaining weeks of the year were also the end of the decade. The coming of the 1890s were to mark a distinct change in Willie's life. It began with illness. Madame Blavatsky had warned him about shaving off his beard, promising him a bad illness in three months as a result of the loss of all the mesmeric force that collects in a beard.[33] And indeed very early in the New Year he came down with a bad case of Russian influenza.[34] The

New Year also saw historical change in Ireland where the Irish Home Rule cause was abruptly deprived of its momentum when Parnell's relationship with the wife of his parliamentary follower Captain O'Shea became an issue in the divorce court. The Irish Party at Westminster split over the matter and Gladstone and the Liberals gave up their alliance with Parnell. A markedly new mood entered politics in Ireland, as it entered literature in England. W.B. Yeats was affected by both, and as the decade wore on, was increasingly influential in both.

Over in France, in this year when Van Gogh died and Monet settled at Giverney, there was an important development in Maud Gonne's life, though Yeats would know nothing of it for some time.

III

THE CALCULATING
DREAMER

The last decades of the nineteenth century witnessed the spread of a poetic move-ment across a Europe invaded by machines. The movement resembled a dense forest; its branches sought to hide the factories and the railways, its pungent fruits held the key to 'anywhere out of the world' and its luxuriant blossoms inspired Art Nouveau. The roots of the trees thrust themselves deep into the subsoil of Celtic and Norse legends, while the saplings, taken from exotic species of trees issuing from Florence, Byzantium and even India, produced poisonous blossoms side by side with healthy ones originating in England. Most of the trees had been planted in England by the Pre-Raphaelites, and in Germany by the Nazarenes and, later, by Wagner. The principal literary streams which fed them were Edgar Allen Poe, E.T.A. Hoffmann, Coleridge and Swedenborg . . . This forest had been planted with trees from the forest of Broceliande and with flowers from the garden of Klingsor. It is here that one finds the well of Pelléas, the swan of Lohengrin, the fauns of Verlaine . . . from about 1880, the blue shadows of the forest of Broceliande sheltered two new and distinct species, the Decadents and the Aesthetes who together united all those 'souls' fascinated by mystery, the occult, bizarre eroticism and exotic archaeology.

PHILIPPE JULIAN, Introduction to *French Symbolist Painters*, 1972

It is among such men with cultivated intellects, sensitive nerves, and bad diges-tion, that we find the prophets and disciples of the gospel of Pessimism . . . Accordingly Pessimism is not a creed which is likely to exert much moral influ-ence on the strong, practical, Anglo-Saxon race, and we can only discern some faint traces of it in the tendency of certain very limited cliques of so-called Aestheticism to admire morbid and self-conscious ideals, both in poetry and painting.

S. LAING, *Modern Science and Modern Thought*, 1896

ARLY IN 1890 THE TWO YOUNG BACHELORS WHO HAD BECOME friends at Kelmscott House, Ernest Rhys and W.B. Yeats, decided at one of their frequent meetings that they would found a poets' club. The members would meet to eat and drink wine, read and discuss their poetry and the state of their art. The society was called the Rhymers' Club and proved to be an important feature of the literary history of the 1890s. The initiative marked a major development in Yeats's career. It showed in him a new confidence and it gave him a new social and professional standing. At the Rhymers he was no longer a dependant, a guest, as he had been at the Contemporary Club or at Kelmscott House. He was now the patron and the organizer and the others came at his invitation and under his auspices. At the age of twenty-five he began forging a new relationship for himself with the literary community of London.

Two years on when the Rhymers were still going strong he took a pride in telling the readers of the *Boston Pilot* how 'remarkable a thing' his Club was: 'Into this little body, as about a round table of rhyme, have gathered well nigh all the poets of the new generation who have public enough to get their works printed at the cost of the publisher, and some not less excellent, who cannot yet mount that first step of the ladder famewards.' He conceded that the society was not like a French 'school' of poetry; it did not have an 'ism' like the four 'isms' flourishing virtually simultaneously in Paris. 'In France literature divides itself into schools, movements and circles. At one moment the Decadents, at another the Symbolists, today the Parnassians, tomorrow the Naturalists, hold the public ear and win acceptance for their theory and practice of literature.' But the Rhymers had no such theory; at most they wanted to be rid of small, limited lyrical forms and to return to a larger notion of poetry: 'they all believe that the deluge of triolets and rondeaus has passed away, and that we must look once more upon the world with serious eyes and set to music – each according to his lights – the deep sound of humanity.'[1] In the year in which Yeats wrote these words and recorded these ambitions Tennyson died; two years earlier, not long after Yeats had first met Maud Gonne, Browning had died. Yeats thinks his group of young poets able to succeed them: 'All, despairing, cry of the departing age, but the world still goes on, and the sound of man is ever young, and its song shall never come to an end. The names of some few of the Rhymers may have already been blown across the Atlantic.'[2]

To have founded such a club satisfied a non-literary part of Yeats's personality; he was far more than the lovelorn, melancholy and introverted figure that his poetry of the time so often suggested. Within his complex nature there was also a clubman. His career as a writer began at the Contemporary Club and throughout his life he would found or join a succession of organizations. In the last years of his life, in Dublin, he greatly enjoyed the comforts and the distinction of membership of Ireland's leading gentleman's club, the Kildare Street Club. For the first meetings of their Rhymers' Club Yeats and Rhys decided to reserve a supper room at the Cheshire Cheese, an ancient inn in Wine Office Court, just off Fleet Street. Here they were on the edge of the old City and at the centre of Britain's newspaper industry, then rapidly expanding as improved public education extended literacy. Virtually all the Rhymers had some contact with the press. The choice of venue also signalled the self-assurance with which Yeats and Rhys began the Club. For this pub, of which the origins were so old as to be unknown and which had last been rebuilt in 1667 after the Fire of London, had for centures received major figures in the English literary tradition. Here, in all probability, had come Ben Jonson, Samuel Johnson, Oliver Goldsmith and Charles Dickens. And here Yeats now brought that group of men which, as an autobiographer thirty years later, he would define as *his* generation. A few were his elders in years but his equals in energetic concern for literature. T.W. Rolleston who came to live in Wimbledon was virtually a founder member; John Todhunter, the dedicated practitioner of poetic drama, was a regular attender, and so was Yeats's partner in Blake research, Edwin Ellis. But the majority of the Rhymers were young men closer to Yeats's age. Ernest Rhys brought along several aspirants whom he knew from his wide experience in London's literary Bohemia.

There was Lionel Johnson, later remembered by Yeats as one of the figures who most characterized the 1890s. The two swiftly became friends. Johnson was a handsome young man, dapper and most fastidious about his clothes, but disconcertingly small. Yeats, with his long, lank hair, 'wore a brown velveteen coat, a loose tie and a very old Inverness cape, discarded by my father twenty years before'.[3] Johnson, who came from a prosperous family, insisted on dressing in the conventional and sober style of 'an English gentleman'. Yet in other respects Lionel Johnson's life was far from conventional. Some two years younger than Yeats, and physically frail, Lionel Johnson had spent some of his boyhood in Wales which made a strong impression upon him and began his lifelong interest in things Celtic. His public school was Winchester where, it has been said, he had been part of a homosexual group. His academic record was a brilliant one and he became a Scholar of New College, Oxford, where he read widely and voraciously in English and classical literature. At Oxford Lionel Johnson was taught and much influenced by Walter Pater of Brasenose College, who early in Johnson's undergraduate career had published *Marius the Epicurean*. This was a work which further articulated Pater's assertion of the amorality of art and the primacy of the sensations it afforded, an anti-Ruskinian view which had informed his *Studies in the History of the Renaissance* published twelve years earlier.

When he had completed his studies at Oxford, Lionel Johnson went to live in Bloomsbury in a shared house at 20 Fitzroy Street, near the northern end of Charlotte Street. His fellow residents had considerable reputations in the arts. Arthur Mackmurdo, in his fortieth year in 1890, was one of the most progressive architects and furniture designers of the day. Trained by Ruskin, he had reacted against the ponderousness of mid-Victorian design, producing furniture characterized by slender lines making for a light, mannered vertical elegance. This tall, linear emphasis contrasted with the sinuous art nouveau designs of the fabrics which he also created to adorn and upholster his furnture. He established the Century Guild, the first of such craft organizations within the larger tradition of the Arts and Crafts Movement. Based in the house in Fitzroy Street the Guild was, in effect, Mackmurdo and his young architect friend Herbert Horne. The Guild also produced a magazine, *The Hobby Horse*, to which the designer and poet Selwyn Image contributed much artwork. Horne and Image also both lived in the Fitzroy Street house.

Yeats remarked on 'the exquisite taste' of this little colony of artists. Lionel Johnson brought the refined, choice literary sensibility of one schooled under Walter Pater to this group, and also to Yeats who lacked a higher education. Like many who have recently graduated, Johnson still used words and phrases favoured by his teacher. Yeats remembered some of Johnson's favourite words which came to mean much to him: 'Life should be a ritual, and we should value it for "magnificence", for all that is "hieratic".'[4] When Yeats went for the first time to call on Johnson, he knocked at the door at five o'clock in the afternoon. The door was opened by a manservant who informed him that Mr Johnson was not yet up. Disappointed, Yeats asked whether his fellow Rhymer was ill. 'Oh no, sir,' replied the manservant and then added as though admiring the feat, 'but he is always up for dinner at seven.'[5]

Sleep was one of the ways in which Johnson, physically fragile and with a highly responsive nervous system, sought to avoid the world. Other ways were books, and at the last, in ever vaster amounts, alcohol. Johnson's need to minimize his contact with life is reminiscent of his near-contemporary Marcel Proust isolated in his cork-lined flat, or of the young Paul Valéry, or Thomas Mann's early heroes such as Tonio Kröger. Yeats saw in Johnson the pre-eminent instance of 'the tragedy of that generation', writing of him that Johnson had rather refused to live than failed.[6] Incapacity in the face of life is the subject of one of Johnson's best known poems, 'The Dark Angel'. As Philip Larkin's 'Churchgoing' articulates something peculiar to the 1950s and Auden's 'Spain' has been taken as an expression of a distinctively 1930s attitude, so has 'The Dark Angel' gained a reputation as a text that epitomizes what was distinctively of the 1890s. The poem is an address to the dark, evil power which, the poet declares, has possessed him. The language used suggests a possession at once spiritual and sexual:

> *Dark Angel, with thine aching lust*
> *To rid the world of penitence:*
> *Malicious Angel, who still dost*
> *My soul such subtle violence!*

Another stanza proclaims the unmitigated pollution of the poet's consciousness:

> *Because of thee, no thought, no thing,*
> *Abides for me undesecrate:*
> *Dark Angel, ever on the wing,*
> *Who never reachest me too late!*

Yet one more exclamation declares how the Dark Angel turns even the poet's art into horror and perversion, a perversion of melodramatic proportions:

> *Through thee, the gracious Muses turn*
> *To Furies, O mine Enemy!*
> *And all the things of beauty burn*
> *With flames of evil ecstasy.*

The self-loathing and disgust that are here proclaimed led Johnson into an alcoholism that would kill him by the age of thirty-five. His drinking shocked and dismayed Yeats because he had become for a time his closest friend.[7] What drew Yeats to this small, handsome, epicene young man was, he said, an elegance of mind which corresponded to his frail but beautifully formed body. He seemed to Yeats to have the features of a Greek carving.[8] In turn the comfortably off Johnson respected Yeats for his powers of survival. He once said to Yeats, 'I need ten years in the wilderness and you ten years in a library.'

To a friend from Winchester and Oxford days Johnson wrote a disparaging letter about a gathering of the Rhymers in his rooms at 20 Fitzroy Street: 'We entertained the other night eighteen minor poets of our acquaintance from Oscar Wilde to Walter Crane, with Arthur Symons and Willie Yeats between. They all inflicted their poems on each other, and were inimitably tedious, except dear Oscar.'[9] The Rhymers also met occasionally in other members' homes, but for the most part they conversed in their sand-strewn room upstairs at the Cheshire Cheese once a week. There they smoked and talked and hoped to get all the younger writers of verse to join them. Those who had the money dined there at seven and the others turned up later.[10] Yeats saw the Club as a means of bringing his generation together, though in the event the membership proved to be limited to writers with a Celtic background. Just about all those who attended had connections with Wales, Cornwall, Scotland or Ireland.

Years later, when so many of the Rhymers had died young or burned out, they would continue for Yeats as a romantic memory. They were made to serve as an important part of the backdrop to his depiction of himself and his development when he came to write his volumes of prose autobiography. A quarter of a century after he founded the Club, in his poem 'The Grey Rock', he would invoke and salute those youthful associates, those 'Poets with whom I learned my trade / Companions of the Cheshire Cheese'. Arthur Ransome, subsequently a highly successful children's writer, wrote a book in the early years of this century supplying a guided tour to London's Bohemia, and felt it obligatory to draw attention to the Cheshire Cheese, 'still the dirty-fronted, low-browed tavern, with stone flasks in the window'. For here, 'Up a winding crooked, dark stair-case there are other rooms, with long tables in them stained with wine and ale, and in one of them the Rhymers' Club used to meet, to drink from the tankards, smoke clay pipes, and recite their own poetry.'[11] Ten years after Arthur Ransome wrote this, Ezra Pound in his long poem 'Hugh Selwyn Mauberley' would also return to the Cheshire Cheese with an incisive critique of the Rhymers and of the decadence and aestheticism which informed their best known art.

But in 1890 the Rhymers were a long way from becoming a legend or a moment in English literary history requiring critical analysis. Initially their Club existed to provide some practical help to young poets starting to make their way in London. Those who had managed to establish themselves as reviewers helped those who had not. Ernest Rhys reviewed for the

Pall Mall Gazette, Rolleston for the *Academy*, Richard Le Gallienne for the *Star* and the ebullient and bewigged Scotsman John Davidson for the *Daily Chronicle*. And, of course, Yeats himself wrote regularly about books for the *Boston Pilot*. The presence of so many reviewers in the group meant that they all had a better chance of getting their work noticed, praised and publicized. Yeats was quick to exploit such contacts. Little over a year after the meetings at the Cheshire Cheese began, Yeats felt able to tell Katharine Tynan that because of the Rhymers' Club he had some influence with reviewers and could probably get her a note in the *Speaker* at least and certainly in the *Queen*.[12]

He was very career-conscious and now, in this same year of 1890, one member of his generation and like him one of 'Henley's young men', his exact contemporary Rudyard Kipling, had an overnight success and became instantly a household name. The publication of the enormously popular *Barrack Room Ballads* established him as *the* poet of the British Empire. The cocksure imperialism and the rabble-rousing tone of these poems were in strong contrast to the spirituality and aestheticism of the Rhymers.

Yeats was closer to some of the Rhymers than to others. John Davidson was kindly and helpful but Yeats could never 'get behind' his 'Scottish roughness and exasperation'.[13] It also took Yeats some time to become friendly with the fair-haired, lightly built Arthur Symons, the son of a Methodist minister and, like Lionel Johnson, greatly interested in Sin. Symons was exactly Yeats's age and had also published poetry and prose. Another colourful figure among the Rhymers was Symons's friend Ernest Dowson whose life was driven by two manic appetites, for drink and for prostitutes. Yeats found him vague and drifting, someone who gave him always a sense of weakness as well as of the virtues of sweetness and of courtesy.[14]

During the early years of the Rhymers' Club, as his friendship with Lionel Johnson developed, Yeats admired more and more the astringency of his mind, the delicacy of his sensibility and his great erudition. And Johnson, as his respect and affection for Yeats grew, became interested in Irish matters. He discovered that he had Irish ancestry, and one of his most substantial essays in literary criticism was a long piece entitled 'Poetry and

Patriotism in Ireland'. In it he praises Yeats's originality as an Irish poet and rebukes English critics for their parochialism, their insistence on judging work with reference to English models, their inability to appreciate Irishness. Johnson writes, 'My friend Mr Yeats has been informed that he is a disciple of Rossetti and of Tennyson; now, no two poets could be less alike than Rossetti and Tennyson; and no one could be less like either of them than Mr Yeats. But he dares to write in his own style, upon his own themes; and because they are not the style and the themes familiar to us from old associations we rush to the conclusion that he is treading in the footsteps of some English poet, despising Irish art.'[15] Johnson's rapidly developing enthusiasm for things Celtic led him to go over to Dublin where, through introductions from Yeats, he was able to meet members of the Contemporary Club and other figures in the Irish literary revival.

But for all their increasing closeness there was one matter on which Johnson and Yeats were always at odds: Yeats's involvement with spiritualism. The year after the Rhymers' Club was founded Lionel Johnson was received into the Roman Catholic Church. He was a connoisseur of ritual, vestments, incense and hierarchy. His notions of the spiritual were confined entirely to the orthodoxy of the Church. For the frail, sexless Lionel Johnson as for that much more robust and masculine friend John O'Leary, Yeats's ventures into occultism seemed theologically and socially perverse. Spiritualism, as Yeats himself discovered, had a special attraction for crackpots and charlatans. Johnson, Yeats remembered, did not care for spiritualism, though he understood why it attracted his friend.[16]

Yeats's speculations took a radical turn in the early months of the new decade. For at the same time as he was organizing the Rhymers' Club he was preparing for initiation into a mystical society which was far more abstruse in its notions and practices than Madame Blavatsky's Theosophical Society. Indeed by the end of 1890 Yeats's notions of the occult had become such that Madame Blavatsky and her associates insisted on his resignation from the Esoteric Section of their Society. The mystical order into which Yeats made a ritualistic entrance in March 1890 was called 'The Hermetic Order of the Golden Dawn'. The Order derived from Rosicrucianism, a mystical tradition which originated in early seventeenth-century Germany. Its earliest texts told of the travels and spiritual quests of Christian Rosenkreutz, the son of a German nobleman. Brought up in a monastery, he went on to found an Order whose members across the centuries would find affinities sometimes with alchemists, sometimes with freemasons. In the mid-1880s two or three adherents of this tradition reformulated their beliefs and organized the Golden Dawn. A historian of the society records that 'By the middle of the nineties the Golden Dawn was well established in Great Britain with a membership of over one hundred drawn from every class of Victorian society.'[17] One of the members of this new version of a venerable, though often underground, tradition was W.B. Yeats. Joining it proved to be one of the most important moments in his career as a mystic.

It all began with a chance meeting at the British Museum. Yeats was working one day under the great dome of the Reading Room when his attention was seized by a striking man, some ten years older than himself, 'who seemed . . . a figure of romance'. The man wore a brown velveteen coat and had 'a gaunt resolute face, and an athletic body'.[18] The man returned regularly to the Reading Room and Yeats came into conversation with him. His name was Samuel Liddell Mathers but he altered this to MacGregor Mathers because, like Lionel Johnson, he wanted to associate himself with the new Celtic consciousness of the 1890s. Though born into a poor family in London, this tall intense man with the burning eyes believed himself the descendant of one of the great Scottish Highland chieftains' families. Soon he would call himself simply MacGregor. And when in four years' time he settled in Paris, he would take to wearing Highland dress and style himself the Comte de Glenstrae. He was a passionate campaigner on behalf of the claims of the Stuart descendants of Bonnie Prince Charlie to the British throne.

Mathers had been a soldier and was keenly interested in military hierarchy, rank and discipline: he had in fact published a book on the organization of infantry. But the central concern of Mathers' life was the occult, occult societies and the hierarchical ordering of such societies – subjects on which he had already published three books. He had been one of those involved in drawing up the complex, hierarchical system of the Golden Dawn and it was his continuing research into such matters that brought him to the British Museum.

Mathers saw himself as a born commander and was authoritative and arrogant. But the elaborate rituals, ranks, examinations and secret lore which he had helped formulate for the Order of the Golden Dawn intrigued and attracted Yeats, as they did others. A wealthy heiress, Miss Annie Horniman, whose family ran a large tea business in Lancashire, financed Mathers and regarded him as her guru. Florence Farr, an attractive, gifted and successful West End actress who lived in the vicinity of Bedford Park, was another member of the Order. When Yeats came under his powerful influence Mathers was living with Moina Bergson, a beautiful woman much younger than he, and the sister of the French philosopher Henri Bergson, who wrote about time and consciousness. Moina, who had psychic ability, had studied art at the Slade and had a studio at 17 Fitzroy Street close to Lionel Johnson's house. And it was here in early March that Yeats went through the secret ceremony of initiation into the Golden Dawn. Like every other member Yeats was endowed with a mystical Latin motto and initials. The four letters, recalling Lionel Johnson's dark angel, were DEDI, standing for Demon Est Deus Inversus: the Demon is God Inverted.

There was a megalomaniacal side to Mathers which became ever more apparent over the years in which Yeats was associated with him. But for the moment Mathers and his group gave the young and spiritually restless young man something which the Esoteric Section of Madame Blavatsky's Theosophical Society could not. This latter group, he concluded, dealt too much in discussion and abstraction.[19] But Mathers offered ritual, physical and bodily ritual, which Yeats found emotionally stimulating. In the Order of the Golden Dawn Mathers directed members to focus their eyes and their minds on concrete images. Yeats, for instance, was told to look at a coloured geometric form and then to close his eyes and see it again in the mind's eye. Then he was shown how to allow his mind to drift, following the suggestion of the symbol. The result of employing Mathers' technique was that this new apprentice to Rosicrucianism was able to see a desert, and a gigantic Negro arising from among great stones.[20] This kind of opening of the mind to unsought images became an important part of the young man's mental life. It was, he later wrote, for many years an important influence on his life.[21]

Such explorations into a world of images believed by Yeats to exist outside and beyond the individual consciousness related closely to the work he was doing with Edwin Ellis on Blake's Prophetic Books. The edition they were preparing was a big task and they worked hard and long at it. Sometimes their collaboration was put in jeopardy by the suspicions of Ellis's German wife. At times this wealthy and emotionally volatile lady became alarmed by the shabbily dressed mystical poet who would throw his arms about rhythmically in her drawing-room, as though conducting an orchestra. On one occasion she even threw him out of the house for, said Yeats, she was entirely convinced that he had thrown a spell upon her.[22] After a lengthy banishment Yeats was finally able to persuade Frau Ellis that 'she had mistaken for the making of symbols a habit I have of beating time to some verse running in my head'. She relented and by way of compensation fed him with a very rich cake covered with almond paste which he did not enjoy at all.[23]

As summer and autumn 1890 wore on Yeats became increasingly exhausted by the work he had to do with the mass of Blake material. He longed to go to Ireland where he could relax and live as the guest of his relatives. Many problems, especially financial ones, continued to plague him and his family. He and his father had quarrelled violently about Parnell and his involvement with Kitty O'Shea and for some weeks would not speak to each other. On this occasion Jack sided with his brother. Lolly, on whom the burden of looking after her invalid mother fell, was tense and irritable; she was approaching her examinations to become a Froebel teacher. Lily was becoming estranged from May Morris and was unhappy at Kelmscott but feared to lose the family's only secure income. In November Yeats had to write a letter to John O'Leary confessing that he simply could not yet pay back the money which his old friend had lent him, because the family was in financial difficulties.[24] Still the work on the Blake ground on. Ellis had secured a contract with Bernard Quaritch, a German *émigré* antiquarian bookseller and publisher with a shop at 15 Piccadilly. Yeats, always a careful reader of contracts, had approved its terms. But still the two collaborators could not complete the work. Then, in that November, Willie, very much run down, caught 'a bad influenza cold' and some ten days later had to tell Katharine Tynan that he was in a state of near collapse.[25] His doctor told him that as a result of his many activities he had been wearing himself out; he urged him to take life more easily: an impossibility for one of Yeats's temperament.[26] Such wide oscillations in his life and health would recur throughout his career; ambitious, energetic initiatives would dissolve in exhaustion and illness. ⌐

$[1890 - 1894]$

IN THE FIRST WEEK OF DECEMBER 1890, AS THE IRISH PARTY IN Committee Room 15 at Westminster argued about the future of Charles Stewart Parnell in the aftermath of the O'Shea divorce case, Yeats met his old schoolmate Charles Johnston once more. The two friends now had illness in common: the brilliant Johnston after only eighteen months in Bengal had been invalided out of the Indian Civil Service and sent home. They talked of the great crisis in Irish politics currently playing itself out. Events climaxed on 6 December when forty-five members of the Irish Party dramatically withdrew from the Committee Room leaving Parnell with only twenty-seven supporters. The Home Rule cause was fractured, its dynamic lost.

Yeats and Charley Johnston discussed the possibility of Yeats visiting the Johnston family home in Ulster, Ballykilbeg in County Down, since Yeats was almost frantic to get away from London and all his various commitments there. But the Blake book still prevented him. He was now beginning to find his collaboration with Edwin Ellis to be something of a problem. For all his awkward, bumbling exterior, the older man brought a great deal of wilfulness to the project. He had his own strong views on Blake and Yeats felt he had to resist them, to the point where he felt he was investing all his time and energy in the fight. He told John O'Leary that he had been working desperately hard on the Blake to the exclusion of everything else. He was driven, he told his friend, by the fear that in his haste to complete the work Ellis might try to write some of the chapters assigned to Yeats and ruin them through his ignorance of mysticism. Sadly, Yeats felt that he could not arrange a visit to London until the first half of the book had been sent to the printer.[1]

The procedure of the two collaborators was to write drafts which each then submitted to the other for correction or rewriting. There is, however, one passage of some twelve pages which had minimal alterations made to it by Edwin Ellis. This is the opening of the third section of the first volume, entitled 'The Symbolic System'. These pages were originally an essay by Yeats entitled 'The Necessity of Symbolism' and help explain his recent involvement with MacGregor Mathers and his entry into the Golden Dawn. They are an important early statement by Yeats on the subject of images and the nature of the individual and individualism. Some of the allusions used here long remained in his mind and recurred even in his very last poems:

The materialist sees only what belongs to his contracted consciousness. The creative visionary or man of genius has all thoughts, symbols, and experiences that enter within his larger circle. If he has developed his perception of mental sound it will give him music; if his perception of thought, philosophic generalisations; and if his sense of mental insight, visions, strong or faint, according to his power of concentration upon them. The mood of the seer, no longer bound by the particular experiences of his body, spreads out and enters into the particular experiences of an ever-widening circle of other lives and beings, for it will more and more grow one with that portion of the mood essense which is common to all lives. The circle of individuality will widen out until other individualities are contained within it, and their thoughts, and the persistent thought-symbols which are their spiritual or mental bodies, will grow visible to it. He who has thus passed into the impersonal portion of his own mind perceives that it is not a mind at all but all minds. Hence Blake's statement that 'Albion', or man, once contained all 'the starry heavens', and his description of their flight from him as he materialised. When once man has re-entered into this, his ancient state, he perceives all things as with the eyes of God. The thoughts of nature grow visible independent of their physical symbols. He sees when

the body dies the soul still persisting and ascending, perhaps as Blake saw
his brother Robert's, clapping its hands with joy. He discovers by 'his
enlarged and numerous senses' the 'spiritual causes' that are behind 'natural
events'. It was in this way that Blake perceived those spiritual forms with
which . . . he talked and argued as with old friends. But most men can only
see the thoughts of nature through their physical effects.[3]

Yeats wrote a good deal of prose during 1891 but most of it did not take up
such deep issues. A lot of it was printed in W.E. Henley's *National Observer*
and consisted of essays deriving from his work on Irish fairylore and folklore. Perhaps Henley, the staunch Unionist, was confirmed in his pre-
conceptions that Yeats was prone to present Ireland in a fanciful, whimsical
way, showing it as a place of superstition and obscurity. But Yeats was also
fast developing his skills as a prose humorist. One essay is a jesting riposte
at the Scots in general and perhaps Henley in particular: 'A Remonstrance
with Scotsmen for Having Soured the Disposition of Their Ghosts and
Faeries'. The bantering tone continues throughout:

In Scotland you are too theological, too gloomy . . . You have discovered the
faeries to be pagan and wicked. You would like to have them all before the
magistrates . . . In Scotland you have denounced them from the pulpit. In
Ireland they have been permitted by the priests to consult with them on the
state of their souls . . . The Catholic religion likes to keep on good terms
with its neighbours.[4]

As he sent this sequence of pieces to Henley, Yeats was already thinking of
them as a basis for a volume of prose and, indeed, two years later *The Celtic*
Twilight was published.

As 1890 drew to an end, and Yeats continued to contend with Ellis, he
tried to make some money by placing his autobiographical novel *John*
Sherman, a venture into fiction that had begun some years before. John
Sherman lives in Ballah, a city on the west coast of Ireland that is recogniz-
ably Sligo. Worldly considerations prompt him to leave both this place
where he is quietly contented and his loving friend Mary Carton. ('They
were such good friends they had never fallen in love with each other.'[5]) He
goes to London, where he works as a clerk in his uncle's business and

becomes involved with the frivolous, fashion-conscious Margaret Leland who lives close to him in St Peter's Square in Hammersmith. Half-heartedly he becomes engaged to this vain, superficial girl, who brings to mind Laura Armstrong. He then feels it necessary to return to Ballah to tell Mary Carton. In so doing he comes to realize his disillusionment with London and with Margaret, who is herself becoming interested in someone else. He returns to the worthy and principled Mary but after a night on the bare mountain of Knocknarea realizes that the happy innocence of their former relationship cannot be restored. Mary's last words are, 'We have shipwrecked. Our goods have been cast into the sea.'[6]

The desolation and suffering which the novel genuinely articulates have little to do with love between a man and a woman. In treating such matters the young, inexperienced novelist can only try to feign the magisterial wisdom (and the antithetical sentences) of a Dr Johnson. 'Perfect love and perfect friendship are indeed incompatible; for the one is a battlefield where shadows war beside the combatants, and the other a placid country where Consultation has her dwelling.'[7] Nevertheless as it mounts to its conclusion the novel does convey genuine emotion. It has to do with a subtle sense of loss and of being compromised. Ballah/Sligo is the hero's love, but London is his necessity. And the experience of London forever deprives him of the innocence and unselfconsciousness that those he knows in Ballah possess. London and Margaret Leland have had their effect upon him, and neither John nor Mary can return to being the people they were before. It is Yeats's most extended statement so far about the painful effects upon an Irish sensibility of living in England. It is a novel about cultural and also psychological division.

Or rather it is a novella. For when published it ran to well under two hundred very small pages and had to be eked out by the addition of 'Dhoya', Yeats's story about a giant in the Ireland of prehistory. After some rejections Yeats finally managed to get Fisher Unwin to publish the two pieces, thanks to a reader's report from Edward Garnett who later assisted the careers of Joseph Conrad, Ford Madox Ford and D.H. Lawrence. Yeats's two short fictions appeared in a series which, to provoke curiosity and interest, was published under pseudonyms. Since he was required to present himself as a figure that would cater to the London fashion for Irish subjects, he reluctantly adopted the pseudonym Ganconagh. He says of himself in an introductory 'Apology': 'I am an old little Irish spirit, and I sit in the hedges and watch the world go by . . . I care for nothing in the world but love and idleness.'[8] It was another ludicrous and irritating experience of being compromised as an Irishman. Yeats, ever anxious for literary fame, made no effort to respect the pseudonym and in his letters of the time was keen to reveal the identity of the author. But he was disappointed in the terms Fisher Unwin offered: he was to earn no royalties until the book had sold a thousand copies.

Financial rewards for all his many literary activities came with tormenting slowness. And his deep desire to get away from London and spend some time in Ireland continued to make him restless. So too did the thought and image of Maud Gonne, for despite his resolve to face the fact that he could have no future with her, he continually thought and wondered about her. In this respect his life, like his poetry, centred on images remembered rather than the reality in front of his eyes. He wanted to know about her travels and her whereabouts: in the spring of 1891, for instance, he writes to John O'Leary in Dublin begging him to let him know whether Maud had returned to Dublin.[9]

By mid-July 1891 Yeats at last felt able to set off on that trip to Ireland which he had so long promised himself and others. When he arrived at the Tynan home at Clondalkin he learned that Katharine Tynan was engaged to Henry Hinkson, an old schoolfellow of his and a law graduate from Trinity, and that Maud Gonne was in Dublin, staying at a hotel in Nassau Street. The moment he could, he went to sit in the hotel lobby and wait for her. When Maud came in, he was greatly shocked to see the immense change in her appearance. Quite simply, she had lost her beauty. Her face was so pale and emaciated that the bones showed through. Her vitality and high spirits had entirely left her. Seeing Maud like this Yeats was struck by a great surge of feeling, so that he felt almost drunk with pity.[10] He knew that he was as intensely in love with her as ever. But this time he would not try to fight against it. Renunciation, such a recurrent feature of nineteenth-century operas, plays, stories and poems about love, was no longer possible for him. As his eyes studied her ravaged face, he longed passionately to do something to protect her and bring her peace.[11] As they talked on in her sitting-room overlooking the summery green gardens of Trinity College, there developed a new closeness between them. Maud hinted at some unhappiness, some disillusionment that had befallen her. Her mood was subdued, as he had never known it before. Her former truculent manner of speaking was gone; she was now gentle and without energy.[12]

Frustratingly he was required to travel on from Dublin the very next day, to visit Charley Johnston in Ulster. On the following morning, his head aflame with thoughts of Maud, Yeats took the train to County Down. Here at the Johnston family home he found Charley, now recovering his health, keen to engage in physical activities. He had a craze for making fire balloons and chasing them over the countryside, and Yeats had to join in. They also went for long rambles and explored ruined castles. After all the difficult and unrewarding months of work in London and then the massive emotional upheaval he had just experienced in Dublin, Yeats found that he was happy to be spending a few days in Ballykilbeg with Charley Johnston. It was a pleasure to these two students of the occult to be away from their books enjoying an outdoor life.[13]

Then there came a letter from Maud. She wrote about her continuing sadness and told him of a dream she had had in which she and he as brother and sister had been sold into slavery somewhere on the outskirts of the Arabian desert.[14] There had been a long journey over endless deserts. Maud's letter renewed and redoubled Yeats's passion for her. He left immediately for Dublin. Just minutes after she had greeted him in her sitting-room at the Nassau Hotel he began to ask Maud to marry him. He took her hand and made his proposal vehemently. When he stopped speaking he continued to hold her hand but soon felt his confidence lapse. Maud drew her hand away and told him that she liked him but that 'she could not marry – there were reasons – she would never marry'. And then in words 'that had no conventional ring', she asked if they might be friends.

The following day they travelled out to Howth Head together. They walked the hilly, wooded paths with the broad views over the sea. They talked of dreams and second-sight and fairy-tales and folklore and theatre and politics. They had a meal at the little cottage near the Bailey Lighthouse where Maud's old nurse still lived. Yeats had a deep pang of sadness when he heard the nurse ask Maud if they were engaged. They continued to meet day after day. He read her the still unfinished play which she had inspired in him some two and a half years earlier, *The Countess Kathleen*. He told her that at those first meetings he had, through her, learnt to understand the story of a woman who would sell her soul to buy food for a starving people'.[15] In a more cautionary tone he spoke of the relationship between the Countess and Maud. The heroine of his play, he said, was 'a symbol of all souls who lose their peace, or their fineness, or any beauty of the spirit in political service, but chiefly her, Maud's, soul that had seemed so incapable of rest'.

Then she was gone again. She left just as abruptly and unexpectedly as on the first occasion in London. She had responsibilities in France, she said. She had to obey an urgent summons from a secret political society to which she belonged. But this was not the truth: her hasty return to Paris was necessitated by an event which Maud kept secret from her young Irish admirer. Maud's relationship with Lucien Millevoye had been more than political. She had been his mistress and, three months after her last brief October meeting with Yeats, she had borne Millevoye's child. The terrible news that her little son, George, now about eighteen months old, had fallen ill and had been diagnosed as having meningitis, was what really drew her back to France. Overwhelmed at once by shock, fear and guilt, Maud returned to Paris as fast as she could and on 29 July, a few days after she arrived, her baby son died.

Yeats knew none of this as he stayed on in Dublin. Maud was constantly in his thoughts and he wrote a series of poems about her in which he presents her as an idealized, spiritualized figure. The 'Rose' poems, such as 'The Rose of Peace', 'The Rose of Battle' and 'The Rose of the World', associate Maud with Rosicrucian emblems of beauty and peace that Yeats had come to know through his membership in the Order of the Golden Dawn. The mood of the poems is a sad, dreamy melancholy. In 'The Rose of Peace' Yeats's love shows itself in extravagant, even blasphemous, hyperbole. In other poems to Maud at this time such as 'The Sorrow of Love', 'The Pity of Love' and 'When You Are Old' there is an intensely poignant sense of loss crafted with extreme, even self-indulgent, delicacy of language. Yeats kept these poems so that he might have them bound to give her on that longed-for day when they should next meet.

Left on his own in Dublin Yeats took a cheap room in a lodging house at 54 Lower Mount Street. His money ran out and again he had to borrow from the ever supportive John O'Leary. He tramped about the city trying to sell articles and found the editors of *United Ireland*, the staunchly Parnellite paper, kindly disposed to him and his work. As the autumn came on, he reduced his expenses by going to live in a communal house run by theosophists at 3 Upper Ely Place. Here there was ample opportunity, day and night, for talk of the occult, and of theosophy and Rosicrucianism and the differences between them. One of the residents of the house was George Russell, or AE, and he and Yeats grew close again.

In the first week in October Yeats was distracted from talk of the spiritual and of spiritualism by sensational news from England: Parnell was dead. Denounced by the Catholic hierarchy in Ireland for marrying the divorced Mrs O'Shea and repudiated in by-election after by-election, the proud Parnell had become run down and ill. After campaigning in a heavy rainstorm for what was left of his political party, he returned to England where he had developed a fever and died. Dublin was shocked by the news and stirred by the prospect of his body being returned to Ireland for burial in Glasnevin Cemetery in the city. At this very same time Yeats had another shock. He received a letter from Maud announcing that she was returning to Ireland. It turned out that she crossed over to Dun Laoghaire (or Kingston as it was then called) on the same boat that brought Parnell's body. As would so often be the case, a major occasion in Yeats's personal life was a major occasion in the history of Ireland.

Not long after the first light of dawn on that autumn morning Yeats took the train from Dublin to Dun Laoghaire to greet Maud on the quayside when she disembarked. She was dressed in black from head to foot, as a mark of mourning for her child. Believing her mourning clothes to be for Parnell, Yeats found them extravagant. Others in the crowd assembled to see Parnell's coffin brought from the ship also thought they signalled her grief for the dead Irish leader. Yeats escorted her to her customary hotel in Dublin where they had breakfast together. In a letter to Yeats Maud had written of her misery at the death of a child, a child that, she said, she had recently adopted. Still maintaining that pretence, she now proceeded to tell him the minute details of the child's illness and death. And when she had finished she went over the story again. When they met the next day and on following days she once again repeated the story. She was clearly very ill, Yeats could see, and it was a relief to her to talk.[16]

He brought George Russell to see her one evening and the conversation soon turned to the subject of reincarnation. Maud was intensely interested in what AE had to say, but Yeats decided that the ideas, beliefs and techniques of the Order of the Golden Dawn would be more helpful to her in her suffering than theosophy. He intimated that there was an evil spirit troubling her life, making her crave power and excitement.[17] He also thought that if this spirit could be made visible to her, she would be better able to understand it and so able to exorcise it.[18] So Yeats resorted to the techniques he had learned from MacGregor Mathers: 'I made a symbol according to the rules of my Order.' The process of evocation brought little to Yeats but an uncertain impression.[19] But for Maud Gonne the technique worked: for her the problematical spirit became visible. 'Maud Gonne saw it almost as if palpably present. It told its story, taking up what was perhaps a later event of her dream of the desert. It was a past personality of hers now seeking to be reunited with her.' This experience brought relief to Maud and she wanted to know more about the procedures of the Golden Dawn. From then on such practices became an important part of her conversations with Yeats and a new bond between them.

By the end of the month Maud had calmed sufficiently to go and stay with her younger sister Katharine, who was now married and living in Hans Place, just off Sloane Street. Yeats decided to return to London too. His assessment of their relationship now was that Maud had shown that she needed him and that she would soon come to love him.[20] In London as in Dublin he saw her every day. He would travel up from the shabby family home in Bedford Park to visit Maud and her sister in the large luxurious house on the edge of Belgravia. There he presented Maud with a vellum-bound book into which he had put the poems he had written to her in Dublin. They talked a great deal about what they were beginning to realize were Maud's considerable gifts of clairvoyance and mystical understanding. Yeats escorted her to a meeting of the Order of the Golden Dawn and she became an initiate.

The day after her initiation she left to return home to Paris, where

Willie wrote letters to her every day. Once he accidentally met Maud's cousin, who had also been staying in the house in Hans Place. As they stood talking on a London street she implied strongly that Maud was receptive to Willie's courting. Why then, asked the cousin in some puzzlement, was he not in Paris with her? The answer was a simple and bitter one: he had not the money to go. His love was the love of a penniless young poet for a stylish young woman with nobility, money and the habit of money. At this time money also became an urgent problem in Yeats's literary career. Indeed, there now came a sad, sordid ending to the story of his first volume of poetry containing the 'epical' account of Oisin, the great romantic hero. The publishers Kegan Paul had not received their subscription money in full, there were copies remaining and they threatened Yeats with lawyers. He had to appeal yet again to John O'Leary, who settled the troublesome debt for him.

Towards the end of 1891, which had seen the publication of Oscar Wilde's *The Picture of Dorian Gray*, Hardy's *Tess of the D'Urbervilles* and the first volume of Conan Doyle's Sherlock Holmes stories, Yeats turned his energies to the founding of an Irish Literary Society. The splitting of the Irish party in the House of Commons and the death of Parnell had brought confusion to the political forces behind the new Irish consciousness. Yeats and other energetic young nationalists now felt that it was all the more necessary to develop Irish cultural institutions. Two days before New Year's Eve he held a meeting at the house in Blenheim Road to plan the new society. Among those who attended were John Todhunter, T.W. Rolleston, and D.J. O'Donoghue, the young clerk from the Southwark Irish Literary Club. Two weeks later the new society was formally established at a meeting at the Reform Club in working-class Clapham. The rest of 1892 was taken up in great part by Yeats's keen promotion of this new initiative, including going over to Dublin in the summer to help found a similar Irish Literary Society there. His passion for this work was intensified by the involvement in it of Maud Gonne. He timed his visits to Dublin to maximize his chances of meeting up with her, John O'Leary noting with fatherly indulgence that when Maud was in Dublin Yeats would be sure to turn up.[21]

In the new society founded in Dublin in June 1892 Maud took responsibility for developing a scheme to establish reading rooms and libraries throughout provincial Ireland, but she also felt the need to campaign for the Irish cause outside Ireland. Her beauty and her considerable gifts as a speech-maker had made her famous in France and beyond. As Yeats told the readers of the *Boston Pilot*:

> *Thousands who come to see this new wonder – a beautiful woman who makes speeches – remain to listen with delight to her sincere and simple eloquence. Last week at Bordeaux, an audience of twelve hundred persons rose to its feet, when she had finished, to applaud her with wild enthusiasm. The papers of Russia, France, Germany and even Egypt quote her speeches, and the tale of Irish wrongs has found its way hither and thither to lie stored up, perhaps in many a memory against the day of need.*[22]

The Irish literary revival showed itself in another new venture this year. This was a plan to found a national publishing company to bring out books on Irish subjects by Irish authors. The organization was to have been financed by a selling of shares but this eventually fell through and it was decided to develop a programme of Irish books through an arrangement with an established publishing house. As the scheme progressed Yeats found himself increasingly caught up in a bruising and time-consuming political struggle for the control of it. He could not accept that the choice of books to be published should be under the control of the 76-year-old Sir Charles Gavan Duffy who, for reasons of health, spent by far the greater part of every year in the South of France. He could not trust the taste or the judgement of this highly respected veteran of the old 'New Ireland' and founder of *The Nation* who was, at this time, about half a century older than he. Yeats wanted ultimate editorial control to be in the hands of a committee of younger people, one of whom, he made no bones about it, would be himself.

In arguing the case in speeches and in letters to the Dublin press the 27-year-old Yeats, looking very much the young man in a hurry, soon came up against J.F. Taylor, his old adversary from the Contemporary Club. The harshly commonsensical Taylor argued forcefully that Duffy would show much greater impartiality than would Yeats, whom Taylor regarded as leading a mutual admiration society. In a letter to the press Taylor included a satirical poem about Yeats and his fellow reviewers and their mutual backscratching. Mocking Yeats's new Rosicrucianism as well as his log-rolling, Taylor wrote, 'A poet, not of the Della Cruscan school, has commemorated such things in moving verse.

You'll praise and I'll praise
We'll both praise together, O!
What jolly fun we'll have
Praising one another, O![23]

In another letter to the press Taylor suggested that Yeats was motivated by 'febrile vanity' and insisted that Duffy was immensely preferable, as director of the new organization, to 'the freaks of any coterie of select and kindred spirits'.[24]

In temporary lodgings at 53 Mountjoy Square and then at 3 Ely Place, Yeats wrote replies stoutly defending himself and his views on the organization of the Irish Library project. The controversy developed a bitterness that was intensified by the involvement of Maud Gonne, who shuttled back and forth between Dublin and Paris, working for Ireland's cause, but took little interest and certainly did not take Yeats's side in the dispute. He later recalled that Maud did not appear to take his work or the dispute seriously. She did not share his concern that the issue would determine the intellectual future of Ireland.[25] Worse still, his enemy Taylor seemed to be gaining in influence over her. Maud, who had shared so many psychic experiences with Yeats and who so easily went into trance and semi-trance with him, was now allowing the objectionable Taylor to become her Svengali. Yeats couldn't bear the idea of someone else possessing her thoughts: he confessed that he was jealous of Taylor not as a suitor but as one who had undue influence on Maud's mind.[26] He and Maud had their first serious quarrel. When Maud fell ill Dr Sigerson, who was attending her and who was a Duffy supporter, would not allow Yeats to visit her in her lodging. Love and literary politics were now miserably intermixed. Yeats was also aware that unpleasant rumours were circulating in Dublin concerning the flamboyant Maud and his relationship with her. He persevered against Duffy and his followers but he was tormented by a mixture of passionate love, jealousy and resentment.

As his profile in Dublin literary life grew higher he also faced attacks from another quarter. His second volume of poems, had been published that summer under the title *The Countess Kathleen*, and several reviewers and readers had seen in it evidence of a very immodest and brash young man. They criticized him for lack of due respect for his elders and predecessors in Irish poetry. The lines that particularly gave offence were from the poem he had entitled 'Apologia addressed to Ireland in the coming days' but which in later collections of his work he would retitle 'To Ireland in the Coming Times'. The lines ran:

> *Nor may I less be counted one*
> *With Davis, Mangan, Ferguson,*
> *Because to him who ponders well*
> *My rhymes more than their rhyming tell*
> *Of the dim wisdoms old and deep,*
> *That God gives unto man in sleep.*

The reviewer for Dublin's *Sunday Sun* voiced the irritation of others when he asked, 'Is it not rather soon for him to rate himself – and somewhat queer to do so himself – as "one with Davis, Mangan and Ferguson," names, we believe, rated among the highest in Ireland? . . . He is young, and modesty will the better become him.'[27]

In the autumn, after forcefully defending himself and his poem, Yeats, hard up as ever, abandoned Dublin and went to stay with his Unionist uncle, George Pollexfen, who was now living at Thornhill, a substantial Georgian house on the road leading south-west out of Sligo. He and his uncle were looked after by the old servant with the gift of second-sight, Mary Battle. While Yeats was living there as his uncle's guest, his grandmother Elizabeth Pollexfen died. Yeats was the only representative of the Bedford Park family at the funeral; even if his mother, Elizabeth's daughter, had been well enough to travel to Sligo, she could not have afforded to attend. After the burial Yeats stayed on to keep company with his uncle, while the two of them had to watch the widower, the once terrifying William Pollexfen, throughout the last weeks of his fatal illness. Yeats later told Robert Louis Stevenson that his grandfather, a very active retired sailor, who rarely read a book, had on his death-bed taken pleasure in reading *Treasure Island*.[28] With the old man's passing the relationship with Sligo that had existed for Yeats since childhood was at an end. His grandparents and their once powerful presences survived now in memory alone.

Living with his Uncle George, who had the manner of a testy old army officer and who was preoccupied with horses and horse-racing, Yeats had ample time to get on with his writing and was able to improve his income by doing more literary reviewing. Through the Henley circle he had come to know Sir William Robertson Nicholl who for Hodder and Stoughton had just launched the *Bookman*, a monthly publication that targeted the book trade. Yeats was invited to be a contributor and over the next six years would write scores of reviews for it. His protracted stay in Sligo also provided an opportunity to seek out more of the 'faery' element in the life of the area. In a letter to his fellow Rhymer Richard Le Gallienne he described an interesting magical adventure he had in the company of his cousin Lucy Middleton and his Uncle George, 'a hard-headed man', according to Yeats. The three of them, Yeats maintained, surely straining Le Gallienne's credulity to the utmost, had a lecture from the queen of the fairies on the economic policies and structure of fairyland. They had set off, Yeats reported, to a well known locality at Rosses Sands and there, having made a magic circle, called on the fairies to appear. Uncle George had said that he could hear sounds of boys shouting and distant music. Cousin Lucy, however, had seen a bright light and many little creatures wearing crimson. She also had been able to hear the music and voices. Yeats continued by saying that there had been a loud noise which seemed like the fairies cheering and stamping their feet. Then, wrote Yeats, they had seen the queen of the fairies and had talked to her for a long time. She had, Yeats claimed, written in the sand a warning against trying to know too much about them. But, Yeats said, before she did this she had told them a lot about the economy of the fairy kingdom.[29]

It was not long before such trancelike experiences in the Sligo countryside were disturbed by annoying news from Dublin and London. Since he now had to accept that there were not funds to establish a special company to publish Irish books, Sir Charles Gavan Duffy, abetted by T.W.

Rolleston, had approached Fisher Unwin to negotiate an arrangement whereby they might publish through him. The newly formed Irish literary societies, they argued, virtually guaranteed a readership. Sometime earlier Yeats himself had discussed such a possibility with Unwin and they had made some progress in their talks. To learn that Duffy and Rolleston had hijacked his negotiations with the publisher was highly irritating to Yeats, who wrote strong letters of protest from Sligo to Edward Garnett and to Fisher Unwin himself. As November approached he began to think that he would have to go back to London to defend his rights and claims. Whoever had charge of the proposed Irish Library would be in a position of considerable influence for himself and for others. However, the lingering death of his grandfather, which finally occurred in the second week of the month, delayed his departure.

On 20 November he took the train to Dublin, the first stage of his journey to London. Here he was in time to hear the inaugural lecture of the National Literary Society of Dublin. Delivered by Douglas Hyde and entitled 'The Necessity for De-Anglicizing Ireland', it became a famous text. Hyde argued that the Irish would only recover their identity if they used the Irish rather than the English language. He also urged the need to revive Irish sports, music, place-names and personal names, and the speech did help to bring about the creation of the Gaelic League in the following year. But to Yeats, whose artistic medium was the English language, Hyde's demands were disconcerting. He wrote a letter to the press making the case for an Irish literature in English, a literature that would have nothing to do with England. 'Can we not', he asked, 'build up a tradition, a national literature, which shall be none the less Irish in spirit for being English in language?' He pointed to American literature as an example of such a possibility and added, 'It should be more easy for us, who have in us that wild Celtic blood, the most un-English of all things under the heaven, to make such a literature. If we fail it shall not be because we lack materials, but because we lack the power to use them.'[30]

His urgent letter was published in *United Ireland* just a week before Christmas. By that time Yeats was back home in Blenheim Road. He renewed contact with Moina and MacGregor Mathers and progressed to a higher standing in the Golden Dawn, but much of his time was spent in negotiations with Fisher Unwin. The publisher was reluctant to side either with Yeats or with Duffy. He was not prepared to become involved at all unless the dispute was settled, Yeats reported to John O'Leary.[31] After Yeats returned to Ireland in late January 1893 discussions with Unwin and Edward Garnett still continued by letter, but in the long run the publishers allowed the control of the series to slip into the hands of Duffy. An agreement with him was signed before the end of March.

Back in Dublin Yeats again devoted himself to the work of the Irish Literary Society in that city. But after about a month in a north Dublin lodging house in St Lawrence Road, Clontarf, he was compelled to return to Uncle George in Sligo for free board. Here he remained for several months. He was still in Ireland in May when the marriage of Katharine Tynan took place in London. No longer could his letters be addressed to 'My Dear Katey'. Form required that he address her as 'Dear Mrs Hinkson'.

During this time in Sligo Yeats worked at a project that was a spin-off from all his hard work with Ellis on the Blake edition, which was at long last published in 1893. This was an anthology of Blake's lyric poems which he had been invited to put together by the recently founded publishing company headed by two young men of wide intellectual interests, Harold Lawrence and A.H. Bullen. This firm continued to be receptive to Yeats and his work until the two partners dissolved the company at the end of the 1890s. To John O'Leary, to whom he still felt obliged to report on his finances, Yeats was able to announce that Lawrence and Bullen were paying him twenty-five pounds for his Blake volume in their series, the Muses' Library. Also during these spring months in Sligo Yeats planned a new enterprise to further the Irish literary revival: an Irish literary periodical. He solicited many of his acquaintances and friends for promises of contributions, telling Lionel Johnson that the 'projected Irish Magazine' was 'intended to be the organ of our literary movement'. Johnson, whose interest in Ireland continued to intensify, was a keen supporter of his friend's scheme which, finally, Yeats did not succeed in implementing.

In the summer he was back in London where one of his projects was to place the collection of essays on Irish fairy-lore which he had assembled from his contributions to Henley's *National Observer*. Writing to the beautiful Constance Gore-Booth who lived with her family at Lissadell, a mansion near Sligo where his father had once painted portraits, Yeats told about the day he had spent tramping between library and publisher.[32] But again Lawrence and Bullen were kindly disposed and they brought out the collection under the title *The Celtic Twilight* by the end of the year. The book confirmed Yeats's reputation as an Irish folklorist, and the lyric poem with which it concludes also declared him to share much of the sensibility associated with the 1890s. (Other poems of this time make it clear that much was also due to his tortured relationship with Maud.) The 28-year-old Yeats here addresses himself as someone emotionally spent in a nearly exhausted century, a *fin de siècle* in which moral categories are a snare and in which only subdued, attenuated, dreamy emotions of half light are possible. The first stanza of 'Into the Twilight' runs:

> *Out-worn heart, in a time out-worn,*
> *Come clear of the nets of wrong and right;*
> *Laugh, heart, again in the grey twilight;*
> *Sigh, heart, again in the dew of the morn.*

In the course of his summer stay in London Yeats's friendship with Lionel Johnson deepened. When Yeats returned to Dublin in September to fulfil his commitments to the Irish Literary Society, Lionel Johnson went with him. They lived out their ideals in shabby surroundings, sharing lodgings with an old acquaintance of Yeats, Joseph Patrick Quinn from Mayo, the former secretary of Michael Davitt's Land League and now, at the age of thirty, a medical student. The three men, all consumed by a grand vision of a free Ireland, lived in a cheap rooming house, geographically and socially at some distance from the Trinity College milieu. Here Yeats and Johnson worked away at launching the proposed periodical. Here too they spent time with Douglas Hyde who with his bride was in Dublin that December. There was much excited talk of the Gaelic League, an organization which had originated as a subcommittee of the Literary Society and which Hyde had now turned into an independent group. Yeats, the literary operator, found a publisher in London for Hyde's collection of poems, *Love Songs of Connaught*, which constituted, said Yeats, the first example of the English dialect of the Connaught country people being used in literature.[33] Fisher Unwin brought out the collection in this same year, 1893.

When Yeats returned to Blenheim Road at the end of the year, he renewed his acquaintance with another of the women who were so important in his life. This was Florence Farr, who lived close to the Yeats family in the Bedford Park area. Like Laura Armstrong and Maud Gonne, she had gifts as an actress, but had developed her talents to a far greater extent than they, having played major roles on the commercial stage in London. She had recently acted in *Rosmersholm* by the fashionably avant-garde Norwegian dramatist Henrik Ibsen. She had also taken a leading part in John Todhunter's *A Sicilian Idyll* in the elegant little theatre in the clubhouse at Bedford Park. And she had played in the first production of *Widowers' Houses* for George Bernard Shaw, with whom she had a passionate affair.

At the time Yeats had his important encounter and conversation with her, Florence was about to divorce her husband Edward Emery, who was also an actor but far less successful than she. Conventional Victorian reticence about sex was not for her. A beautiful, shapely brunette 'with semicircular eyebrows', Florence was extremely attractive to men and, it was often said, unable to say no to them. Shaw remembered her as being extremely forward. She 'lost all patience with the hesitating preliminaries of her less practised adorers. Accordingly, when they clearly longed to kiss her, and she did not dislike them sufficiently to make their gratification too great a strain on her excessive good nature, she would seize the stammering suitor firmly by the wrists, bring him into her arms by a smart pull, and saying, "Let's get it over", allow the startled gentleman to have his kiss and then proceed to converse with him at her ease.'[34]

There is no evidence, however, to suggest that she had a sexual relationship with Yeats at this time. She was five years older than he and far more experienced, but his lovelorn state and sexual diffidence were probably such as to place him beyond even her powers. What is certain is that he greatly respected her theatrical knowledge and skills, and as one aspiring to write poetic drama he went to her for advice. When he had first started drafting his play *The Countess Kathleen* four years earlier, he had shown his work to Florence and had been much reassured by her judgement that it was both worthwhile and stageworthy. Perhaps it was because she was impressed by that script that she now, meeting him shortly after the publication of *The Celtic Twilight*, made the suggestion that proved to be a turning point in his career.

Florence Farr was currently in charge of the season of productions being offered at the Avenue Theatre just down from Trafalgar Square in Northumberland Avenue. She had made up her mind that she would like to offer, as part of her season, a one-act play in which her niece, ten-year-old Dorothy Paget, who, Florence Farr believed, had great acting talent, might make her professional début. So Florence now asked Yeats whether he would be interested in writing such a play for her. Immediately and enthusiastically he agreed to do so. The result was a very successful playlet, *The Land of Heart's Desire*, in which the ten-year-old actress played the 'Faery Child' who seduces the young peasant bride Maire Bruin away from her husband with promises of extravagant experiences beyond the life 'of this dull house'. The Faery Child, whom Yeats later in a letter to Sarah Purser called an 'imp', tells Maire:

> *You love that great tall fellow there:*
> *Yet I could make you ride upon the winds,*
> *Run on the top of the dishevelled tide,*
> *And dance upon the mountains like a flame!*

Maire, with her extreme expectations and hopes of life, is a Maud Gonne figure. When her young husband, Shawn, speaks of her the image that first comes into his mind is that of blossom.

> *Do not blame me: I often lie awake*
> *Thinking that all things trouble your bright head –*
> *How beautiful it is – such broad pale brows*
> *Under a cloudy blossoming of hair!*

The play was powered by Yeats's strong sense of how he too came a poor second to other concerns in the life of the woman he loved. Remembering the occasion of Florence Farr's invitation he later wrote that he had put into *The Land of Heart's Desire* all his bewilderment at Maud's rejection of him. He could only surmise that, like his heroine, Maud was in search of excitement and an impossible kind of life.[35]

Yeats worked hard at this script through January and early February. The play went into production immediately and was staged, together with John Todhunter's *The Comedy of Sighs*, at the Avenue Theatre during the first couple of weeks in April. Then for the next three weeks Yeats's faery play was performed as a curtain-raiser to George Bernard Shaw's *Arms and the Man*. This was Yeats's most pleasing experience of success in the commercial theatre.

Florence Farr's was not the only invitation that would bring new prospects into Yeats's life. His spiritual tutors Moina and MacGregor Mathers asked him to stay with them at their home in Paris, an invitation Yeats accepted. At the end of the first week in February 1894 he crossed the English Channel for the first time. When the overnight boat-train from London arrived at the Gare du Nord Yeats made his way out of the station looking very much the artist. He wore a black sombrero, soiled shirt, floppy black silk tie, untidy black trousers and long black cloak. He was nervous for, of course, whatever else it was, Paris was the home of Maud Gonne. This was really the main reason he had come. Would she see him? And if she agreed to, how would they get on? But the visit was to be crucial for quite a different reason too.

In Paris that month, Yeats, the consciously, even aggressively Irish writer, suddenly perceived how his literary sensibilities and assumptions had affinities with a larger international movement which had its centre there. This movement later became known as modernism. When, thirty-seven years on, the great American critic Edmund Wilson offered his pioneering account of the movement, he called his book *Axel's Castle*. The phrase came from *Le Château d'Axël*, the title of a drama by Villiers de l'Isle-Adam that was playing in Paris that February. This play, which Wilson regarded as a founding document of the movement, had a massive impact upon Yeats. He took a copy back to London where he studied it so painstakingly, slowly and with much difficulty. As a result some passages gained particular importance for him, while the whole was as impenetrable as some Sacred Book.[36] The performance of *Axël* revealed to him that as an artist he belonged not only to an Irish but also to a European tradition. His first stay in Paris lasted less than three weeks but it had a momentous effect upon his literary and intellectual career. So far the story of Yeats's life had been the story of three cities: Dublin, Sligo and London. But now came the fourth, Paris.

I T WAS THE MOST GLAMOROUS OF TIMES; IT WAS THE MOST
dangerous of times. It would later be romanticized as *la belle époque.*
But in actuality it was a time of bitter social and racial antagonism in
French society. The French Republic was still under threat of destabliza-
tion just as it had been five years before when Maud's hero General
Boulanger had attempted his *coup d'état.* There was outrageous financial
and political corruption. Much of the scandal centred on de Lesseps, the
creator of the Suez Canal, whose subsequent Panama Canal Company had
failed disastrously. There was great public disillusion. The year before Yeats
arrived there had been violent disturbances in the Latin Quarter and large
demonstrations led by the Socialists. Recurrent acts of terrorism spread
fear throughout French society. In December 1893 the anarchist Vaillant
had hurled a bomb into the Chamber of Deputies; during the weeks Yeats
spent in Paris in February Vaillant was sent to the guillotine. At the end of
that year a Jewish army officer, Captain Alfred Dreyfus, was court-martialled and sent to Devil's Island for allegedly passing French military
secrets to the Germans. What proved to be a complete and gross injustice
divided French society into two ever more bitterly hostile camps over the
next twelve years.

In the arts there were also strident confrontations. To Yeats it was all
very novel. Neither in Dublin nor in London had he seen groups and
schools of artists define themselves with the intensity, the fine discrimina-

tion, and the hostility towards others, that he now encountered in Paris. Painters such as Monet, Gauguin and Toulouse-Lautrec still had to fight against the mocking incomprehension of those whose views and tastes derived from the Académie. And a young composer, in later years recognized as the creator of a major new phase in the history of both French and European music, caused an uproar at the Paris Conservatoire by the supposed formlessness of a composition he completed during the year of Yeats's first visit. The composer was Claude Debussy, a friend of Impressionist and Post-Impressionist painters. The highly controversial work was his *Prélude à l'après-midi d'un faune*. The *Prélude* referred to a poem by Stéphane Mallarmé, the central figure in the contemporary school of poets known as *les symbolistes*. At the time Yeats was in Paris Debussy was also engaged in composing an opera which was the setting of a text by another of the *symbolistes*, the Belgian Maurice Maeterlinck. This opera to which Debussy would devote ten years of his life was *Pelléas and Mélisande*. Three years after it was first staged Jean Sibelius, a member of the Yeats generation, would also compose a nine-part suite of incidental music to Maeterlinck's text. Play, opera and music, each evoking an experience of unhappy love in a dreamy, medieval setting, all show similarities with the mood and manner of Yeats's work at this time.

In practical terms the visit to Paris meant for Yeats a chance to approach again that object of his own unhappy love. He proceeded very cautiously. He did not on that first day in Paris go straight away to Maud's apartment, and this was wise, because he soon heard that Maud was ill. Only years later did he learn that her illness had to do with her being two months pregnant. In the coming August she would bear a second child by Lucien Millevoye, a daughter who would be named Iseult. During Yeats's time in Paris Maud did not tell him about her continuing affair any more than about her new pregnancy. And still he was too unworldly to have any suspicions. All that he noticed when she finally received him, and they went paying social calls together, was that the once highly energetic Maud mounted stairs slowly and with difficulty. But his delicacy in approaching her brought its rewards. They did not recover that intimacy that they had known together on Howth Head, but as his visit proceeded they did share experiences which made for friendlier relations than they had had when she was last in Ireland.

Yeats spent time with the Mathers in their apartment in a wedge-shaped building south of the grand eighteenth-century Ecole Militaire. Moina Mathers' brother, Henri Bergson, also paid a visit to Paris at this time. He was Professor of Philosophy at the University of Angers; it would be another six years before he reached the peak of his academic career and received his professorship at the Collège de France. At this time Bergson was writing his book *Matter and Memory* which was published two years later, and his views ought to have interested Yeats, but all the visitor saw was an obscure professor.[1] MacGregor Mathers, the philosopher's brother-in-law, was exasperated with Bergson, telling Yeats of his failure to influence him with any of his magic.[2] On Sundays, dressed in the robes of a high-ranking member of the Golden Dawn, Mathers would dedicate himself 'to the evocation of Spirits'. On other evenings in that apartment not far from the Invalides Mathers would wear Highland dress and dance the sword dance. Mathers said that in Highland clothes and with daggers in his stockings he felt 'like a walking flame'. But the visitor sometimes doubted whether Mathers had seen the Scottish Highlands at all. During Yeats's stay he and his host and hostess would also play a curious game of four-handed chess, allowing Mathers to deploy his powers as a magician. Yeats would always partner the beautiful Moina while the dictatorial Mathers, who throughout the game spoke a good deal about imminent Apocalypse, had a spirit for his partner. Mathers 'would cover his eyes with his hands or gaze at the empty chair at the opposite corner of the board before moving his partner's piece'.

During his stay in Paris Yeats also set out to visit some of its literary figures. He was especially keen to meet Mallarmé, the most profound and innovative of the *symbolistes*, a poet to whom he had brought recommendations from his fellow Rhymer Arthur Symons and also from W.E. Henley. Mallarmé, the chanter and evoker of the etherial, earned his living as a schoolmaster teaching English. He knew the language well and wrote articles for Henley which appeared in the *National Review*. Yeats crossed over to the right bank of the Seine and made his way up the rue de Rome to the apartment building close to the Gare Saint-Lazare where Mallarmé held his famous 'Tuesdays' at which writers sympathetic to his radical poetic and linguistic theory would gather. Unfortunately Mallarmé had just set off to

England where he was to deliver a series of lectures organized by Yeats's Bedford Park friend, the francophile York Powell, and in whose rooms at Christ Church in Oxford Mallarmé stayed. So on this visit Yeats met only Mallarmé's wife and his daughter Geneviève. Mademoiselle Mallarmé marvelled that such an enthusiastic student and admirer of her father's poems apparently understood very little French.

Yeats had better luck in making contact with Paul Verlaine, of whom he had learned a great deal from Arthur Symons, an expert in French poetry. Symons it was who organized a reading tour for this symbolist poet whose work was intellectually and prosodically less demanding than Mallarmé's. Verlaine, the poet of *états d'âme*, states of the soul, mostly ones of plangent melancholy, was now fifty years old. It was almost a quarter of a century since he had begun his affair with Arthur Rimbaud which had led to Verlaine shooting and wounding his lover and consequently serving a two-year jail sentence.

Yeats went to visit him in his tiny apartment on the Left Bank, high up in the rue Saint-Jacques, not far from the Sorbonne and the bookshops of the boulevard Saint-Michel. They smoked cigarettes together and Verlaine's middle-aged mistress made coffee. She was very much in charge and her taste dominated the attic room. There were canaries in cages and sentimental lithographs on the walls. Also pinned up were newspaper cartoons of Verlaine showing him as a monkey. The two poets talked about Victor Hugo, the French writer Yeats had read in translation since boyhood. Verlaine considered Hugo 'a supreme poet, but a volcano of mud as well as of flame'.[3] They also spoke of the *symbolistes* and especially of Maeterlinck and of *Pelléas et Mélisande*. Verlaine did not esteem Maeterlinck as highly as Yeats did, saying of him that despite his good qualities he was something of a mountebank.[4] But Yeats thought that Maeterlinck's poetic dramas were important in providing alternatives to realist and naturalist theatre; the Belgian *symboliste*, he believed, was of great importance in helping people to understand the new drama.[5] They also talked of Villiers de l'Isle-Adam and of his current play, *Le Château d'Axël*. Here Verlaine was entirely admiring. As a connoisseur of French style Verlaine praised especially the excellent way in which Villiers used the language. Verlaine's overall judgement of the author of *Axël* was '*exalté*'.

When Yeats himself went to see the play at the Théâtre de la Gaieté, in the company of Maud Gonne who helped him with the French, his admiration for the piece outran that of Verlaine. Rooted as it was in Rosicrucian lore, the play had an immediate appeal for Yeats. Rosicrucianism, under the leadership of the art critic and novelist Josephin Péladan, was a distinct force in the cultural life of Paris at this time. In Brittany there were other students of Péladan, among them some of the painters who gathered around Gauguin in the remote coastal village of Pont-Aven. The division in Yeats's experience between life in London and life in the west of Ireland was replicated for certain artists in France at this moment by the contrast between life in Paris and life in Brittany, with its dolmens, its ancient and often mysterious carved stones, its mystical Catholicism, its extensive, pagan superstition and its wealth of folklore. One of the painters who joined Gauguin at Pont-Aven was the Irish artist Roderic O'Conor, who had been at art school in Dublin just a couple of years before Yeats. But the member of the Pont-Aven group who was most knowledgeable about Rosicrucianism and Péladan was Paul Sérusier, who in the 1890s painted sets and designed costumes for *symboliste* theatre.

In *Axël* there unfolds a story and poetry of ideas which had an overwhelming effect not just on Yeats's evolving understanding of the drama but also on his understanding of experience itself. The play, briefly summarized, develops as follows: Axël is a young German nobleman of ancient lineage living in his ancestral castle deep in the Black Forest. He is attended only by a few ancient retainers and by Master Janus, a Rosicrucian and cabbalist. The crisis of Axël's life is the temptation to forsake his secluded life of mystical contemplation and to enjoy worldly experience. To Axël's castle there come two visitors who, each in a different way, try to induce him to give up his isolation and 'live'. Commander Kaspar, a courtier and worldling, seeks to persuade him to look for the great treasure which legend says is buried on Axël's estate and then to return with him to use the wealth to enjoy the various pleasures of court life. Axël's refined sensibility is grossly offended by this suggestion and he challenges Kaspar to a duel and kills him. Yet Kaspar's visit has, against his will, excited Axël's interest in the external world. He finds himself unable to undergo the final initiation into the occult mysteries at the hands of Master Janus. The second temptation, represented by the arrival of Axël's distant kinswoman Sara, is less easily resisted. Brought up in a French convent, Sara has also evaded the claims of the spiritual life by refusing to take the final vows of a nun. She and Axël fall in love. They find the hidden treasure and dream of travelling together through the world and of experiencing all that life has to offer. But at the end of the play Axël returns to his contempt for such 'living' and convinces Sara that the actual experiences would be greatly inferior to the dreams and imaginings of them which they have just shared. He proposes that they kill themselves. Life in the external world, he maintains, has nothing to offer which would not be but a vulgar travesty of the supreme moments of consciousness which they have just envisioned together. 'From now on, to agree to live would be no more than a sacrilege against ourselves. Live? The servants will do that for us.'[6]

These are famous lines expressing an extreme example of late nineteenth-century world-weariness and they lingered for a long time in Yeats's memory. In his review of *Axël* for the *Bookman* he wrote that 'the play throughout gives a noble utterance to those sad thoughts which come to the most merry of us, and thereby robs them of half their bitterness. We need not fear that it will affect the statistics of suicide, for the personages of great art are for the most part too vast, too remote, too splendid for imitation. They are merely metaphors in that divine argument which is carried on from age to age to age, and perhaps from world to world, about the ultimate truths of existence.'[7]

As he left Paris for London Yeats had to accept a truth about his own existence that found an echo in *Axël*: his deep, enduring love for Maud Gonne could continue only as a matter of memories, images and dreams. True, there had been no quarrels between them in Paris. They had gone about together; had smoked hashish and summoned visions together; had gone to a memorable play together which she with her command of the French language had helped him to understand. Nevertheless there was a distance between them. The Order of the Golden Dawn and its rituals were no longer a bond, since Maud had become disillusioned with Mathers, objecting to his absorption in biblical and masonic symbolism. Yeats still loved her, obsessively, but he could no longer come close to her spiritually, emotionally or physically.

So, painfully frustrated as a lover but highly stimulated as a writer, Yeats returned to London and his family in Bedford Park. He quickly began a new work which speaks eloquently of the power of Maud and Villiers over his art. This was *The Shadowy Waters*, a poetic drama which would take him some five years to complete. Set in ancient Celtic times, the play had for its hero Forgael, the captain of a ship who, to the bitter resentment of his crew, sails in quest of the place where 'the world ends', for there the mind finds 'miracle, ecstasy, the impossible hope'. When his men capture another ship they bring to him as a prisoner the beautiful Queen Dectora. Eventually the Yeats/Axël figure persuades her to renounce ordinary life and join him in his quest for the supreme happiness he imagines. Aibrie, his officer, the voice of common sense, declares such happiness to be an illusion. If it exists at all, it can only be in death.

> *And if that happiness be more than dreams,*
> *More than the froth, the feather, the dust-whirl,*
> *The crazy nothing that I think it is,*
> *It shall be in the country of the dead,*
> *If there be such a country.*

But Dectora ignores this and turns to Forgael asking him to take her with him on his quest.

> *O carry me*
> *To some sure country, some familiar place.*
> *Have we not everything that life can give*
> *In having one another?*

The Shadowy Waters is a renewed assertion of the Romantic possibility that Villiers had confirmed. Of *Axël* Yeats wrote that 'In a decade when the comic paper and the burlesque are the only things sure to awaken enthusiasm, a grim and difficult play by its mere grimness and difficulty is a return to better traditions, it brings us a little nearer to the heroic age.' It also helps to uplift the taste of the theatre-going public 'by reminding it very forcibly that the actor should be also a reverent reciter of majestic words'.[8]

The Shadowy Waters was planned as a work that would further such literary and cultural objectives, but another reason Yeats was moved to begin his new play on his return from Paris was the success of his *The Land of Heart's Desire* at the Avenue Theatre. Yeats took much pleasure in attending the performances and overhearing the responses of the audience. He was beginning to have a sense of himself as a man of the theatre. One of those who came to his play was Oscar Wilde. Wilde's *Salomé*, originally written in French and considered by some London critics to exhibit French decadence, had been banned in London by the Lord Chamberlain's office in 1892 on the grounds that it portrayed biblical characters on stage, so did not receive its first performance until 1896, in Paris. It was *Lady Windermere's Fan* and *A Woman of No Importance* for which he was now famous. Yeats was grateful that Wilde, such a success both in the theatre and in society, should trouble to come and see his one-act play.

In April Yeats found himself one of the fifty or sixty people from the literary world who were invited to a formal dinner which proved to be one of the great occasions in the cultural history of the 1890s. The dinner was held at the Hotel d'Italia, a somewhat shabby restaurant in Old Compton Street, Soho. In late Victorian London Soho was by far the most cosmopolitan and raffish quarter in the West End, so appropriate for a celebration of the founding of a new magazine called *The Yellow Book*. Yeats would have seen the arrogant John Lane who was the publisher of *The Yellow Book*. He ran The Bodley Head, the publishing firm from which his partner, the far more gentle Elkin Mathews, was in the process of withdrawing. Beside Lane sat Henry Harland, a dark, handsome young American writer who was the literary editor of the new periodical. Beside him sat a striking figure, a slender, 21-year-old man in an elegant dinner jacket. He had a pale face and reddish hair – cut unconventionally in a fringe and parted down the middle. This was the art editor of *The Yellow Book*, Aubrey Beardsley. He was accompanied by his sister, the actress Mabel Beardsley, to whom he was very close and with whom he had had a sexual relationship since childhood.

Beardsley was the sensation of the year in London in 1894. A former office clerk with scant training in art, he had produced illustrations for the English translation of Oscar Wilde's *Salomé* that had astonished Elkin Mathews and John Lane when they had first been shown them. The drawings' serpentine art nouveau lines, their elements of caricature (which

Wilde did not like) and of perversion (Salome about to kiss the severed, dripping head of John the Baptist) combined to create a scandalous originality. John Lane was in no doubt about the commercial viability of such art, and the founding of *The Yellow Book* was to a considerable extent inspired by the (in two senses) drawing power of this *enfant terrible*, this outrageous young man, Aubrey Beardsley. As with so many of the young talents that emerged in the 1890s, Beardsley's career would be a short one. He would be dead in four years.

As the dinner proceeded Yeats's attention was drawn away from his three hosts. He became increasingly intrigued by an unknown woman sitting opposite to him in a group of successful novelists that included Arthur Symons's friend, the Irish writer George Moore, who had scandalized society with his naturalistic novels. Yeats could tell that the beautiful lady was interested in him also. Her face, he thought, was Greek in its regularity, though no Greek would have had such dark skin. Her hair was also very dark, he noticed.[9] She had full, sensuous lips and large, soulful eyes. Yeats thought that her style of dress, with what appeared to be very old lace at her breast, was exquisite. He saw in her a likeness to Constance Gore-Booth's younger sister: she had the same sensitive look of distinction that he had admired in Eva Gore-Booth. The two studied each other covertly across the long table. When *The Yellow Book* dinner came to an end, the beautiful lady rose and for a moment looked at him directly and enquiringly. She hesitated, but there was no one to introduce them, so she turned away and slowly left the room.

As Yeats was leaving the restaurant, an acquaintance told him that the lady had asked to be told his name. In some frustration he took the underground back to Bedford Park. The only thing to do was to put her out of his mind and get on with his work. There was a good deal to do. As he worked away at *The Shadowy Waters* he also wrote a strongly critical review of two recently published volumes in Unwin's New Irish Library series, of which Duffy had finally gained control. Yeats's worst fears were borne out and in his piece for the *Bookman* he deplored the taste of the old Young Ireland which the books under review exemplified. 'The truth of the matter is that Sir Charles Gavan Duffy has let that old delusion, didacticism, get the better of his judgement.' The books that Duffy selected were such that

not even 'the most skilful advertising, the most eloquent appeals to patriotism, the most energetic canvassing will make the Irish people read'.[10]

Another literary job this spring was to assist in bringing out the *Second
Book of the Rhymers' Club*, which meant Yeats saw a good deal of his friend
Lionel Johnson. As with the first Rhymers' collection two years before, this
was to be published in a limited edition by John Lane's The Bodley Head.
On one of the days on which Yeats went to visit Lionel Johnson, he found
that his friend had with him another visitor, the beautiful lady from *The
Yellow Book* dinner. The lady was Lionel Johnson's cousin, Olivia
Shakespear. Like Lionel Johnson she came from a well-to-do family and
her father had been a major-general in the British army in India. Just over
eight years before this meeting with Yeats, she had married a London
lawyer, Henry Hope Shakespear, who was some fourteen years older than
herself. They had a daughter, Dorothy, who was now approaching her
eighth birthday. But Olivia was by no means happy; she once said that
Henry Shakespear 'ceased to pay court to me from the day of our marriage',
and she moved about London on her own, as she did to the famous dinner
in Soho. She found some solace in friendships with women, in her enjoyment of the arts and in writing fiction. The year she was introduced to
Yeats also brought the publication of her first novel, *Love on a Mortal Lease*.

Olivia and Yeats were strongly drawn to each other and quickly
arranged to meet again. Their chief topic of conversation was literature and
their writing. As Yeats began sending Olivia letters offering advice on her
novels he developed a new prose form that could be called literary criticism
as flirtation, or perhaps even wooing. He suggested describing a character
they could both agree to patronize, who was so much Yeats's antithesis that
he defined Yeats's attractions. Gerald was vigorous, fair-haired, and fond
of boating and cricket. His fondness for physical activity made him
appear manly, but he lacked any drive in emotional and intellectual matters.[11]

Financial considerations compelled Yeats to retreat yet again to his
Uncle George's house in Sligo, but their correspondence continued. In
their letters they exchanged admiration for Lionel Johnson's book on
Thomas Hardy. Yeats, a great admirer of Johnson as a literary critic and
prose stylist, thought that his friend had praised Hardy in a style superior

to Hardy's own.[12] Yeats wished that his friend 'had written instead of Dante or Milton'. But gradually, during his absence in Sligo, Yeats's letters began to show a predominance of personal feeling for Olivia over issues of literary criticism. Of her fictional characters, for instance, he observed that her 'own character and ideals are mirrored in them'; that is why they are 'refined, distinguished, sympathetic'. Her letters to him in Sligo brought him a 'half-conscious excitement'. But he gained the impression from them that she had had many lovers and was disillusioned. He wondered whether she was perhaps, like her increasingly drunken cousin Lionel Johnson, someone for whom the ordinary life seemed empty, someone for whom all that was left was either sanctity or dissipation.[13] But he put these doubts aside. He also determined that he would not be held back by his problematical love for Maud, which had gone on for more than six years now. He decided that since he could not get the woman he loved, he would take comfort even if only for a short time in devoting himself to another.[14] At Sligo his mind dwelled on the exciting possibilities that these decisions created.

Before he left London in October 1894 for his seven-month stay as a dependant of Uncle George in Sligo, Yeats attended two ceremonies. On 16 July he was one of a thousand people who witnessed the unveiling of a portrait bust of John Keats in Hampstead Church. This honouring of the poet who had meant so much to Yeats as a young writer and who would still be a reference point in a late poem such as 'Ego Dominus Tuus' was organized by Yeats's American friends Louise Imogen Guiney and the Boston publisher Fredrick H. Day. Just over a month later Yeats was in the recently built Emmanuel Church in the west London suburb of Gunnersbury for the wedding of his brother Jack. Within days of his twenty-third birthday Jack was marrying Mary Cottenham White, who had been one of his fellow students at art school. Always known as Cottie, the bride was a few years older than Jack, from the west of England, and had a small private income. Though the couple never had any children the marriage was a contented one. The improvident John Yeats was both proud and pleased at the way his younger son had applied himself to his work. Years later John Yeats wrote of Jack that during 'winter time and every morning from six o'clock till late at night he worked in a fireless room producing black and white drawings for comic journals etc. At the end of three years he had made enough money to marry the young lady and have a comfortable house very beautifully situated on the banks of the Thames some miles from London.'[15] The house was near Chertsey in Surrey, then a pleasant little riverside market town. Yeats stayed with them there briefly in the following year.

In Sligo that autumn Yeats continued with *The Shadowy Waters*, but his chief and most demanding task was the preparation of an edition of most of his poetic works to date, which he had contracted to publish with Fisher Unwin. As he proceeded he found himself making extensive revisions to major pieces such as 'The Wanderings of Oisin' and *The Countess Kathleen*. His daily routine was a simple one: a good deal of work in the mornings and the afternoons, and two 'constitutional walks' with gruff Uncle George, one after lunch and one after dinner to the same gate at Knocknarea; and at Rosses Point, to the same rock upon the shore. There was also a time set aside to study and improve his French.

The great social gulf that had once existed between the aristocratic Gore-Booths of Lissadell and the middle-class Yeatses and Pollexfens of Sligo was now bridgeable as a result of Yeats's friendship with Constance Gore-Booth in London after she became an art student at the Slade. In June Yeats had made arrangements for the 26-year-old Constance to have her fortune told by an expert Kabalist,[16] Moina Mathers. Now in December Constance invited him to stay at Lissadell. He enjoyed his visit greatly. He gave a lecture on fairy-lore to an audience of family retainers, who were mostly Orangemen.[17] Yeats thought that he had been tactful in choosing 'nothing but humorous tales'. Nevertheless some there were concerned about Yeats giving the impression that the fairies really existed.

Yeats was impressed by the Gore-Booth family and was especially drawn to Constance's sister Eva. Despite his old and enduring entanglement with Maud and his new fascination with Olivia he started to develop a serious relationship with Eva, who had a delicate gazelle-like beauty. She quickly became his close friend and he told her of all his failures in love.[18] He even thought of proposing marriage to her. He threw the Tarot cards and, discouragingly, the Fool turned up. He also realized full well that Eva's family would be shocked by the idea of a penniless poet as her suitor. He did not proceed.

The Gore-Booths were, on the face of it, a conservative 'county' family but Yeats found them a very pleasant, kindly, excitable family. They were always ready to be interested in new ideas and new things. For instance, they had had no previous experience of folklore and had not known it existed.[19] He was also very pleased, he told his sister, that he had been able to interest them in the new Irish writing, including his own. On the day after Christmas he wrote to his sisters thanking them for their presents and apologizing for not sending anything to them. All he had, he told Lily, was a two shilling piece and a halfpenny. He would have nothing until the anthology *A Book of Irish Verse*, which he was putting together for the publishing firm of Methuen, was accepted and published.

The letter is a marker in Yeats's early life: at this Christmas of his twenty-ninth year he was virtually a pauper, kept by his uncle who, he admitted, continued to treat him as a boy.[20] While his young brother had his own home and his marriage, Willie was still a dependant. Unable to support himself financially, he could not realistically contemplate marriage. But Yeats did not falter, such was the strength and the single-mindedness of his commitment to his art. A Goethean daemon drove him as it drove the larger Irish consciousness. While that quiet Christmas at Uncle George's came and went and his thirtieth birthday loomed, Yeats, with nothing to show materially and financially from his first decade as a writer, worked on with steely determination.

IN EARLY JANUARY 1895 SLIGO WAS RACKED BY VIOLENT STORMS AND the long table mountains of Knocknarea and Ben Bulben and the grey shadowy coastline were flickeringly illuminated by lightning. At Thornhill Yeats practised astrology with Uncle George, who grew daily more fascinated by it. After nearly three months in Sligo, however, Yeats's thoughts turned again to London and he wrote to Lily asking her to send him a copy of the *Westminster Gazette* so that he could read a review of Oscar Wilde's new play *An Ideal Husband* which had just opened at the Haymarket Theatre. He also kept his eye on literary Dublin. At the end of the month he was quick to respond with a letter to the press criticizing some remarks in a lecture by Edward Dowden which Yeats considered disparaging to the new Irish literature. The controversy continued in the pages of the *Dublin Daily Express* well into the next month. Then he told his publisher Fisher Unwin that they needed a new controversy, to continue from the one on 'Prof Dowden and Irish Literature'.[1] Yeats hit upon the idea of sending a letter to the *Express* defining the canon of Irish literature by offering a list of the Thirty Best Irish Books. That should surely provoke disagreements, upset and debate, and draw attention to himself. To get his letter published he enlisted the aid of his old mentor, the Tory Democrat Standish O'Grady, who was on the staff of the *Express*. The letter appeared in the first week of February and, as he had hoped, it provoked a good deal of controversy which included a rejoinder from Edward Dowden.

In Sligo, as the spring approached, the gruelling work of rewriting many of his major poems for the new edition continued. In dealing with Fisher Unwin, Yeats was fastidious and demanding about the physical appearance of this new collection. For his designer he demanded Charles Shannon who had designed and decorated many of Oscar Wilde's books. Shannon and his lifelong companion the artist Charles Ricketts were prominent figures in the London art world of the 1890s. At their elegant home in Chelsea Yeats made many important contacts. Yeats also insisted to Fisher that the designer's task should be to make the book a work of art.[2] Keen to distance his book from the productions of Duffy and the old Young Ireland, he also prohibited the use of green and of shamrocks.[3]

The end of February was bitterly cold in Sligo. There was a skating party out at Lissadell to which Yeats was invited. 'We had great skating,' he told Lily, 'the river up to the lake being frozen as far as the windmill. The Miss Gore-Booths were there and made coffee on the shore.' Then when the spring came Yeats travelled a little way inland to County Roscommon to visit Douglas Hyde and his wife at their new home near the little town of Frenchpark. Lucy Hyde had a private income and the couple lived in a large, beautifully kept Georgian house overlooking Lake Gara with a fine view of the mountains to the north. The Gaelic League had prospered way beyond Douglas Hyde's hopes and expectations. It had suited a mood in Ireland and quickly attracted a large membership. It made links with similar organizations in Scotland and Wales, and when an organization was formed in Brittany to defend and preserve the ancient culture of that region of France, it was modelled on the Gaelic League.

Yeats's bruisings in his struggles with Duffy and his associates and his recent experiences in Paris had led him to begin thinking of himself in an international rather than a solely Irish context. A few months earlier he had written, 'it is often necessary for an original Irish writer, to appeal first, not to his countrymen, but to that small group of men of imagination and scholarship which is scattered through many lands and cities.' He told John O'Leary that 'as long as the Irish public knows nothing of literature, Irish writers must be content to write for countries that know nothing of Ireland'.[4] A dialogue between the Irishness of Yeats and his European and international interests continued to develop, but with Douglas Hyde this spring the former reasserted itself. They went on a trip to Lough Key, some miles east of Lake Gara. They had themselves rowed down the lake and stopped at Castle Rock, an island with a castellated building from the early years of the Gothic Revival at the beginning of the century. Yeats was taken with the place and started to plan an Irish mystical order which would buy or rent the castle and use it as a place where the members might retire for contemplation and engage in secret rites that resembled the Eleusinian mysteries.

One reason Yeats had been interested in Lough Key was to find out whether any of the local people could give him a version of the tale of Tumaus Costello, the central character of a story Yeats was then writing entitled 'Proud Costello, MacDermot's Daughter, and the Bitter Tongue'. It became a part of a collection of stories which he was now putting together and later published under the title *The Secret Rose*. For the most part they are sad, painful tales of suffering and sacrifice. The epigraph from Villiers, 'As for living, the servants will do that for us', establishes at the outset their preoccupation with the inner life. Yeats told Olivia, before he set off for County Roscommon, that these 'wild Irish stories' were not mere phantasies but 'the signatories – to use a medieval term – of things invisible and ideal'.[5] They are also a blending of Yeats's concern with the supernatural and with Ireland.

In the early summer of 1895, he returned to London for the publication of his *Poems* by Fisher Unwin. He arrived back in Blenheim Road just as the greatest scandal of the 1890s was coming to its head. Oscar Wilde was about to stand trial on charges of homosexuality. Having lost his libel action against the Marquis of Queensberry, the father of Lord Alfred Douglas with whom he was besotted, Wilde had been arrested and then released on bail. His trial, which created a sensation in the press and in society, started in the third week of May. Both Yeats and his father felt dismay and sorrow for the great Irish wit, socialite and dandy whom they saw as humiliated by a brutal social and legal code. Yeats tried to help, gathering letters of support for Wilde from various people. He had heard that Wilde was staying at his mother's house in Oakley Street in Chelsea, and the day before the trial began Yeats went there with the letters. But Wilde had left the house after assuring everyone that he would neither flee nor kill himself, but would face his accusers. Yeats managed to speak only with Wilde's brother. During the coming weeks he, like everyone else, followed the drama of the trial, the conviction and the sentencing to hard labour. The ruin of Oscar Wilde was one more instance (and the most highly publicized) of the artist as victim, a notion that was to become a part of the definition of the decade.

But for Yeats this summer of the famous trial was a time of happiness, of new and vital possibilities. For him there was Olivia. Their relationship was quickly renewed. Their feelings for each other grew stronger each time they met. And they met often. There was a slight sense of delirium in the relationship. After a couple of weeks he asked her to abandon her lifeless marriage and go away with him, giving her, as his pledge, a kiss that was spiritual and in no way erotic. Olivia was touched by such 'beautiful tact' in giving her 'but a brother's kiss'. However Yeats later admitted that at the age of thirty this was the only way he knew how to kiss. A day or two later, full of ideas about how to manage their future relationship, they took the train out to Kew Gardens on the south-western edge of London. (In the coming days and weeks suburban trains provided one of the best means of meeting discreetly.) As the train approached their destination, Olivia kissed him sensuously, startling him with this first experience of a passionate kiss.[6] Puritan that he was at heart, he was also a little shocked by her forwardness.

As they walked together through the long sequence of gardens they were full of plans and possibilities. It was a fine summer's day on which to see the Orangery and the Pagoda, designed some twenty years before the beginning of the American War of Independence. In the gardens were the thousands of plants that Captain Cook's botanist Joseph Banks had brought here from all around the world. As they wandered, the beautifully dressed lady from upper middle-class Kensington and the thin, sallow, bespectacled poet with lank dark hair and shabby Bohemian clothes talked on and on about the practicalities of their coming affair. For a woman of Olivia's social standing, with a husband, a child, a house and servants, to enter into a relationship with a young man with no home of his own was problematical. Above all, scandal, with its incalculable consequences among the strait-laced Victorian bourgeoisie, had to be avoided.

They considered delaying the relationship, waiting until Olivia's elderly mother, for whom she felt responsible, had died. Then Olivia changed her mind and said they should not wait and that openness was the best policy. She would tell her husband the truth and ask him for a separation.

When she broke this news to Henry Shakespear, he was extremely upset, and became ill. Olivia then told Yeats that it would be better from now on to deceive him. At one point in this summer of passionate but confused expectations Yeats received a strange letter from Maud Gonne[7] who was suddenly interested in him again. She wanted to know whether he was ill or whether something had happened. She had had a vision of him walking into her room in the Nassau Hotel in Dublin where she was talking to friends. She had told him to return at midnight and he vanished. He did return at the appointed hour, appearing 'in some strange, priest-like costume, at her bedside'. Then they had found themselves wandering round the cliffs of Howth as they had done over four years before, when they had tried to sustain a purely spiritual friendship. Yeats was thrown into turmoil by this letter: suddenly his old love seemed to threaten the new.[8]

But the new love was strong; it persisted and composed and readied itself. Still the most difficult problem was to find a place for their assignations. Their meetings always had to be in public places and as a result Olivia was under a social obligation to have a chaperone, or sponsor, as she called her friend Elizabeth Fox who tactfully helped her in this. To Olivia Yeats brought poems: 'The Travail of Passion', 'A Poet to his Beloved', 'He bids his Beloved be at Peace' and 'He gives his Beloved certain Rhymes', this last containing the piningly erotic lines, very much in the 1890s manner:

> *You need but lift a pearl-pale hand*
> *And bind up your long hair and sigh;*
> *And all men's hearts must burn and beat . . .*

Olivia brought to him new experiences in art; at Dulwich Picture Gallery she communicated to Yeats her feeling for the paintings of Watteau. Another time they went to the National Gallery where she showed him her beloved Mantegnas. And always there were train journeys in and around London. Then in September the problem of where to meet was eased.

Yeats's fellow Rhymer Arthur Symons told him that Havelock Ellis, the literary critic and writer on sexuality with whom Symons shared rooms in one of the Inns of Court, was going to be away for a while. Symons wondered whether Yeats would like to take over Ellis's share of the lodgings in Fountain Court, Middle Temple, close to the Thames at the eastern end of the Strand.

Yeats had serious misgivings about his ability to support himself away from the family home. But chiefly because of Olivia he finally decided to take the chance and in October moved into the two rooms which Symons had to offer. The medieval Knights Templar, protectors of pilgrims to the Holy Land, had their London headquarters here until they were dissolved in the early fourteenth century. Gradually the lawyers had taken over the property as a place where they could live and work communally. Down the centuries many of those residing here had also been writers: Wycherley and Congreve, Evelyn, Burke and William Wilberforce. Fountain Court where Symons lived is a quiet quadrangle reminiscent of an Oxbridge college. In the dining hall great revels, masques and plays were performed, including, in 1601, Shakespeare's *Twelfth Night*.

One of the pleasures of the months Yeats spent in this bachelor's establishment in Fountain Court was his close literary and personal relationship with Arthur Symons. The friendship with Lionel Johnson was now less close because Yeats could not bear to see his fastidious friend become intoxicated day after day. Symons, who was preoccupied with the music hall and especially with dancers and the dance, had a verbal delicacy that interested Yeats. As a critic he was extremely well versed in French literature and his book *The Symbolist Movement in Literature* introduced the French *symbolistes* and their contemporaries to the English-speaking world; it was a book of prime importance for the later generation that included Ezra Pound and T.S. Eliot. Symons helped Yeats to sustain that interest in French literature really begun on his first visit to Paris. Yeats later wrote of his eight months in Fountain Court in daily contact with Arthur Symons that 'my thoughts gained in richness and in clearness from his sympathy, nor shall I ever know how much my practice and my theory owe to the passages that he read me from Catullus and Verlaine and Mallarmé.'[9] In hindsight Arthur Symons stands out as, after Yeats, the member of the

Rhymers' Club with the most considerable literary achievement. But his career, like that of so many other Rhymers, was a tragically short one; twelve years later he would go mad.

Lolly had been mockingly sceptical about her brother's ability to leave home, telling Lily who was on one of her treasured visits to Sligo that he 'has taken a room says he can live on 10/- a week. Let him try.' But when Lily returned to London she was pleased to see that he was making a go of it.[10] Above all it meant that he could receive Olivia and they could become lovers. Parts of his emotional life that had been markedly arrested were now, at the age of thirty, opened up to adulthood. The months at Fountain Court mark the beginning of Yeats's belated maturity.

I N THE EARLY SPRING OF 1896 YEATS GAVE UP HIS ROOMS IN FOUNTAIN Court and rented a place that was entirely his own where he and Olivia could be together in complete privacy whenever they wished. This was at 18 Woburn Buildings (now 5 Woburn Walk) on the northern edge of Bloomsbury, south of Euston Station and close to Tavistock Square. It was a modest flat on the third storey of a terrace of Regency shops built in the 1820s all to the same pleasing design, in a quiet little alley in a then unfashionable part of London. A shoemaker lived on the ground floor and above him a workman and his family; above Yeats there was an attic where an old pedlar lived. Yeats rented his rooms from a working-class couple, Mr and Mrs Old; the husband was a carpenter and Mrs Old, a tall, brawny woman from rural Oxfordshire, acted as Yeats's housekeeper and cook. Urchins in that shabby run-down neighbourhood soon referred to him as 'the Toff what lives in the Building'. Illiterate themselves, they were impressed to see the postman deliver so many letters to Yeats's address.

Olivia helped Yeats to set up and furnish this first home of his own, as she had helped him to become her lover. The process was difficult. She had to trump up reasons for her absence from home, afraid that scandal might mean losing her daughter Dorothy. She could not direct the cabbie to go direct to Woburn Buildings for fear her servants might hear this outlandish address, and instead she changed hansoms in central London. The awkward, nervous poet needed instruction in the many intricacies of the female dress and underwear of the time. It was important for her to return to her house fully buttoned and laced, and his help was needed to achieve this. Discrepancies of this kind, noticed by servants, could be cited as evidence in late-nineteenth-century divorce cases. Then there was the problem of contraception, the choice between *coitus interruptus* and rudimentary mechanical devices. Yeats was no help at all. As a writer on this relationship has noted, 'These were problems unknown on Danaan shores. Oisin had never been required to unlace a corset in near-freezing temperatures, or wrestle with a nineteenth-century condom, and Yeats's knowledge of these subjects was very much the same as Oisin's.'[1]

Nevertheless Olivia persevered, showing great patience and delicacy. At the first attempt Yeats failed completely, being so nervous that he was impotent.[2] Some days later she returned, but again his tension was so great that they tacitly agreed simply to sit and talk and have tea together. Yeats was grateful that his inadequacy did not damage her interest. He was touched to see that Olivia was only 'troubled by my trouble'. Happily when she visited him next time, he could control his nervousness. At last they became lovers. And so began 'many days of happiness'. One of their many pleasures was furnishing his new home together. They went about London searching for cheap furniture that could be thrown away when he became more prosperous, as he was confident he would. Yeats's puritanism, gentility and poverty all contributed to his embarrassment when they went to a shop in Tottenham Court Road to buy the bed. Under the eyes of the knowing salesman they had to decide exactly how wide it should be. Love favoured width but 'every inch increased the expense'.

His long-standing worries about money were lessened somewhat at this time by the founding of a new magazine that promised to pay its contributors well. This was the *Savoy*, edited by his friend Arthur Symons, which first appeared in January 1896. To John O'Leary, to whom he still owed money, he felt able to say of his financial position: 'I have I believe definitely turned the corner thanks partly to the *Savoy* which came in the nick of time to let me raise my prices and to keep me going until I get the new prices generally accepted.'[3] The new magazine also provided a position as art editor to Aubrey Beardsley, who had been dismissed by John Lane from *The Yellow Book*. The mood of moral indignation sweeping society in the aftermath of the Oscar Wilde trial was intense, and Beardsley's provocative drawings drew much criticism. Soon after the sentencing of Oscar Wilde Mrs Humphry Ward, a best-selling novelist with a heavy moral line, took the lead, writing a letter to John Lane deploring Beardsley's work and demanding that he no longer continue as an editor. Mrs Ward said that she wrote because 'She owed it to her position before the British people.'[4] Beardsley was thought by the public also to be a homosexual, which greatly distressed Beardsley and led him, as Yeats observed, to engage in a conspicuous, manic heterosexuality, aggravating the tuberculosis from which he was already dying. Yeats and Symons were both indignant at the injustice done to Beardsley, and Symons made it a condition of his editing the *Savoy* that Beardsley should become the art editor.

Yeats was pleased to be a contributor to the seemingly well-funded magazine, but also uneasy about the publisher. Leonard Smithers had started life as a solicitor and then become a successful publisher of under-the-counter pornographic books. He was also to publish two volumes of drawings by Aubrey Beardsley, a book of caricatures by another noted 1890s wit, Max Beerbohm, as well as Oscar Wilde's last three books. Plump, sweaty Smithers now wished to get rid of his image as a purveyor of pornography and the *Savoy*, a fashionable, quality magazine, was his means of doing so. Yeats had no illusions about the dubious reputation attaching to Smithers's name. His reservations would be justified in a few years' time when Smithers entered into a highly disreputable relationship with Yeats's fellow student from Dublin days, Althea Gyles. But at the beginning of 1896 Yeats felt that, after what had happened to Wilde and Beardsley, he and other serious artists were necessarily at war with the British public. In their fight they must use any means to hand. Yeats's involvement with the magazine nevertheless led to letters of protest and criticism from two people who had known him for a very long time, AE and T.W. Rolleston.

Certainly, thanks to its owner and some of its contributors, the *Savoy* had a reputation for being risqué. It was one of the cultural products of the decade that helped to create the phrase 'the Naughty Nineties'. Along with Rhymers such as Dowson, Symons, Lionel Johnson and Yeats, the *Savoy* published Bernard Shaw, Joseph Conrad and Max Beerbohm. The artwork in the magazine was of a high standard, too. One illustrator for the *Savoy* was William Thomas Horton, a dedicated mystic whom Yeats counselled on initiation into the Order of the Golden Dawn. A quarter of a century later, Yeats, remembering the 1890s, would evoke Horton's delicate spirituality in his major poem 'All Souls' Night'. Horton illustrated a translation from the French medieval poet François Villon for the magazine. In the *Savoy* as in *The Yellow Book* there was much reference to France and its literary tradition. Paris was in its heyday as the world capital of art. In the next few years it would attract Pablo Picasso from Barcelona, Constantin Brancusi from Rumania, Rainer Maria Rilke from Prague and James Joyce from Dublin.

George Moore, the established Irish novelist, now in his forties, also wrote for the *Savoy*. He was a friend of Symons and like him had rooms in the Middle Temple. He contributed a translation of a work by Mallarmé, which of itself was not a matter for disapproval. Rather it was his previous career that added to the scandalous reputation of the *Savoy*. As a very young man he had left his Ascendancy home in County Mayo to study art in Paris. He soon turned from painting to literature and became a follower of Zola and a writer of naturalistic novels. Just as Zola's theory of fiction demanded, these novels showed lives usually lived in sordid conditions, determined by the forces of environment and heredity. Before he was thirty George Moore had published *A Modern Lover*, a novel which, for the time, was startlingly frank about sexual behaviour. This was followed by *A Mummer's Wife* and *Esther Waters* which were also indebted to the example set by French naturalism. Rather loud in his manner, Moore pulled rank by claiming a far greater knowledge of the ugly realities of life.

He boasted a great deal about his womanizing and treated women brutally. One of his lovers was Pearl Craigie, a friend of Olivia Shakespear's who, under the pseudonym of John Oliver Hobbes, also published novels. George Moore ended his affair with this society lady by publicly kicking her bottom, very hard, in Hyde Park. It was probably to Pearl Craigie that he referred when he called on Symons and Yeats after an assignation, threw himself down in a chair and exclaimed disgustedly, 'I wish that woman would wash.' Yeats and Symons, both far gentler men than George Moore, were shocked for they knew the lady to be accomplished, fashionable and witty. Yet for all Moore's arrogance and grossness women responded to this rather ugly man with the sallow face, drooping moustache and small, wet mouth. One of his current lovers was Lady Cunard, the wife of a shipping magnate. Lady Cunard, he boasted, on first meeting him at a lunch at the Savoy Hotel, had cried out, 'George Moore, you have a soul of fire!' The affair continued for some time. Lady Cunard's daughter Nancy, who became a prominent figure in the literary life of Paris and London in the 1920s, long phantasized over the possibility that George Moore, and not her mother's husband, was her father.[5]

In the coming years George Moore was to become an important, if often annoying figure in Yeats's life. So too did a cousin of George Moore's who visited London early during the one-year lifespan of the *Savoy*. This was wealthy Edward Martyn, a devout Catholic, whose home was Tillyra Castle in County Galway. He was George Moore's opposite in many respects: spiritual rather than worldly, a misogynist and not a lecher, an ascetic rather than a bon viveur. Edward Martyn did not look to Paris as his cousin did. Unlike Moore, who had written a savage attack on the country, *Parnell and his Island* (1887), Martyn was a passionate supporter of the Irish Revival and devoted his time and his fortune to assisting its various manifestations: Sinn Fein, the Literary Society, Douglas Hyde's Gaelic League and the revival of Irish music. In Loughrea not far from Tillyra Castle a new cathedral was being planned; the foundation stone would be laid the following year. Edward Martyn interested himself in and gave generously towards its construction and decoration, especially to its stained glass and works of art. He went so far as to persuade Sarah Purser to open An Tur Gloine (the tower of glass) in Dublin, a studio in which the cathedral windows were designed and made by Irish artists. He also had aspirations to write plays about Ireland.

Martyn and Yeats, therefore, had much in common and when Yeats spoke of travelling in Ireland with Arthur Symons in order to show his friend the country, Edward Martyn invited them to stay with him and his mother at Tillyra. This summer expedition would mean a separation from Olivia, but in fact Olivia too would be absent from London; she still had to keep up appearances as a wife, which entailed a holiday in Italy with her husband and daughter Dorothy. Yeats and Arthur Symons went first to Dublin, then took a train the few miles south to Dalkey on Dublin Bay where Ernest Dowden was now residing. Despite his public disagreements with the distinguished Trinity College professor, Yeats was still sufficiently sure of a welcome from his father's friend to feel able to introduce Symons. The two of them then stayed with Uncle George in Sligo, before setting off for Galway where Symons was keen to make contact with Paul Bourget, a successful French novelist staying there. From there they went on to Tillyra Castle. This journey through Ireland showed Symons a landscape and a people such as he had never seen or imagined. In his vivid account of their travels which he later published in the *Savoy*, he returns continually to the foreignness of Ireland, its differences from England. He is especially taken by the difference in the dress and appearance of the people.

> *I remember in the curve of a rocky field, some little way in from the road, seeing a young woman, wearing a blue bodice, a red petticoat and a gray shawl, carrying a tin pail on her head, with that straight flexible movement of the body, that slow and formal grace, of Eastern women who have carried pitchers from the well. Occasionally a fierce old man on a horse, wearing the old costume, that odd precise kind of dress-coat, passes you with a surly scowl; or a company of tinkers (the Irish gipsies one might call them) trail past, huddled like crouching beasts on their little, rough, open carts, driving a herd of donkeys before them.*[6]

Tillyra Castle also made a strong impression on Symons. It was a large building dating from the Gothic Revival with a tower from a much earlier time. In the evenings the party would put out the lights and sit talking in the shadows as though, as Yeats said, upon a stage set for Wagner's *Parsifal*. Martyn had a 'monklike' bedroom in the ancient tower where he prayed fervently. When Yeats attempted some of his own invocations in a room near the tower Martyn became very upset, fearing that the images solicited by Yeats might obstruct the upward passage of prayer. In his isolated tower room Martyn also kept his collection of paintings by Degas, Monet and Corot, and prints by Utamaro, which his cousin George Moore had helped him choose. At different times during the day Edward Martyn would retire from the company and play religious music by Roman composers of the sixteenth century, Vittoria and Palestrina, on the organ that had been built into the high lancet-windowed entrance hall. All the time his old mother, who was of peasant stock, tried, as she had done for years, to interest her heavy, unworldly son in a possible bride. The latest candidate was a pretty, slightly brash girl with a ruddy face. But Edward Martyn, whom his ribald cousin George declared to be a homosexual, preferred to read Swift and the saints and would have none of her.

After a few days at Tillyra, Yeats and Symons set off on a further excursion, making first for Cashlan Bay on the Galway coast and there boarding one of the sailing boats peculiar to the region and known as 'hookers' which took them across to Inishmore, an island some five miles long and two miles wide, the largest of the Aran Islands. Here on this western outpost of Ireland which for months at a time was blasted by gales from the Atlantic, the two friends stayed at a small and primitive lodging-place made up of three whitewashed cottages. Again Symons was interested in the people in this bleak, remote place. 'The women of Aran almost all dress in red, the petticoat being heavily woven,' he reported. The dress of the men was similarly distinctive. The guide they employed was typical. He 'was dressed, as are almost all the peasants of Aran, in clothes woven and made on the island; loose rough woollen things, of drab or dark blue or gray, sometimes charming in colour; he had a flannel shirt, a kind of waistcoat with sleeves, very loose and shapeless trousers, worn without braces, an old discoloured hat on his head, and on his feet the usual *pampooties*, slippers of undressed hide, drawn together and stitched into shape, with pointed toes, and a cord across the instep.'[7] These shoes were favoured on Aran, Yeats learned, because they were the only ones which the sharp rocks did not immediately cut to pieces.

As the two friends moved about the bleak windlashed islands, seeing the tiny fields marked out by unmortared stone walls, Yeats inquired of the local people about their experiences of the fairies and of 'silkies', seals who could shed their skins and turn into human beings. The replies were none too helpful but Yeats was powerfully affected by the great prehistoric fort of Dun Aengus on Inishmore, by the chamber tomb of Diarmuid and Grainne on Inishmaan and by the elemental life of the islanders. They had a fascination which he communicated to his brother Jack who, some years later, also set off to Aran and painted the islands and their people. Aran gave Yeats a sense of a more ancient and primitive Ireland than he had known before. Aran was also an entirely new experience for Symons and it effected radical changes in his consciousness and prose style. The following passage of description inspired by his stay on the island is uncharacteristically poetic.

> *The sea on these coasts is not like the sea as I know it on any other coast; it has in it more of the twilight. And the sky seems to come down more softly; with more stealthy steps, more illusive wings; and the land to come forward with a more hesitating and gradual approach; and land, and sea, and sky to mingle more absolutely than on any other coast. I have never realized less the slipping of sand through the hour-glass; I have never seemed to see with so remote an impartiality, as in the presence of brief yet eternal things, the troubling and insignificant accidents of life. I have never believed less in the reality of the visible world, in the importance of all we are most serious about. One seems to wash off the dust of cities, the dust of beliefs, the dust of incredulities.*[8]

The two friends sailed through rough seas to return to the mainland. Symons proceeded almost immediately to London and the editorial offices of the *Savoy* in Old Bond Street, but Yeats stayed on with Edward Martyn at the Castle. Not far away from Tillyra there was another large and famous house of the Ascendancy belonging to the Gregory family. Sir William Gregory, who had been Governor of Ceylon (today Sri Lanka), had died some four years before. He left a widow, Augusta, who was thirty-five years younger than he, and a son, Robert, who was now just fifteen. One day that August, as Yeats lingered at Tillyra after his visit to Aran, Augusta Gregory came over from Coole Park in her two-wheeled jaunting car drawn by a pony. As Yeats and this new visitor, thirteen years older than he, conversed, there came a quick, strong feeling of sympathy born of shared interests. Thus began, that day at Tillyra, by far the most important and creative of the many friendships in Yeats's life.

They had actually met briefly at a social occasion in London some two years before, and had not been greatly interested in each other. Yet now, meeting in County Galway, they felt differently. Yeats found that this rather dumpy, plain-looking and plainly dressed woman of forty-four had a high regard for the new Irish literary movement. They talked of his interest in fairy-lore and before long Augusta offered to assist his researches by going into the cottages of the peasantry around Coole to see what stories she might be able to collect for him. He told her about his work on *The Shadowy Waters* and his belief in the need for a Celtic drama. Augusta Gregory and Edward Martyn both shared his enthusiastic vision of founding a theatre in which such plays might be performed.

Augusta invited Yeats to come and stay at her home, Coole Park, and he promptly accepted. During this visit their shared interests quickly cemented a comradeship and a friendship. With no difficulty at all the poet and literary journalist who lived in the cheap flat near Euston Station took to life in the great mansion. He luxuriated in Sir William's library with its calf-bound editions of the classics,[9] and he took great pleasure in studying the paintings which Sir William, once a Trustee of the National Gallery in London, had acquired. There were works by Stubbs and Guardi, Zurbaran and Canaletto. Coole showed the evidence of generations of wealth, luxury and taste, including Sir William's cellar of fine wines. When his widow offered them at mealtimes, Yeats enjoyed them greatly.

Like her dead husband, Augusta was from an aristocratic background. She was born Augusta Persse and had grown up at Roxborough Hall between Loughrea and Gort. Because she was not good-looking, people had assumed she would never find a husband. But when she was twenty-seven she unexpectedly received a proposal. It came from the 62-year-old widower Sir William Gregory, well known in London and Irish society for his worldliness and his passion for horses, gambling and the arts. Her marriage took Augusta beyond the Ascendancy world of western Ireland; she became the mistress of a fashionable establishment in London. The couple travelled to several countries including Egypt, then part of the British Empire in all but name. Here she met the poet and compulsive seducer Wilfrid Scawen Blunt who was a vociferous supporter both of Egyptian and of Irish nationalism. Augusta had an affair with him. She wrote a sequence of poems about the relationship and under the title 'A Woman's Sonnets' they were published anonymously, as part of Blunt's *Love Lyrics and Songs of Proteus*. This was in 1892, the same year in which Yeats published *The Countess Kathleen* and *Various Legends and Lyrics*. It was also the year in which the 75-year-old Sir William died. His widow then returned to Ireland with the eleven-year-old Robert and set about managing Coole and its extensive estate in such a way as to pay off the inherited debt created by her husband's gambling.

At the time she had her first serious conversation with Yeats at Tillyra, Augusta was seeking a fuller life. The Irish cultural revival interested her even though she was still, in the tradition of her family, a staunch Unionist. When Yeats, the young star in the renaissance, first came to Coole Park, she asked him if he could find some way for her to help the new intellectual movement.[10] She was a little hurt that all he could suggest was that she should read the books produced by the Revival. He remembered that he had told her, 'If you get our books and watch what we are doing, you will soon find your work.' In any event he was proved right. In mid-life she was to begin a career as a dramatist, dramaturge and theatre manager that constituted one of the leading achievements of what Yeats called 'our movement'. But on this first visit to Coole there seemed little for Sir William's energetic widow to do except wait on the pale, undernourished young poet who was her guest and attend to his physical needs. From the outset of their long friendship one of the roles that Augusta assumed for him was that of a mother.

As the time came for Yeats to leave Coole, they talked of him returning the next year, and indeed he did, spending some twenty summers at Coole. The great house would become a part of the rhythm of his life into late middle age. But now he went back to Tillyra and thence to London and to Olivia. Her visits to his Bloomsbury apartment resumed. Throughout that autumn they experienced the old happiness together, but then Maud Gonne once more made her presence felt in Yeats's life. During the summer Maud had gone to Bayreuth to hear Wagner's *Ring*. In August she had written to tell him how 'wonderful' the performances had been. She also encouraged him to come to Paris again. 'I wish Irishmen would come oftener to Paris. There is lots of interesting work to be done there. We want to have Ireland better known.'[11] Some weeks later she wrote to say that she would have loved to be with him during his time in the west of Ireland. She suggested that they could have participated in a quest similar to that of the hero and the heroine in *The Shadowy Waters*. 'I would have loved to have spent a week in Sligo while you were there, we could have tried if the fairies would have been good to us and shown us some glimpses of that lovely world which we so seldom see.'[12]

Under the influence of his experience of the Aran Islands Yeats was now planning a novel, _The Speckled Bird_, with two contrasting settings, Paris and Aran. He told Maud about this in a letter, and her response was virtually an invitation to him: 'I shall hope to see you in Paris in the winter, when your story takes you there.'[13] This revitalization of his relationship with Maud soon affected that with Olivia. He felt a loss of sympathy for his first lover; they no longer shared the same moods so readily. One day when she came to his rooms he could not read love poems to her as he usually did at the beginning of her visits. Olivia burst into tears, and when she recovered herself a little she said simply that she recognized that he loved someone else.[14] Then she left him. It was the moment remembered in the poem 'The Lover Mourns for the Loss of Love', in which Yeats, addressing Maud, recalls his 'beautiful friend' who 'looked in my heart one day / and saw your image was there; / She has gone weeping away.' By December 1896 Yeats was back with Maud in Paris. Here, for the second time, Yeats came into stimulating contact with the literary, political and intellectual life of France.

I N PARIS MAUD GONNE WAS LIVING IN GRAND STYLE AT 7 AVENUE
d'Eylau, across the Seine from the Eiffel Tower and close to the spectacular Moorish-style exhibition hall of the Trocadero, built twelve
years earlier. When Yeats arrived he settled into something much more
modest, a small room in a students' hotel on the rue Corneille, with the
Luxembourg Gardens across the street to the right and the Sorbonne a
short distance to the left across the boulevard Saint-Michel. Since Maud
was busy, he often ate on his own at one of the cheapest restaurants on the
rue Saint-Jacques. He also spent a good deal of time at a café near the
boulevard Saint-Germain where he could linger and smoke and read the
Irish news in *The Times*.

In this busy Latin Quarter there were students and scholars, painters
and writers from all over the world. One day Yeats went to visit Stuart
Merrill, an American *symboliste* poet who wrote in French and was a
devoted follower of Mallarmé. At Merrill's apartment Yeats met a Jewish
Persian scholar with a large ring which the owner claimed was made of
alchemical gold. Yeats also fell in with some cultists who were followers of
the eighteenth-century mystic Saint-Martin. With them Yeats smoked
hashish, talked into the night, laughed a great deal and watched some
members of the group dancing. Hashish was more readily available in Paris
than in London, though Symons' friend the sexologist Havelock Ellis
could supply Yeats with both hashish and mescalin.

As on his first visit to Paris, Yeats had a memorable experience in the theatre, at the first night of *Ubu le Roi* by Alfred Jarry at the Nouveau Théâtre in the rue Blanche on the southern edge of Montmartre.[1] Debunking high seriousness and tragedy, the masked actors performed as dolls, toys, marionettes. The masks and set designs in this early example of absurdist theatre were done by Toulouse-Lautrec, Sérusier, Vuillard and Bonnard. The audience quickly divided into two noisy groups, those who were receptive confronting those who were hostile to the outrageously avant-garde play. Yeats and those with him shouted with the pro-Jarry group. But when he crossed back over the Seine and returned to his little room in the Hotel Corneille Yeats reflected sadly that his own dramatic aesthetic was now being challenged not only by grim naturalism but by an idea of drama based on things conspicuously lacking in his own work to date – humour and irony. Through Jarry 'comedy, objectivity, had displayed its growing power once more'.[2] Seeing *Ubu* he sensed that *symboliste* poets and painters would soon be left with no further agenda. 'After Stéphane Mallarmé, after Paul Verlaine, after Gustave Moreau, after Puvis de Chavannes, after our own verse, after all our subtle colour and nervous rhythm, after the faint mixed tints of Condor, what more is possible?'[3]

As he moved about the Latin Quarter, one day Yeats found himself in company with the Swedish dramatist and fellow occultist, August Strindberg. On another he talked to Georg Brandes, the Danish literary critic, historian and author of the then well-regarded *Main Streams of Literature in the Nineteenth Century.* Here was the great commender of the liberal rhetorical tradition from Schiller to Victor Hugo. To Yeats, the poet of the local, the inward and the hermetic, the views of Brandes were lacking in finesse. After he had settled into the Hotel Corneille Yeats was told that there was another Irishman living in a room on the top floor. This was the 25-year-old John Millington Synge, a former student of Trinity College Dublin, a player of the violin, an aspiring poet and at that moment a student of French literature at the Sorbonne, who hoped to make a career as a literary critic. Yeats quickly came to like Synge for his genuineness and the breadth of his culture and, though only six years older than this son of a well-to-do Ascendancy family, he soon became a mentor to him. With his mop of hair and moustache and a touch of beard under his lip Synge looked very much the young Left Bank intellectual. His fine eyes were wide-set and dreamy and suggested his uncertainty about himself and his future. Yeats confidently set about putting him off a career as a critic. Arthur Symons, he maintained, was *the* critic of the day. Instead Yeats proposed another activity for Synge, one that would not immediately condemn him to being second best. Still full of his enthusiasm for Aran, Yeats urged the younger man to leave Paris, to abandon the international and comparative view of literature taken by such as Georg Brandes, and return to his Irish roots. Nowhere was more elementally Irish than the Aran Islands. Yeats urged his rather lost and melancholy compatriot to go home and spend some time on this distant outpost of Ireland, indeed of Europe. It would be a valid and worthwhile literary task to give expression to the life and traditions of these ancient Irish islands.

Yeats took Synge across the Seine to visit Maud Gonne in her spacious apartment in the sixteenth arrondissement. Yeats and she had drawn closer on this visit, but while Yeats still wanted to be her lover, what chiefly drew them together was political camaraderie. As she told him directly some months later, 'I don't want you to give me so much place in your life.'[4] So for the present they talked for hours about their visions of Ireland: Yeats's continuing dream of a community in the island castle of Lough Key where Celtic mysteries might be celebrated; her work as an orator for the Irish cause. She told him of her work lobbying for an amnesty for Irish political prisoners doing penal servitude in such harsh British prisons as Portland and Dartmoor. They discussed the divisions within the nationalist movement and the plans to raise funds for a monument in Dublin to Wolfe Tone, who had been at the head of the French-supported invasion of Ireland in 1798. The centenary of his death was two years away.

As Yeats stayed on in Paris over Christmas and into the New Year of 1897, he and Maud decided to found a Paris branch of the Young Ireland Society. One of the dozen or so founding members of the new organization was John Synge, but this gentle, unfailingly courteous young man soon withdrew. He did not share Maud Gonne's radical and passionate anti-British attitudes. Indeed he rarely spoke of politics. Years later, remembering his first meeting with Synge in Paris, Yeats marvelled that it had not made a greater impact upon him, 'that we can meet unmoved some person, or pass some house, that in later years is to bear a chief part in our life. Should there not be some flutter of the nerve or stopping of the heart?'[5] Yeats also recruited Fiona Macleod, whose career as a writer and poet had been involved in the advancement of the cause of Celticism in Scotland. It would seem that for years Yeats did not know that Fiona Macleod was the pseudonym or, more accurately, the second identity of William Sharp, a fat, red-faced journalist with bristling hair whom Yeats had first met in London a dozen or so years before. In correspondence about literary matters Yeats and Sharp both referred to Miss Macleod as an actual person. And now, in Paris, Yeats wrote to her hoping that she might be able to supply some 'short, direct prose plays' for the new society to perform. Such plays, he declared, 'would be far more effective than lectures and might do more than anything else we can do to make the Irish, Scotch and other Celts recognize their solidarity'.[6] Yeats thought that his own plays were too elaborate for the essentially propagandist aims of the Young Ireland societies. *The Shadowy Waters*, for instance, was 'magical and mystical', its purpose spiritual, to create 'a kind of grave ecstasy'.[7]

When he returned to London in late January 1897 Yeats's attention was quickly diverted by trouble in the Order of the Golden Dawn. Around the time he had gone to Paris MacGregor Mathers had decided that Annie Horniman should be expelled from the Order. Like other members of the London branch Yeats felt that this decree was unfortunate and he joined in an attempt to have Miss Horniman reinstated. He involved himself in a petition to Mathers which asked for 'a Merciful Judgement of her failings, whatever they may have been'. He also wrote a letter which concluded with an allusion to the niceties of hierarchy within the Order: 'I write this letter by direction of the Higher Members of the Second Order.' This turned out to be only the first stage in a developing conflict with Mathers that became by turns comic, grotesque and physically violent.

Maud too involved Yeats in the politics of personalities. She was increasingly at odds with some of the fellow nationalists who were planning the monument for Wolfe Tone and she was even accused of being a British spy. There were also divisions among the Irish Americans involved in the planning of the memorial. Yeats, of course, was always on

Maud's side in the infighting and it was surely to help her and perhaps to win her that he now let himself be lured into nationalist politics. He deluded himself into thinking, so he later wrote, 'that if I accepted the Presidency of the '98 Commemoration Association of Great Britain, I might be able to prevent a public quarrel, and so make a great central council possible'.[8] So the poet turned to organizational politics once again, but with limited success and at the cost of great exhaustion to himself. During that year, often with Maud, he attended discordant meetings of Irish nationalists round England. He soon became sick of the wrangling, telling John O'Leary in May that 'I am hoping against hope that the London committee will not want me to go to the Dublin convention on the 20th or that I shall discover a good excuse for not going. I want simply to think and write and forget these brawls.'[9] Later that month he managed to get across to Sligo to stay with Uncle George. But then in June he was in Dublin for one of the great occasions in Maud Gonne's career as agitator and orator. On the 22nd, the day of Queen Victoria's sixtieth anniversary as Queen, Maud and other nationalists took flowers to decorate the tombs of heroes of the Irish cause in St Michan's Church near the Four Courts. A caretaker informed Maud that the chuch was locked because of the royal Jubilee. The following day Maud delivered a passionate and rousing speech to a large crowd in Dame Street. The emotional climax was her rhetorical question, 'Must the graves of our dead go undecorated because Victoria has her Jubilee?' The crowd cheered her wildly and long.

Anti-imperial feeling continued to run high in Dublin that day. In the evening outside the National Club in what is now Parnell Square a magic lantern show was rigged up to show statistics of emigrations, acts of violence and evictions in Ireland during Queen Victoria's long reign. There was a procession with a coffin marked 'The British Empire'. Members of the crowd started tearing down the red, white and blue Jubilee decorations. The crowd also began breaking windows. As matters grew worse the police organized a baton charge against the crowd. The *Irish Times* reported that some two hundred people were injured and one person was killed.

Yeats and Maud were having tea in the National Club as the violence

escalated outside. A man ran in to report the batoning of the crowds by the
police and immediately Maud rose up to go out to her followers, but Yeats
would not let her. Showing a new authority which now, at the age of thirty-
two, he felt towards her, he ordered the doors to be locked for her safety.
He was no longer the malleable, lovesick young man he had been at their
first meeting more than eight years before. He loved her still, but now he
could and did contradict her in word and deed, for her own good, of course.
But Maud did not like being saved on the evening of the Jubilee Riots. A
few days later she wrote him a letter of stern reproof, saying that 'everyone
who remained in the club and did not go to the rescue of the people who
were batoned by the police ought to feel ashamed of themselves . . . you
made me do the most cowardly thing I have ever done in my life.'[10] She
went on to say that they could never again work together where there was
likely to be physical danger. She knew that he was not a physical coward
himself but also knew that he could become one on her behalf. The friendship (the word Maud always insisted on) still existed but on different terms.
Yeats should no longer involve himself in what she called 'the *outer* side of
politics'. That was her job.

With these new and unhappy memories now part of their relationship they went their separate ways for a while. Maud went on with her
centennial fund-raising which took her to America in the autumn, and
Yeats set off for the first of his extended summers amidst the many comforts that Lady Gregory provided at Coole. In June, whilst he enjoyed
strolling through the seven woods that were part of the great estate,
Lawrence and Bullen in London published a limited edition of three
stories, 'Rosa Alchemica', 'The Tables of the Law' and 'The Adoration of
the Magi'. The last of these is the story of a pagan rather than a Christian
nativity. (Lawrence and Bullen insisted on a limited edition for fear that
ordinary publication might invite charges of blasphemy.) It is also a story
in which Michael Robartes figures, one of the several fictional characters
Yeats created at this time who would recur in his writings for years to
come. In the story 'Rosa Alchemica', a highly wrought piece of *symboliste*
prose, Michael Robartes is introduced as the great pagan magician with
'wild red hair, fierce eyes, sensitive tremulous lips and rough clothes' who
is 'something between a debauchee, a saint and a peasant'.[11] He and the

first-person teller of the tale have known each other in their student days in Paris. This story, like the two others in the volume, refers back to Paris and to Yeats's own intellectual experiences there. The narrator of 'Rosa Alchemica' is very much the world-weary connoisseur of sensations in the manner of Axël and des Esseintes in Huysmans' *A Rebours*. Michael Robartes, whose character clearly owes something to that of MacGregor Mathers, offers the narrator initiation into unfamiliar, pagan and mystical states of understanding. Possibilities first intimated in Paris begin to be developed in a temple of mysterious rites on the western coast of Ireland. But ultimately the storyteller reneges on this adventure into new spiritual consciousness and returns to the limitations of a strict Catholic orthodoxy.

Another, though different, instance of a quester is the impious Owen Aherne, the central figure of the story 'The Tables of the Law', who also recurs in Yeats's *oeuvre*. He is the passionate heretic, 'half monk, half soldier of fortune'. Like Michael Robartes he is a seeker of extremities of consciousness, but Catholic rather than pagan. His hubris leads him at last to the recognition that 'I have lost my soul because I have looked out of the eyes of the angels.' For him the human condition has come to mean the tormenting question, 'I have seen the whole, and how can I come again to believe that a part is the whole?'[12]

Like Michael Robartes, Owen Aherne is an instance of the kind of radical exploration of the possibilities of heightened consciousness that Yeats had known and prized in the work of Villiers de l'Isle-Adam, Mallarmé and other *symbolistes*. Owen Aherne subverts orthodoxy, setting out on a quest for a spiritual understanding beyond what God and His Church allow. Neither he nor Robartes is Yeats but each is a possible image of selfhood Yeats contemplated. Each offers a vision of religion larger than that proposed by Catholic Christianity. Within the spiritual and metaphysical turmoil that prevailed at the end of the nineteenth century Yeats creates and presents Robartes and Aherne as roads not followed, options vividly imagined but not finally taken up.

In this same year Yeats also published a sequence of six related short stories that create still another possible but not actual Yeatsian self. These are the *Stories of Red Hanrahan* which present an artist rather than a mystic or a religious visionary. Some years later, with Lady Gregory's help, Yeats was to excise from the first version of the stories 'that artificial, elaborate English so many of us played with in the nineties',[13] and in so doing created a masterpiece of prose. Around this time much serious fiction concerned itself with the nature of the artist, and Yeats's fifty-page work offers, within its small compass, some delicate insights into the subject. In several respects Red Hanrahan, the hedge schoolmaster, is the artist that Yeats was not. He is close to the soil and the country roads, the landscape, the weather and the people of Ireland. He is also naturally at ease with women and the lover of many of them. But there is also in the stories a Yeatsian sense of external powers impinging on human life, of the fatedness of the artist, of the female principle as problematic and of the deep sadness which is the inevitable heritage of the Irish artist. The storylines are enriched by the unobtrusive use of repetitions, rhythm and highly crafted phrasing. The stories read well as narrative but they are also endowed with dramatic force and emotional resonance by the employment of 'that simple English' which Lady Gregory 'had learned from her Galway countrymen'.[14]

During that summer at Coole in 1897 Yeats and Lady Gregory began to work seriously at their literary anthropology. Visiting peasant homes around the communities of Gort and Kiltartan they discovered a great deal about the oral tradition of storytelling in the area. The two researchers then began to collaborate on articles on Galway folklore. Yeats, undernourished and prone to colds and minor illness, grew healthier and put on a little weight, enjoying his large, comfortable bedroom at Coole and Lady Gregory's good food and wine, basking in her admiration and her enthusiasm for his work and his research. When he returned to Dublin in the late autumn and Augusta sent a food parcel after him, his gratitude burst out in his letter of thanks. 'How extraordinarily good you are – wine and all manner of biscuits and bottled fruit have just come. Nobody has ever shown me such kindness. Everybody tells me how well I am looking, and I am better than I have been for years in truth. The days at Coole passed like a dream, a dream of peace.'[15]

Congenial visitors had come to join them at Coole, including AE. He was soon, with Yeats's encouragement, to distance himself a little from the theosophists of Dublin and to become one of the organizers of a scheme developed by Horace Plunkett for co-operation among peasant farmers. AE, now engaged to be married, was fine company. Both Lady Gregory and Yeats admired his simple goodness and intense spirituality and missed him when he left. Another regular visitor was Edward Martyn from nearby Tillyra Castle. Among the three of them the idea of an Irish theatre was always under discussion. They generated an enthusiasm between themselves this summer that impelled them to action. When Yeats finally left for Dublin in late October he went with the idea of recruiting supporters for the new theatre company and of booking a theatre in which its first production might be mounted. He made some progress, but before anything could be settled negotiations with publishers and commitments to the '98 Committee required that he go yet again to London.

As 1898 began Yeats started to feel the comforting influence of Augusta Gregory on his still poorly furnished apartment in Woburn Walk. He was beginning to be able to entertain the new friends he was making. One of these was the painter William Rothenstein, who did a portrait of Yeats this year. Another was Thomas Sturge Moore, a poet and engraver, who designed the covers for some of Yeats's most important books. An intense, dedicated aesthete with a huge beard and an awkward lumbering body, Sturge Moore now began a lifelong friendship with Yeats. Lady Gregory brought Yeats things that made his apartment more comfortable. She gave him a large blue curtain for the front window, a striking piece which many of his many visitors over the years would remember. She later sent him a fine leather armchair, and once, she having returned to her *pied-à-terre*, a small suite of rooms in Queen Anne's Mansions, north of Oxford Circus, Yeats found that she had left twenty pounds tucked between the mantelpiece clock and the wall. Also the folklore articles which she helped him to produce could command ten or fifteen pounds each from the monthly reviews. At long last his financial difficulties were easing.

He was not only making more money from his writing but, above all, had become the recipient of generous patronage both in money and kind. In literary history Augusta Gregory's enduring support of Yeats compares in importance with that given to James Joyce by Harriet Shaw Weaver.

Modernist literature was in considerable part a literature of patronage rather than of the market-place. And it was a patronage undertaken by women just beginning to experience economic and personal independence. Yeats, like Joyce after him, pursued his career sustained by female feeling, understanding and financial generosity.

One of the first fruits of this patronage was the founding of the Irish Literary Theatre. In March Yeats returned to Dublin to see about renting one of the commercial theatres in the city. When it proved difficult to obtain the use of a major house such as the Gaiety, he looked about for other rooms in which the new company might perform. But first he needed a theatre licence from the Lord Chancellor's Office in London. Established Dublin theatres opposed his application, regarding it as a threat to their own box office. Yeats, therefore, had to work hard as a lobbyist in order to obtain the necessary licence. Preparations for the great Irish anniversary of 1898 also involved him in much toing and froing between Dublin and London this year. And in the spring he was once again in Paris. Increasingly he was a man of three cities.

On this visit to the French capital he stayed again with the Mathers, who had moved out to Auteuil, west of the Bois de Boulogne. Though the little country place still had some vineyards, it was being transformed into a suburb embellished by the great art nouveau block of flats known as the Castel Beranger. One of the crazes of the decade was bicycling, and the lanky, bespectacled Irish poet in the loose black suit with a large floppy tie had great pleasure pedalling his way among the trees of the Bois, now coming into blossom. A main aim of his visit was, of course, to see Maud, but she was suffering badly from bronchitis and looked ill and tired. She was so weakened that for once she had to curtail her political activities. But she did manage to travel out to Auteuil in order 'to see visions' with Yeats. William Sharp wrote to say that there was a chance that Miss Fiona Macleod might come to this occasion. But she did not.

Then both Yeats and the ailing Maud had to be off to London and thence to Dublin to help finalize the arrangements for the '98 centennial celebrations. They planned on arrival to go to the prehistoric site of Newgrange to collect sacred earth with which to evoke the forms of gods and spirits of Ireland, but at the last moment Maud found she had too many commitments and as on numerous other occasions stood Yeats up. Then at a demonstration in Dublin Maud was thrown from a horse-drawn wagon on which she was to address the crowd. Her arm was broken and her face bruised and scratched. Yeats, who had made arrangements to go on to Coole, remained with her, fussing and worrying a great deal. It concerned him that Maud was so self-reliant that she would allow no one to tend her, but in the end she allowed herself to be taken in by the kindly, practical Sarah Purser and belatedly Yeats was able to go on and join Lady Gregory.

By early August Yeats was back in London for the celebration of the centennial of Wolfe Tone and the French expedition to liberate Ireland. There was a banquet at Frascati's restaurant in Soho on 9 August, and a meeting the following day at St Martin's Hall, at which Maud Gonne made the main speech, with Yeats acting as her chairman. She denounced the British Empire from the very centre of its capital city. In under a week they were back in Dublin for the noisy and successful celebrations there. Yeats and Maud Gonne were joined on the platform by leading members of the different factions of the Irish parliamentary party at Westminster.

Things quietened down at last when, once again, Yeats arrived in Sligo to spend some time with Uncle George. With age his uncle was becoming less cantankerous, but he was irritated when he took his nephew to a Masonic concert in Sligo and Willie hissed a performer who did a 'stage Irishman' act. Yeats's passion for the cause was also stimulated by two gifts from Maud Gonne. She had finally gone to Newgrange without him, and now sent him some earth from the ancient site and water from the River Boyne flowing nearby, urging him to try some experiments with them. She thought that if he touched his lips, ears and eyes and breast with them, they would bring him special dreams. Yeats's preoccupation with the Celtic next prompted him to engage in an exchange with his former schoolmate W.K. Magee, who published under the name of John Eglinton. In the press Magee had asked the question 'What should be the subject of a National Drama?' Yeats, keen as ever to publicize himself and his cause, responded forcefully. He also thought that such polemics would be a useful preface to the formal announcement of the founding of the Irish Literary Theatre.

He, Edward Martyn and Augusta Gregory had decided that this should take place in December.

From Paris Maud wrote to say that she would be back in Ireland very soon; she wondered 'where we can see each other and talk over the things which interest us'.[16] Yeats immediately left for Dublin, and while awaiting her arrival, he worked at setting up the first production at the new theatre. This was to be a dual offering made up of his own play *The Countess Kathleen* and Edward Martyn's *The Heather Field*. The coming opening caused some excitement in Dublin society. *Tableaux vivants* or still-life representations of certain climactic moments in plays were very fashionable in high society at this time, and Lady Balfour, a prominent member of Castle society, took it upon herself to plan *tableaux* from *The Countess Kathleen*. Interest in the forthcoming productions was further spiced by the rumour going about Dublin that Catholics would find Yeats's play heretical.

As Yeats assumed the role of theatre impresario, and waited for Maud, he had a most exciting dream: he dreamt that he kissed her on the lips. When Maud crossed over to Ireland and he told of her of this, she told him, as she had often done before, of a dream of her own on the same night as his dream: that she had left her body and been carried off by the Celtic god Lugh who had clapsed her hand and declared them married. After Maud had recounted this dream to Yeats, she did something entirely unexpected. She moved towards him and for the first time she kissed him.[17] After nearly ten years their relationship had seemingly become something other than friendship.

The following day Maud regretted her impulse. She apologized to him, said she could never be his wife in a physical sense, and began to tell him about Lucien Millevoye and some of the events in her life which she had kept secret from him all these years. Millevoye still needed and depended upon her but they no longer lived together. After she had become his mistress, sexual love soon began to repel her. She would never marry Lucien or indeed anyone for she was horrified by and afraid of physical love.[18] She grew upset as she talked on. It would seem that her upset on this day and the following days was to some extent caused by Yeats's response. Yeats, having been kissed on the lips by her the previous day, was now confounded by Maud's 'pathetically plain sexual overtures'.[19] He had sustained two major shocks. First, 'The Rose of the World' had acknowledged a twelve-year career as the mistress of a middle-aged, married French politician. Second, the woman he had assumed to be a virgin, to whom 'with reverent hands' he had brought the books of his 'numberless dreams', now revealed herself as the mother of two illegitimate children, one of them, her daughter the five-year-old Iseult, living. Maud suddenly became to Yeats a daunting female.

Maud finally decided that she should go back to Iseult in Paris, even though she was worried about the turmoil in France as the Dreyfus case approached one of its several climaxes. Zola, the great champion of Dreyfus and author of *J'Accuse*, had felt it necessary to flee to England. What was virtually a Fascist party, the Action Française, had grown up overnight. The Republic again appeared to be tottering. Maud was distraught as she left Dublin for France.

There now began for Yeats a period in which he was 'tortured by sexual desire and disappointed love'.[20] The Maud he had loved was an illusion, but still he loved her. How could he propose marriage and thus become the stepfather of a five-year-old child, a family man? His memories of family life were not happy ones. Even so it was impossible for him to forget Maud. He was in torment. He later remembered that never in his life, either before or after, had he been so miserable and upset as then. Since Olivia Shakespear had left him he had had no shared sexual experience. And now his emotional and sexual frustration with Maud and his guilt about his occasional masturbation made him physically ill. He clearly came close to a breakdown. The act of getting dressed in the morning was enough to exhaust him. At Coole an anxious Lady Gregory sent up cups of soup immediately after he was awakened. Maud and Lady Gregory had met and talked in Dublin earlier in the year and Yeats's patroness had not liked what Yeats's beloved had said of him. To her friend Lady Layard in Venice Augusta Gregory wrote of Maud, 'I am afraid she is only playing with him, from selfishness and vanity.' She added, 'I don't wish her any harm, but God is unjust if she dies a quiet death.'[21]

Yeats spent time at Thornhill to recuperate from his emotional crisis and to recover physically from general weakness and a series of heavy colds.

At last, this Christmas, he had the money to send a present to each of his sisters. He could also have his life enriched by that 'mine of fairy lore', his Uncle George's servant Mary Battle. He told Lady Gregory that Mary 'is really a kind of saint and is supremely happy'.[22] Yeats also talked less guardedly to his uncle these days. As he told him about the startling occasion of Maud's kiss and his subsequent disillusionment, uncertainty and misery, his uncle began to encourage him to see this recent development as something that held promise. The old man finally urged him to go back to Maud, to take the initiative and reopen the issue with her. As 1899 began Yeats finally made up his mind to go again to Paris and persuade Maud Gonne to become his wife.

He was there by the last day of January and settled into a cheap hotel at the sourthern end of the boulevard Raspail, close to the Montparnasse Cemetery. The Dreyfus affair continued to embitter and destabilize French society. But Paris also had new charms to offer. There were the art nouveau entrances to the Métro just now being completed, designed by Hector Guimard. And in this year in which Bergson published his book entitled Laughter, a great hit in the Paris theatre was the exuberant French farce La Dame de Chèz Maxim, by the master of comedy Gustave Feydeau. But for Yeats his fourth stay in Paris brought little pleasure. When he arrived there Maud made no difficulties, inviting him to come to the rue d'Eylau. But her mood was markedly different from what it had been in December. She was cold and distant and the great intiative pondered and decided upon with his Uncle George got nowhere: Maud rejected his proposal of marriage. He reported to his confidante Lady Gregory, 'I have had rather a depressing time here.'[23] But Maud did continue the story of her secret life that she had begun relating to him in Dublin. For all his disappointment, Yeats felt for her: 'I do not wonder that she shrinks from life,' he wrote to Coole. Maud's life had 'been in part the war of phantasy and of blinded idealism against eternal law'.[24] At the same time, the things he had learned lately made his long-enduring love for Maud 'the bitterer, and the harder'.

He and Maud planned to cross the Channel together, but then Maud discovered that she had to stay in Paris. So after a brief meeting with John Synge, who was now learning the Breton language, Yeats set off, defeated and demoralized, back to London on his own. Here a letter informed him that AE and his wife, despite having what Yeats called an 'aerial Theosophic marriage',[25] now had a baby son. After the trip to Paris, Yeats had no money, so wrote to Uncle George in Sligo asking for a loan of seven pounds, but said little of his disappointment. However at Thornhill the old man, racked by headaches and depression, became even more cast down as he sensed what had happened. 'I was in hopes,' he wrote, 'but suppose affairs did not culminate favourably.'[26]

Rehearsals were to begin very soon for the first season of the Irish Literary Theatre under the direction of the actress Florence Farr, Yeats's old friend from Bedford Park. It had been agreed that professional actors should be cast for the parts in London and that the rehearsals should also take place there. The company would only go over to Dublin shortly before the first night, scheduled to take place early in May. All went well until the fastidious, unworldly Edward Martyn made the mistake of inviting his cousin George Moore to one of the rehearsals of Martyn's play *The Heather Field*. Loud and overbearing as ever, George Moore made it abundantly plain that he did not like the performance of a Dublin actor who had been given a leading part. Moore's interruptions and sneers so outraged the actor that he kicked chairs around the stage. He also swore at Moore, and the prompter threatened to use physical force to evict him if he persisted with such foul language in front of Florence Farr and the other ladies in the production. George Moore's career as a maker of strife in the Irish Literary Theatre had begun.

But then the first production faced a more serious crisis. *The Countess Kathleen* continued to be talked about as a heretical work. An old enemy of Maud Gonne and thus of Yeats, Frank Hugh O'Donnell (whom Yeats called 'the mad rogue'), published an article in the *Freeman's Journal* developing this charge. He then wrote a further piece along similar lines, made the two into a pamphlet and distributed it into letterboxes all over Dublin. Such malice added greatly to Yeats's fame and notoriety. The elderly Cardinal Michael Logue, who had not read the script, published a letter saying that if the charges against the play were valid, no Catholic should attend its performance. Edward Martyn, whose money largely funded the production, was a devout Catholic, and under no circumstances would he allow himself to be implicated in heresy. Yeats became extremely anxious.

He wrote to Martyn at Tillyra Castle offering to excise or rewrite any offensive passages. He asked that his text be submitted to the judgement of qualified theologians with some literary understanding. Martyn, a student and devotee of that most ascetic of saints St John Chrysostom, responded with peremptory bullying letters that show his fright at the accusations of heresy. George Moore, gleeful and delighted as always at his cousin's discomfort and doing his best to aggravate it, planned to write an essay on the controversy entitled 'The Soul of Edward Martyn'.

Finally, however, with some ill humour Martyn allowed himself to be reassured about the play and did not withdraw his financial support. So at the beginning of the second week in May the two plays had their first night in the Ancient Concert Rooms in present-day Pearse Street. Yeats, remembering the Jubilee Riots a couple of years before, asked for police protection. Some twenty officers duly appeared for the opening, but everything passed off quietly; the opposition stayed away. He was not sure how to rate the success of *The Countess Kathleen* on the stage. However, one thing was absolutely sure: the companion piece on the double bill, Edward Martyn's *The Heather Field*, enjoyed an excellent reception.

Martyn was very pleased with himself. When the few weeks of this first season of the Irish Literary Theatre ended, and he, Yeats and Lady Gregory returned to the west of Ireland, he immediately set about writing another play, *The Tale of a Town*. When the manuscript was sent over to Yeats and Augusta Gregory at Coole, neither of them could admire it or think it worthy of production. But George Moore confidently took over the manuscript and said he would improve it. While Moore stayed at Tillyra doing the rewriting, he became angry that his cousin absolutely insisted that he accompany him to Mass. This meant going to a distant church because the local priest had been caricatured by Moore in a novel and had promised to have the notorious womanizer thrown into the village duckpond if he ever dared to show his face.

All this amused Yeats as he spent an otherwise quiet summer at Coole, ministered to by Lady Gregory. He continued to work on *The Shadowy Waters* and in the autumn entered into a collaboration with Moore on a play about the love story of the legendary Irish figures Diarmid and Grania. In the future there would be a great falling out between Yeats and the over-

bearing George Moore, who 'lacked manners but had manner',[27] but at the
moment Yeats was extremely pleased with what they had written together.
The first draft, he told his sister Lily, had 'a very powerful plot and arrangement of scenes. It will be a wonderful part for a great actress if she can be
found.'[28]

Yeats left Coole briefly for a subdued meeting with Maud who was also
in the west of Ireland, campaigning against evictions. And when the Boers
of South Africa went to war with the British Empire in the September of
1899 she immediately set out on another campaign to dissuade Irishmen
from enlisting in the British army. In October she and Yeats went on a historical and spiritual pilgrimage together. They met in Belfast and climbed
Cave Hill, which is topped by a prehistoric fort where Wolfe Tone, the
hero of 1798, had founded the freedom movement known as the United
Irishmen. Then Maud went back to the courthouse at Ballina to assist in
the eviction cases.

When Yeats finally returned to London in mid-November he crossed
the Irish Sea with Maud, who went on immediately to Paris, to Iseult and
to her political concerns in France. As Yeats picked up his social life in
London the Puritan in him was shocked to see what he regarded as the
scandalous behaviour of Althea Gyles, the artist who had been his fellow-
student at the Metropolitan Art School in Dublin. He was quick to share
with Lady Gregory the full story of how Althea had 'taken up' with the
pornographer Leonard Smithers and was 'throwing off every remnant of
respectability with an almost religious enthusiasm . . . She gave an at home
the other day and poured out tea with his arm around her waist and even
kissed him at intervals. I told her that she might come to my "at homes" as
much as she liked but that I absolutely forbade her to bring Smithers.'[29]
But to another scandalous figure Yeats was more accommodating. His
admiration for George Moore, the francophile who dressed like the Mayo
country gentleman that he was, continued to increase. He considered
Moore's rewriting of Martyn's *Tale of a Town* to be 'extraordinarily fine'.
Commending the piece to Lady Gregory, Yeats told her, 'It is now a splendid and intricate gospel of nationality and may be almost epoch-making in
Ireland.' George Moore finally took the play out of his cousin's hands, retitled it *The Bending of the Bough* and had it produced at the Gaiety Theatre

in Dublin a couple of months after Yeats's return to London. In the billing
the contributions of Yeats and Martyn were not mentioned. Moore's name
alone appeared as the author.

But at this time practical problems rather than literary ones took prece-
dence for Yeats. Life in the apartment in Woburn Buildings was none too
comfortable in December, despite the food parcels and bottles of port
which Lady Gregory at Coole arranged to have delivered to him. Mrs Old,
the middle-aged housekeeper and cook who 'did' for Yeats, made it clear
that she wanted a number of days off over Christmas. Yeats was incapable
of fending for himself so he had to look about for somewhere else to stay.
He finally had to settle for spending the holiday with his family in Bedford
Park. It proved to be the last Christmas that they would see as a complete
family.

$$\left[\mathit{1900}-\mathit{1901}\right]$$

EARLY ON THE THIRD MORNING OF 1900, AFTER SPENDING AN evening with his father at the home of George Moore, Yeats was awakened to be told that his mother was having serious difficulty with her breathing. Not long after, with her husband and her elder son at her bedside, Susan Pollexfen Yeats died. There had been no indication that she was close to death and her two daughters were away from home. Lolly was in Germany with an older woman friend on a sketching holiday paid for by her earnings as a Froebel teacher and by the royalties from her three little books on brushwork technique in painting. Lily, no longer an embroideress for May Morris, was in Sligo dealing with family matters: violent, brutal Uncle Frederick Pollexfen had been divorced and his daughter Ruth had been placed by the court into the custody of her cousin Lily Yeats. It was thus only the male members of Susan's family who, three days after her death, attended the burial of the daughter of the great house of Merville in the cemetery in the raw Victorian suburb of Acton. The family had to club together to pay the three pounds and eight shillings for Susan's grave plot. Her young son Jack was greatly upset by his mother's death and ceased painting for some months. But her elder son was less affected. His mother, whose mental and physical activities had been greatly curtailed by her second stroke some twelve years earlier, was never a force in his life in the way that the mothers of George Bernard Shaw or D.H. Lawrence were. To all the members of the family she was completely undemonstrative. Her husband once recalled in a letter to his elder son that 'I often said to your mother that her affection was a matter that one *inferred*. No one ever saw it or heard it speak.'[1] In later years Lily, remarking that her mother was 'not at all good at housekeeping and childminding', agreed that 'She was prim and austere, suffered all in silence. She asked no sympathy and gave none.'[2]

Remembering her death eight years later, Yeats wrote that 'My mother was so long ill, so long fading out of life, that the last fading out of all made no noticeable change in our lives.'[3] Immediately after the funeral Yeats returned to Bloomsbury and his involvement with Augusta Gregory. Thirteen years older than he, and thus not quite old enough to have been his mother, Augusta nonetheless had mothered him far more than Susan had done. They had afternoon tea together, and dinner together, and planned the second season of the Irish Literary Theatre. One of their concerns was a magazine which the organization now published from time to time. It bore the title *Beltaine* – meaning in Gaelic, the Spring Festival – and Yeats carried chief editorial responsibility. A year or so later he began a successor magazine under the title *Samhain*, the Festival of Harvest. As Yeats and Lady Gregory considered what should be included in their theatre's magazine, they also discussed problems with the organization. They pondered what they would do if Edward Martyn carried out his renewed threat to withdraw support from the coming season, and awaited in some anxiety the consequences of another terrible quarrel between Martyn and George Moore over *The Bending of the Bough*.

Within Ireland at large there blew up another bitter row early that year. It was caused by the announcement from Buckingham Palace that the 81-year-old Queen Victoria was to pay a visit to Dublin. The British government maintained that this was to commemorate the hundredth anniversary of the creation of the Union. To Irish nationalists such a celebration was offensive enough; but they also saw it as an attempt by the imperial government and its Irish Unionist supporters to promote the recruitment of troops in Ireland to oppress the rebellious Boers of South Africa. Yeats and George Moore both published strong letters of protest in the press. In Paris Maud Gonne assisted the campaign by bringing out a special 'Queen's Visit' issue of her magazine *L'Irlande Libre*. Though seriously ill with enteritis Maud also made plans to travel to Ireland to join the protest meetings and to boost support for the Boers in their struggle against the British.

One object of fervent nationalist admiration at this moment was the Irish Brigade, which had been formed by Irishmen in South Africa to fight alongside the Boer farmers against the troops of the British Empire, some of whom were Irish. The founder of the Brigade, and soon a popular hero of nationalist Ireland, was 32-year-old John MacBride. A member of the Irish Republican Brotherhood and a follower of John O'Leary, MacBride had left Ireland in his early twenties to become an assayer in the gold-mines near Johannesburg. Here he met a compatriot, the young journalist and radical nationalist Arthur Griffith, and together they organized '98 clubs in South Africa. After the Boers went to war against the British, MacBride immediately offered his services and was commissioned a major in the Afrikaner army by the leader of the newly proclaimed Boer state, President Kruger. When news of Major MacBride's exploits with the Boer commandos reached Ireland, his name immediately became a rallying cry for the nationalists. Writing to Maud Gonne, Yeats enthusiastically suggested that in the next general election Major MacBride should be nominated to contest one of the Dublin constituencies.

During this time, Yeats in London suddenly found himself distracted from politics by a painful personal conflict concerning the Order of the Golden Dawn. MacGregor Mathers now had as his closest associate in Paris a bullet-headed young man with a strikingly cruel mouth called Aleister Crowley. Energetically bisexual, as well as sadistic, Crowley's subsequent garish career as an occultist and satanist would show him to be a crook and an exploiter, chiefly of women. But Mathers greatly admired the young man and requested that he be initiated into the London branch of the Golden Dawn, which was known as the Isis-Urania Temple. Yeats considered Crowley, who used dozens of false names and who was wanted for debt, to be 'a mad person', 'a person of unspeakable life', and in agreement with other members of the London branch declined to initiate him. This refusal came at a time when Mathers was angered by what he thought was a schism within the London group created by Florence Farr. He also alleged that one of his co-founders of the Golden Dawn, Dr Wynn Westcott, Queen's Coroner for north-east London, had forged certain of the texts on which the Order was based. Instead of responding to Mathers directly and immediately, Yeats, Florence Farr and four other members of Isis-Urania set up a committee to investigate their leader's accusations.

When they decided to suspend Mathers from the London branch, he was infuriated. He ordered Crowley to go immediately to the Golden Dawn premises in London, dingy rooms painted with mystic signs in a basement under a building on Clipstone Street not far from Fitzroy Square. Crowley was to take possession of both the rented rooms and the documents they contained. Yeats and his supporters confronted Crowley at the door and forced him to leave. But Crowley returned, dressed up in the style of Mathers himself, in full Highland costume with a silver dagger in his stocking top. Again they managed to make him go, whereupon he went to law and took out a summons for the recovery of the papers and the property. These events and the prospect of a court action worried Yeats a great deal. He also felt it necessary to patrol the area around the headquarters of the Golden Dawn for fear Crowley might try to break in. For several nights in succession Yeats, more and more worked up, got very little sleep. Finally Crowley withdrew his suit and paid money towards the legal costs of Yeats and his friends, who had retained the son of the Lord Chief Justice to represent them.

Clearly Yeats felt a keen personal antipathy towards Crowley and regarded the struggle with him as an important spiritual battle. The near-hysterical upset, sleeplessness and worry was the price that had to be paid to prevent 'the whole system of teaching' of the Golden Dawn from being ruined. This system, he claimed in tones of aggressive sentimentality, he must defend in the interests of old friends and especially his Uncle George in Sligo. To such people the hierarchical system of the Golden Dawn was the only basis for a religious life. If it had been perverted by Crowley's evil influence, they would have experienced 'a great grief'. So Yeats fought, and finally won, showing the mystic and dreamer had his hard, obstreperous side. Crowley in defeat settled for making wax images of the Yeats group and sticking pins into them. In Paris Mathers is reported to have taken dried peas and baptized each one with the magical name of a London rebel. Then shaking the peas together in a sieve, he called up Beelzebub to make his enemies fall upon each other and argue and fight.[4] Unaware of this, Yeats set off for his summer at Coole, reassured that the London branch was now fully independent and had a new organization in which Yeats and his friends Florence Farr and Annie Horniman (whom he had helped readmit to the Order) had considerable influence. But the new-found harmony within the Order was not to last long; the dried pea treatment seems to have worked.

Summer at Coole was again a pleasure and a recuperation from these exhausting exertions. Maud Gonne, though, was much on his mind; he worried about her involvement with wild radical members of the national-ist cause. When he wrote telling her again of his desire to protect her, she replied that she could not accept protection from anyone, though she fully understood the generous and unselfish thoughts behind his offer. Later in the year Maud and other Irish nationalists in France were excited to meet the heroic Major John MacBride on his triumphant arrival in Paris from South Africa in the company of President Kruger. There was a grand occasion in the state reception room of the Hôtel Seine at which the 70-year-old John O'Leary, speaking in fluent French, presented the Boer President with an illuminated address written in Irish, Dutch, French and English. Later that year Maud would travel to Ireland to receive the freedom of the City of Limerick, and to lecture on Major MacBride and the achievements of the Irish Brigade in South Africa.

In mid-October Yeats returned to London where he continued to collaborate with George Moore on their play about Diarmuid and Grania. But as the year drew to its end there were signs of strain in the relationship. At one point Moore asked Yeats to accept Arthur Symons as umpire and mediator in the literary disagreements between them. Nevertheless by the New Year they had a script to show around among the theatre companies of London. They had hopes that the flamboyant and successful actress Mrs Patrick Campbell might decide to do their play. But in the end it was the Benson Company, which also enjoyed great prestige in the English theatre at the turn of the century, which took it up. At this time Frank Benson and his wife Constance and their troupe were not confined to the West End; they were also responsible for the Shakespeare season at Stratford-upon-Avon. And in the spring of 1901 they invited Yeats up to the redbrick Gothic theatre beside the river to attend their productions. Their new dramatist saw all the Shakespeare history plays from *King John* to *Richard*

III performed in chronological order. They made a strong impression upon him. He wrote that in Stratford the theatre had moved him more than ever before. He had been almost overwhelmed by the vivid evocation of an extended period of history and the people who had played a part in it.[5]

The year 1901 was one of memorable theatre-going, productions and performances. Yeats also now began to introduce a performance element into his poetry. One of his growing band of devotees, the future poet laureate John Masefield, frequently attended these performances of poetry. He later wrote:

> *I often heard Yeats's method. It is not easy to describe; it would not be easy to imitate; probably it influenced all who heard it either for or against. It put great (many thought too great) yet always a subtle insistence upon the rhythm; it dwelt upon the vowels and the beat. In Lyric, it tended ever towards what seemed like Indian singing; in other measures towards an almost fierce recitativo. When reading or reciting verse to a friend, he was frequently dissatisfied with the rendering of a line. He would then say, 'no, no' and would repeat the faulty line with a more delicate rhythm, helping it to perfection with the gestures of his (most strangely beautiful) hands.*[6]

With Florence Farr, famed for the beauty of her voice, Yeats began to develop still further a theory and a practice of chanting poetry for an audience. It was an attempt to resuscitate the art form of poetry as performance, as it might have been experienced prior to its transmission through manuscripts and printed books. Poetry as an aesthetic experience should, Yeats believed, become public again rather than private. At first, Florence Farr and a fellow performer Anna Mather were accompanied by a harp or a piano. But the enterprise developed further when Yeats and Florence attended a concert given by Arnold Dolmetsch and were afterwards introduced to him. A dedicated musician and a maker and repairer of musical instruments, Dolmetsch had been born in France of Swiss parents. He had begun to study music in Brussels and then had come to London where he became a student at the Royal College of Music. Passionately interested in the revival of early English music and a pioneer in employing proper period instruments, he would go on to establish a workshop for the repair and manufacture of harpsichords, viols, recorders and lutes. When Yeats and

Florence Farr first talked to him about the relationship between poetry and music and their 'chanting', Dolmetsch was intrigued by their ideas and proceeded to design a special instrument with which to accompany the chanting. This was a version of the medieval psaltery; it was shaped like a lyre, was made of satinwood and had metal strings. For the next few years Yeats and Florence Farr would use this instrument to contribute to many a literary occasion in Edwardian London.

Towards the middle of the decade, as Florence approached fifty, the two old friends also began an affair. But Florence, as Yeats later recalled, 'got bored' and they returned to a relationship based on their poetic theory and performance. Yeats would open the proceedings with some remarks about this new, or renewed, art form and then Florence, in flowing robes, would gently caress and pluck the strings and chant poems in a voice just a little lower than her singing voice. The first of such performances took place at the Fellowship of the Three Kings, a new and predominantly Irish literary club which Yeats organized after the gradual dispersal of the Rhymers. The new club, like Yeats himself, had moved up in the world; it met in a pub in fashionable Mayfair not far from Claridge's Hotel.

Only a month or two after he met Arnold Dolmetsch, Yeats encountered someone else who also enlarged his ideas about the potential of theatre. On a Saturday afternoon at the end of March Yeats set off to attend a production of Purcell's opera *Dido and Aeneas* at the Coronet Theatre in Notting Hill Gate. He had for a long time given much thought to the question of appropriate scenery, lighting and costumes for his *symboliste* drama, and was overwhelmed by what he saw at this matinée. Unlike the ornate, lavish stage furnishing that was the convention in late Victorian theatre, the set designed for Purcell's baroque masterpiece by Edward Gordon Craig was arrestingly simple, even stark. Yeats enthused to Lady Gregory, that it was the best scenery he had ever seen and that it realized an idea he had long had. He described for her the strange effect of purple robed figures against a purple backcloth.[7] Yeats went home to Bloomsbury full of excitement. He wrote to a friend who knew the designer and asked him to forward a note of congratulation and admiration. Resolving initially to write an article on the amazing stage set, Yeats then decided he simply had to meet Craig, so he wrote to him directly and invited him to dinner.

Craig, some seven years younger than Yeats, was the illegitimate son of Edward Godwin, the architect of Whistler's house and interior designer of Oscar Wilde's house in Chelsea, but also himself a theatrical designer. His mother was Ellen Terry, one of the great stage stars of the second half of the nineteenth century, the leading lady opposite Sir Henry Irving in his opulent productions of Shakespeare at the Lyceum Theatre in the Strand. She had then taken leading roles in the plays of her friend of late years, George Bernard Shaw. Gordon Craig himself had first appeared on the stage at the age of six. All of his long life was to be dedicated to the theatre, but when Yeats first met him he was only beginning to make his name. Yeats was keen to get him to work for the Irish Literary Theatre in its approaching third season. And, unremittingly attentive to money matters as usual, Yeats saw in this possibility a financial snip. Having Gordon Craig, he told Lady Gregory, would attract a lot of attention since it would be the first time that the ordinary theatre had undertaken anything so new. The cost might be no more than for other scenery, since Gordon Craig had his name to make and might work cheap.[8]

That summer at Coole Yeats worked on a new play which he contemplated making available for the third season. This was the piece which he eventually entitled *On Baile's Strand*. It shows a marked development over *The Shadowy Waters* in Yeats's dramatic writing. In this play the lush incantatory language of the dream vision reminiscent of Villiers de l'Isle-Adam now gives way to a language that articulates homely psychological realities in the legendary conflict between the two kings Cuchulain and Conchubar. A poetic drama, *Baile's Strand* also contains prose passages spoken by the Fool and the Blind Man. In none of Yeats's earlier dramas had there appeared such lowly characters using down-to-earth language. This play began a trend that was to continue in Yeats's art throughout this new decade, a movement away from the preoccupation with inwardness and dream towards the formulation of larger, external realities. A long poem he wrote at Coole this same summer about two lovers, 'Baile and Aillinn', looks back to the 1890s and to *Axël*, concluding as it does with an affirmation of love in a world other than this: '. . . for never yet / Has lover lived, but longed to wive / Like them that are no more alive.' But *Baile's Strand* is the first product of the Yeats of the Edwardian decade, the writer who is newly aware of the practicalities of running a theatre, of appealing to audiences and of putting his artistic preoccupations – love, mysticism, Ireland – in a distinctly public context.

Another more realistic play written this summer was a collaboration with Lady Gregory entitled *Cathleen ni Houlihan*. It was based on a dream Yeats had and which he related to Lady Gregory. She wrote the dialogue, he wrote chants for the heroine and allowed his name to appear as that of the sole author. Patroness and poet also tried their hands at comedy, working together on *The Pot of Broth*, a light piece about the gullibility of the Irish peasantry.

In the July in which Yeats began this new type of play Maud Gonne was back from a fund-raising tour of the United States, exhausted. She treated herself to a favourite theatrical experience by going to Bayreuth to attend *Parsifal*, Wagner's final statement about transcendental love. In an enthusiastic letter she told Yeats that 'It did me more good than I can tell', it was 'worth travelling round the whole world to hear'.[9] Not long after this the two of them were able to share another memorable evening in the theatre. For by the time the Yeats–Moore collaboration *Diarmuid and Grania* was first performed in Dublin, Maud had arrived in the city and attended the opening night with Yeats. The occasion pulsated with patriotic feeling. Yeats's co-author, George Moore, was nervously excited. Just a few months before, a still small voice, as he relates in his volume of autobiography *Ave*, had prompted him to abandon England because of the brutal war against the Boers. So he had taken the difficult step of leaving his home in London and committing himself to Ireland by coming to live in Ely Place in Dublin. *Diarmuid and Grania* was a script designed to promote the Irish cultural cause to which the once cosmopolitan Moore had now determined to dedicate himself.

The Bensons' performances were excellent and there was some fine incidental music. For though Edward Martyn refused to spend his money on employing Gordon Craig, he did allow the promising English composer Edward Elgar to be retained for the musical side of the production. The company had looked for an Irish composer, but without success. So they settled for the imperialist composer who in this same year produced the first two of his *Pomp and Circumstance* marches. But Elgar showed great sensitivity to this Irish play. Yeats later wrote admiringly of the heroic melancholy of Elgar's incidental music and hoped that the composer would set other texts of his.[10] For years the notes of the horn in Elgar's dirge for the dead Diarmuid would remain in Yeats's memory. So too would the wild enthusiasm of those watching the play from the gallery. After the performance had ended and Yeats and Maud Gonne mounted into a cab to go to a first night supper-party, excited members of the audience started to unharness the horse from the shafts so that they might themselves drag these two great figures in the Irish cause to their destination – such was the celebrity and acclaim enjoyed by Maud Gonne and Yeats in Dublin in their mid-thirties. But Maud, still weary from her American tour, appealed to their noisy admirers to let the cab proceed.

This was a time of great excitement and activity in Dublin theatre generally, where two of the leading figures were the brothers Frank and William Fay. A few years younger than Yeats, they were the sons of a lowly government official who sent Frank to work for a firm of accountants. But Frank Fay, like his brother, was thoroughly and incurably stagestruck. They founded an amateur dramatic group which they called the Ormond Drama Company after the street in which they lived. William then started getting small professional parts in various Dublin theatres and Frank became theatre reviewer for Arthur Griffith's nationalist newspaper, the *United Irishman*. He reviewed a performance of *The Land of Heart's Desire* and thus began a correspondence about Irish theatre with Yeats. In August, a night or two before *Diarmuid and Grania* was produced, Yeats saw the Fay brothers acting and was overwhelmed by their talent. He said that he 'came away with my head on fire'. AE, also caught up in the current enthusiasm for the theatre, completed his play on an Irish theme, *Deidre*, for the Fays and their associates to perform. AE and Frank and William Fay were interested, too, in *Cathleen ni Houlihan* and asked if they might produce it. But Yeats, always circumspect in his literary business dealings and unsure of his future in the theatre now that the three years' experiment of the Irish Literary Theatre was completed, withheld his agreement and pondered what he should do.

Back in London in November Yeats used the resources of the British Museum to complete his more ambitious play *On Baile's Strand*. He wrote essays for an extended and revised edition of *The Celtic Twilight*. He also entertained a good deal in his Woburn Buildings apartment. This was the time when his 'Mondays' began. On Monday evenings he was at home to his friends and their friends from eight until two or three in the morning, and his rooms soon became one of the major literary centres of London. John Masefield later remembered, in free verse, those who came.

> *The writers and the painters and the speakers,*
> *The occultists, the visionary women.*
> *Astrologers with Saturn on their moons,*
> *And contemplative men who lived on herbs*
> *And uttered gentleness and sanctity,*
> *The poets of the half-a-dozen schools,*
> *Young men in cloaks, velvet, or evening dress;*
> *Publishers, publicists and journalists,*
> *Parliament men, who served the Irish cause,*
> *And every Irish writer, painter and thinker.*[11]

That November of 1901, Masefield, the young sailor-poet, had paid the first of many visits to Woburn Buildings and was entertained to a dinner of stewed steak and apple pie cooked and served by Mrs Old, whom Yeats would summon to table by striking an unusual oriental gong.

Their table talk was of the prose romances of William Morris and of the decade now ending. Yeats did an impromptu parody of Maeterlinck. He also spoke of Villiers de l'Isle-Adam and praised his three-scene play *La Révolte*, which had been revived at the Théâtre Antoine in Paris the previous year. This domestic tragedy constituted a powerful statement of the superiority of a wife's world of dream over her husband's dedication to bourgeois reality. Offending the conventionally minded in Paris and provoking polemics, *La Révolte* had attracted the support of writers such as Alexandre Dumas fils, Lecomte de Lisle and Théophile Gautier and composers such as Franz Liszt and Richard Wagner.

Yeats's sitting-room, the 22-year-old Masefield thought, was 'the most interesting room in London'. It was covered with brown wallpaper and hung with drawings by John Yeats and with Blake engravings, including the first Dante engraving, *The Whirlwind of Lovers*. There was also on the wall behind the tall dark settle Aubrey Beardsley's poster for the Florence Farr production of *The Land of Heart's Desire* of six years before, as well as pastels done by Yeats himself of the hills and lake near Coole.

Amidst all his London activities Yeats kept Coole and Lady Gregory very much in mind. He helped her with the publication of what was her first work deriving from their friendship and literary activities together, a collection of folk stories entitled *Cuchulain of Muirthemne*. Her relationship with Yeats brought the aristocratic widow to life as a writer. After some misunderstandings which Yeats helped sort out, her book was published by the distinguished London publishers John Murray, who had also brought out Augusta's very first book, her edition of her dead husband's papers entitled *Sir William Gregory, An Autobiography*. Yeats encouraged his patroness at every stage of publication and assisted her through her literary difficulties. Deciding on a subtitle proved difficult and Yeats finally suggested that it read 'Cuchulain of Muirthemne / Being traditional stories / of the Champions of / the Red Branch; / rearranged and put into English / by Lady Gregory'. Yeats also contributed a Preface to the book for which Lady Gregory paid him in advance. As he worked on this in London in midwinter, he must have been reminded of their many discussions at Coole at midsummer. Muirthemne, Cuchulain's place of origin, which gives Lady Gregory's book its title, also figures in 'Baile and Aillinn', Yeats's long poem of that summer. The two texts, like other later ones, are an indication of the literary intimacy by now established between them.

IV

THE EDWARDIAN
IMPRESARIO

The Edwardian Theatre, both in the West End and the provinces was almost as far removed from the mainstream of European Drama as it would have been if it had been taken to Afghanistan. Masterpieces appearing regularly in foreign capitals were either ignored altogether or given an occasional tentative matinee performance.

What the Theatre offered was done well – the musical shows, the faintly satirical or sentimental comedies, the costume-and-rapier 'tushery' – with a high standard of acting, very strong in superb character actors.

So far as there was any movement at all in the Edwardian Theatre what was central, creative and influential in it moved from the actors' to the authors' Theatre . . . in short, what the author had written came first.

J.B. PRIESTLEY, *The Edwardians*, 1970

The Abbey Theatre Company from Dublin had visited Oxford during the summer term . . . As a Conservative I was opposed to Home Rule, but Yeats and Synge and Maire O'Neill could convince me where the eloquence of all the Irish members of the House of Commons would have failed.

DUFF COOPER, *Old Men Forget*, 1953

WEEK AFTER THE EVER-GENEROUS AUGUSTA GREGORY PAID HIM
ten pounds in advance for her Preface, Yeats wrote to tell her that
Maud Gonne was anxious to play the lead in *Cathleen ni Houlihan*.
He recognized that Maud with her high political profile would certainly be
'a draw' and Lady Gregory was inclined to agree with him. By the end of
January 1902 he finally went along with Maud's view that the Fays should
be allowed to stage his play. She thought that a production involving such
gifted Irish performers would be better than one with English actors. The
first performance took place on 2 April and though Yeats arrived in Dublin
only a week before, the preparations for the production were very much on
his mind during the first three months of the year. Maud, in Paris, wrote
to him enthusiastically about her forthcoming role and sent him a detailed
description of the costumes she had in mind for herself. On her way to
Dublin in March she came over to Bloomsbury from her cousin's fine
house in Hyde Park Gate to discuss her interpretation and performance of
the role with him.

The play, set in the west of Ireland in 1798 at the time of the French
military expedition there, has for its protagonist an old, wandering woman
who is received into the house of a prosperous peasant family where the
son, Michael, is about to be married. The old woman laments that there
are strangers in her house and that her four beautiful green fields have been
taken from her. The symbolism by which the old woman stands for

oppressed and dispossessed Ireland is not initially obtrusive. At first the play further confirms that movement towards realism begun in *On Baile's Strand*. But when the old woman inspires Michael to follow her and help her, leaving his family and bride behind him, and then casts off her ragged cloak and appears beautifully robed as a queen, the allegorical intention of the play is dramatically revealed.

George Moore appeared at one of the rehearsals and his criticisms and suggestions were, as on previous occasions, numerous and loud. But Maud went her own way and on the opening night she and the Fays and their company had a great success. At a time of a succession of famous theatrical occasions in Dublin, the double bill comprising *Cathleen ni Houlihan* and AE's *Deidre* was outstanding. Large numbers of people had to be turned away from St Teresa's church hall, behind Grafton Street, the only venue the Fays had been able to book. Yeats was moved to see the patient enthusiasm of crowds of people prepared to stand up at the back of the hall even though they could hardly see because of the people in front.[1] Maud, he thought, played her part 'magnificently and with weird power'.[2] One of Maud's fellow actresses shared his enthusiasm and later wrote:

Watching her, one could readily understand the reputation she enjoyed as the most beautiful woman in Ireland, the inspiration of the whole revolutionary movement. She was the most exquisitely fashioned creature I have ever seen. Her beauty was startling . . . In her, the youth of the country saw all that was magnificent in Ireland. She was the very personification of the figure she portrayed on the stage.[3]

After this heady evening Yeats started negotiations with Frank and William Fay to establish a new Irish theatre so as to continue the initiative begun with the Irish Literary Theatre. By August they managed to take over a modest hall on Camden Street just south of Stephen's Green for the first productions of the new organization.

In June of that year, 1902, Yeats's patriotic feeling found another outlet. News came that an Englishman, a member of a sect known as the British Israelites who believed the English to be the lost tribe of Israel, was employing labourers to excavate the Hill of Tara, the site of Ireland's ancient capital, in hopes of finding the Ark of the Covenant there. With

Douglas Hyde and George Moore, an outraged Yeats travelled to Tara, a remote country place some fifty miles north-west of Dublin, and was horrified to see the extent of the digging. The crude, amateur archaeologists had destroyed the contour of the sacred Hill. The three visitors immediately wrote a letter of protest to *The Times* and ten days after it appeared they returned to Tara. They found the Irish owner of the site sitting on the hillside with a gun, a bottle of whiskey and a number of ferocious-looking dogs. But the three men of letters were not to be intimidated. Yeats especially was in one of his fighting moods. Ignoring the loud, bullying menaces of the drunken landlord the three forced their way onto the property. Douglas Hyde threatened that a mass protest meeting would be held on the site, organized by the Gaelic League. After much altercation and argument it was at last agreed that the English tenant should suspend the diggings at Tara, and finally they were abandoned altogether.

A month after his theatrical triumph in Dublin, Yeats travelled from London to Oxford where he had been invited to lecture on 'The Theatre' to the Essay Society of St John's College. The subsequent discussion lasted late into the night but Yeats found the dons' questions 'commonplace'. However, the visit did enable him to spend time with Augusta's son Robert, now an undergraduate at New College and looking forward to his twenty-first birthday celebrations at Coole in the coming summer. Yeats reported to Lady Gregory that Robert moved in what seemed to be 'a clever set'.

When Yeats reached Coole in August for his summer holiday he found that Augusta had invited other guests: his brother Jack came and so too did Douglas Hyde. Another visitor was the respectful Cornelius Weygandt, a professor of English at the University of Pennsylvania who had written admiring letters to Yeats over the last few years requesting information about the Irish literary movement. Then there arrived another far more dynamic and forceful American visitor, a lightly built man who wore an expensive suit with a waistcoat. Five years younger than Yeats, he carried himself with quiet confidence. Already balding, he had a narrow face and deep-set eyes that were both shrewd and intense. He also was an admirer of Yeats's work and had written him letters which made no great impression on the recipient. But now, meeting for the first time face to face, the two men quickly took to each other. Yeats thereby gained the patron who was second only to Lady Gregory in promoting his fortune and his fame during his approaching middle age.

This new patron was John Quinn, a 32-year-old Irish American deeply interested in the homeland of his parents, who had been emigrants to Ohio. Highly intelligent and energetic, Quinn had worked his way up from humble origins and studied law at the universities of Michigan, Georgetown and Harvard. By the age of thirty he was junior partner in a prosperous law firm and had ample money to indulge his interest in Ireland, history, literature and painting. He had got in touch with John Yeats regarding the purchase of some pictures. Now at Coole it was his great pleasure to talk poetry and philosophy with the portraitist's son. The enthusiasms they shared made for a quick friendship and Quinn soon proposed that he should help Yeats organize an extended speaking tour of the United States towards the end of the following year. Yeats, always eager to promote himself, readily agreed and Quinn set to work. The visit to America brought Yeats a good deal of money and extended his fame. In this way the relationship with Irish America which had helped launch Yeats's career in the days of his contributions to the *Boston Pilot* was renewed. A famous man in Ireland, an established man of letters in London, Yeats, by courtesy of John Quinn, would soon become a literary star in the United States.

Quinn's contributions to Yeats's career were intellectual as well as managerial and financial. Shortly after their first meeting in County Galway he sent Yeats a book which, like *Axël*, was to have an important effect on his thought and art. This was Nietzsche's *Thus Spake Zarathustra*. Like so many others Yeats was greatly impressed by Nietzsche, calling him a strong enchanter, one who had the same power as Blake.[4] Yeats was also reminded of the heroic vision and the 'curious astringent joy' in the stories of William Morris. The influence of *Zarathustra* on Yeats's thinking shows clearly in his next play *Where There Is Nothing*. Lectures on Nietzsche also became a part of Yeats's repertoire as he pursued his career as a public speaker.

He was becoming a cult figure on the lecture circuit, creating a band of devotees, including young composers such as Arnold Bax and Havergal Brian who wished to set his lyrics, and young journalists eager to promote and make the critical case for his work. One of the keenest of these was H.W. Nevinson, an adventurous military and political correspondent as well as a literary critic who took it upon himself to help build Yeats's reputation. Nevinson became something of a groupie, feeling highly honoured to be invited to Woburn Buildings and attending all the lectures he could. He was especially impressed by one of Yeats's first lectures on Nietzsche. 'Very excellent and true and fresh he was,' noted Nevinson, 'he has only to shake himself and beautiful things fall out.' Reporting the lecture in the *Daily Chronicle*, Nevinson wrote:

> *Mr W.B. Yeats followed out the distinction which Nietzsche drew between the Dionysic [sic] and the Apollonic moods of poetry, which went to make up the perfection of the Greek drama. The folk poetry, corresponding to some extent to the Greek chorus, is the extravagant cry, the utterance of the greatest emotions possible, the heartfelt lyric of an ancient people's soul. With the heroic poetry comes the sense of form, the dramatic or epic proportion of the work of art, the heroic discipline.*

As Yeats enthusiastically developed this line of thought inspired by John Quinn's gift, he was also assisted by Florence Farr, 'whose illustrations, chanted to the psaltery, were drawn from anonymous English ballads, Morris's translation of the Odyssey, and best of all, the splendid lament of Queen Emer over Cuchulain, which Mr Yeats described as the finest poem that ever came out of Ireland'.[5] The last item was a translation made by Lady Gregory that appeared in her *Cuchulain of Muirthemne*.

The year he first met Yeats, John Quinn also took an interest in the doings of the other members of the Yeats family. By October 1902, Yeats's father, his sisters Lily and Lolly and their cousin Ruth Pollexfen had moved from London to Gurteen Dhas, a largish redbrick house in Dundrum, near Churchtown on the southern edge of Dublin. It was an act of commitment to Ireland. Established in this house, the two sisters began new careers for themselves as associates of Dun Emer industries, an Irish arts and crafts company in the tradition of the William Morris firm. The greater part of the capital had been provided by Evelyn Gleeson, whom the sisters had first met through the Irish Literary Society. She came from a prosperous family, her father having founded the Athlone Woollen Mills to boost employment in Ireland, and was a prominent campaigner for women's suffrage as well as for the Arts and Crafts movement. Determining to found an entirely female handicrafts company in Ireland, Evelyn Gleeson took over a large house in Churchtown not far from Gurteen Dhas. The house was originally called Runnymede, but this allusion to Magna Carta and to English history was quickly erased when the property was renamed Dun Emer. In Irish, Dun means a fort, whilst Emer in Irish legend was the wife of Cuchulain and renowned for her beauty, wit and skills. So with this name the company proclaimed itself to be a stronghold of Irish women's arts. Lily and Lolly brought to Dun Emer not capital but energy. Lily, the former pupil then employee of May Morris, brought her considerable expertise in embroidery. Lolly had to cast about to decide what skill she should develop. She decided on hand printing and set about teaching herself this craft. It was an act of high idealism on her part to give up her teaching career in London to participate in the women's craft movement in Ireland. In becoming a printer and then a publisher Lolly also entered into a new relationship with her older brother. The year after the sisters returned to Ireland the Dun Emer Press published its first book, Yeats's collection of poems with a title alluding to Coole, *In the Seven Woods*. From then on an important part of the business side of Yeats's career as a writer was his often difficult, even stormy, relationship with his younger sister who continued as one of his publishers until the end of his life, while he was to become editorial director of her press.

In the Seven Woods was one of only two volumes of poems published by Yeats in the decade of the 1900s. The other was *The Green Helmet and Other Poems* of 1910, published by Lolly after she and Lily had parted company with Evelyn Gleeson and founded their own company, Cuala. The years between Yeats's thirty-fifth and forty-fifth birthdays were his least prolific decade as a lyric poet, when the greater part of his time and energy went into theatre rather than poetry. Nevertheless, *In the Seven Woods* shows his art as a lyric poet developing with the same rapidity as his theatrecraft. 'Adam's Curse' is generally, and rightly, regarded as a turning point in that it shows a distinct shift in diction, idiom and tone away from the poems in the preceding volume, *The Wind Among the Reeds*. The poem recalls a conversation that Yeats had had in 1901 with Maud and her sister Kathleen.

Yeats had congratulated Kathleen on her dress and her appearance and she had remarked that it was hard work being beautiful. The poem speaks of the way women and artists alike must serve, and work for, beauty. The very last line, in which Yeats laments that he and Maud now lack the energy to work for a beautiful love, that they have grown as 'weary hearted as that hollow moon', looks back to the melancholy, enervated style of the 1890s. But the remainder of this substantial poem of nearly forty lines is made up of a more robust language, one of common sense and practical, homely allusions. This is not the language of youthful dreaming and posing, rather of thoughtful exchanges and kindly reflections remembered from the conversation between the speaker and the two women. Lolly's new publishing venture introduced a new Yeats to the poetry-reading public.

Lolly's printing press, bought second-hand from a provincial newspaper, arrived at Dun Emer in the pouring rain on 24 November 1902. Two days later over in London, in his flat in Woburn Buildings, Yeats, despite continuing difficulties with his eyesight, gave a reading of his new play *Where There Is Nothing* to a small invited audience. This group included a number of fashionable women interested in the arts, their carriages and coachmen awaiting them in the lamplight at the end of the alley. The ragged children living in this still run-down area of Bloomsbury gathered to marvel at the expensive equipages used to bring the grand ladies to visit 'the Toff'. Also present that winter evening was Yeats's old friend Ernest Rhys from Camelot days and more recent friends such as the scholarly Lawrence Binyon, who worked in the Department of Prints and Drawings of the nearby British Museum, and Thomas Sturge Moore, elder brother of the Cambridge philosopher G.E. Moore whose *Principia Ethica* was to be such an important text for the Bloomsbury Group, the writers and artists who would soon come together in the terraces close to Yeats. Shy, heavily bearded and gentle, Sturge Moore was an artist and designer as well as poet and dramatist. Like the designer Charles Ricketts, and in later years Edmund Dulac, Sturge Moore, as a student and painter of visual images, was important to Yeats, the maker of verbal images. He was also strongly sympathetic towards Yeats's aspirations to create a heroic art.

Where There Is Nothing is a play about a heroic anarchist and nihilist. Paul Ruttledge is an Irish country gentleman who renounces the lifestyle and the falsities of his class and, ultimately, of the monastery where he is forced to end his days. Anarchists and nihilists were an ever more prominent element of European life. Winston Churchill, when Home Secretary, pursued them unrelentingly in the famous siege of Sidney Street in the East End of London, and Joseph Conrad in *The Secret Agent* wrote a horror comedy about them. But Yeats's hero is a more complex figure than Conrad's vicious, destructive Professor. Paul Ruttledge is a thoroughgoing and honest heretic, capable of contemplating the extremes of nihilism such as Yeats would have encountered in Nietzsche. His utter honesty gives Ruttledge, as Yeats told John Quinn, a magnetic quality, a 'power of making people love him and of carrying them away'.[6] He has something of the charisma of that role model for the young Yeats, William Morris. The play is also a further pondering of the spiritual extremism described by Yeats in 'Rosa Alchemica' and 'The Tables of the Law'.

One week after his reading of this play to friends Yeats entertained James Joyce, whom he had first met in Dublin in October just before he returned to London. AE had recommended this highly gifted, though sometimes very rude young man. So Yeats invited the willowy poet and would-be medical student to the smoking room of a restaurant in O'Connell Street, where they had a long conversation. In the course of it the 20-year-old who so passionately admired the realism of Ibsen told his 37-year-old host that the latter's recent plays based on Irish folklore showed that he was 'deteriorating'. In a famous instance of a younger generation knocking brusquely on the door he also remarked, as Yeats later remembered, that he thought Yeats was past being helped. 'I have met you too late. You are too old.'[7] But Yeats bore no grudge and a few weeks later let the young man rest at Woburn Buildings on his way to stay in Paris for the first time. He breakfasted, lunched and dined with him and took him around literary London, paying for all the hansom cabs and the buses. He tried to help his career by introducing him to editors who might publish his poems and reviews. When Joyce passed through London on his way back to Dublin early in 1903 Yeats managed to arrange for him to meet the editor of the *Academy*. But when Joyce discovered that the man was indifferent to him and his work, he became insulting and caused Yeats much embarrassment.

Yeats was much occupied with theatre matters this January and February. About to become the founder-president of the Irish National Theatre Society, he worked on plans for the new company to make an early visit to London. He had discussions with his wealthy friend from the Society of the Golden Dawn, Annie Horniman, who sometimes did secretarial work for him in London and who now expressed an interest in funding a theatre building for him in Dublin. He had discussions with his agent A.P. Watt and with his publisher Arthur Bullen about the publication of his Irish plays. He took an interest in Synge's dramatic writing, entertaining him and listened to him read *Riders to the Sea*. He gave lectures about the theatre. It was just before he went on to the platform to give one such lecture that he received the telegram that blighted his life.

The shock caused by the news it contained started a roaring in his ears that he simply could not control. Nevertheless he forced himself to go ahead and give the impromptu lecture. But afterwards he could not remember a single word he had said. When he left the hall, he wandered the streets for hours, unseeing, unhearing, utterly numbed. The telegram in his pocket was from Maud Gonne and informed him of her marriage to Major John MacBride.

THE CIVIL CEREMONY HAD TAKEN PLACE IN PARIS AT THE BRITISH Consulate, where MacBride kept his hand on his revolver for fear there might be an attempt to arrest him as one who had fought with the King's enemies in South Africa. The wedding was held at Maud's parish church of Saint-Honoré d'Eylau on 21 February 1903, four days after Maud had joined her husband's faith and become a Roman Catholic. As the marriage vows were exchanged, the best man held aloft the flag of the Irish Brigade in the Boer War. The wedding breakfast, served in a hotel, was set out on a table decorated with violets and shamrocks. Comradeship in Ireland's cause was the chief bond between the newlyweds but it did not sustain the marriage for long. Penniless John MacBride with his narrow-minded Catholic view of women was easily provoked by a wife who had her own money and the habit of having her own way and going wherever she wished. He drank to excess and abused his bride verbally and physically. Seven-year-old Iseult hated him. By the end of April when Maud found herself pregnant, the marriage was doomed.

Unaware of Maud's unhappiness, Yeats hurried away to Coole to try to overcome his own pain. In letters to Maud earlier in the month attempting to dissuade her from the marriage, he said he believed that she had lowered herself, lost caste in the eyes of the Irish people and that this imperilled her part in their mission to inspire the nation.[1] Around the time of Maud's wedding hurricanes had devastated the west of Ireland and great damage had been done to the woods at Coole. The ravaged landscape was an apt symbol of the emotional damage done to Yeats, which he experienced as a deep physical malaise.

He sought escape in work. He began a play, *The King's Threshold*, which celebrates the calling of the poet despite social and political rejection and the seductive, siren voice of a lover. He prepared for publication a collection of essays, written over the last seven years, which he entitled *Ideas of Good and Evil*. He returned to London and lectured and gave poetry recitals with Florence Farr. In the last week of March he threw himself with feverish energy into an attempt to found a new theatre company in London that would be devoted to staging poetic drama. This was the Masquers Society, the founding meeting of which was held in the theatrical costume shop of Gordon Craig's sister Edith, close to St Paul's Church in Covent Garden. The artist and designer Walter Crane chaired the meeting and those constituting the society included Arthur Symons, Sturge Moore and the distinguished classical scholar Gilbert Murray. A year younger than Yeats, Murray had been Professor of Greek at Glasgow University and resigned to dedicate himself to the revitalization of the theatre. His translations of Euripides had been performed with success at the Court Theatre in Sloane Square. His version of Euripides' *Hippolytus* was one of the plays the Masquers planned to put on. Others were Yeats's *The King's Threshold*, Maeterlinck's *Les Aveugles*, Ibsen's *Peer Gynt* and Villiers de l'Isle-Adam's *La Révolte*.

Gilbert Murray, who four years after the founding of the Masquers Club became Regius Professor of Greek at Oxford, was married to Lady Mary Howard, a daughter of the Earl of Carlisle, owner of Noworth Castle in Cumberland and of Castle Howard in Yorkshire, the Vanbrugh house which is one of the grandest homes in England. During the Edwardian years Yeats's literary contacts slowly but surely brought him entry into the highest levels of English society. In the weeks after the devastating news about Maud, Yeats greatly enjoyed the visits to Woburn Buildings of the daintily pretty Lady Margaret Sackville. This 22-year-old poetess who sought Yeats's help in bringing out her short-lived magazine, *The Celt*, was the daughter of the 7th Earl De La Warr.

In the summer Yeats was back at his aristocratic base at Coole where

he worked with Augusta on rewriting and improving the diction and style
of the Red Hanrahan stories. He moved around restlessly. He went to stay
with his old friend Douglas Hyde at Frenchpark and then on to see a sympathetic Uncle George at Moyle Lodge on Rosses Point. To Hyde he spoke
of his enthusiasm for John Synge's script *In the Shadow of the Glen,* which
Yeats thought of staging in Dublin in the autumn. The play depicts a young
Irishwoman with an elderly husband preparing to run off with a younger
man and then being charmed into travelling the roads of Ireland with a
tramp. But Synge's comedy did not entertain Hyde; he disliked the way
Irish womanhood was portrayed. Just before the play was produced in
October the leader of the Gaelic League felt obliged to resign from the
board of the Irish National Theatre Society. So too did Maud Gonne, who
by now had resumed an uneasy correspondence with Yeats. Neither she nor
Hyde could condone the performing of Synge's play, which they believed
did a serious disservice to the image and reputation of Ireland.

These two nationalists were not the only objectors to *In the Shadow of
the Glen,* which provoked a wider controversy when it was finally staged.
And Yeats's theatre venture in London, the Masquers Club, was failing for
lack of money. So it was something of a relief for him when the time came
to set off on the American tour he had planned with John Quinn. He sailed
from Liverpool in the first week of November and was to remain in the
United States for some four months. On disembarking in New York City
he found that Quinn had organized some excellent publicity for his visit. A
succession of journalists came to interview him, some of them very aggressive. At times he felt harassed, but they were impressed by him. A writer for
the *New York Daily Tribune,* for instance, who interviewed Yeats in his room
at the Plaza Hotel, described the poet, now in his thirty-ninth year, as

> *Gaunt of body, with a classical, finely chiselled face and a heavy shock of*
> *black hair, finely sprinkled with silver . . . He listens to one in a dreamy*
> *sort of way, but as soon as he himself begins to speak he talks with a stress*
> *of voice and a play of expression which show his intensity . . . He . . . sat*
> *on the brass bar of the bed, and was apparently entirely oblivious of any*
> *uncomfortableness. With his right hand he emphasized each sentence with*
> *a grace which showed him to be as much an actor as a playwright.*[2]

1. William Pollexfen of Sligo, Yeats's maternal grandfather: a man of few words and violent temper who frightened Yeats as a child

2. Elizabeth Pollexfen, Yeats's maternal grandmother: a lady of genteel tastes who alone could calm her irascible husband

3. The poet's father, John Butler Yeats, at the time of his engagement to Susan Pollexfen

4. Susan Yeats, the poet's mother, drawn by John Yeats early in the marriage

5. Lily (Susan) Yeats, the poet's favourite sister, painted by John Yeats at the time she worked for May Morris at Kelmscott House

6. A portrait of Lolly (Elizabeth) Yeats drawn by John Yeats for the frontispiece of 'Ye Pleiades'

7. The 24-year-old bearded Yeats painted by the family's
Bedford Park neighbour Henry Marriott Paget

8. A self-portrait of W.B. Yeats's brother Jack Yeats whom Lolly described as
being inclined to tell people too little about himself

9. John O'Leary, the widely respected Fenian who was the intellectual mentor and financial supporter of Yeats as a young man

10. Katharine Tynan, 'dearest Katey', the poet's closest literary intimate in his early twenties

11. George Pollexfen, Yeats's uncle who gave him room and board when he was penniless and who came to share Yeats's occult interests

12. Maud Gonne, the love of Yeats's life, in 1897,
the year of the Jubilee Riots in Dublin

13. W.B. Yeats in 1902, the year *Kathleen ni Houlihan* was produced in Dublin with Maud Gonne in the title role

14. The house in which the Cuala Press operated. Here Lolly handprinted and published many of Yeats's works

15. Olivia Shakespear whom W.B. Yeats met in 1894 at *The Yellow Book* dinner

16. Woburn Buildings where Yeats lodged for nearly a quarter of a century

17. Maud Gonne with her children Sean MacBride and Iseult Gonne in 1905, the year she sued John MacBride for divorce

18. Lady Augusta Gregory, Yeats's patroness, collaborator, comforter, adviser and friend

19. John Quinn, the successful
Irish-American lawyer who was the
patron of the entire Yeats family

20. Ezra Pound, the iconoclastic
American poet who argued
poetics with Yeats during the
last thirty years

21. Yeats on his seventieth birthday with his old friend, the Poet Laureate
of the day, John Masefield

22. Margot Ruddock, Yeats's lover
in old age. He remained loyal to her
long after she became insane

23. Ethel Mannin, another of Yeats's lovers
in his old age. Wine helped bridge their
wide political differences

24. Yeats in the late 1930s with the artist and designer Edmund Dulac and the last of his lovers, Edith Shackleton Heald

Yeats also proved himself to be a hard-working, reliable and successful speaker on a long and gruelling lecture circuit. Based in Quinn's large apartment with its many fine works of art, Yeats first set off for Yale and then went on to Smith, Amherst, Mount Holyoke and the University of Pennsylvania. Numerous lectures later, at the beginning of the next month he spoke at Harvard where he was pleased and interested to meet the distinguished psychologist, philosopher and fellow supporter of psychic research, the 61-year-old William James, whose writings he had once studied in the British Museum and whose *Human Immortality* had been sent to him by Quinn.

Everywhere he went in America Yeats was strongly supported by Irish American organizations. It was perhaps to demonstrate his sympathy with this political constituency that the President of the United States, Theodore Roosevelt, invited Yeats to lunch at the White House. At table, in a dining-room brightly ornamented with Christmas decorations, Yeats, possibly tired by his ceaseless travelling, was for once quiet and unforthcoming. The President, to make him feel at home, spoke of his own strongly anti-imperialist views. He had of course led the American Roughriders into Cuba in the war against the Spanish Empire five years before. He believed, he told his Irish guest, in preserving, at all risks, the autonomy of little peoples. Yeats was at last roused to reply, 'Sure, you'll find little people all over Ireland. Every old man that's raked the hay in the meadow has seen one of the little people. I have seen some of them myself.' President Roosevelt, reported one of those present, 'looked as if he had been struck suddenly by a thunderbolt'.[3]

Back in New York on 2 January 1904, Yeats spoke in Carnegie Hall on 'The Intellectual Revival in Ireland'. A large delegation of Clan na Gael attended and entertained him after his speech. The following day he took the sleeper train west to St Louis and from there travelled on to other Midwestern cities. He was impressed by his visit to Notre Dame University in Indiana; the tolerance and kindly worldliness of the priests who taught there revealed to him possibilities in Catholicism that he had never imagined before. By 26 January, the day Maud Gonne's son Sean (or Seagan) was born in Paris, Yeats had arrived in San Francisco. The following day he delivered two lectures, and the tiring schedule continued as he moved on to Stanford and Sacramento. By the end of the first week in February he was back in Chicago from where he travelled to many venues in the Midwest. Though he was growing weary of lecture halls, his need to make money drove him to accept extra bookings. After his return to New York via Toronto the Irish societies paid him an especially good fee to give a lecture on Robert Emmet on the centenary of the death of this Irish patriot. More than four thousand people assembled in New York's Academy of Music to hear him speak. Just over a week later John Quinn threw a grand farewell party for Yeats, who sailed for England on the liner *Oceania* on 9 March. Yeats had liked America and had been stimulated by it, agreeably surprised by the cultivation of so many of the people he met, and touched by the kindness and hospitality he had received. In his first days back in London he found that he annoyed English people by his enthusiastic praise of America.

The financial success of his tour through the United States meant that for the first time in his life he had money to spare. He wrote to John Quinn for advice on how to invest four hundred pounds. He soon had a success in the West End too. His theatre company retained the Royalty Theatre to give a season of Irish drama, the programme comprising a play by Padraic Colum, one by Synge and Yeats's *The King's Threshold*. The first-night audience was socially 'the most distinguished' that Yeats had ever seen in a London theatre. The plays were well received and the season was a success in every way.

Yet the most exciting concern for the remainder of 1904 was first the leasing and then the refurbishing of the Dublin building which would open its doors to the public as the Abbey Theatre. After consulting the Tarot cards, Annie Horniman, who had resumed her duties as Yeats's volunteer part-time secretary, agreed to put up the necessary capital. In April, prior to her annual trip to Bayreuth to indulge her passion for Wagner, she and Yeats travelled to Dublin to study the feasibility of renovating the old Mechanics Institute, presently being used as a cheap music hall. They went ahead with the lease and the improvements and during the summer Yeats had excited discussions with Synge and AE and Lady Gregory at Coole about the new theatre. In August he worked on the application to Dublin Castle for the necessary licence. Miss Horniman, stimulated as ever by her Wagner pilgrimage, joined him at Coole, as did John Quinn. At the end of August they all went over to Dublin and were excited to see the first rehearsals taking place on the new stage. A week before Christmas Eve the company had its first dress rehearsal and on 28 December 1904 gave its first public performance. It comprised four one-act plays: Lady Gregory's farce *Spreading the News*, Synge's *In the Shadow of the Glen*, Yeats's *Cathleen ni Houlihan* and his new work *On Baile's Strand*.

Early in the following year the excitement and triumph were cut short when Arthur Griffith launched another attack on Synge's play. The editor of *United Ireland*, a staunch nationalist who in the near future would found the organization later known as Sinn Fein, declared that 'Mr Synge's adaptation of the old Greek libel on womankind – "The Widow of Ephesus" – has no more title to be called Irish than a Chinaman would be if he printed Patrick O'Brien on his visiting card.'[4] *In the Shadow of the Glen*, asserted Griffith, was a libel on Irish womanhood. Yeats quickly went to Synge's defence and in the ensuing polemical exchanges in the press showed himself extremely adroit.

There was a much more painful development at this time, of which Yeats was a helpless witness rather than a participant. By January Maud Gonne felt she had no choice but to seek a separation from her husband. While she had been away on a visit to Ireland, MacBride's drinking had increased and he had behaved in a sexually threatening way towards the female members of Maud's household in France, including her cook. What troubled Maud most, however, was that MacBride had threatened the delicately beautiful Iseult with sexual abuse. Maud was miserable and humiliated to have to report her separation from her husband. She told Yeats, 'Of a hero I had made, nothing remains and the disillusion has been cruel. I am fighting an uneven battle because I am fighting a man without honour or scruples who is sheltering himself and his vices behind the National cause.'[5] A few weeks later she began telling Yeats more about MacBride: 'My husband is insanely jealous . . . On one occasion he told me he had intended to kill you – Even Russell he declared was my lover and that Mrs Russell was mad with jealousy!!'[6]

Despite the excesses of which Maud accused him, MacBride determined to contest her petition for a separation and for custody of their baby Sean. To Maud's dismay her husband rallied some of the members of the Irish nationalist groups to his support. The dispute continued bitterly throughout that year. In the springtime Maud found some diversion by practising drawing at the Academie Julien and by going to the Gustave Moreau Gallery to make copies of paintings by this *symboliste* master whose art, especially the jewel-like colouring, she and Yeats found fascinating.

In his letters to Maud Yeats did all he could to comfort her. But he was tormented on her behalf, and it was a relief to him that spring to go to Stratford to stay with his publisher, the courtly, wine-loving Arthur Bullen, who had a passion for Elizabethan literature. One of Bullen's friends and fellow Stratford residents, the popular romantic writer Marie Corelli, called and invited Yeats to share an outing with her on the River Avon in her Venetian gondola. It was, she said, just about big enough to accommodate herself, Yeats and Yeats's large floppy tie.[7] But Bullen's womenfolk warned that the publicity-hungry Marie would arrange for gossip columnists to do a story about their trip in the gondola, which might detract from the *gravitas* that was now becoming an aspect of Yeats's image.

Always mindful of his finances, Yeats agreed that Bullen should bring out a volume of his poems of the last six years, and they also planned an edition of his collected works. Yeats also accepted Bullen's offer of forty volumes of Balzac's works at a very good price. Yeats's fortieth birthday was fast approaching and these were his present to himself. John Quinn, Lady Gregory and other friends and admirers gave him the famous edition of Chaucer produced at the Kelmscott Press, designed by William Morris and illustrated by Edward Burne-Jones.

That summer at Coole Yeats read this beautiful book every morning immediately after breakfast. Then he would walk in the gardens for twenty minutes before settling down to three hours of hard work in the library. Lunch was at two and lasted for an hour; then he would go fishing for a couple of hours. (On Fridays, if there were Catholic company invited to dinner, it was his responsibility to catch a sufficient number of perch from the lake.) After fishing he would read or write letters before dining at eight with Lady Gregory and the guests who often joined them. This pleasant, calming routine helped him to work even harder than usual. *Yes, again*

His mind was very much on his writings for the theatre. He was stimulated by a long essay, 'The Ideas of Richard Wagner', published by Arthur Symons in the *Quarterly Review* in July, which his close friend of the 1890s had sent him. Yeats rewrote his plays radically, making thoroughgoing revisions to *On Baile's Strand, The King's Threshold* and that dense text, first drafted eleven years before, and which George Moore had once tried to help him simplify, *The Shadowy Waters*. He and Lady Gregory also had lengthy discussions about the administrative problems beginning to develop at the Abbey Theatre. They drew up plans to get rid of the present unwieldy board with its time-consuming democratic procedures and to convert the Abbey Theatre into a limited liability company with themselves and John Synge as directors. By the summer's end they were in Dublin arguing their case and by October they had achieved their objectives.

The introspective poet who a few months earlier had been fine-tuning the spiritual language of *The Shadowy Waters* now became a truculent, uncompromising administrator who treated his fellow board members to some nasty, brutal language and outbursts of bad temper. The attractive young actress Maire nic Shubhlaigh received an especially vicious tongue-lashing and fled from his presence distraught. AE, who was one of those who dissociated themselves from the Abbey Theatre at the time of the Yeats–Gregory takeover, wrote Yeats an angry letter reproaching him for his bullying and saying, 'There is probably not one of the younger people of whom you have not said some stinging and contemptuous remark.'[8]

Back in London Yeats again demonstrated his pushy single-mindedness and his business acumen as he wrote forceful letters to his publisher Bullen about the right way to price and promote the book of poems they had planned back in May. Yeats also took a great deal of pleasure in his success as a lecturer. In early February 1906 he went on a remunerative speaking tour in Scotland which included appearances in Edinburgh and St Andrews. To Florence Farr, to whom he was drawing closer at this time, he commented on the unusual way in which his career as a public speaker had become so successful. The lecture agencies had shown absolutely no interest in acting for him and he had made his way by accepting any and every invitation he was offered. But this policy had, over the years, built him a reputation as a public speaker and now this part of his career made him 'hundreds of pounds'. Yeats's self-confidence at this time is also apparent in a letter to Russell in which Yeats allowed that he was 'a fairly strong and capable man' who could gather the strong and capable about him. By contrast Russell, because of his 'religious genius to which all souls are equal', gathered the weak and inadequate about him.

During 1906, the year in which British politics were rocked by the Liberals' landslide victory in the General Election, Yeats was to need all the confidence he could summon. For his career as a theatre manager and impresario faced a serious threat when the cultural life of Dublin was riven by the founding of a new theatre that offered a nationalist alternative to the fledgeling Abbey. The Theatre of Ireland was organized by some of the people who had abandoned the Abbey in protest against the Yeats–Gregory takeover. Its chairman was Edward Martyn and the Abbey defectors included Maire nic Shiubhlaigh, the young dramatist Padraic Colum and the fervent nationalist poet and teacher Patrick Pearse. The new enterprise was an ideological challenge; more unfortunately it was a threat to the Abbey's box office receipts. For a time the Abbey Theatre struggled, and audiences were often small, but Yeats and his associates persevered. By October Yeats claimed that the Abbey was a success. Performances were sold out and people were willing to stand, both in the stalls and in the gallery. Most important of all, the Abbey Theatre was profitable.

There was just one occasion to mar his triumph. This was in October on the first night of Lady Gregory's tragic play about patriotic self-sacrifice, *The Gaol Gate*. The audience sat waiting expectantly for the curtain to rise. But there was a delay. And still more delay. Then, as Padraic Colum's wife-to-be later recollected, Yeats entered hastily, accompanied not, as usual, 'by the short Queen Victoria-like figure of Lady Gregory, but a tall woman dressed in black, one of the tallest women I had ever seen. Instantly a small group in the pit began to hiss loudly and to shout, "Up, John MacBride!".' But Maud was not afraid of her husband's supporters. Mary Colum continued. 'The woman stood and faced the hissers, her whole figure showing a lively emotion, and I saw the most beautiful, the most heroic-looking human being I have ever seen before or since . . . she was smiling and unperturbed. Soon a counter-hissing set up, the first hissers being drowned by another group, and then I realized who she was . . . She was a legend to us young persons in our teens.'[9] Maud this year had finally obtained her legal separation from John MacBride and she was in a subdued mood. She kept away from the rivalry between the two theatres. The Abbey, she told Yeats, was not quite the theatre she had wanted but it was beautiful nevertheless. She thought that in Dublin there was room enough for both theatres.

Summering at Coole, Yeats had concentrated his energies on creating a major new piece for the Abbey. This was *Deidre*, his own dramatic version of the story of the great tragic heroine of Irish legend on whom AE had also based a play. During these months he also spent a great deal of time and emotion on a violent quarrel with Lolly about the editorial policy of the Dun Emer press. At issue was a volume of poems by George Russell which Lolly had agreed to publish. Off in America promoting Dun Emer products with the help of John Quinn, Lolly engaged in an extended correspondence with her brother which provoked his high-handed resignation from his position as editorial director. This particular quarrel showed again the arrogant and combative Yeats. Even John Yeats, Lolly's severest critic, protested to his elder son on her behalf, reproaching him for behaving as if he were a demi-god. But this conflict was finally smoothed over and the poet reassumed his title and continued his always tricky relationship with his publisher sister.

By the time he left Coole in the early autumn, *Deidre* was completed. It was staged at the end of November despite Miss Horniman's ever less muted grumblings about the Abbey policy of performing exclusively Irish plays. It was a great success with its first audiences, gripping them, as Yeats noted, as powerfully as *Cathleen ni Houlihan* had done in the past. He regarded it as his best dramatic poetry so far and it brought him special pleasure, because, as he told his old friend Katharine Tynan who had recently written to him again, it was far more difficult to keep an audience's attention with a play written in verse than one in prose.[10]

Early in January 1907 Yeats presided enthusiastically over the production of another play which he took to be a masterpiece and which he thought would boost the fortunes of the Abbey Theatre. This was John Synge's *The Playboy of the Western World*, a comedy about a witty and talkative young man who by claiming to be his father's murderer fascinates the girls in a small community in the west of Ireland. It seemed likely that the nationalists would see the play as yet one more slur on Irish womanhood. But on the first night there was calm during the first two acts and in the interval Lady Gregory sent a telegram of relief to Yeats, who was away in Scotland fulfilling a commitment to lecture at the University of Aberdeen. The wire read: 'Play great success.' In the third act, however, when the playboy declares, 'It's Pegeen I'm seeking only, what'd I care if you brought me a drift of chosen females, standing in their shifts', members of the audience became incensed by what they regarded as improper language, and hissing, booing and general pandemonium broke out. Synge and Lady Gregory hurried to the telegraph office and sent another wire to Aberdeen; it read: 'Audience broke up in disorder at the word shift.' Sensing serious trouble ahead Yeats at once took the train to Glasgow, crossed to Belfast and hurried on anxiously to Dublin. He did not arrive in time for the second staging of *The Playboy*, at which the rioting was so bad that the performance had to be terminated before the end, and the audience had its money returned. On the third day of the play, Yeats was determined not to be bullied by the mob. He took Synge to lunch at the Metropole Hotel where they gave an interview to a reporter from the *Freeman's Journal* with the combative Yeats doing most of the talking. He said, 'We will go on until the play has been heard sufficiently to be judged on its own merits. We had only announced its production for one week. We have now decided to play all next week as well, if the opposition continues, with the exception of one night, when I shall lecture on the freedom of the theatre, and invite our opponents to speak on its slavery to the mob if they have a mind to.'[11]

That evening in the Abbey after the curtain-raiser, Synge's *Riders to the Sea*, had ended, disturbances began. Yeats strode on to the stage and sought to quieten the audience, some members of which were drunk. He repeated his intention of opening the theatre the following Monday for a debate about the play, to which all might contribute. He then left the stage and for the third time the curtain went up on *The Playboy of the Western World*. Instantly there was uproar and threats to invade the stage. From a side door

Yeats immediately led out a body of policemen who ranged themselves around the walls of the theatre. Yeats's manner was uncompromising, even truculent, and there were arrests. Then under very conspicuous police protection the play proceeded. The following day Yeats gave evidence in the Northern Police Court against those arrested. This 'witnessing for the Crown' against Irish nationalists led to bitter reproaches from Maud Gonne.

After some less disturbed performances later in the week, the day came for the promised debate about the play. The Abbey was packed and all the literary personalities of Dublin were present, except for Synge, who was ill. All the reports by those present indicate that this was a brilliant and courageous moment in Yeats's life. The debate was at times physically violent. Speeches mostly denouncing the Abbey directors and their anti-Irish play were at one point interrupted by a young man who forced his way up on to the stage, attempted to attack Yeats, then dropped and broke a whiskey bottle on the stage. Then, as the poem 'Beautiful Lofty Things' later admiringly recalls, Yeats's father rose to make a speech. At first he was well received. But when John Yeats went on to speak of his high regard for Synge he was booed loudly. When his son rose to make a final speech the booing became much worse. But Yeats, wearing elegant evening dress, was full of confidence and disdain. Though suffering from an acute sore throat he spoke well and succeeded in refuting the charges of his opponents. Mary Colum, who was again at the Abbey that night, remembered with what force and effect he reminded the opposition that he was the author of *Cathleen ni Houlihan*: 'The audience, remembering that passionately patriotic play, forgot its antagonism for a few moments and Yeats got his cheers . . . I never witnessed a human being fight as Yeats fought that night, nor knew another with so many weapons in his armoury.'[12]

After this climax to the rioting and controversy Yeats was exhausted. Two months later he was further depleted by the news of the death of John O'Leary, the great and generous mentor of his youth who had schooled him in an Irish nationalism founded on literary and cultural scrupulousness. Worried to see Yeats so run-down, Lady Gregory suggested that he accompany her and her son Robert on a tour of northern Italy. Yeats readily accepted the invitation. This began a new and important phase in his experience and appreciation of Europe. Their time in Italy Lady Gregory remembered as 'a beautiful month'.[13] They visited Florence where Yeats developed his understanding of Michelangelo, who would become an important point of reference in some of his major poems in the future. In ramparted Ferrara, a riverside city of turrets and towers delicately illuminated by the spring sunshine, Lady Gregory, a contemporary patroness of the arts, and her son and her poet saw the lavishly decorated castle of the Este family, great patrons of the arts during the Renaissance. Some forty-five miles away lay the city of Ravenna where Yeats visited Dante's tomb and became acquainted with an art form prominent in that stately ancient city, one which also strongly affected some of his later poetry, the hieratic Byzantine images rendered in mosaic. ∠

Some of the most memorable of these were in the tomb of Galla Placidia, sister of the Emperor Honorius, who abandoned Rome and moved the imperial capital to Ravenna in 402 AD. To Yeats, to enter the mid-fifth-century tomb and to see the many deep blue and gold mosaics representing Christ, the Apostles and attendant animals glittering in the light, was a new and startling experience that was to remain imprinted in his mind. Nearby is the church of San Vitale, built a hundred years later when the Byzantines had conquered the city, and richly decorated with mosaics showing their influence. These mosaics generally depict more secular figures, grandly dressed personages from the court of the eastern Roman Empire ruled from Constantinople, including the Emperor Justinian and his wife Theodora. Yeats's feeling for mosaics was enhanced by his stay in Milan, where he studied those in the beautiful Romanesque basilica of St Ambrose. In the introductory pages to a philosophical work of his later years, *A Vision*, he remembered coming out into the courtyard of this building with its two brick campaniles and saying to Lady Gregory, 'That is my tradition and I will let no priest rob me.'[14]

Yeats and his two companions also visited Urbino, birthplace of Raphael and Bramante, which made a special impression on him. Lady Gregory read aloud from Castiglione's *Book of the Courtier* with its passages in praise of Urbino and its Renaissance court at the beginning of the sixteenth century. Yeats delighted in the hilltop city with its brick and pale stone buildings and towers and domes, dominated by the ducal palace whose quiet spacious architecture exuded the Renaissance feeling for harmony and grace. The images of civility and culture which the place conveyed to him differed greatly from what he had just experienced in Dublin. In five years' time, as part of another confrontation with his fellow Dubliners over cultural matters, Yeats would write a mocking poem to Lord Ardilaun of the Guinness family, reminding him of Guidobaldo da Montefeltro, Duke of Urbino at the time Castiglione was writing. Guidobaldo was one of those who in matters of patronage had the assurance, magnanimity and dash that Lord Ardilann so conspicuously lacked.

The Italian tour was a quick one, perhaps too quick. On his return Yeats did not feel physically renewed. His condition continued to deteriorate and he worried Maud Gonne when he wrote of his fears of a nervous breakdown. She urged him strongly to devote less time to the Abbey Theatre. And indeed in this, its third year of existence, problems and conflicts within the organization proliferated. Miss Horniman was increasingly at odds with Lady Gregory and discontented with the way the company's repertoire was evolving. The Fays were also restless and volatile and in the second week of 1908 they finally resigned. This was just after John Yeats had arrived in New York on a visit. His friends had created a fund to enable him to visit the great art centres of Italy but he decided to use the money to accompany Lily to America where she in turn went to promote sales of Dun Emer products. He quickly took a liking to New York and refused to sail home with his daughter; he never returned to Ireland again.

Not long after her return Lily, together with Lolly, ended their association with Dun Emer. There had been increasing disagreements with Evelyn Gleeson, and finally the two Yeats sisters broke away to found their own organization, Cuala, named for the ancient barony in which Lackeen Cottage was situated, the property they had rented to house their entirely female workforce. One of Cuala's founding assets was the right to publish in limited editions the new poetry of W.B. Yeats.

In the early months of 1908 Yeats continued to work hard on the eight-volume edition of his *Collected Works* which Bullen began bringing out in September of that year. Miss Horniman had made the large project possible by pledging £1,500. Yeats and Bullen did not always work smoothly together. Yeats fussed a great deal about the pictures of himself that were to appear in the volumes. He sat for Shannon and then to the fashionable portrait painter John Singer Sargent, whom the clubman side of Yeats found entertaining and more like a businessman conversant with the arts than an artist.[15] Yeats fretted about the use of his father's drawings of him, saying that they were sentimental and too obviously the work of a fond father.[16] Yeats preferred the way he was pictured by the Dublin artist Mancini, whom he greatly admired. He enjoyed being made to look joyous, feckless, immoral, like an Italian bandit or bohemian.[17] Though recognizing its accomplishment, he was not so pleased with the portrait supplied by Augustus John. It made him look disreputable and without pleasure in life.[18]

And indeed Yeats was not especially enjoying his life at the time. In a letter to his old friend Florence Farr he spoke of his profound loneliness. He had a wide range of acquaintance and he was happy to be seeing Olivia Shakespear. During this decade they quietly become lovers again, but without any of the grand plans for elopment of years before. Olivia, however, was often away and in those cold winter months of late 1907 there was no one in London to whom he felt he could talk intimately. He spent his time going to bad plays and hurting his weak eyes reading by candle-light, both out of boredom. Early in 1908 he went to Ireland for a break. From Dublin he wrote Bullen a succession of bad-tempered letters about the new edition of his collected works. He travelled on to Coole and in the west had at least one stirring and restorative experience. This found expression in the finely moving lines of the poem 'At Galway Races' which would become part of the volume *The Green Helmet and Other Poems* published by Lolly at the end of the decade. It communicates the delight of the jockeys as they race and of the crowd that watches them. The emotional unity of performer and spectator is for the poet a saddening reminder of his lack of such unity with his audience. Yet the image of the lively, happy race meeting also comes, in the gentle but insistent hoof beats of the final lines, to serve as a portent of future release from such alienation.

That spring on his return to London there came a diversion from his lonely preoccupation with himself. A young woman in her mid-twenties, young enough to be his daughter, offered himself to him, and an intensely

physical love affair began. Her name was Mabel Dickinson and she worked
in London as a masseuse. She had attended Yeats's lectures and readings
and become obsessed with him. Yeats was delighted by her lithe, athletic
figure and by her ready compliance in pleasuring him sexually. In time he
would tire of her, finding her sexuality coarse. But that spring she brought
him companionship and release. She was a far less complicated person than
Maud, with none of Maud's other-worldly concerns. When Yeats went to
Paris in June to see Maud and to renew their essentially spiritual relationship, he found it reassuring to have the prospect of returning to Mabel in
London. From Paris he wrote to Mabel telling her how he and Maud had
talked over old things, 'always old things that have drifted away'. He went
on, 'I shall return to London on Monday morning . . . I am hoping to hear
from you in the morning . . . For the moment I am tired of modern mystery
and romance and can only take pleasure in clear light, strong bodies –
having all the measure of manhood.'[19]

Nonetheless, Yeats and Maud drew close again during the summer
visit, though Maud still deplored his commitment to the Abbey Theatre;
she thought it wasted his best energies, dragged him down, involved him
in petty quarrels and resurrected his old class prejudices. She was especially
upset at the dismissive way in which he spoke of AE's dramatic version of
Deidre. Yeats's own play about this tragic heroine of Ireland had had a great
success a few months earlier when the most distinguished actress of the day,
Mrs Patrick Campbell, performed the title role first in Dublin and then in
London. Subsequently a grateful Yeats dedicated the play to her, thanking
her for playing the part 'in the generosity of her genius'.

After such success Yeats found the energy to return to a play that had
been giving him trouble. He took the unfinished manuscript of *The Player
Queen* with him when he returned to Paris in December. On this visit the
relationship with Maud became still more intense. As some writers on
Yeats have suggested, it may have included sexual experience. It is even
possible that Maud feared she might have become pregnant, for in January
she wrote to Yeats that 'the anxiety I spoke to you of when you were in Paris
is now at an end'.[20] But it is also clear that their future as she envisioned it
was to be entirely non-sexual. After his departure from Paris, she wrote to
him calling him 'beloved' and telling him that she was 'glad and proud

beyond measure of your love, and that it is strong enough and high enough to accept the spiritual love and union I offer'. She said she was praying 'that the bodily desire for me may be taken from you'.[21] However Yeats may have felt about this, there is no doubt that there is a new warmth in Maud's letters after his December visit. No longer are the letters addressed to 'Dear Willie'; the new greeting is 'Dearest'.

But 1909 brought a series of setbacks and Maud worried that Yeats did not write to her. Outwardly Yeats might seem assured, the dedicated careerist, measuring himself against his contemporaries. When he met his sister Lily on O'Connell Street he talked with her about Swinburne's recent death, concluding triumphantly, 'Now I am King of the Cats.'[22] But for all his sense of success, in this his forty-fourth year Yeats also had to face insecurity. It was one of those pivotal years in his life marked by clear-cut endings and beginnings.

The first shock came early in February 1909 when Lady Gregory was stricken by a cerebral haemorrhage and lay for a day and a night in her room at Coole, her eyes resting on the bust of Dante which had been her husband's gift to her years before. When Yeats received the news from Robert Gregory, he was distraught. His feelings at this time found expression in the poem 'A Friend's Illness'. To his immense relief Augusta slowly recovered but as she did so, there came another blow. The day before her seizure John Synge, suffering from the cancer known as Hodgkin's Disease, had been forced to enter Elpis Nursing Home in Dublin and in March he died there. The loss affected Yeats deeply. As his journal shows, his thoughts turned time and time again to his colleague's heroic career, literary achievement and unhappy ending. For Yeats this death marked the end of the first phase of the history of the Abbey Theatre.

Another important friendship appeared to have come to an end in 1909 when Yeats quarrelled with his loyal, energetic patron John Quinn. In Paris the previous year Yeats had met Quinn's mistress, the American Dorothy Coates. He had taken an interest in her because she claimed to have psychic powers. After leaving France Yeats spoke indiscreetly about her and his remarks got back to Quinn. Dorothy herself had described Yeats to Quinn as a would-be seducer and the hot-tempered lawyer abruptly terminated his relationship with the poet. In a few years' time there would be a reconciliation, but to Yeats at the time, rejection from Quinn came as one more major loss.

However, as one dynamic American exited from Yeats's life, another came into it. A brilliant and vital young man served to confirm Yeats's sense of himself as someone of middle age, and of eminence. When Yeats himself was young, he was very receptive to what his elders, especially John O'Leary, had to teach him. It was part of Yeats's genius that his susceptibilities, his range of intellectual and emotional responsiveness did not shrink with age. Now, at the age of forty-four, he started to learn from a younger generation.

V

WARS AND REVOLUTIONS

Things fall apart; the centre cannot hold;
Mere anarchy is loosed upon the world.

W.B. YEATS, 1919

The terrible, terrible war, made so fearful because in every country practically
every man lost his head, and lost his own centrality . . .

It was in 1915 the old world ended. In the winter 1915–1916 the spirit of the
old London collapsed; the city in some way perished, perished from being a heart
of the world, and became a vortex of broken passions, lusts, hopes, fears and
horrors. The integrity of London collapsed and the genuine debasement began .

D.H. LAWRENCE, 'The Nightmare' in Kangaroo, 1923

THE FIGURE WHO MADE SUCH AN IMPORTANT ENTRANCE INTO Yeats's life towards the end of 1909 was the 24-year-old American poet from Philadelphia, Ezra Pound. His appearance was striking, especially to women. He had a mass of hair of an unusual shade of auburn or golden brown; it curled up and back in soft waves. He had a high fore-head, a pale face, a strong, square jaw and piercing grey-blue eyes. He exuded energy and talked with passion about poetry and poets, and partic-ularly his current enthusiasm, the medieval troubadours of Provence. His American accent was very pronounced; he was gregarious, to the point, some thought, of being brash.

Pound had thrust himself quickly into the literary world of London. After gaining degrees in Romance literature from Hamilton College and the University of Pennsylvania he had gone to Venice where he arranged, at his own expense, to publish his first volume of poems, *A Lume Spento*. His many unsold copies he brought with him when he moved to London in 1908, going straightaway to Elkin Mathews' shop off Regent Street where he asked him to sell some. Through Mathews, Pound met a young Australian poet, Frederic Manning, and through him Mrs Eva Fowler, a wealthy hostess greatly interested in the occult, who had a grand house in Knightsbridge. One of Mrs Fowler's friends was Olivia Shakespear with whom Ezra Pound also became friendly. Olivia's daughter Dorothy, now twenty-two, was overwhelmed when she met this lively young American who had got himself employed at the London Polytechnic Institute to deliver a series of lectures on 'The Development of Literature in Southern Europe'. She was impressed by his wide-ranging erudition and entranced by his appearance. Of this most unconventional young man, who five years later would become her husband, Dorothy wrote in her private journal immediately after their first meeting: 'Oh! Ezra! How beautiful you are! With your pale face and fair hair! I wonder – are you a genius? or are you only an artist in Life?'[1] She ached to see him again, and her reaction was not unusual; many women were susceptible to him. In the coming decade of the 1910s in which he became a central figure in making the modernist aesthetic and poetic, he was also, among society women of artistic interests, a great sexual predator.

Pound spoke to the two ladies of the Shakespear family at length about his admiration for Yeats: he considered him one of the Twenty who have 'added to the World's poetical matter'.[2] With what seemed very American informality, the young visitor slipped off his chair in the Shakespears' drawing-room, extended himself on the hearthrug and with a voice full of emotion read the ladies a poem by Yeats. Pound was greatly impressed to learn that Olivia knew Yeats and grateful to her when she said she would introduce him. Their first meeting in May 1909 was brief: Yeats was then off to Ireland. It was not until the second week of October that they met again and had the lengthy conversation that set the friendship going. Pound wrote proudly to his father back in Pennsylvania that he and Yeats had talked for five hours. Yeats, now in his forty-fifth year, was impressed by the young man's knowledge of Provençal literature and by his keen concern for the sound and performance of poetry. Remembering his own experiments, Yeats concluded that Pound had got closer to the right sort of music for poetry, with effective speech which was yet definitely music with time strongly marked.[3]

From there on Ezra Pound was a regular at Yeats's 'Mondays' at Woburn Buildings. And the forward young man, of an age to have been Yeats's son, progressed rapidly from being a silent admirer to being the centre of attention. Some were shocked to see him silence some of Yeats's oldest friends, such as the gentle, golden-bearded Sturge Moore. One visitor was astonished too at the way in which Pound soon 'dominated the room, distrib-

uted Yeats's cigarettes and Chianti and laid down the law about poetry'.[4]
In the coming months, as Pound published volumes of poetry in quick
succession and then in 1910 his critical book, *The Spirit of Romance*, which
dealt with, among others, Villon, Arnaut Daniel and Dante, the friendship
between these two poets of different generations became increasingly one
of literary equals.

At the same time that he started to draw close to the gangling, raffish
young American with the turquoise earring and shabby boots, Yeats was
also mixing with the most powerful in the land. In mid-November
Edmund Gosse, who was Librarian to the House of Lords and a middle-
man between the world of letters and the world of power, gave an all-male
dinner party where Yeats found himself seated next to the Prime Minister,
Herbert Asquith. The Prime Minister, a suave lawyer, had been a brilliant
classicist when at Oxford, and Yeats was impressed by the extent of his
reading, especially in poetry. Asquith asked him many questions about the
condition of Ireland; Yeats enjoyed their conversation. On Christmas night
Gosse gave another dinner which Yeats attended, along with England's
leading Impressionist painter and connoisseur of the London music halls,
Walter Sickert. By now Yeats had become aware that Gosse's hospitality
was calculated to serve the larger purpose of changing and improving his
life.

In the meantime Yeats had again to turn his attention to the Abbey
Theatre. In January 1910 Yeats set off for Dublin in freezing weather and
with a bad cold. He and Lady Gregory were keen to reduce their workload
at the Abbey and they agreed to appoint a manager. Yeats plumped for
Lennox Robinson, a young man of about Ezra Pound's age who came from
Cork and was himself a dramatist. Yeats, ever a man of intuition in human
dealings, later claimed that he 'chose Lennox Robinson as manager before
we had exchanged sentences by the shape of his back'.[5] But he quickly
observed the young man's theatrical talents and noted that he was no older
than Ibsen when he moved from a job in a chemist's shop to take over his
theatre in Norway. Lennox Robinson would have a long and distinguished
career at the Abbey; thirteen years later, in 1923, he became its director.

Yeats and Lady Gregory had also to discuss the models of some strikingly elemental stage sets which Gordon Craig had prepared for the Abbey.

But the most pressing issue they had to take up during these dark winter days was the purchase of Miss Horniman's holdings in the theatre which, she had indicated, she was now ready to sell for just over £1,400. To Yeats and Lady Gregory the purchase would mean a great financial and administrative challenge. From Paris Maud Gonne wrote sympathizing with Yeats for the additional responsibility and worry which a takeover of the Abbey would entail. In the spring, with theatre matters still unsettled, Yeats found time to go over to Normandy to see Maud at her house at Colleville. It was one of their calmer times together. They visited Mont Saint-Michel, churches and chateaux. He was impressed by Maud's religious devotion as she prayed in each of the churches they visited. They talked a good deal about old times and the occult, and got into their old argument about Sinn Fein and its attack on Synge. However, when Yeats left, they parted as good friends.

In Britain trouble awaited him. In the first week in May King Edward VII died. As was customary, theatres closed as a mark of respect and mourning, all, that is, except the Abbey Theatre in Dublin, much to the delight of the Republicans. Miss Horniman, when she learnt of this slight to the monarchy, was incensed. A violent row broke out between her and the Irish directors, and her departure from the Abbey board seemed more likely than ever.

The new king, George V, exactly the same age as Yeats, was a conservative, and the monarchy became far less colourful and more troubled than it had been in the Edwardian decade. During the reign of George V would come the First World War, the secession of Ireland, the General Strike of 1926 and the great Depression of the 1930s.

One of Yeats's literary acquaintances within the Establishment, Edward Marsh, who was Winston Churchill's secretary, launched a series of poetry anthologies intended to promote new literary talents for the new reign of George V. But during its near ten years of existence the *Georgian Anthology* contained little more than backward-looking nature poetry, a prosodically tired and mechanical repetition of one of the great Romantic themes. It was rather Yeats and his younger associates, Ezra Pound and T.S. Eliot, and other modernists whose art would face up to and be vivified by the devastating realities of the post-Edwardian age.

In 1910 Britain found herself in her gravest political and constitutional crisis in decades. Prime Minister Asquith's Chancellor of the Exchequer, the radical Welsh Liberal David Lloyd George, had presented a People's Budget, which Tories in the House of Lords voted down. Asquith took the case to the people in two elections during 1910 and won, though with reduced majorities. The Liberals then introduced the Parliament Act, which would limit the Lords' right to veto legislation from the House of Commons. The Tory diehards resisted fiercely. The confrontation was a dramatic moment in the political democratization of Britain; eventually the Tories backed down when George V let it be known that he would create enough Liberal Lords to outvote them if they continued to block the passage of the Act. Asquith had won but again with a narrow majority. He could continue to govern but only if the Irish MPs supported him in the House of Commons. Amidst all the constitutional excitement Home Rule for Ireland emerged as a hot issue once again.

In this historic year Yeats was suddenly the recipient of a good deal of formal public recognition. A few weeks before he went to see Maud, he learned from Gosse that he was to be named as one of the thirty members of the newly created Academy of Letters. Among those similarly honoured were Joseph Conrad, Thomas Hardy and Henry James. When Yeats returned from Colleville to London he also learned that there were those in Dublin proposing him as a successor to the ailing Edward Dowden as Professor of English Literature at Trinity College. On his way to Coole for the summer Yeats met and conferred with these supporters in Dublin. Then at Coole he received the news from 10 Downing Street that Asquith had recommended him for a government pension of £150 a year. Gosse's creative hospitality had finally paid off: Yeats's habitual financial precariousness was now eased and his fame further institutionalized. At the age of forty-five he was formally identified in London, as in Dublin, as a distinguished man of letters.

But the award of the pension also involved some pain. Gosse had asked Lady Gregory to write a letter of recommendation, which she did. Then, unaccountably, Gosse had sent her an extremely rude letter declaring that what she had written was pointless. Yeats wrote a letter to Gosse to protest, but did not put it in the mail. Was this because he did not wish to offend an influential man who could continue to assist his career? For a long while he brooded about his failure to defend an old and generous friend and on what this revealed about his character. He knew that Lady Gregory's son Robert, now in his thirtieth year, saw him as self-serving in the matter. It was the most painful time in Yeats's relationship with Augusta Gregory since she had first become his patroness.

Whilst he was at Coole in 1910 one who had also sustained him while he was struggling to establish himself as a writer, Uncle George Pollexfen, died. Yeats travelled north to Sligo for the funeral and his brother Jack, who had recently returned to live in Ireland, also came. Yeats found it difficult entering Uncle George's house, decked out with all the trappings of mourning. The funeral, held at the Protestant church, 'was as George would have wished it for he loved form and ceremony'. Eighty Freemasons attended and each threw acacia leaves into the grave, while two Masons who, like Uncle George, had a higher degree of rank, each threw in a white rose. Yeats was pleased by the stately proceedings. *cf. TV today 2013*

Wearied by bereavement Yeats returned to Dublin and thence to England where he had been engaged to do a lecture tour of large northern cities including Manchester, Leeds and Liverpool. He spoke a great deal about drama with a view to creating a public for the Abbey Company when it went on tour in Lancashire and Yorkshire. As Christmas approached he returned to Dublin to work for the Abbey on the spot. He assisted Lady Gregory with the complex legalities involved in obtaining a new patent for the theatre, without which they could not continue to give public performances. He had to negotiate with Miss Horniman about the purchase of her shares. He supervised the installation of the new permanent set which Gordon Craig had designed, which would, Yeats thought, give them a beautiful but strange stage.[6] Craig had done all the costumes and scenery for Yeats's play *The Hour Glass*.

In time for Christmas Lolly at Cuala published *The Green Helmet and Other Poems*, a volume containing some fine poems by Yeats expressing his now more resigned and philosophical attitude towards Maud Gonne. It is customary to regard poems such as 'A Woman Homer Sung', 'Words' and 'No Second Troy' as constituting an advance in the Yeatsian lyric: earlier verbal lushness here gives way to language that is more conversational and intellectually taut. Ezra Pound, now spending some time back in America, was the first to applaud the change revealed in the drafts Yeats had shown him. To his wealthy girlfriend and generous patroness Margaret Cravens, Pound wrote: 'Yeats has been doing some new lyrics – he has come out of the shadows and has declared for life . . . That is to say that the movement of the . . . nineties for drugs and shadows has worn itself out.'[7] With uncharacteristic modesty Pound did not claim that he was the one to effect this change in the older poet. 'There has been no "influence". Yeats has found within himself the spirit of the new air which I by accident had touched before him.' Pound felt a new solidarity with the older artist; 'he and I are now as it were in one movement, with aims very nearly identical.' Yeats's art had 'now a note of personal and human triumph that will carry him to more people'. In another letter to Margaret in Paris Pound copied out an early version of 'No Second Troy' and told her, 'That is the spirit of the new things as I saw them in London. The note of personal defeat which one finds in the earlier work has gone out of it.'[8]

In the early weeks of 1911 the subject of 'No Second Troy' heard nothing from Yeats. So at the beginning of the second week in February Maud wrote to him to ask what was the matter. She hoped that his long silence was not a sign that he was going to get married. He was not. With his newly declared eminence he was spending a good deal of time as a guest in some of England's great aristocratic houses. At one of these he met the most pugnacious member of Asquith's Liberal government, the Home Secretary Winston Churchill. This stocky 35-year-old with sandy hair presently taking an aggressive line with striking miners, anarchists and suffragettes would, ten years on, intrude significantly into the history of Ireland. Meeting him in early 1911 Yeats found this young comer in British politics extremely impressive. Then his old friend, the retiring, innocuous Sturge Moore, had been threatened with prosecution for obscenity in a story he had published in the *English Review*, so Yeats rallied to his support. There was also a dispute involving some of his Abbey plays in Manchester which he had to settle.

But late in February he found time to choose a ring to send to Maud. She was delighted with it and wrote him a warm letter of thanks. That same month there came another pleasing letter, this time from his father in New York. It told of a meeting with Ezra Pound who was just about to return to Europe from America. John Yeats liked the young poet who, he wrote to Willie, quoted 'quantities of your verse'. John Yeats also introduced Pound to John Quinn and thus, without knowing it, provided the modernists with their leading patron and paymaster. John Quinn would subsidize not only Pound but through him T.S. Eliot, Wyndham Lewis and James Joyce.

In the first days of March Pound was back in England and immediately called on Yeats before setting off for Paris. As the winter came to an end Yeats, feeling overworked and dispirited, decided that he needed a break. So he too chose to have some time in Paris. He met Pound there and the two passed a pleasant afternoon dawdling around Notre Dame together. Yeats also spent a good deal of his time in Paris with Lady Gregory, helping to complete the final draft of a book of folklore they had worked at, on and off, for some fifteen years, *Visions and Beliefs in the West of Ireland*. When she went on to London to stay with her nephew, the art dealer Hugh Lane, in his beautiful Chelsea house full of fine paintings, Yeats went too. There he attended a grand dinner for the flamboyant Gordon Craig, at which he was to have made a speech, but when he discovered that this also would mean proposing a toast to the King he quickly got William Rothenstein to substitute for him. He thought this refusal might damage his prospects for the proposed Chair at Trinity College, but was still not sure that he wanted the job.

In July he and Lady Gregory were suddenly faced with another task. An American theatrical agency offered excellent terms for a tour of various cities in the United States by the Abbey company. The agents were especially keen that the still controversial *Playboy of the Western World* be one of the plays performed. The offer was too good to refuse, so Yeats and Lady Gregory set about organizing the tour and creating a second, stand-in company to perform in Dublin. Given the trouble *The Playboy* was likely to cause among Irish Americans, Yeats agreed to accompany the actors but managed to persuade Lady Gregory to follow him later, and take over, so that he would not have to stay in America for the duration of the tour. Maud Gonne was extremely angry about his going. She told him there were hundreds of competent theatre managers but very few great poets; he should not dissipate his energies and time on lesser activities like theatre management. She went on to say that his poems were the children of Yeats and herself; the theatre company was the child of Yeats and Lady Gregory, and that child took a lot of looking after. Maud confessed that she was sometimes jealous on behalf of her children, the poems.

In America the Abbey company certainly did need a lot of looking after. But the worst difficulties occurred only after Yeats had returned to England. He was in Boston for the opening night of the tour, and made arrangements for his own plays and publications for and about the theatre to be on sale at this and future performances. Then, six weeks later, after a brief meeting with his father in New York, he boarded the grand Cunard liner the *Lusitania*, launched five years before, and sailed for England. Though he had to face angry charges of blasphemy and political treachery from various American Gaelic societies, it was after he was back in London that the attacks on Lady Gregory and Lennox Robinson in America grew far worse. At one performance of *The Playboy* in New York City the stage was invaded and the set wrecked. In Chicago Lady Gregory received a death threat letter containing menacing symbols of a revolver and a coffin. The climax came when the whole Abbey company was arrested in Philadelphia in January 1912. At the insistence of some local Irish societies the company was held awaiting bail for five days until John Quinn finally obtained their release. The tour agents in New York had gained all the publicity they could ever hope for.

By this time Yeats had crossed over to Dublin to take charge of the replacement Abbey company there and also to develop the organization further. It had been decided that a theatre school should be established at the Abbey, to recruit and train additional actors for the second company. For some time Yeats had been impressed by the energies and ability of the 34-year-old actor-producer Nugent Monck, who specialized in mounting Elizabethan plays and who had achieved many great successes with the company he ran at Norwich. He had staged a revised version of *The Countess Kathleen* in London in 1912, presenting Yeats's play as a medieval pageant set against the 'screens' that Gordon Craig had created for his Moscow Art Theatre production of *Hamlet*. Nugent Monck was also renowned for his skills as a teacher of acting. So Yeats set out to persuade him to come and teach for a while in the new Abbey school. The fashionable young director agreed and during the winter months of 1912 Yeats devoted all his time to working alongside Monck to develop the school. Poetry was set aside; Yeats was now entirely a man of the theatre and pleased with the results that he and Monck produced. The young entrants learned fast and by March he could take pride in the seventeen young actors selected and engaged from the school.

He was glad to be away from London, for England in 1912 was undergoing further startling political convulsions. Militant suffragettes were intensifying their acts of violent protest. In the early spring there was also a nationwide coal strike, Winston Churchill going so far as to suggest that the strikers were being assisted by 'German gold'. Without coal fuelling the trains troops could not be moved, and Britain would become vulnerable to the Kaiser's armies. Irish politics were also becoming a divisive issue. In June a Home Rule Bill for Ireland was debated in the House of Commons. The prospect of such legislation caused uproar among the Protestants of Ulster led by the forceful Edward Carson, the lawyer who had played a prominent role in the prosecution and conviction of Oscar Wilde.

When back in London Yeats was introduced to a venerable-looking Bengali poet, Rabindranath Tagore, at the house of his friend, the painter William Rothenstein. From the start Yeats was greatly taken with this distinguished Indian writer who would win the Nobel Prize the following year. He found inspiration in Tagore's poetry and communicated his enthusiasm to Ezra Pound who even thought of learning Bengali in order better to understand Tagore's work. Pound and Yeats now became still closer friends as the younger man sought to become engaged to Olivia's daughter, Dorothy. The only problem was that Dorothy's father was far from convinced that Pound had enough money to support a wife. But Yeats approved of the relationship between the two young people who had nicknamed him 'Eagle'. At tea one sunny June day in the Shakespears' house in Brunswick Gardens near Kensington Palace Yeats appeared with a copy of the *English Review*, the magazine edited by Ford Madox Ford. The *Review* contained two poems by Pound which Yeats read to mother and daughter 'with due music'. Pound's pioneering work in free verse, 'The Return', was, Yeats told the ladies, 'distinguished' and 'flawless'.[9] The poem would linger for years in 'the Eagle's' mind and he recalled and quoted it in full in the introduction to *A Vision*, the major prose work of his later years.

There were times, however, when Yeats put up resistance to the dynamic young writer and his fervent ideas. A young American woman remembered how Pound took her to the Aldwych Theatre to see a Shaw play, where they ran into Yeats and Olivia Shakespear. After the matinée Pound, lordly and debonair, invited the two older people to tea at Prince's Restaurant in Piccadilly and there a heated argument broke out between the two men. Pound, who like D.H. Lawrence and T.S. Eliot had a gift for languages, maintained that it was important for a poet to know several. No great linguist himself and in a 'cantankerous' mood, Yeats expressed contempt for this idea, saying that it was no more than a bus conductor's ability to memorize a string of words. The argument was fierce and ended in stony silence. Then when it was time to pay the bill, Ezra, the rash host, was dismayed to discover he had not enough money. He asked his young companion in a whisper to help, but she did not have enough. When Yeats was not looking she whispered in turn to Mrs Shakespear whom she scarcely knew, to explain the difficulty. The kindly Olivia laughed and slipped her a sovereign under the table, averting a scene. But Yeats, very much on his dignity, bade the young people 'a rather formal farewell' as he left with Olivia to rejoin Dorothy in Brunswick Gardens.[10]

Partly to earn some money in order to become engaged to Dorothy, Pound accepted the post of 'foreign correspondent' for a new magazine called *Poetry* edited by Harriet Monroe in Chicago. It was one of the 'little magazines' in which new forms of poetry were nurtured and published, poetry we have come to know as modernist. In his new capacity Pound sought poems from Tagore; he also persuaded Yeats to let him have some for Miss Monroe. Presumptuously Pound made changes to Yeats's work without consulting him and the Eagle became extremely angry, but he relented and even accepted the changes. In December Pound wrote an essay for *Poetry* on the condition of art in London. Yeats, he concluded, was 'the only poet worthy of serious study', one who was 'already a recognised classic'.[11]

In the later months of 1912, Pound and Tagore had intense discussions about poetry at Yeats's 'Mondays'. Pound, already beginning to regard himself as a student of 'world literature', collaborated with Tagore's pupil Kali Mohan Ghose on translations from the fifteenth-century Hindi poet Kabir. And Yeats set about writing an introduction to Tagore's *Gitanjali*, published in English as *Song Offerings*, a collection of poems translated from Bengali. One of the ways in which the modernism of the 1910s differentiated itself from Edwardian and Victorian literature was through the extent of its concern for the literature of Asia. Writing from China and Japan would soon follow that from India in stimulating Yeats and Pound. In his essay introducing Tagore's poems Yeats makes no secret of how powerfully these translations had affected him. He describes how he carried the manuscript around with him constantly, reading it on top of trams and omnibuses and in restaurants, always holding it close so that strangers should not see how deeply moved he was. The subtleties of rhythm and of metrical invention in Tagore's poetry which Indian friends praised to Yeats were, inevitably, lost in translation. Nevertheless, he declared passionately, these lyrics 'display in their thought a world I have dreamed of all my life long'.[12] This was a world with a unified culture in which 'poetry and religion are the same thing' and in which there is 'carried back again to the multitude the thought of the scholar and of the noble'. It was an ideal which Pound, T.S. Eliot and D.H. Lawrence soon joined with Yeats in urgently commending, and became one of the chief icons of modernism.

When the collection of Tagore translations was published it occurred to Yeats that the eighteen-year-old Iseult Gonne might enjoy it, so he sent her a copy. Her mother wrote back saying how much pleasure it had given Iseult. Maud went on to say that Iseult, now a very beautiful young woman, had recently sat for an artist who wanted make a study for the head of the angel of the Annunciation. John Quinn, then on a visit to France, had hastened to buy it. Iseult had broken several hearts lately, but Maud thought that her daughter's own heart was quite untouched as yet.

In the latter part of this year Yeats came to know another attractive young woman just two years older than Iseult. Olivia Shakespear's brother Henry had married a widow, Nellie Hyde Lees, who had a daughter, Georgiana. The three of them lived in a house in fashionable Montpelier Square near Harrods and they also owned a house on the Devonshire coast where Yeats and the Shakespear ladies were invited to stay. Yeats was very taken with Georgie, as close friends such as Dorothy Shakespear called her. Twenty-seven years younger than he, Georgie had pronounced colouring, an attractive, rather square face and flashing dark eyes. She had much in common with Yeats: she loved the arts and was intrigued by the occult. Now began, however distantly at first, a relationship that in six years time would lead to a complete reordering of Yeats's life.

The London to which Yeats returned after his Devon visit continued to be politically troubled. Under the leadership of the burly, truculent Carson, the Protestants of Ulster gathered to commit themselves at a great rally to a solemn league and covenant; they would resist, by force if necessary, the imposition of rule from Dublin. Yeats felt demoralized. He was also unwell. He had nervous indigestion and he was starting to suffer from rheumatism. He felt he needed to be taken care of, so he set off for Coole where he could rest, fish for pike, write poems and enjoy the ministrations of Lady Gregory.

During his stay there occurred one of the great moments of literary transmission in modern poetry. Herbert Grierson, then Professor of English at the University of Aberdeen, published his famous edition of John Donne which rescued the seventeenth-century poet from neglect and placed him in a position of importance and influence in contemporary literary culture. Grierson sent Yeats a copy of his historic edition and Yeats was overwhelmed by it. He told Grierson that the book had given him the greatest pleasure.[13] Unquestionably the book had a major impact on Yeats's art. Here is a source of the poetry sometimes called 'the late Yeats', that rich mixture of sensuous imagery and intricate ideas. The newly revealed Donne spoke immediately to Yeats's concerns as he read him at Coole, and in this metaphysical poetry he saw how 'the more precise and learned the thought the greater the beauty, the passion'. Like the young American poet T.S. Eliot, whom he would soon meet through Pound, Yeats revelled in the Grierson edition and in a poetry that preceded what Eliot called 'the dissociation of sensibility'. Tagore's art assisted Yeats in his resistance to modern, atomized society; Donne's poetry, as now made known to him, assisted him in his efforts to escape modern atomized consciousness.

In late November Yeats left Coole and returned to Woburn Buildings

feeling restored, indeed buoyant. Energetically he developed a plan for his
father to earn some money by writing his memoirs, which Yeats would then
place with a publisher. He was confident that John Yeats could attract a
considerable readership with memories of the figures of his generation,
Isaac Butt, York Powell and the Dublin painter J.T. Nettleship, along with
his many entertaining anecdotes and his 'pictures of Old Ireland'. These
would certainly contrast with the picture of the Ireland of today that Yeats
now had to contemplate. In January 1913 Orangemen in Ulster had formed
themselves into a military organization, the Ulster Volunteer Force, to
resist rule from Dublin. If the Home Rule Bill reached the statute book
civil war in Ireland looked like a definite possibility.

As he followed these events from his Bloomsbury flat, Yeats also
involved himself in a new cultural venture in Ireland. Lady Gregory's
nephew Hugh Lane had recently offered to donate a collection of distinguished paintings to the city of Dublin on condition that a suitable
gallery was built to house them. Dublin Corporation voted to expend
£2,000 a year on the project but Lane insisted that wealthy individuals
should contribute too. Lord Ardilaun, the Guinness heir, subscribed but
said he would give no more until it was shown that there was a popular
demand for the paintings. This qualification elicited an indignant poem of
protest from Yeats, 'To a Wealthy Man who promised a Second
Subscription to the Dublin Municipal Gallery if it were proved the People
wanted Pictures'; the poem is an insistent declaration of how high culture
had been and could again be funded as it was in fifteenth-century Italy by
Cosimo de' Medici, Guidobaldo da Montefeltro, Duke of Urbino, and
Ercole d'Este, Duke of Ferrara. These men, their Italian names musical-
izing the text, were, the poem proclaims, indifferent to hostile public
opinion, and were moved to finance literature, architecture, philosophy and
libraries by their exultant hearts, their vibrant sense of the role of the arts.
They did, and Ardilaun should, Yeats concludes, build for the future of
culture. The three dozen lines are propaganda as well as art. Yeats sent the
poem to the *Irish Times* where it appeared in the second week of January.
When it later appeared in the volumes of poems *Responsibilities* the note of
social criticism was sustained by the poem that immediately followed,
'September 1913', a piece provoked by mean-spirited middle-class attitudes

to the Lane gallery. The tone is sneering but, in contrast, the two-line refrain at the end of each stanza is a rouser, a ringing reminder of Romantic Ireland and its visionary, the brave and generous John O'Leary who had been such a dominant figure in Yeats's development.

At the same time as Yeats was using poetry for purposes of social and political comment he was starting to write a sequence of poems of a very different kind. Since Aubrey Beardsley's death, Yeats had kept in touch with his sister Mabel who continued her career as an actress and who occasionally attended his 'Mondays' at Woburn Buildings. Now came the shocking news that at the age of forty she was dying of cancer. Yeats immediately went to visit her and was troubled and impressed by her courage in the face of pain and helplessness. Propped up on pillows with her pale, ravaged face well rouged, she was charming and wanted gossip, jokes, laughter. Beside her were four dolls that Charles Ricketts, the Chelsea artist, had made to divert her, dolls resembling people in her brother Aubrey's drawings, women with baggy trousers and boys that looked like women. It must have taken Ricketts days, Yeats thought, to model the faces and sew the clothes. Conversation around her bedside turned to people they had known in the 1890s. Mabel, notorious for her scandalous lifestyle, was amused that Florence Farr, who, she recalled, had often said things that made even Mabel herself blush, was now in Ceylon, soon to be headmistress of a girls' school.

The poignant image of Mabel Beardsley had a strong effect on Yeats. He lay awake most of the night until finally a poem began to shape itself in his mind. It proved to be the first in a sequence of seven with the overall title 'Upon a Dying Lady' which belong to a characteristic part of Yeats's oeuvre: poems deriving from a highly particularized occasion evoked and assessed with great sensitivity. 'Occasional poems' in this sense, the seven lyrics are united in an aesthetic whole by some common concerns. There is the delicate realization, for Mabel, the poet, and for the reader, of the tension between looking back at this world and looking forward to death; there is in these poems respect and admiration for their subjects and carefully formulated compassion.

Yeats found it strange that Mabel had brought the 1890s back to his attention in this way, for he had also recently been at work on a poem entitled 'The Grey Rock', a substantial piece of more than 130 lines addressed directly to his old associates the Rhymers, his companions at the Cheshire Cheese in Fleet Street. He salutes them, especially Ernest Dowson and Lionel Johnson, for staying true to 'the Muses' sterner laws', and relates for them a story from eleventh-century Ireland involving Murrough, son of King Brian Boru, which also takes up issues of faithfulness as opposed to betrayal. An intricate parallel is established between the ancient story and that of the self-destructive 1890s generation, with Yeats, the survivor, at the end presenting himself, contrary to the view of many of his critics, as a man of fidelity. Ezra Pound, who had learned a great deal about the 1890s from Yeats, admired this poem and included it among those he sent to *Poetry* of Chicago, where it was published in April 1913.

Another of Yeats's literary projects was a selection of his love poems to be published in an expensive limited edition by Cuala. He wrote to Bullen to get the publisher to agree to such an undertaking, saying that his chief motive was to feed 'my sister's hungry press'.[14] But besides assisting Lolly he also wanted to do something to draw attention to his more recent poems. He was tired of his image among the reading public, an image which, he said, was founded on what he had written before his thirtieth birthday. Weariness, discontent and a desire for change were the chief features of Yeats's mood during these winter months in early 1913. Later in the year he told Maud Gonne how lonely he had felt. Those of his own generation were disappearing from his life: Florence Farr was in Ceylon and he had fallen out with Miss Horniman. There was Mabel Dickinson, but she was only his mistress and could not give him a home. He was weary of his London bachelorhood, finding it ever harder to be the lively man about town. He was a 47-year-old single man who got nervous indigestion when compelled, as often happened, to dine alone at restaurants. Also his eyesight was very bad and his favourite activities, reading and theatregoing, only caused more strain. As the days started to lengthen he felt a little better and hurried off to Coole, but he had not been there long when there came a shock. A telegram from Mabel Dickinson informed him that she was pregnant.

Yeats went into a frenzy. What should happen now? He was always sensitive to women and anxious to be a gentleman, but how could he deny that this was a loveless relationship? What were his obligations to the unborn child? In a fever of anxiety he hastened back to London, and met with Mabel outside the redbrick mass of the Victoria and Albert Museum. When he discovered that Mabel's announcement had been a false alarm, Yeats's tension gave way to a surge of anger; they had a violent quarrel and parted. In coming weeks the resentment between them eased and there was something of a reconciliation, but Yeats had been seriously affected by the trauma.

A few days after this meeting in June, there came yet another shock, but this one was entirely different, bringing only exhilaration. Though recently Yeats's involvement in the occult had not been as intense as at other times in his life, he still attended séances. At one of these he came into contact with Elizabeth Radcliffe, a simple young girl who was also an astonishing medium. Consciously, she knew only English and a little French. But when she went into a trance she would do automatic writing, transcribing messages from the dead in Greek, Latin, Chinese, Italian, Provençal and Hebrew. Yeats was staggered but, as always, was determined not to be gullible. He did careful research into the various dead who identified themselves through the automatic writing, taking the papers with him to a country house at Brasted in Kent owned by Eva Fowler, the friend of Olivia Shakespear and Ezra Pound. Here, and on trips to the British Museum, he carefully checked out these messages from the beyond and concluded that they were genuine, being consistent with the life histories of their subjects; this was, he wrote solemnly to Maud Gonne, 'the most irrefutable evidence of the survival of the soul and the power of the soul'. He was greatly affected and his interest in the occult was rekindled. At this time he introduced his young friend, Miss Georgie Hyde Lees, into the Order of the Golden Dawn, while to his sceptical father in New York he wrote saying that he was developing a curious theory of spirit action which would make a rational study of mediums possible.

In the same letter he put a new literary idea to John Yeats. For years he had been impressed by the philosophical and critical sections of his father's letters, and now proposed that John Yeats allow a collection of such passages to be put together and published by Cuala. It was Pound who made the selection, which was published some years later. Collaborations between Yeats and Pound increased when Yeats, his eyesight ever worsening, decided to employ the lively young American as his secretary. At the beginning of November Yeats rented Stone Cottage at Coleman's Hatch, a small country place amidst woods and heather in the moorland close to the Ashdown Forest in Sussex, where they settled in. Yeats's correspondence was extensive and there was plenty of work for Pound to do – one Sunday Yeats dictated twenty-one letters. But the relationship was much more than that between an employer and an employee. The winter weeks in the remote Sussex woods became a poets' retreat. They talked for hours at a time; they argued about the art of poetry. Pound asserted his imagist poetics of *vers libre*, a poetry free of *a priori* rhythms, lineation, metre and rhyme schemes. But Yeats would not accept this part of modernist poetics; *vers libre*, he maintained, was no more than prose. On and on the arguments went, but companionably and creatively.

That November, as Ezra Pound prepared his contentious anthology *Des Imagistes*, Yeats suggested that James Joyce, now living in exile in Trieste, might have something to contribute. Pound immediately wrote off and the result was the inclusion of Joyce's poem 'I Hear An Army Charging' in the collection. That letter also initiated a literary relationship between Pound and Joyce that was to be highly productive for the modernist movement.

In coming winters Yeats and Pound were happy to return to their Sussex retreat, and 'Stone Cottage' came to signify an important phase in the history of modern literature. To spare Yeats's eyesight Pound also read aloud to him, getting through a substantial booklist including William Morris's versions of the Icelandic sagas and the Hindu *Mahabharata*. Yeats had managed to interest his young friend in astrology but Pound was wary of the spirit world, 'the spooks' as he called them. Nevertheless he persevered with the reading of Joseph Ennermoser's *History of Magic*, a work with an 'Appendix of the Most Remarkable and Best Authenticated Stories of Apparitions, Dreams, Second Sight, Somnambulism, Predictions, Divination, Witchcraft, Vampires, Fairies, Table-Turning and Spirit-Rapping'. Pound also got through a volume of spells and wizardry, *The Grimoire of Pope Honorius* of 1629, and a French occult novel of the late seventeenth century, *Le Comte de Gabalis*. Yeats later passed this on to Olivia Shakespear who translated it into English.

At Stone Cottage that first winter Pound also brought to Yeats one of the most important literary gifts that the older poet ever received. A couple of weeks before going to Sussex, Pound, ever on the move through literary London, had been introduced by the Indian poet Sarojini Naidu to an American widow, Mrs Mary Fenollosa. Her husband, who had died some five years before, had taught philosophy at the Imperial University in Tokyo. Ernest Fenollosa had become passionately interested in the art and literature of China and Japan and at his death he left a good deal of manuscript material which his widow was determined should not be lost. Out of his papers she compiled and edited a two-volume work, *Epochs of Chinese and Japanese Art*. Having read Pound's poetry she asked Naidu to arrange for her to meet the leader of the new imagist school of poets. Following this meeting Mrs Fenollosa made up her mind that Pound was the person to make use of her husband's translations of plays and poems and she entrusted him with the manuscripts, which he then brought to Stone Cottage. Yeats took an immediate interest in Fenollosa's versions of Japanese Noh plays, discovering in them new and exciting possibilities for his own writing for the theatre. They provided models for a more stylized, hieratic and archetypal drama than he had written hitherto. It was yet another important instance of the transmissions that helped make for modernism. Yeats's first play in the Noh style was *At the Hawk's Well*, a one-act rendering of the human condition through the use of masked and generic characters such as An Old Man, A Young Man, Three Musicians. A couple of years later, in 1916, Yeats saw it performed in the large drawing-room of Lady Cunard's house.

During their Sussex winter of 1913–14 the two poets made frequent trips up to London to keep in touch with goings on in the literary world. There was an important occasion at the end of November when Yeats, who had accepted Gosse's invitation to serve on the Academic Committee of the Royal Society of Literature, had to attend a large public meeting at Caxton Hall at which he was to award the Polignac Prize to his fellow Dubliner, 31-year-old James Stephens, for his book *The Crock of Gold*. A reporter for the feminist magazine the *New Freewoman*, soon to be renamed *The Egoist* and another of the important 'little magazines' of this period, gave an account of Yeats at this ceremony. The amused young writer was probably

Richard Aldington, one of Pound's fellow imagists. 'Mr Yeats,' he wrote, rose to speak and

> explained with Dublin Theatre gestures and parsonic elocution that he had no manuscript to read from. He had given his to the press. He smiled benignly, and recited his memorised speech perfectly. He spoke in his beautiful voice; he expressed Celtic love with his more beautiful face; he elevated and waved his yet more beautiful hands. He blessed us with his presence. He spoke of spirits and phantasmagoria. He spoke of finding two boots in the middle of a field and the owner of the boots listening for earth-spirits under a bush . . . He praised Mr Stephens' Crock of Gold. He read one of Mr Stephens' poems, which was admirable as he read it . . . Mr Yeats concluded the performance by giving Mr Stephens a hundred pounds.[15]

Later, Yeats went on with Olivia and Dorothy to a puppet theatre in Chelsea to see a performance of Maeterlinck's *Ariadne et Barbe Bleue*. Dorothy wrote to Ezra suggesting that the four of them should create a puppet theatre: 'O.S., you and I and WBY could manage one beautifully. You two to read and us to pull Craig cardboard scenery, WBY plays, dresses by DS.'[16] The suggestion is a good indication of the closeness between the mother, her former lover, her daughter and her daughter's suitor at this time.

The world outside this intimate, cultured circle grew ever more turbulent. At the time Yeats and Pound were settling into Stone Cottage Dublin was paralyzed by a bitter industrial dispute. A strike by the transport union had led to a lock-out by the employers who were organized by William Martin Murphy, the proprietor of two newspapers, the *Irish Independent* and the *Evening Herald*. Murphy embodied all that Yeats despised in modern Ireland. An anti-Parnellite and an opponent of the plan to house the Lane picture collection, Murphy provoked Yeats to write a letter to the *Irish Worker* protesting against the lock-out. The city was at a standstill. Non-unionized workers who could not count on the support of trade unionists in England, Scotland and Wales were without wages and their children were without food. Maud Gonne hurried over from France to help with a programme of children's dinners. She sold the last remaining piece of her once large jewellery collection, her diamond necklace, to help finance them. Yeats sent her a cheque which she thought generous. The lock-out dragged on as the year approached its end. There was a good deal of violence, especially on the part of the police, resulting in the socialist and nationalist James Connolly founding the Irish Citizen Army to enable people to protect themselves against the brutality of the Royal Irish Constabulary.

In the early weeks of 1914 the confrontation petered out. Workers drifted back to work accepting hard terms. There was a pervasive sense of defeat and demoralization. Over in Sussex, Yeats prepared to set out on a lecture tour of the United States where his reputation continued to grow. *Poetry* of Chicago, at Pound's urging, awarded him a prize of fifty pounds for 'the best poem published during the magazine's first year', which they declared to be 'The Grey Rock'. Yeats, now feeling a little more prosperous, in great part because of his royal pension, suggested that he retain just ten pounds to commission a bookplate from Sturge Moore to remind him of the magazine's generosity. He asked that the remaining forty pounds be awarded to some young indigent poet and recommended Ezra Pound. He told the editors that he thought Pound's poetic experiments were perhaps errors but he went on to say that he 'would always sooner give the laurel to vigorous errors than to any orthodoxy not inspired'.[17]

Shortly before sailing for New York Yeats took part in a ceremony, part literary, part political, held at the instigation of Pound. On 18 January on a bitterly cold winter's day he led a group of poets across Sussex in a hired car to Newbuildings Place, the country estate of Wilfrid Scawen Blunt. This 73-year-old white-bearded patriarch, the husband of Byron's grand-daughter and the lover of many women, including Lady Gregory, was to be honoured for his poetry and his progressive politics. He was a strenuous opponent of British imperialism and a long-time supporter of the Irish cause. For this he had been imprisoned a quarter of a century before. The poets now presented him with a stone reliquary carved by Pound's sculptor friend Gaudier-Brzeska; it contained manuscript poems by each of the poets present. An aristocrat with a grand manner, Blunt received them courteously and invited them to dine on roast peacock. The guests represented two generations of poets following that of Blunt. Yeats, Victor Plarr and Sturge Moore were of the 1890s generation and Pound and his imagist associates F.S. Flint and Richard Aldington were of the next.

Two weeks after this ceremony Yeats left for America, where he would remain for nearly three months. When the liner *Mauretania* docked in New York, he went first to the Algonquin Hotel and then to stay for a few days with his father at the Petipas sisters' rooming-house. John Yeats owed his landladies a considerable sum of money which his vexed, embarrassed son set about paying off. A conciliatory letter arrived from John Quinn. Dorothy Coates, who had caused the breach between Yeats and Quinn, was now in the grip of a serious illness and anxious that the two men be reconciled. So Quinn wrote to say that he was ready to 'shake hands with you and let by-gones be by-gones'. Yeats quickly agreed and they began to co-operate on a number of projects, the chief of which was the returning of John Yeats to solvency. Quinn's part was the purchase of manuscripts from Yeats, the money going straightaway to reduce the old painter's debts. John Butler Yeats was, however, incorrigible. When the debts were finally paid off in the following year he immediately invited all his friends out to dinner and drank three glasses of Jameson's as a mark of celebration. He was soon in debt again.

Yeats's American tour was a great financial success and with the proceeds he was able to pay off his own long-standing debt, amounting to some £500, lent to him over the years by Lady Gregory. After a grand farewell dinner in New York organized by John Quinn on 1 April, Yeats sailed for England, arriving in time for the marriage of Ezra Pound and Dorothy Shakespear in Kensington's large Victorian parish church, St Mary Abbotts. Yeats, more prosperous now than he had ever been before, gave them a sum of money as a wedding present. To his delight Dorothy and Ezra used it to give a commission to Arnold Dolmetsch, who had made the psaltery for Florence Farr decades before. The newlyweds asked him to make them a clavichord. This keyboard instrument was 'the size of a suitcase', Pound told Quinn, and the prize possession of the musically minded young poet and his wife.

In the month of the wedding there appeared in *Poetry* of Chicago Pound's highly favourable review of Yeats's recent volume of poems, *Responsibilities*. Pound commended the book above all for its nobility, which he saw as 'the very core of Mr Yeats' production, the constant element of his writing'. Like many subsequent readers he saw it as showing a distinct evolution in Yeats's art; it is indeed a turning point, for in comparison with *The Green Helmet and Other Poems* of four years before it shows a marked intensification of social concern and satirical tone. There are new and deeper levels of contempt in 'On those that hated *The Playboy of the Western World*, 1907' and in 'To a Shade' which mocks those, and William Martin Murphy in particular, who opposed Lane as they opposed Parnell. The opening and closing poems in the volume are responses to George Moore. In January 1914 this sometime friend published in the *English Review* an article entitled 'Yeats, Lady Gregory and Synge' in which he ridiculed Yeats for his social pretensions and for his doting attention to Maud Gonne. When Maud got wind of the article, she had been determined to come to London to give Moore a 'horsewhipping'. But when she read it, she decided that it was not a personal attack, just cheap, yellow journalism. Yeats's responses to the attack in these two poems are more complex. The first shows him strongly, unrepentantly proud of his ancestry; the last responds to Moore with a careful definition of Yeats's hard-won confidence in his art and his stoical, lofty indifference to those who show it disrespect.

Responsibilities is by no means entirely polemical, also containing narrative poems of Irish history, two thoughtful lyrics addressed to the eighteen-year-old Iseult Gonne, and many more such as 'Fallen Majesty', 'That the Night Come' and 'A Memory of Youth' expressing Yeats's latest and more distanced feelings for Iseult's mother. 'The Cold Heaven' comes closer to the unhappy love story and evokes, memorably, its agony. 'The Peacock' is a proud, triumphant assertion of the value of the creative process; it is the poem which Pound, in a comic passage in *The Pisan Cantos*, recalls Yeats composing at Stone Cottage that winter, his voice booming up the chimney as he repeatedly chanted the lines to get them right.

Not long after the Pound wedding Yeats set off to stay with Maud Gonne at her house in Normandy. They took a trip south to Mirebeau, a little town near Poitiers, to investigate a miracle that had been reported. A representation of the Sacred Heart in a crude oil-painting had begun to drip blood. Yeats and Maud, both fascinated by this occurrence, were permitted to dip their handkerchiefs in the blood. When the samples were sent to the Lister Institute for chemical analysis, the verdict was that they contained no human blood. The priest who owned and made the claims for the painting, the Abbé Vachère, was summoned to Rome and finally excommunicated.

Yeats's feelings for Maud were reanimated as he saw her approaching her fiftieth birthday, and on his return from France he wrote a number of fine poems sparked by memories of her on this visit. 'Her Praise' begins in an excited rush of admiration before it slows down to stress her generosity to the poor, now as 'in the old days'. 'Broken Dreams' is an assertion of the continuing power of Maud's presence even as she ages and her hair turns grey; and also of the power of the memories she created when she was young. 'A Thought from Propertius' in eight lines recalls the heroic quality of Maud's beauty, simultaneously high-minded and compellingly sensuous. The phrasing of the poem is assisted by the example of the Roman love poet who was the subject of one of Ezra Pound's major poems of this decade, his 'Homage to Sextus Propertius'. Pound's many love affairs and his recent marriage made Yeats aware of the generation gap between himself and his young friend. But in the lively, good-natured poem 'His Phoenix', in which he lists some of Pound's many girlfriends and in which his refrain, to the young is 'let them have their day', he consoles himself with another refrain, that in Maud 'I knew a phoenix in my youth'.

The poem 'The People' is a far more serious piece, a difficult dialogue with the beautiful ageing phoenix he had stayed with in May. The poem recalls an occasion nine years before when Yeats, despondent about his work in and for Ireland, had contemplated a life of courtly, cultured exile in some old Italian city. The Phoenix reproves him, asserting her faith in the Irish people despite her experiences of dishonesty and ingratitude. Yeats attempts to explain their differences by contrasting those who live by thought and those who live by deeds. But he does not have the last word. Her words about the people make his heart leap in spite of himself. He was abashed by her words then; he is abashed to remember them, seeing her nearly a decade later. 'The People' is a delicately managed representation of the victory of words as feeling over words as argument. It is a treatment of an issue that greatly concerned Yeats's younger literary contemporaries.

When Yeats was in France with Maud, Ireland was approaching a condition of civil war. In May 1914 the Government of Ireland Act was finally passed by the British Parliament. There was to be Home Rule with the six north-eastern counties excluded for an unspecified period of time. But the Ulster Volunteer Force, for which Rudyard Kipling wrote inspirational poetry, was preparing to create their own government that would keep the province free from Dublin for ever. The previous month huge quantities of arms had been landed at Larne to increase the firepower of the Ulster army. When the National Volunteers, the defenders of Home Rule, also landed a large consignment of arms from Erskine Childers's yacht *Asgaard* at Howth, they were discovered and the troops called out. There followed a demonstration in Dublin in favour of Home Rule and the National Volunteers. Troops helping the police were mocked and tormented by demonstrators, became panicky and eventually fired into the crowd, killing three people and wounding thirty-eight. There was shock throughout and beyond Ireland. From Maud Gonne it produced a surge of sympathy and compassion for the rioters. From Yeats's brother Jack, a strong Republican, it elicited a major painting, *Bachelors' Walk*. But then, the bitterly contentious arguments over Ireland had suddenly to be put on hold. A world war had long threatened and on 4 August 1914 it began. Three great European imperial powers, Britain, France and Russia, were ranged against Germany and Austro-Hungary, who would soon be joined by the Ottoman Empire ruled from Constantinople. The war was the devastating beginning of a new epoch in the history of Europe and the North Atlantic basin. When after four years of unprecedented slaughter the war ended, the condition of England, of Ireland and of Yeats himself would be utterly transformed.

D
URING THE AUTUMN MONTHS OF 1914 WHILE THE WAR IN
eastern France was settling into horrific trench warfare, Yeats was
enjoying the comforts of Coole and writing his account of his
early years, *Reveries over Childhood and Youth.* This short prose work of
some seventeen thousand words (the ideal size for Lolly's press[1]) was completed on Christmas Day. The book was intended for the market in Irish
reminiscences of a particular generation established and exploited by
Katharine Tynan, Lady Gregory and George Moore. Yeats's memoir
begins with his earliest recollections and ends in 1892, the year in which he
was twenty-seven and his grandfather William Pollexfen died. His grandfather is the dominant figure in the book, by far the most considerable male
forebear in that ancestral Irish world which it evokes, and it is with him
rather than with his father that Yeats is most deeply involved. The selective bias of Yeats's narrative is such that his development, his *Bildung*, is
shown as something that occurs almost entirely through his interaction
with males. To be sure, there are women in the story but they are not
prominent. Yeats's mother and Lily are pictured rarely, Lolly not at all: the
two sisters who in 1892 were still contributing to his keep do not figure.
Neglectful, like most autobiographies, of many areas of the subject's experience, *Reveries* concentrates on a young man's spiritual, cultural and artistic progress. It is a finely written work with many delicate passages
presenting a chronological, if sometimes disjointed, narrative. Occasion-

ally however, as in the seventh section, Yeats follows Pound's example and abandons chronology in favour of a collocation of images, or of what Pound would call luminous details. Developing this technique further over twenty years, Yeats was to write two more volumes of autobiography, and this trio of books is the work which more than any other establishes him as one of the masters of twentieth-century English prose.

After leaving Coole with the completed manuscript of *Reveries* Yeats proceeded to Stone Cottage in Sussex where he again took up residence with Ezra Pound and Dorothy. Once more Pound acted as his secretary and engaged him in further intense literary discussion and study. In January 1915 Pound began to read aloud all seven volumes of the edition of Wordsworth prepared by Ernest Dowden of Trinity College Dublin, who had recently died. Yeats did not finally like Wordsworth, seeing him as one who made insufficient distinction between poetical experience and intellect.[2] Pound at Pisa commented that Yeats only listened to the Wordsworth 'for the sake of his conscience' and really preferred hearing Ennermoser on witches.

In this once quiet, remote wooded place the loud thuds from the guns of the Royal Artillery training nearby on the south coast sounded over Pound's drawling voice as he read on and on to Yeats. Another of the works they chose to hear was C.M. Doughty's *Travels in Arabia Deserta* and his epic poem *The Dawn in Britain*. Yeats like Pound and most of the other young modernists, 'the men of 1914' as Wyndham Lewis called them, was preoccupied with the nature and possibility of the epic in modern times. It was one way to be rid of the aesthetic and the ethic of realism.

After Yeats and his young companions returned to London, the capital had its first experience of being attacked from the air as the long silver spheres of German airships, the Zeppelins, let their bombs fall. There was much damage and loss of life. In May came the news that the liner *Lusitania*, on which Yeats himself had once travelled, had been sunk in the Atlantic by German submarines. Among the 1,153 drowned, 128 of them citizens of neutral America, was Lady Gregory's nephew Hugh Lane who had insisted on giving his lifebelt to a woman passenger. His death was a blow to Lady Gregory, and the complexities of his will also created a long-lasting problem for her, for Yeats and for Ireland. Irritated by the grudging, inadequate response to the gift of paintings he had offered

Dublin, Lane had willed his art collection to the National Gallery in London. Then, when he became director of the National Gallery in Dublin, he changed his mind and three months before he died wrote a codicil to his will bequeathing the collection to Dublin. But the codicil was not properly witnessed and the London National Gallery insisted it was invalid. Off and on, for the remainder of their lives, Yeats and Lady Gregory struggled to have Hugh Lane's final intentions respected, but both were long dead when a compromise settlement was at last agreed.

In a letter explaining the problem of the Lane pictures to John Quinn, Yeats portrayed himself as living a rather quiet life as a middle-aged bachelor in sombre, anxious, wartime London. Certainly a production of *On Baile's Strand* with excellent costumes by Charles Ricketts had been an exciting success and fired him to proceed with his heroic cycle of plays. But socially he was often at a loose end. He still had his 'Mondays' and he went to visit Ricketts a good deal 'to discuss painting'. But there was little else to report except a visit to Robert Bridges in the country. After his return, Yeats, ever keen to promote Pound's career, sent Bridges, now Britain's Poet Laureate, his protégé's latest volume, *Cathay*, made up of poems from the Chinese and deriving from the draft translations of Ernest Fenollosa.

This summer Pound recruited Yeats to assist him in another of his many enterprises. The young American had come to admire increasingly the work of James Joyce; he also feared for Joyce's material well-being in Trieste in the midst of war. Always energetic in his support of talents he respected, Pound set about obtaining some money for Joyce from the Royal Literary Fund. He got Yeats to approach Edmund Gosse and ask him to use his considerable influence in government circles. Throughout the summer Yeats engaged in correspondence with Gosse, supplying information as requested, commending Joyce as a man of genius and bracketing him with James Stephens as 'the most promising people we have in Ireland'. By the autumn Pound's strategy had worked and Joyce received a grant of seventy-five pounds.

Back at Coole, Yeats received letters from Maud describing the miserable life she was leading in war-torn France where absolutely no criticism of the French and British involvement in the war was tolerated. She and Iseult were working as volunteer nurses and both were horrified by the appalling wounds and amputations with which they had to deal. By November Maud was in a strange psychological state. Her consciousness, she reported, was taken over by a wild dance tune, a reel. It reminded her of passages in one of her favourite operas, Wagner's *Siegfried*. She also had a strong sense that the thousands of Irish soldiers killed in the war were all dancing to this wild reel.

Yeats for his part tried his best to ignore the war. When Henry James, entering the last year of his life, wrote to ask him for a poem for a collection being assembled by his friend Edith Wharton for war charities, Yeats sent a brief piece that insisted that the poet should remain silent about times like these. This apolitical attitude did him no harm in London society. In early December he was able to report to Lily that he had been offered, and had declined, a knighthood. Flattered by the offer, he had, as a believer in Ireland's independence, no choice but to turn it down. He remembered how Wordsworth had betrayed the principles of his youth through accepting government patronage and he did not want someone to write of him, as Browning had of Wordsworth, 'Just for a handful of silver he left us/Just for a medal to pin on his chest'.

He was very much involved with his family and wanted Lily to have an embroidery exhibition. He was keen 'to keep her needle busy' and had commissioned a design for a table centre from Sturge Moore which he wished her to embroider. It was to be a present for Olivia Shakespear, but further versions could be marketed by the Cuala embroiderers. Like his friend Charles Ricketts Yeats was well aware of how Bakst's designs for the Russian ballet had dramatically affected public taste and he urged his sister to use stronger colours. He was also concerned about his father's responses to the account of the Yeats family life in *Reveries*. The picture of Dowden was the one he feared might give his father greatest offence. Writing in January 1916 Yeats conceded that Dowden was always charming in private, but in public, Yeats insisted, the Trinity College professor was the most serious opponent of 'my movement in Dublin'. He went on to acknowledge that one of the strategies of *Reveries* was to commemorate 'my movement' and to show Dowden as insubstantial, merely a foil to the very vivid image of Yeats's mentor and sustainer, John O'Leary.

During the third and final winter at Stone Cottage shared with Ezra

Pound, one of their new enthusiasms was the *Imaginary Conversations* of Walter Savage Landor, a writer from the Romantic period who in old age had been befriended by the young Robert Browning and his wife. Yeats and Pound alike were intrigued by Landor who in this work, like Pound in his Cantos, put together voices of characters from different periods of history. But their discussions of the persona as a poetic device were rudely interrupted when two low-ranking members of British military intelligence knocked on the door of the remote cottage and demanded to be told what an American alien was doing so close to the artillery batteries on the coast. Ezra and Dorothy suddenly found themselves facing prosecution, but Yeats contacted the Poet Laureate Robert Bridges, Pound appealed to Ford Madox Ford's friend, the Liberal MP and minister C.F.G. Masterman, and eventually the matter was dropped. Yeats and Pound were able to return to one of the main shared tasks of this winter, the first of Yeats's Noh plays, *At the Hawk's Well*, dedicated to his enthusiastic secretary.

Returning to London at the time when the German artillery was engaging in unprecedented shelling of the French fortress of Verdun, Yeats prepared to supervise the rehearsals of this new work. The first performance was scheduled for 2 April 1916 before an invited audience in the drawing-room of Lady Cunard in Cambridge Square. The play concerns the quest of the hero, Cuchulain, for the wisdom and immortality to be obtained by drinking from a well watched over by a mysterious guardian. Cuchulain, instinctive and passionate, meets an old man, the embodiment of Reason, who for fifty years has been fooled by the guardian every time he attempts to drink from the well. On the rare occasions when the waters bubble up, the guardian turns into a hawk and entices the questers away. When they return, the waters have receded and the well is dry again. In this first production the Old Man was played by Allan Wade, a young admirer of Yeats's work who would one day edit the first major collections of the poet's letters. The part of the guardian Hawk was played by Michio Ito, a Japanese actor-dancer known to Ezra Pound. During rehearsals Yeats frequently took Ito to London Zoo in Regent's Park to study the hawks in their cages. Bystanders were amused to see the small Japanese man flapping his arms in mimicry of the birds and receiving careful, precise direction from the tall black-suited Irishman with the pince-nez.

Rehearsals did not go smoothly. A difficult member of the production team was Edmund Dulac, a 33-year-old Frenchman from Toulouse. Dapper and always formally dressed, the witty Dulac had won fame as an artist by his striking illustrations to an edition of *The Arabian Nights* published in 1914. He had met Yeats at the home of Ricketts and Shannon, and Yeats, admiring his many talents and his sharp, uncompromising intelligence, soon counted one more practitioner of the visual arts among his close friends. Dulac designed the costumes for *At the Hawk's Well* and composed the play's music – which was remote and archaic in character, rather like the *Gymnopédies* of Erik Satie whom Dulac had known in Paris years before. Dulac had violent quarrels with the lady guitarist who did not wish her instrument to be covered with a cardboard disguise to make it look ancient and Irish. After some nasty scenes the fastidious and irascible Dulac had his way. He changed the scoring so that one musician played a harp, another a series of bamboo flutes with different scales which Dulac had made, whilst the composer himself played a gong and a drum. The urbane orchestral conductor and impresario Thomas Beecham, who directed a concert in the drawing-room prior to the play, was much impressed by *At the Hawk's Well* and its music, and talked of mounting a theatre season in the West End with Yeats, Ricketts and Dulac. Yeats himself was delighted with this new, stripped down theatre. He had discovered a new form, he enthused to Lady Gregory. He expressed his wonder at the success of the dancing and masks.[3]

Some three weeks after the performance any residual pleasure and excitement Yeats might have felt were abruptly ended by news from Ireland of an uprising. On Easter Monday in front of Dublin's General Post Office, Patrick Pearse had read out the proclamation of the Irish Republic. The Post Office and other key public buildings were quickly seized and main streets barricaded. In the next six days there was streetfighting and the centre of Dublin was devastated by British artillery fire and by shelling from a Royal Navy gunboat on the River Liffey. On the Saturday after Easter Pearse and James Connolly were forced to agree to unconditional surrender. In less than a week they were court-martialled and shot by a firing squad. Other leaders of the Rising, including Maud Gonne's estranged husband John MacBride, were also executed.

[handwritten marginalia: "That would be good to me,"]

[handwritten marginalia: "Easter 1916!"]

Yeats, staying at the Gloucestershire home of his friend the painter William Rothenstein, was overwhelmed by the news, telling Lady Gregory that he had no idea that a public event could move him so deeply. Eight days after the first executions in Dublin he tried to express his contradictory and complex feelings by embarking on the poem which would later bear the title 'Easter 1916'.

The news of the Rising and its suppression reached Maud in Normandy, where she was working as a nurse. The experience of 'taking care of some terribly mangled wrecks from the Verdun battle'[4] had brought a pervasive sense of horror into her mind which the reports from Ireland intensified. She was consumed with anger against the British and with compassion for the victims. Her feelings were such that she was ready to forgive John MacBride for all his abuse. She declared to Yeats that 'Those who enter Eternity by the great door of Sacrifice atone for all.'[5] Iseult came over to London to stay with her aunt, Maud's sister. Yeats was worried by the account she gave of her mother's emotional state, but he entertained Iseult royally, introducing her to his friends and acquaintances including Bernard Shaw and the Pounds.

Ezra was greatly taken with Iseult's etherial beauty and would soon have an affair with her. But Yeats's mind was on Maud and he decided to go over and see her, hoping that MacBride's death had created new possibilities in their relationship. After a brief trip to battle-scarred Dublin in early June he travelled on to Colleville, where he stayed for most of the summer. With the young Iseult, who was now an aspiring poetess, he spent much time studying the new generation of French Catholic writers – Paul Claudel, Francis Jammes and Charles Péguy – the last of whom Iseult was keen to translate into English. Yeats also asked Maud to marry him and to work with him to promote Ireland's cultural and literary renewal in the aftermath of the recent catastrophe in Dublin. But Maud was no more minded to accept this latest proposal than she had been his first, nearly a quarter of a century before. Deeply disappointed, fearful of returning to his essentially solitary life in Bloomsbury, Yeats asked Maud if he might have permission to propose to Iseult, now twenty-one and some thirty years younger than he. Maud consented but Iseult, very much in awe of Yeats, felt unable to respond when he began to talk about their marrying. She was flattered and charmed, but also shy and uneasy, simply unable to envisage such a possibility. Yeats did not pursue the matter and in a state of considerable depression he returned to his bachelor quarters in Woburn Buildings.

With his increasing prosperity he had taken over and furnished the floor below so that he now had quite a large apartment. But it gave him little pleasure. In the months after the Rising he felt greatly drawn to his own people. He wanted to root himself in Ireland. On a trip there towards the end of the year he began negotiations for the purchase of a tumbledown castle and cottage at Ballylee not far from Coole Park. The place would become an important subject in his later poetry. ∠

Shortly after he returned to London in November he received a forthright letter from Maud strongly criticizing the final version of 'Easter 1916' which he had sent her. She said that it wasn't worthy of him or of the subject. 'Too long a sacrifice' had not made stones of the hearts of Pearse, Connolly and MacDonagh. The poem ought not to have censured them but ought to have avenged their defeat by creating a monument of spiritual beauty to them. Though not referred to in the poem, Maud of course saw herself as one of those who, according to Yeats, had restricted their range of consciousness, restricted their involvement in the larger life process in order to sustain the willpower and single-mindedness necessary to achieve political objectives. As always, she could not be content with his lofty, long-term pondering of political motivation, violence and courage. For Yeats though, 'Easter 1916', as well as being a complex meditation on these matters, represented an evolution in his thinking about his fellow countrymen. The title itself is clearly a rejoinder to 'September 1913', but now the scorn is gone. Yeats has been taught humility towards and respect for those in Dublin who have given their lives for their country, those who have created 'a terrible beauty'. But the oxymoron formed by that adjective and noun encapsulates the ambivalence that runs through the poem. It is a work of inquiry, and the fourth and final section of twenty-four lines contains no less than four question marks. There is an anxious probing of uncertainties, yet the last six lines are an entirely unambiguous assertion of the heroic status of Connolly, Pearse and MacDonagh and, yes, MacBride. Yeats owns up to his doubts about the political prudence of the Rising, about the emotional condition of its leaders and the role of the poet in its tragic aftermath but he is, at the last, assertively loyal to the men executed as criminals just a few months before.

In 1917 there were suddenly two important new players on the world scene, neither of whom was attractive to Yeats. In the first week in April America was led into the war by her idealistic Democratic President, Woodrow Wilson. Ten days later Lenin arrived in St Petersburg from exile in Switzerland and set to work to bring about a Bolshevik government in Russia. These developments signalled the displacement of the European empires from the centre of global power, and began that crisis in Europe which was a condition of Yeats's art in his later years. Throughout the spring and summer his mental state deteriorated from unhappiness to depression, to crisis and thence to an intense, panicky fear of imminent nervous breakdown and insanity.

In the spring of 1917 he was at Coole, having gone there earlier than usual in order to complete the purchase and to help plan the renovations of his tower at Ballylee. He also wanted to steady himself and recover from the many blows of the previous year. He had not seen the spring at Coole before. It was beautiful but it did not lift him, and the best he could say to Olivia Shakespear was that 'I am not in the best of spirits but when the day is fine life is endurable.'[6] But he was managing to do some work. He completed a small volume of philosophy first called 'An Alphabet' and then retitled with a phrase from Virgil, *Per Amica Silentia Lunae*. The first of the two essays it comprises, 'Anima Hominis', is a series of random thoughts about consciousness, the self and the anti-self. He gives as an example Walter Savage Landor, 'who topped us all in calm nobility when the pen was in his hand, as in the daily violence of his passion when he laid it down'.[7] The second essay, 'Anima Mundi', is a pondering of Wordsworth's 'immortal sea which brought us hither' and of the images constituting 'a Great Memory passing on from generation to generation'.[8] Yeats thought of these prose pieces as 'a kind of prose backing to my poetry'; they were parts of his persistent quest for a vision of transcendent order beyond the spectacularly developing chaos of the times.

At Coole he also worked at his writing for the theatre. He made more revisions to *The Player Queen* and began another play in the Noh style which he would later entitle *The Dreaming of the Bones*. It is another

response to Easter 1916. A young, dedicated ideologue who had participated in the Dublin Rising flees to the west of Ireland and in a remote place
encounters the spirits of the legendary lovers Dervorgilla and Diarmuid,
traditionally blamed for inviting the English into Ireland in the middle of
the twelfth century. The bitterness endures as the intransigent Republican
confronts the lovers, hears of their difficult fate but finally refuses to forgive
them.

In June Yeats went over to England on a brief visit and gave lectures at
Edinburgh and Birmingham. He had ambitious plans for his new enthusiasm, the tower at Ballylee, and was keen to make extra money. He also
received an invitation from an agency of the French government to deliver
lectures in Paris later in the year and he hoped that these would pay enough
to roof the castle. He spent a few days in London and saw and admired a
performance in English of *L'Annonce faite à Marie* by Paul Claudel, whose
work Iseult admired so intensely. But in London he was oppressed by the
war-weariness of the place and by the bleak, lonely prospects for his future
life there.

Returning gladly to Coole, he stopped off for a few days in Dublin and
spent time with the witty, entertaining doctor and man of letters, Oliver St
John Gogarty, and with those friends from earlier years, Douglas Hyde and
AE. He enjoyed and lived in 'a whirl of excellent talk'. But when he arrived
back in County Galway his long-standing depression returned, despite
Augusta Gregory's affectionate attentions. He had made up his mind to
propose to Iseult again. Despondently he showed Lady Gregory the new
clothes he had bought in Dublin to wear when he went courting. Then he
suddenly mentioned the possibility of proposing marriage to Georgie Hyde
Lees if Iseult turned him down. Georgie had none of Maud's flamboyance
or her strong opinions. She listened respectfully to Yeats, glad to learn from
him about art and the occult. She was also sensible and practical, down-to-
earth in a way Iseult could never be. But Georgie had none of Iseult's pale
etherial beauty that Yeats admired so much; her features were more robust,
her colouring was almost as dark as a gypsy's. Lady Gregory could see that
if Yeats married Iseult he would have to take care of an unstable young
woman. If he married Georgie, a competent young woman would take care
of him, and the frank Lady Gregory doubtless made this clear to Yeats. But

then Yeats had second thoughts about Georgie. He wondered about his half-heartedness in pursuing the idea of marrying her. He did not know what to do with himself; his plans for ending his unhappy bachelorhood were leading nowhere. He had got to the point, he told Olivia Shakespear, where only work was of interest any more. *Yes!*

When Yeats joined Maud and Iseult at Colleville, the daily routine with the two dogs, the caged birds, the monkey, the seven rabbits and the parrot was pleasant enough – even when the monkey tried to pluck feathers from the parrot. But it became increasingly and depressingly plain to Yeats that Iseult would not, could not, warm to the thought of marrying him. By the first week in September he began to accept the inevitable and prepared to return to London. He also pursued negotiations with Mrs Tucker and her daughter about the possibility of his proposing to Georgie. For weeks Maud had exhausted herself in vitriolic diatribes against the British for denying her the special wartime passports necessary to travel to Ireland, but she finally obtained permission from the British passport office in Paris for Iseult and herself to proceed as far as London. Yeats and the two women he loved agreed to travel together via Le Havre and Southhampton. At Le Havre Iseult, in one of her violent mood swings, burst into heavy sobbing, protesting that she had been selfish in refusing Yeats and that she was sure that despite his assurances their friendship was threatened. Then she rushed off and hid herself. After she had been found and to some extent calmed down they had a tense sea-crossing. When they stepped on to the dock at Southampton, immigration officials immediately approached Maud and Iseult, took them aside and, while the boat train was kept waiting, subjected them to a long and thorough search as possible spies. Mother and daughter were subsequently served with a written notice issued under the Defence of the Realm Act forbidding them to go on to Ireland. Maud was humiliated and furious. Staying at his club in London, Yeats worried that she would do 'something wild'.

He himself was in turmoil. What should he do now about Georgie Hyde Lees? He did not want to abandon Iseult in her near enforced imprisonment in London with Maud, but he recognized there was no future with her. He felt unstable, desperate and unable to go on alone. His only salvation was a wife, a companion. Two days after his return from France he decided to accept Mrs Tucker's invitation to join her and Georgie at their home in the country. In their first discussion Mrs Tucker made it plain that she was far from being sure about the advisability of her daughter marrying a man so very much older. But Georgie at the age of twenty-four was eager to be married and become free of her mother. She was flattered by the proposal from someone so eminent and so admired by her friends and contemporaries, Dorothy and Ezra. The couple became engaged. However, Yeats was uncomfortable with the disagreement between mother and daughter and, as on other occasions, hastened to Coole to ask Lady Gregory for advice. His old friend urged him to marry as soon as possible, and did not change her mind when Mrs Tucker wrote asking her to persuade Yeats to terminate the engagement. Lady Gregory regarded Maud and Iseult as women who brought only distress and disruption into Yeats's life, but Georgie she saw as a gentle and unassuming young woman who would not threaten her own long-standing friendship with Yeats. She sensed that Georgie, with her private means, would be able to make a stable home where the troubled poet could settle to his work, and so she threw her considerable influence behind the marriage, writing reassuringly to Mrs Tucker. The engagement was not broken.

At long last the feverish crisis of Yeats's late middle age began to abate. Sir Denison Ross, one of Yeats's colleagues in research into spiritualism, managed to find a job for Iseult and she became less of a concern. Still interested in the work of Tagore, Iseult was happy to accept the position of assistant librarian in London University's School of Oriental Languages. Maud then leased a flat in Chelsea for half a year, and started a course of study in design. Early in October Yeats took Georgie to meet his beloved of almost thirty years. Arthur Symons, perhaps still bitter about the way Yeats had virtually dropped him after he had gone through a period of insanity, took pleasure in reporting Maud's reaction to John Quinn: 'Wish you had heard Maud laugh at Yeats's marriage – a good woman of 25 – rich of course – who had to look after him; she might either become his slave or run away from him after a certain length of time!'[9] But to Yeats Maud wrote encouragingly about his forthcoming marriage. At their first meeting she found Georgie charming, graceful and beautiful, and admired the bright picturesque dress worn by this former art student. She sensed that Georgie had 'an intense spiritual life of her own' and warned Yeats not to disappoint his young bride in this aspect of their marriage. Maud also felt confident that her own relationship with Yeats would not be jeopardized by his marriage to Georgie. Indeed Georgie would add to it. Iseult also took to Georgie at their first meeting, and the young women soon became close friends.

The 52-year-old Yeats married Georgie Hyde Lees three days after her twenty-fifth birthday, on 20 October 1917, in the Victorian Registry Office on the Harrow Road. The occasion was coldly bureaucratic and left Georgie with unpleasant memories. The marriage certificate was witnessed by Georgie's mother and by Ezra Pound, who served as Yeats's best man. At the end of the proceedings a rather flurried Yeats asked his best man to send a telegram to Lady Gregory to convey to her the news that at last he was a married man. Then after a moment or two Yeats bethought himself and hurried after the irreverent Pound, so gifted with the most up-to-date demotic English, and appealed to him not to use words that would be talked about in the post office at Gort for years to come. Lily and Lolly in Dublin were surprised and a little hurt that they had not been informed of the wedding until it was too late for them to attend.

The newlyweds began their honeymoon at a country hotel in the Ashdown Forest not far from Stone Cottage, and almost immediately Yeats had a terrible crisis of conscience. He felt that his proposal to Georgie, or George as he took to calling her, had been wrong and that in making it he had been false to her and also to Iseult and to Maud. Two days after his marriage he wrote the rending poem 'The Lover Speaks' in which he tells of his heart going mad and driving him away from Iseult. In a companion piece written three days later and entitled 'The Heart Replies' he expresses the guilt he feels about his disloyalty to his new wife.

This painful, debilitating tension was suddenly brought to an end by what Yeats called 'a miraculous intervention'. There in the hotel room George, while speaking normally to Yeats, took a piece of paper and, seated at a table, began to do automatic writing. The first message sent through her from beyond was about Iseult and it read, 'With the bird all is well at heart. Your action was right for both.'[10] The effect of this communication on Yeats was astonishing. The physical malaise he had felt for years immediately left him. His rheumatic pains, fatigue and neuralgia all disappeared. Minutes before he had felt more miserable than at any time since the marriage of Maud Gonne; now he felt entirely well and happy.

Many years later George told Richard Ellmann that on that memorable occasion her 'idea was to fake a sentence or two that would allay his anxieties over Iseult and herself, and after the session to own up to what she had done'. But then for George, as George Mills Harper suggests, and as Yeats himself remarked, 'it was as though her hand were grasped by another hand'.[11] To Ellmann she described the experience more fully: 'she suddenly felt her hand grasped and driven irresistibly. The pencil began to write sentences she had never intended or thought, which seemed to come from another world.' Some who knew George, Sean O'Faolain, for instance, have disbelieved this. And certainly George always resisted Yeats's suggestions that third parties might be invited to witness their sessions. However, whether the automatic writing was genuine or fabricated, there can be no doubt that Yeats took it seriously and benefited from it. Formal occasions for automatic writing became a part of their marriage. Questions were put to George's Communicators from whom she, in trancelike state, received and wrote out the answers. They also encountered Frustrators, spirits such as Leo who were hostile to giving knowledge and wisdom to Yeats. Much of the information relayed through George had to do with matters Yeats had already written about in *Per Amica Silentia Lunae,* concerning history, philosophy, psychology and poetry. Some of Yeats's questions were no more than thinly disguised enquiries about Iseult and Maud. Nevertheless the automatic writing seemed to stabilize the marriage and hold it together. During the first three months George produced hundreds of pages of answers from her Controls and Communicators. As the couple moved around restlessly from one place to another, from the Ashdown Forest Hotel to Stone Cottage, then to London for a week, and then back to Sussex, the automatic writing was a constant. It remained so as this turbulent year of 1917 drew to an end, and the couple invited Iseult to spend Christmas with them at Stone Cottage.

B Y THE FIRST WEEK OF 1918 YEATS AND HIS WIFE WERE LIVING in rooms in a fine old house at 45 Broad Street in the centre of Oxford. They were very close to the Bodleian Library, for Yeats one of the great attractions of the university city, where thirty years before, in his days of poverty, he had come up from Bedford Park to work as a copyist. Now, with a wife with a private income, he thought of becoming a resident in this place of learning. Most days he would take the few steps that brought him to the five-storeyed Jacobean tower of the Bodleian and the Schools Quadrangle in which the doors had painted over their lintels in antique lettering the names of the schools or subjects to which they gave access: Metaphysics, Grammar, Moral Philosophy, Rhetoric, and so on. Yeats had his own work-table in the library and spent much time examining the woodcuts and etchings of the English visionary artists of the early nineteenth century, Samuel Palmer and Edward Calvert, both followers of Blake. He also worked at systematizing the insights that had come to him through George's automatic writing. He thought of organizing them into a series of dialogues about an imaginary medieval book. 'The Discoveries of Michael Robartes' was the first title Yeats considered for this, to him, exciting new work.

In February Yeats undertook a literary task of a more melancholy kind. The shocking news had come that Lady Gregory's son Robert had crashed and been killed while flying over the Italian front. Acutely sensitive to the suffering of his old friend, Yeats set about writing two substantial yet different poems commemorating the life of her son. The first was 'Shepherd and Goatherd', a highly literary poem deriving from Edmund Spenser and before him from Virgil. Here Yeats offers his conspicuous poetic erudition and craftsmanship in the making of a verbal funerary monument of classical elaborateness. This pastoral elegy takes the form of a dialogue in which two rural figures from the Coole area talk of life, death and immortality, remember the dead man, grieve for him and feel for his stoically sorrowing mother. Yeats also takes the opportunity to express, in this memorial, his own gratitude for the years of generosity extended to him by Lady Gregory as well as his admiration for her son.

Some weeks later Yeats began his 'In Memory of Major Robert Gregory' in which the poet places the young pilot alongside others of his important dead: Lionel Johnson, John Synge and George Pollexfen, all lovers of Ireland. Each of them had one great quality – scholarship, artistic power, horsemanship. But the young major had within himself all three qualities, and more: he was 'Our Sidney', a Renaissance man. But Yeats does not monumentalize him; rather he establishes a character, a courteous, brave, gifted, courageous young man, as he recollects Robert Gregory's horse-manship, his abilities as an artist, his practical skills, his vital intellect, his love for and understanding of the landscape of County Galway round Coole Park.

Coole was very much in Yeats's mind in these winter days in wartime Oxford. He spoke at length to George about Ballylee and the tower he had bought, the surrounding countryside and the history and romance associ-ated with it. She was enchanted and readily contributed money to help realize her husband's dreams of refurbishing the place. They sent money to the local carpenter, Raftery, to enable him to proceed with the necessary repairs to the woodwork, and excitedly made plans together about what they would do with their unusual summer home when they could go over to Ireland at Easter. They liked Oxford, even though George was starting to feel uncomfortable with some of the dons' wives. Certainly it was a plea-sure to see Robert Bridges and Professor Raleigh and Ezra Pound's girl-friend of years before, the poetess Hilda Doolittle who styled herself HD. Yet as the spring came on, Yeats and his young wife were eager to be off.

They were keen to take up Lady Gregory's offer of Ballinamantane House, a substantial Georgian property she owned in the little town of Gort where they could live while they supervised the renovation of the nearby tower.

They landed in Dublin in March. The protocols of family life at the time required that George be formally presented to her in-laws. So, having dressed up in their room in the Royal Hibernian Hotel, the married couple set out for Gurteen Dhas, the late-Victorian house which was the home of Lily and Lolly in the suburban village of Dundrum on the southern edge of Dublin. As usual, Lily and Lolly were short of money but they laid on an impressive spread for this important evening party: hams and Irish cheeses and soda bread and Lolly's famous potato cake. The sisters had also invited young Joseph Hone, Yeats's future biographer, and his wife who belonged to a family well known in the arts in Dublin. Perhaps this was so that the young bride might have someone more of her own generation to talk to. Or perhaps, as one writer on the Yeats family has suggested, it was a way of minimizing the chances of Lolly and Willie having a row.[1]

Lily and Lolly wore their best clothes and sat nervously in their dark parlour awaiting their guests of honour. Their brother Jack arrived with his shy wife Cottie, who was even more nervous. She was a little uneasy about losing her status as the Yeatses' only sister-in-law, but when Willie led his young wife into the house, everyone immediately relaxed. The Irish hosts were much impressed by George, finding her more mature than her age might suggest; her clothes were pleasing and her manner kindly. Lolly, fidgety and over-talkative, was taken with her intelligence. Lily, quieter and more watchful, noted her tact and delicacy. Lolly wrote to their father in New York that marriage had worked wonders for Willie: he looked young and handsome.

With responsibilities to family properly discharged Yeats next took his wife to meet his colleagues at the Abbey Theatre. He showed her the city and they enjoyed shopping together. Showing her something of the surrounding countryside, they went to Glendalough where they stayed at the Royal Hotel, wandered through the monastic ruins and sat under the ninth-century tower about which Yeats wrote a poem as a souvenir of their happiness there. Proceeding on to the village of Glenmalure in the Wicklow Mountains, they fished together with the new fishing rods they had bought in Dublin. After enjoying these beauty spots the couple finally set off for their chief destination, Yeats's beloved west coast, about which he had told his wife so much. At Coole Lady Gregory, still feeling the pain of her bereavement, was made happier by their arrival. It was vital that George get on with this important friend of her husband's and she did, with great success, rapidly establishing a friendly relationship with Lady Gregory. Taken to see the tower, George again lived up to her husband's expectations, and was immediately entranced by the place. Straightaway she made plans for digging up some of the untended ground nearby and planting a flower garden.

Once established in Ballinamantane House in Gort the couple went every day to hasten along the refurbishment of the tower, eager to live in it before summer's end. From the National University of Ireland their architect, Professor William Scott, whom Yeats considered to be a drunk but a genius, sent them plans.[2] As a source of building materials they bought the complete contents of an old mill, including the beams, planks and paving stones. Raftery, together with the local mason and blacksmith, worked hard to create what Yeats envisioned as the setting for his old age. At the same time he felt that he was realizing an ambition that had first come to him in the far-off days when he was close to William Morris. He told Maud Gonne that he dreamed 'of making a house that may encourage people to avoid ugly manufactured things'.[3] Everything was to be made nearby in Galway or Limerick. His neighbours were pleased that he and George were getting not 'grand things' but rather old, Irish furniture.

As Yeats and his young bride worked in idyllic surroundings to realize his dream, the world beyond was appalled by the ever more horrific reality of the war. After making peace with the Russian Bolsheviks on the Eastern Front the Germans had been able to launch a massive onslaught on the Western Front at the beginning of the third week of March, with an immense German artillery barrage along a forty-mile front. The intricate, long-established network of trenches was obliterated within hours and complete battalions of British soldiers were wiped out. After this devastating breakthrough a German victory suddenly seemed probable. With their new momentum the Germans would push the depleted British forces into the sea and have the French at their mercy.

One response of the Allies to the horrendous loss of men was to extend conscription, and Lloyd George's government now decided that there should be compulsory recruitment in Ireland. In early May Field Marshal Lord French was made Lord Lieutenant of Ireland and directed to proclaim conscription. The British government was well aware that there would be resistance, so in a pre-emptive strike all likely opponents of the new law, leading members of Sinn Fein and the Volunteers, were imprisoned on the questionable grounds that they had been involved in treasonable negotiations with the Germans. Maud Gonne, as she left an evening meeting at George Russell's house in Dublin, was arrested by the police, put on the boat to England and placed in a cell in Holloway, the women's prison in London.

Like so many others in Ireland Yeats was horrified by the arrests and did all he could to help his old friend. When there was trouble between Iseult, now Ezra Pound's lover, and Pound's former girlfriend Iris Barry, who had been sharing a flat with her, Yeats and George went over to London to help organize their separation. Yeats also wrote to Maud in jail advising her on the difficult choice of a school for her son Sean. Along with Stephen Gwynn, a writer and Nationalist MP for Galway, he lobbied Lloyd George's Chief Secretary for Ireland, Edward Shortt, for Maud's release. Over in New York John Quinn also exerted pressure. Finally towards the end of October, after some five months' detention in prison without trial, Maud was permitted to leave Holloway, but only on condition that she did not return to Ireland, which she desperately wished to do. Iseult, who had just ended her affair with Ezra Pound, was unhappy, thin and ill, and wanted badly to go back to Dublin. The months in prison had also had a serious effect on Maud's health. She had a recurrence of tuberculosis which gave her actute pain in her left lung; she was often breathless and unable to stand. Detained in England against her will, she sought shelter in the rooms Yeats still kept on at 18 Woburn Buildings.

As the summer of 1918 turned into autumn Yeats and George no longer enjoyed the great contentment they had known earlier in the year. There was a joyous day in June when George told her husband that she was to have a child, but the pregnancy proved to be by no means an easy one. The virulent flu that was sweeping a war-weary Europe struck her down and when she had barely recovered she became seriously ill with pneumonia. She was unable to face the prospect of going back to Oxford to set up a winter home there. Instead they settled for Dublin where they rented from Maud her large house at 73 St Stephen's Green.

By this time the Great War showed signs of approaching its end. In mid-June Marshal Foch had struck back hard against the Germans at the second battle of the Marne and the initiative passed to the Allies. On 8 August the Germans suffered a devastating defeat at Amiens, what the future Nazi general Erich Ludendorff called 'the black day of the German army'. Six weeks later, in September, the British Fourth Army broke through the Hindenburg Line. It was now clear that the war would soon be over, and at the eleventh hour of the eleventh day of the eleventh month of 1918 an armistice came into force followed by wild rejoicing throughout Britain and France. Europe was in chaos. A Bolshevik revolution in Finland forced Yeats's contemporary Jean Sibelius to flee his home and go into hiding. Just over a fortnight after the Armistice Maud Gonne crept out of Woburn Buildings in heavy disguise and boarded the boat train to Dublin.

Successfully eluding the police she went directly to her house on Stephen's Green. She confidently expected to take up residence there again, for Yeats in a letter had agreed to move out if ever she recovered her freedom. But now, at such short notice, Yeats absolutely refused to go. Ill and weary from the difficult journey, Maud became angry and tried to order him out but Yeats insisted on staying. The illness of his pregnant wife was extremely serious; indeed George and the baby were in some danger, and he would not have Maud in the house with his wife. Eventually Maud left and stayed elsewhere in the city. At fifty-three and married, Yeats was no longer susceptible to the wishes of Maud Gonne as he had been for the previous thirty years.

Two weeks after this there was a hastily arranged General Election. The Prime Minister of the Tory Liberal coalition government, the white-haired, shaggily moustached David Lloyd George, was determined to cash in speedily on the post-war euphoria. He acted fast to exploit electorally his still soaring reputation as 'the Welsh Wizard' and 'The Man Who Won the War'. The plan worked well except in Ireland. Lloyd George's coalition was returned to power but in Ireland his candidates were rejected. The unfulfilled promise of Home Rule made in 1914, the Rising of 1916 and the handling of the recent conscription crisis were not forgotten. Sinn Feiners, many of them in jail, won the majority of the seats. Yeats's old friend from Lissadell, Con Markievicz, was the first woman to be elected to the British House of Commons. But like other victorious Sinn Fein candidates she declined to take her seat at Westminster. Instead, at the end of the first week of January 1919 they assembled in Dublin to establish a parliament for Ireland, Dail Eireann.

George, still weak from illness, was approaching the time when her baby was to be born. Two days before the end of February she gave birth to a daughter. The new baby was named Anne Butler Yeats. Lily and Lolly at once hurried over to the nursing home in Upper Fitzwilliam Street and were ecstatic to see how pretty their niece was. George took her baby home to a furnished house she had rented in Dundrum, near to Gurteen Dhas. As was the custom in those days, the father was very much in the background. The sisters went over every day to see the child and brought her special Cuala gifts. Lolly painted decorations on a wooden cradle and Lily embroidered a christening cloak. The baptism took place in St Mary's Donnybrook, the church where Yeats himself had been christened. At about this time an anonymous poem celebrating Anne's birth appeared in the *Freeman's Journal*, which was edited by the Sinn Fein leader Arthur Griffith, and Lolly hurried about buying up as many copies as possible to send to family and friends.

Some two and a half months after the birth of his daughter Yeats left his womenfolk and set off for London to help with the production of his play *The Player Queen* by the Stage Society. He now ended his tenancy at Woburn Buildings begun over a quarter of a century before, thereby breaking his last connection with his long bachelorhood. He had sub-let the flat to an old literary acquaintance, Douglas Goldring, who had worked with Ford Madox Ford on the *English Review*. Goldring's Irish wife had been uneasy there, feeling qualms about the poet's writing desk which had on it strange chalk marks in the shape of a turkey's claw. She was also put off by the bookcase that contained Yeats's occult library. But Goldring himself stolidly read the mystical books, including one on the phases of the moon which had been published in the United States. Not long after in Dublin, in the drawing-room of his mother-in-law Ellie Duncan, a long-time acquaintance of Yeats, Goldring was staggered to hear Yeats introduce a lecture on the phases of the moon by saying that the teaching he was about to expound to them had been revealed to him 'in a dream by a Moorish initiate with whom he had made contact on the astral plane'. Goldring almost laughed out loud but later concluded that this might have been 'a device for riveting the attention of an audience'. Certainly, 'His listeners, mostly elderly women, stared at him goggle eyed when he made this rather startling opening statement.'[4]

That summer the Yeats family at last took up residence in the tower at Ballylee. It was, he contentedly told John Quinn, a good place for his daughter to grow up in.[5] Here he completed one of his great poems, his 'Prayer for my Daughter'. Loving, protective, entreating gifts of special human qualities for the tiny sleeping child, the poet begins with a strong sense of menacing violence in the world outside her quiet cradle. Understandably so, because tensions between the Sinn Fein Dail in Dublin and its supporters, on the one hand, and on the other, the Unionists of Ireland supported by the British government were increasing every day. In September 1919 it was clear that those who wanted an independent Ireland would have to fight for it. The Sinn Fein government that had established itself in Dublin went underground and guerilla warfare began.

In October Yeats and George did what they had wanted to do the previous year and moved back to Oxford for the winter. Ballylee, prone to heavy winter flooding, could only ever be a summer home. In Oxford they rented a tall house at 4 Broad Street immediately across from the Victorian Gothic façade of Balliol College. The stairs were dimly lit and they decorated the walls with Blake's engravings from the Book of Job. Students and younger dons sought Yeats out. L.A.G. Strong, for instance, the 23-year-old secretary of the Literary Society of Wadham College, came shyly to ask if Yeats would give a talk. The nervous young man long remembered being received by 'the tall legendary figure' wearing a loose-fitting suit of a faintly pinkish tinge and a blue soft shirt. 'He greeted me in a low tone, introduced me to Mrs Yeats, put into my hand a strange-shaped glass – I was much too overcome to notice what was in it – and then, in a surprisingly brisk and business-like fashion, asked me what sort was our society and what we would like him to talk about.'[6] A subject was agreed upon and on the appointed day the undergraduate officials came in a taxi to take him the short distance to Wadham College. Appreciating the respect intended, Yeats nevertheless mildly reproved them for spending their money in this way. The students found the famous man very easy to be with. He dined with them in their Hall and its early seventeenth-century hammerbeam roof and greatly entertained them with his many stories and his 'vigorous, quick-darting talk'.[7] He later disconcerted one of the Fellows of Wadham College by, at sight, dating pieces of early Greek sculpture to within thirty years.

As winter came to Oxford George, though fond of the undergraduates, again began to tire of the dons and their wives and Yeats began to feel uneasy about money. Although he was a celebrity, he was by no means financially secure and like most new fathers was more than ever mindful of the need to make financial provision. Ballylee was their shared passion but it could and did eat up a good deal of money. For Yeats there was one sure-fire way of easing financial difficulties and that was to go on another lecture circuit in the United States. George was also keen to see America. So Yeats got John Quinn to help him make the necessary arrangements with a lecture agency and on 13 January 1920 the couple sailed for New York on the *Carmania*. They would be in the United States for well over four months. Baby Anne, just over ten months old when they sailed, was left in the care of Aunts Lily and Lolly in Dundrum.

The first thing to do in New York City was to take George to meet John Yeats. The eighty-year-old painter was immediately captivated by his new daughter-in-law and she took a great liking to him. Yeats gave his father a guarantee to cover his living expenses in New York and urged him to return to Ireland where he might see his granddaughter, but the old man clung to New York.

Yeats and his wife then set off on a gruelling lecture tour on which they criss-crossed the continent, visiting more than fifteen American states and two Canadian provinces. To save money on train fares George did not go to all the venues. Yeats's most popular lecture was entitled 'My Own Poetry with Illustrative Readings' in which he declaimed a succession of poems, each one prefaced by the story of how it came to be written. In America he continued to project the image that he had created for himself decades before, very much the Irish poet with the lecture focused on his early poems and his early life. He would begin with 'The Lake Isle of Innisfree' and then proceed to 'The Fiddler of Dooney', 'Wandering Aengus', 'Cap and Bells' and 'He wishes for the Cloths of Heaven'. The lectures were well attended with enthusiastic Irish Americans always in the audience.

In Salt Lake City Yeats was interested to talk to the Mormons, especially about their doctrine of continuous inspiration and their insistence that miracles continued to happen.[8] He was also a little regretful to learn that they had abandoned polygamy. In the West he had a memorable encounter with Junzo Satu, the distinguished-looking Japanese Consul in Portland, Oregon. When Yeats had concluded his lecture in that city, the courtly Japanese came forward to the rostrum, bearing a large gift wrapped in embroidered silk. With considerable ceremony Junzo Satu undid the wrapping and produced a sword which had been in his family for five centuries. He showed Yeats the maker's name on the beautifully wrought hilt. Yeats, overwhelmed by the gift, was embarrassed at accepting such an ancient family heirloom, but finally he could not refuse this tribute to himself and to his art and he bore it back to his home at Ballylee, where it would become a subject in the third poem of his sequence entitled 'Meditations in Time of Civil War'. For Yeats in war-torn Ireland the ancient, carefully crafted sword was a compelling instance of the power in life of 'a changeless work of art'.

Back on the East Coast John Quinn took him to a huge rally of Irish Americans in New York City at which the principal speaker was Eamon de Valera, who had assumed the title of President of Ireland in the Sinn Fein government. This famous, much respected figure of the 1916 Rising, who had escaped execution solely on the grounds of his American birth, was in the United States to raise money for the Irish cause. He was also working to persuade the Republican National Convention meeting in Chicago in a month's time to nominate a presidential candidate, to adopt a plank committing the next American government to recognize the Irish Republic proposed by Sinn Fein. At the Chicago convention de Valera was to organize a massive torchlit procession with bands and banners to promote his cause, but in New York that night Yeats listened as the tall, gaunt, unsmiling man with the long pale face explained his cause to the New York Irish. Yeats immediately felt reservations about de Valera, finding the former mathematics teacher too abstract. He was 'A living argument rather than a living man . . . I judged him persistent, being both patient and energetic, but that he will fail through not having enough human life as to judge the human life in others.'[9]

When Yeats and George returned from America she made a quick trip to Dublin to bring the baby, Anne, over to London. For a time they placed her in an expensive crèche in Kensington while they themselves lived in the Pounds' flat just north of the parish church of St Mary Abbotts. Pound, like Ford Madox Ford and D.H. Lawrence, was bitterly disillusioned with London, which he considered to be in a state of political and cultural decay. He and Dorothy were now in the process of removing to Paris. Yeats and George had hoped to summer again at Ballylee but the workmen had not continued with the necessary renovations, and from Lily and Lolly and Lady Gregory they heard worrying stories about the breakdown of law and order as the war continued in the west of Ireland. So they decided to return to Oxford instead and by mid-July they were re-established in their house in Broad Street. Yeats took a special pleasure in visiting his old friend Lady Ottoline Morrell, who had been his neighbour in his Bloomsbury days, in her beautiful seventeenth-century manor house at Garsington just outside Oxford, much frequented by the Bloomsbury Group and other literary figures. Just a few months earlier her friend John Maynard Keynes had published his devastating attack on the financial provisions of the Versailles Treaty, *The Economic Consequences of the Peace*. And the year before that, in 1918, the notoriously affected, gay wit Lytton Strachey had shocked the reading public with his debunking of nineteenth-century values and worthies in *Eminent Victorians*. In the beautiful Italianate garden which Lady Ottoline had created at Garsington Yeats and Lytton Strachey sat and talked at length about history.

The pleasant summer in and about Oxford was disturbed by bad news from Ireland, so worrying that Yeats felt he had to go over to Dublin. Iseult had suddenly married an eighteen-year-old would-be poet from Ulster, Francis Stuart. The marriage was an instant disaster and Maud wrote agonized letters to Yeats describing its horrors. Francis regularly hit Iseult and knocked her down for disagreeing with him. As another punishment he burned her clothes and, in so doing, almost burned down the house. He allowed her no money and sometimes systematically starved her into obedience, or tortured her with sleep deprivation. Iseult, who continued to insist that she loved Francis despite the abuse, soon became pregnant. The violence continued, while Maud looked on mortified, not knowing what to do. Iseult grew worn, pale and listless, while Maud poured out all her anger, frustration and terror in increasingly tormented letters to Yeats. Yeats concluded he had to do more than simply reply to them. He set off.

When Yeats arrived in Dublin he made efforts to persuade Iseult to enter a nursing home in order to recover her health. He also urged her to have no dealings with her husband until a proper settlement concerning the marriage and the expected child should be made. As interim solutions these plans worked, but another suggestion came from George, who suggested that Iseult and her husband should come and stay with them in Oxford where Yeats might use his influence to calm their troubled relationship. Maud was touched by George's kindness but the idea came to nothing. Yeats also engineered an invitation from Lady Ottoline Morrell to Iseult to stay at Garsington. But Maud feared that her daughter had not the right clothes for life in such a grand house, now that Francis had burned her dresses, and Iseult was not allowed to go.

Yeats returned to Oxford where that summer George had a miscarriage. As autumn approached he himself felt unwell with severe pain in his throat. It was determined that his tonsils should be removed and he settled upon Gogarty as the doctor to perform the operation. He crossed over to Dublin again and before going into hospital was one of Maud's guests in her recently acquired country house at Glenmalure, a remote, desolate place among the Wicklow Mountains south of Dublin. Here he completed the poem, made up of twelve-syllable lines, 'On a Picture of a Black Centaur of Edmund Dulac'. Was it the proximity of Maud that recalled to him the old duality he saw in his life? There was his 'half insane' retreat into the 'mad abstract dark' of philosophical speculation, and alongside it a powerful attraction to the physical world of violent sensuous passion that is emblematized by Dulac's centaur and that throbs in the long opening lines of the poem.

Returning to Dublin Yeats presented himself for the operation. Up until the moment when the anaesthetic took effect the jovial Gogarty talked of literary matters and when Yeats came round, feeling weak and close to death, Gogarty was still talking on the same subjects. As he convalesced under George's care in Oxford, letters brought Yeats news of yet more brutalities and outrages in the war in Ireland. Maud's told of another disaster for her and her family, only this time it was her son Sean who was in trouble. A French journalist in Dublin had asked Sean, then studying law and agriculture at University College, to take him to his mother for an interview. Sean agreed and borrowed a car but did not trouble to obtain the necessary permit from the British military to drive. Con Markevicz heard that they were off to see Maud, and insisted on coming along, so when the police officer stopped the car and saw who was inside there were immediate arrests. Sean and the journalist were held in jail, and Maud was terrified about the treatment her son might receive. But he and the French journalist were released after a few days. Sean's detention meant that he missed some university exams and this effectively set his academic career back some years. Con Markievicz, MP-elect, however, was belatedly tried and sentenced to two years in prison for her part in founding the nationalist boys' organization, Fianna Eireann, back in 1910.

After these setbacks Maud reported to Yeats that, like many other Republicans, she returned home one day to find that her house had been raided and searched. She was also outraged by the atrocities perpetrated by the Black and Tans, the police auxiliaries wearing khaki army tunics and black police trousers whom the Lloyd George government had drafted into Ireland to deal with the breakdown of law and order. These men, said Maud, expressing an anger that was pervasive among the Irish, were 'the most debased riff-raff of English jails and war-drunk soldiers'.[10] They burned Irish homes, they flogged and shot unarmed men, they practised torture of the most sadistic kind. Maud felt that Willie over in England did not appreciate the horror of the situation, and towards the end of November 1920 she told him that he should do more for Ireland at this terrible moment in her history.

He did earn Maud's approval and admiration when on 17 February 1921 he was a chief speaker in a debate in the Oxford Union on the motion 'This house would welcome complete self-government in Ireland and condemns reprisals'. Throughout his life, Yeats had moments of brilliant success as an orator, and this was one of them. As he spoke he grew more and more angry. He strode up and down the aisle that divided the 'ayes' from the 'noes', shaking his fists, making his points vehemently, aggressively, eloquently. The assembly listened with hushed attention as the tall figure with the flowing white hair described and passionately denounced the atrocities of the Black and Tans, all those 'horrible things done to ordinary law-abiding people by these maddened men'. He declared that he did not know which lay heaviest on his heart, 'the tragedy of Ireland or the tragedy of England'. He received a long, excited ovation. The motion Yeats supported was carried by 219 votes to 129.

Though responding in this way to the shocking actualities of contemporary history, Yeats, like the great modernist writers who were his younger contemporaries, was also involved in an attempt to present a longer view of history and to define its patterns. George's automatic writing, he told AE, had given him the figure of two thousand years as the basic unit of the historical process. As he worked away at refining his formulation of what he called his 'law of history' he also read a good deal in the theory of history; for instance, he read all the works of the American historian and theorist so much admired by Ezra Pound, Henry Adams. Yeats was greatly taken by Adams's view that cones or spirals provide the best image of the historical process. Adams maintained that history oscillated between extremely subjective civilizations, which are the top of the cone, and extremely objectives ones, which are its base. 'We are at present at the extreme objective width of the base of the cone. We have spiralled outward towards a civilization of apparatus, and are due now to turn inwards again towards the subjective self, the spirit.'[11]

This interest also shows itself in the new volume of autobiography that Yeats was writing, which dealt with his life in the late 1880s and early 1890s. An important organizing principle in this work is Yeats's notion of Unity of Being, a notion that there have been periods in which individuals reconciled and unified within themselves the claims of thought and feeling. It also applied to whole societies: 'their nations had it too, prince and ploughman sharing that thought and feeling.'[12] But, like Eliot's concept of the dissociation of sensibility, Yeats's notion recognizes the loss of such Unity. Yeats, however, dates the loss earlier than Eliot; in a rhetorical question he asks, 'Had not Europe shared one mind and heart, until both mind and heart began to break into fragments a little before Shakespeare's birth?'[13] The first illustration that he gives of this is one familiar from Pound's reading of history in terms of prosody: 'Music and verse began to fall apart when Chaucer robbed verse of its speed that he might give it greater meditation.'[14]

As he wrote this volume of autobiography Yeats chanced upon a phrase that would help underline this idea of moments of shattering change in the history of human consciousness. He recalled that Stéphane Mallarmé, a poet he admired greatly, had characterized his time by employing a biblical image of imminent catastrophe, the trembling of the veil in the Temple at Jerusalem. *The Trembling of the Veil* became the title for Yeats's account of himself and his contemporaries from his early twenties to his early thirties. The book has lively characterization and anecdotes as well as cultural and historical theory. These are the qualities of good narrative prose; indeed extracts soon appeared in Sir John Squire's *London Mercury* and in *The Dial* in New York. Cuala published the section entitled 'Four Years' and then to Yeats's great delight the rising young publisher Werner Laurie offered him £500 for a limited commercial edition of the book.

Money was much on Yeats's mind, as in the August of this year George was expecting her second child. To save money the couple decided to take an opportunity to let their house in Oxford and move to a much smaller place, a cottage a few miles away, in the Berkshire village of Shillingford. Later in the summer they found another temporary place in which to live: Cuttlebrook House, a substantial Georgian house in the centre of Thame, a small and picturesque Oxfordshire market town with one long, wide street lined with a remarkable number of ancient inns and houses. Yeats enjoyed this new furnished home with its bay window giving on to the cobbled street. He admired its contents: old sporting guns, a silver hunt cup, old-fashioned family portraits and interesting engravings. The poet who was forever moving from house to house dreamed of a future with stability and possessions, free from 'the deluge of impecuniosity' that his father John Yeats had brought upon the family. In old and mellow

Cuttlebrook House Yeats dreamed of a legacy and of a house for his daughter such as he had never known: 'As I look at my Anne I get a touch of pleasure when I think that she will be so much further from the deluge, that she will hardly know of its existence, and, if old Isaac Yeats leaves me his treasures, will be familiar with some house – her own or a brother's – that will show itself for the accredit of many generations.'[15]

They were still living in the charming house in Thame in July when there came at last some good news from Ireland. A truce had been agreed by the London and Dublin governments and negotiations were to begin to draft a treaty establishing the political status of Ireland. Just over a month later there was more good news for the Yeatses; on 22 August 1921 their son Michael was born in Thame.

In October the summer let of the Broad Street house had ended and they returned to Oxford for the winter. By the end of the year there was yet another major development in Irish politics when Arthur Griffith and Michael Collins, the leaders of the Irish delegation in London, returned to Dublin with the treaty which, after great difficulties, they had negotiated with the British government. It allowed for something different from the All Ireland Republic demanded by de Valera, giving twenty-six counties in the south of Ireland Dominion status similar to that of Canada, while six counties in the north-east would remain in a United Kingdom. Irish political officials would swear an oath of allegiance to the King and a governor-general would be appointed by London. From December to January 1922 there was an angry debate in the Dail about whether or not to accept the treaty. De Valera, who had not been in the delegation in London, had considerable support when he argued that Collins and Griffith had settled for too little. In January there finally came the vote on whether or not to accept the Treaty that would create a new Irish Free State. Sixty-four members of the Dail voted for acceptance and fifty-seven against. This result signalled what was immediately to become a destructive and bloody division in Irish society: the treaty that marked the ending of Ireland's war of independence also marked the beginning of her civil war. Those opposed to the treaty resorted immediately to violence to destabilize the new Free State government. It was a time of great bitterness among those who had been comrades, and some families were split. It ended, for instance, all remaining feeling between Yeats and his brother Jack. In 1920 Jack had closed an exhibition of his in Dublin in protest against the atrocities of the Black and Tans and the official refusal to recognize the status of political prisoners. He continued a staunch Republican and deplored his elder brother's support for the Free State. They rarely met again and when they did, were distant and formal with each other.

Imperialists and Unionists in Britain were also embittered by the treaty creating the Irish Free State. Rudyard Kipling wrote a virulent letter to his friend Lady Bathurst, an influential newspaper proprietor, denouncing the treaty that Lloyd George and Winston Churchill had helped to negotiate. The most popular and, financially, the most successful poet of his generation, Kipling regarded the treaty as a cowardly capitulation to violent men, a betrayal of those in Ireland still loyal to the Empire.

> And of course it isn't only the Loyalist cause that is betrayed – it is every notion of right and fit and possible Government throughout the Empire. One can see that already in India where . . . the example of the Free State of Ireland is setting the note for Calcutta and Benares, so that the whole of India is set for organized crime and assassination which can now claim to be dealt with by Treaty, as a 'Nation'. In cold truth the Government have created a 'Free State of Evil' wherever Evil exists, or tries to exist in the world.[16]

Yeats felt that the people of Ireland would endorse the treaty when it was put to them in a general election, and he was proved right. He was a backer of Arthur Griffith's new government, but not a happy one. He was gloomy about the immediate prospects for the Free State, feeling that his fellow countrymen would find it hard to rid themselves of bitterness. In February 1922 as the anti-treaty forces, or 'Irregulars' as they were called, stepped up their terrorist attacks against Griffith's government, Yeats received more depressing news. His father had died in New York, peacefully in his sleep. Willie wrote to comfort both Lily and Lolly, who felt unhappy to think of him dying alone, away from his family and in a foreign country. To the last he still had projects and hopes for success as a painter. His final words, to the lady who sat at his deathbed, were to remind her that she had promised to sit for her portrait the following morning. Doubtless remembering his mother's miserable final years, Yeats concluded that his father's death had been a good death.

George, who was upset to lose the father-in-law whom she had known so briefly, was not one to brood long. She felt she had to attend to the living, and worried about her husband, sensing that he was losing direction. In Oxford he was full of pessimistic thoughts about Ireland, but merely watched from afar. He became more and more sunk in his philosophy, 'the mad, abstract dark', which George generally felt was not good for his poetry. In some ways still the youthful admirer of the elderly dignified poet, she also tended more and more to take the initiative in the practical management of the marriage. And now she made up her mind that something must be done. That February, while Yeats in his Oxford study pondered ways of expressing his conical philosophy of history in imaginary dialogues with Michael Robartes, George took it upon herself to uproot and remake their lives.

VI

MEDITERRANEAN DAYS

the problem after any revolution is what to do with

your gunmen

as old Billyum found out in Oireland

    in the Senate, Bedad! or before then

    Your gunmen thread on moi drreams

   O woman shapely as a swan,

Your gunmen tread on my dreams

EZRA POUND, Canto LXXX

'Sligo in heaven' murmured uncle William

    when the mist finally settled down on Tigullio

EZRA POUND, Canto LXXVII

$[1922-1927]$

B Y FEBRUARY 1922 GEORGE COULD STAND OXFORD NO LONGER, and set off for Dublin to look for a new home for her family. Within days she was offered, at a bargain price, one of the great Georgian houses in Merrion Square. She bought it immediately. Just a few weeks later she packed up all their belongings in the Oxford house and the family set off for Ireland. At the age of fifty-six Yeats, who had once lived in the shabby lower-class suburbs of Terenure, now had one of the most fashionable addresses in Dublin. His wife's money and drive had brought him, geographically speaking, right to the centre of power in the new nation.

George had perhaps taken the step sensing that at this crucial moment in the history of Ireland Yeats himself, deep down, wanted to be there. As the general election in the Free State approached, the election that would give the voters' decision on the treaty, Yeats was in no doubt about the dangerous uncertainties that lay ahead. He told Olivia Shakespear that if the treaty were accepted life would be pleasant and energetic but that he was fearful of the consequences should it be rejected.[1] But, he went on, he was glad that he was going to leave England and take his place with his countrymen in their new nation. He was glad that George had so robustly forced the issue. He knew that she had made the right decision because it was necessary for him to be in Ireland to fight for an Irish Academy and even a government theatre.[2]

They decided that they would spend the spring and summer at what Yeats now called Thoor Ballylee, and begin living in the Merrion Square house in the autumn. They were relieved and pleased to discover that scarcely anything had been stolen during their two and a half years' absence from their summer home. Those first sunny weeks at Ballylee were a profound pleasure for them both. They delighted in their country surroundings: the old elm trees, the tinkling river beside the house, the moorhens and the luxuriantly blossoming whitethorn. On an upper level of the partially refurbished tower George painted the new ceiling of a bedroom blue, black and gold. Happily and energetically she planted flowers and vegetables over their acre of land. She delighted to see Anne and Michael and her husband looking healthier than they had ever done in Oxford. They erected a garage near the cottage beside the tower and thought that next year they might buy a car to put in it, a Ford. During these happy months Yeats worked hard to complete his second volume of autobiography, *The Trembling of the Veil.* He made the short journey over to Coole regularly and was pleased to learn that Lady Gregory was working on her memoirs too. In a letter to John Quinn he wrote about how important such memoirs would be in making vivid to young Irish students his own life and those of his contemporaries. He recalled how much Gavan Duffy's *Young Ireland* had meant to him as a young man.[3]

With this good sense of working for a larger purpose Yeats enjoyed his life, as the beautiful spring days led on into a warm summer in this quiet, remote rural place. But then some discordant intrusions began. From England came an unpleasant letter from the 28-year-old Peter Warlock, the pseudonym of Philip Heseltine, one of the succession of composers keen to set poems by Yeats. Warlock's recent setting for voice and ensemble of 'The Curlew' from *The Wind Among the Reeds* was and would remain a major item in the output of this composer, who died young. He was angry that Yeats and his agent failed to respond to his request for permission to do further settings and he threatened to take the matter to court. He also made it clear that he might pirate material. Yeats referred the matter to the Society of Authors.

Far more disturbing were stories of the activities the Black and Tans in the Coole Ballylee area during Ireland's war of independence in 1920 and

1921 while Yeats had been away. An image which Yeats tried hard to get out of his mind was that of the two young Irishmen whom the Black and Tans tied by the heels to the back of a lorry and then dragged along a rough road until they were battered to death; their bleeding bodies were finally dismembered. An old countryman had reported that for one mother all that remained was the head, left by the roadside.

The Ballylee area became increasingly involved in the escalating war between the Free Staters who accepted the treaty and the Republican 'Irregulars' who did not. By July normal life was completely disrupted. There were no trains, newspapers or postal service. The following month came the news that Michael Collins had been shot through the head when ambushed by some Irregulars. That same month the leader of the Free State, Arthur Griffith, often an adversary of Yeats, also died, from overwork and exhaustion. All over Ireland there were appalling incidents of violence. In Thoor Ballylee the Yeats family had visits from both Irregulars and troops of the Free State. In August the bridge over the river at Ballylee was blown up by the Irregulars, as Yeats had feared it would be. This year of 1922, in which T.S. Eliot completed *The Waste Land* and Mussolini and his black-shirted Fascists made their march on Rome, was a year in which nineteenth-century notions of political and artistic order could be seen being violently cast aside.

These unsettled times led Yeats to work on the sequence of seven poems entitled 'Meditations in Time of Civil War', which would become a part of one of his greatest collections, *The Tower*. Only the last three of the seven poems actually allude to the war. The first four refer to earlier experiences. The first meditation, 'Ancestral Houses', recalls times, a year or two before, when Yeats was the guest of the exotic Lady Ottoline Morrell at her beautiful Oxfordshire manor house at Garsington. The next three poems then evoke and ponder life at Ballylee in the early summer. Only in the fifth poem do 'An affable Irregular' and then 'A brown Lieutenant' with his Free State troopers enter the sequence. In the earlier poems Yeats, now the father of two and very much the home owner, dwells on ancestry, lineage, children, descendants. Yeats, the great virtuoso of stanza construction, makes the first three poems' design far more involved and intricate than the fifth and sixth which speak, very simply, of the war. But these, one a simple description, the next a lyrical prayer for renewal, precede a highly crafted finale made up of five eight-line stanzas which articulate a difficult personal struggle against the sudden ethos and influence of violence. Yeats is tempted by feelings of vengeance but resists them. He wonders whether he could not have been partisan and proved himself in 'something that all others understand or share'. But no such easy solidarities can be part of the discipline of the serious artist. As he must transcend vengeance so he must transcend causes and persist in his longer and lonelier enterprise, that study of 'daemonic images' of which he is able, in the final line, to declare: 'Suffice the ageing man as once the growing boy'. The great, profoundly challenging vocation is, amidst all the crazy pressures in this time of civil war, quietly yet strongly reaffirmed.

The seven meditations were put into their final form after Yeats and his family returned to Dublin for the winter at the end of September. The sequence appeared in Sir John Squire's *London Mercury* a few months later. Once established in his study in his grand house in Merrion Square Yeats went back to work on what at this time he called 'the system', his categorization of history and of human personality types deriving from George's automatic writings, the system which would later bear the title *A Vision*. In early December on a quick visit to London Yeats, somewhat to his own surprise, managed to interest his publisher Werner Laurie in bringing out the work. On this same trip he also had two very vinous dinners with Edmund Dulac. Later Yeats felt it necessary to apologize to his old friend for his behaviour on these occasions. Tiredness, he claimed, had been responsible for his garrulousness.[4] Such verbal self-indulgence after wine was, Yeats regretted, 'my refuge from logic, and passion, and the love of God and charity to my neighbours and other exhausting things'.

A more successful social occasion this same week was the lunch to which Yeats invited T.S. Eliot at the Savile Club, a meeting which had been urged by Lady Ottoline Morrell. Though both men were close friends of Ezra Pound, they had not met since the middle of the war, and never before on their own. Eliot was not yet a celebrity like Yeats – the author of the recently published *The Waste Land* was still a clerk working for Lloyds Bank in the City. He was still recovering from a period of mental instability and his marriage was becoming a torment to him, but in the company of the courteous Yeats, the urbane host and clubman with the mass of white hair, the 34-year-old poet of alienation, agony and despair was able to relax and enjoy himself. To Lady Ottoline, Eliot said of the lunch with Yeats, 'I enjoyed seeing him immensely . . . He is really one of a very small number of people with whom one can talk profitably about poetry, and I found him altogether stimulating.'[5]

Returning to Dublin, Yeats found his attention distracted from poetry and from 'the system' by the violence that continued unabated. The city was a war zone. Shooting and explosions were rampant as Republicans persisted in their attempts to undermine the Free State government now headed by William Cosgrave. His ministers fled their homes and lived, protected by loyal members of the army, in the government buildings on Merrion Row. Yeats and George, living close by, found that political socializing could be unnerving. 'One meets a Minister at Dinner,' Yeats wrote, 'passing his armed guard at the doorstep, and one feels no certainty that one will meet him again.' In company with the officials of the Free State government Yeats lobbied tactfully but insistently to have the Abbey Theatre transformed into the Irish State Theatre. Though this did not happen, the political contacts brought about another development. In November 1922 Cosgrave nominated Yeats as a member of Ireland's new Senate. Yeats was one of the fifty per cent of the membership created by appointment rather than election. More than ever before Yeats was a public and political figure.

Ten days after his entry into the Senate that December there came yet another public honour. Like another great man of letters before him, Samuel Johnson, Yeats was awarded a doctorate by Trinity College. There was a grand academic ceremony in the place to which, nearly fifty years before, the threadbare young art student had gone nervously to an interview regarding the publication of his first poem of any length in the *Dublin University Review*. Doctor Yeats! Senator Yeats! 'I feel,' he told Olivia Shakespear, 'that I have become a personage.' His new honours clearly brought him pleasure but they also brought costs. He was now conspicuously established as one of Cosgrave's adherents and as an opponent of the Republicans and Irregulars whom he called 'our wild men'. To Herbert Grierson, who had sent Yeats a copy of his historic book, *The Metaphysical*

Poets, which was the culmination of his work on John Donne and his contemporaries, Yeats said of the state of Irish politics at the end of 1922, 'We are preparing here behind our screen of bombs and smoke, a return to conservative politics as elsewhere in Europe.' In particular, he went on, Ireland was looking to the ultra-conservative example of Mussolini in Italy.

Such attitudes together with his seat in the Senate greatly affected people who had once been close to him. His brother Jack remained a staunch Republican and bitterly deplored Willie's acceptance of political patronage from the Cosgrave government. In identifying himself with Cosgrave Yeats also antagonized Maud Gonne. In January 1923 she was one of the prominent Republicans arrested by the government that Yeats supported. Just before she was taken into custody she wrote to him saying that if he did not denounce the government she would abandon him for ever. His response was to get in touch with Iseult to make sure that Maud had warm blankets in jail. He persevered in his duties as a Senator which, he discovered after his appointment, brought him a good salary. The Senate met in the afternoons which meant that he could devote his mornings, his best time, to the writing of 'the system'. A month after his entry into the Senate, which President Cosgrave had described as a dull but well-dressed crowd, Yeats set off to London to assist in arguing Ireland's case over the Lane pictures. In the spring of 1923 he was back in Dublin for the opening of the Abbey Theatre's highly successful production of *The Shadow of a Gunman,* which established the career of the 38-year-old working-class writer Sean O'Casey as a major Irish dramatist.

But the pleasure brought by his public successes was offset by a new misfortune in the Yeats family. Lily had become seriously ill and the doctor's diagnosis was tuberculosis. So many women died of this disease in Ireland at this time that the news was very alarming to her family. Lolly had little money with which to help her sister so Yeats and George stepped in and decided that they should pay for Lily to be treated in a nursing home on the outskirts of London. The lease on the cottage housing Cuala was also about to end and a decision had to be taken about what to do with all its equipment, especially the Albion Press. George finally made up her mind that it should be removed to the basement of 82 Merrion Square. In Lily's absence George also permitted the embroideresses to come to the house

and work under her supervision in the dining-room. Up in his study,
pondering 'the system', Yeats was uneasy at the thought of Lolly downstairs
in the basement, but through George's bustling good offices they avoided
serious quarrelling. By the end of October Lolly had completed the first
book to be issued from Cuala's new home – *An Offering of Swans* by Oliver
St John Gogarty who, like Yeats, had become a Senator of Ireland. The
title refers to Gogarty's offering of thanks for having escaped capture by
the Republicans. He had been kidnapped naked from his bathtub and
taken to a house beside the River Liffey. The Senator then claimed he was
having a bowel seizure and when the Irregulars took him outside, the
brawny athletic Gogarty leapt into the Liffey and swam away. As he did so,
he made a vow to give the Liffey two swans if she bore him to safety. The
volume of poems contained his swans. The colophon read 'The first book
of Elizabeth Yeats' Cuala Press printed at Merrion Square'.

While family and business problems were being satisfactorily dealt with
in Dublin, Lily in London was slow to convalesce. A great tax on her health
was her perpetual worry about the large sums of money her time in hospital was costing her brother and sister-in-law. Suddenly this unhappy situation was ended by a great stroke of good fortune when, late one evening
in November 1923, the telephone rang in the house in Merrion Square.
Yeats answered it and heard at the other end Bertie Smyllie, the hard-
drinking editor of the *Irish Times* who had often attended parties in the
Yeats home. The journalist was excited and eloquent as he poured out
congratulations. Only after some time did he give Yeats the news that he
had been awarded that year's Nobel Prize for Literature. Yeats halted the
journalist's flow with a short, practical question. 'How much, Smyllie, how
much is it?' The answer was £7,000. Yeats and George searched the house
for a bottle of wine but not find one and cooked sausages instead. For the
first time in his life Yeats felt liberated from long-term financial uncertainty.

At the end of the first week in December Yeats and George set off for
Stockholm, crossing over to England and sailing first to Esbjerg in
Denmark. On the elegantly appointed ship Yeats was confronted for the
first time in his life with a Scandinavian smorgasbord. A conservative eater,
he declined these items of food, some because he couldn't recognize them

and some, such as eels in jelly, because he could. At the railway station in Copenhagen and later at the hotel there were journalists keen to talk to the new world celebrity. In England the novelist Joseph Conrad reported to a friend, 'Yeats has the Nobel Prize. My opinion about that is that it is a literary recognition of the new Irish Free State.'[6] In Copenhagen the newspapermen were keen to question Yeats about Ireland's political and cultural relations with the British Empire. Yeats replied that the work of his generation in Ireland was 'the creation of a literature to express national character and feeling but with no deliberate political aim'. A journalist from Helsinki retorted with an analogy, declaring, 'Finland has had to struggle with Russian influence to preserve its national culture.'[7] Yet in this very year in Finland Jean Sibelius produced his sixth symphony, which shows similarities with current developments in Yeats's art and thought, going beyond extra-musical references and subleties of texture in the use of the orchestra and achieving a greater purity and depth of musical expression. Sibelius has here put the horrors of 1918 behind him and does not seek to console or inspire. He remarked of it that while other composers of the day were composing cocktails of various types, he was offering pure spring water. At the time of his visit to Stockholm Yeats's concerns were becoming very similar. Though he was conspicuously associated with a political party, his mind was occupied not so much with the practical politics of Ireland or of Irish culture but rather with getting 'below all that is individual, modern and restless, seeking foundations for an Ireland that can only come into existence in a Europe that is still but a dream'.[8] Yeats was on the look-out for such abstruse entities and powers in the world immediately about him. In his memoir 'The Bounty of Sweden', he discerns in the face of the Swedish Princess Margaretha, for instance, a 'subtle beauty, emotional and precise, and impassive with a still intensity suggesting that final consummate strength which rounds the spiral of a shell'.[9]

Yeats glimpsed her face at a grand ceremony at which he and the other Laureates received their medals from the King, old, 'intelligent and friendly, like some country gentleman who can quote Horace and Catullus'. The same night there was a banquet and when it was Yeats's turn to address the assembled company, he spoke of Swedenborg, Strindberg and Ibsen. A reception followed at the Royal Palace. Yeats found all the grand costumes almost theatrical, but this, his very first experience of court life, much affected him. 'I who have never seen a court, find myself before the evening is ended moved as if by some religious ceremony.'

On following days he and George visited the art galleries of Stockholm. He was asked to write a piece recommending the many Swedish paintings deriving from French Impressionism. He was disinclined to do so. He was certainly grateful for 'Impressionism's gift to the world . . . when all seemed sunk in convention', and he acknowledged that it 'taught us to see and feel . . all those things that are as wholesome as rain and sunlight, to look into our hearts with an almost mystical emotion whatsoever happens without forethought or premeditation'. Yet this art which he thought coincided 'with a new sympathy for crowds, for the poor and the unfortunate' was not for him in the major tradition of visual art. He looked to artists who penetrated beyond commonplace reality, the 'great myth-makers and mask-makers'. The members of this tradition, 'the men of aristocratic mind', he listed as 'Blake, Ingres in the *Perseus*, Puvis de Chavannes, Rossetti before 1870, Watts when least a moralist, Gustave Moreau at all times, Calvert in his woodcuts, the Charles Ricketts of *The Danaides* and earlier illustrations of *The Sphinx*'.[10]

This tradition and notion of art informed the formal lecture which Yeats delivered to the Swedish Royal Academy. His title was 'The Irish Theatre' and the lecture contained handsome tributes to his two colleagues, Lady Gregory and John Synge. Two days later came the final public occasion, a production of his *Cathleen ni Houlihan* at the Royal Theatre. Yeats was taken with the opulence of the stage setting and the expensive costumes. Neither Irish reality nor Abbey Theatre productions were ever so richly endowed as what he saw here on a stage in wealthy Sweden. But he regarded this as unimportant in 'a symbolic play like *Cathleen*'.[11]

On his return from Stockholm to Dublin Yeats found that the award of the Nobel Prize had brought him a vast number of letters of congratulation and admiration. To answer them all he had to employ a secretary and during January 1924 dictated seventeen or eighteen replies every afternoon. From the ever practical John Quinn, Yeats received a cautionary letter urging him not to squander his newly acquired wealth on developing Ballylee. Yeats reassured his old patron, saying that with his responsibilitites to Cuala and to the Senate he could not spend very much time away from Dublin. The greater part of his prize money, some £6,000, Yeats put into investments. The remainder, something over £1,000, was used to pay Lily's expenses and to improve the furnishings of the Merrion Square house. For his study Yeats purchased a large gold-barred cage that housed fifty canaries which from time to time would all scream, ear-splittingly, in unison. The Yeatses also bought bookcases, stair carpets, plates, dishes, cutlery and something that Yeats had long wanted, the dozen or so volumes needed to make up an adequate reference library.

Yeats was now an even greater celebrity than he had been before and his grand house became one of the leading literary and political centres of Dublin. As a host Yeats dressed the part of the world-famous poet. He wore a black velvet coat and silver buckled shoes, a wide black ribbon attached to his tortoiseshell rimmed glasses. On his little finger he wore a large ring of gold. One of his guests was Sean O'Casey, a gauche, prickly little man wearing a cloth cap and steel-rimmed glasses who had grown up in the poorer neighbourhoods in Dublin. In March 1924 he had a great success when his realistic play about Dublin tenement dwellers, *Juno and the Paycock*, was first performed at the Abbey Theatre. O'Casey was uneasy at the formal social occasions at Merrion Square with the men 'immaculate in shiny black, the women gay and glittering in silk sonorous and brilliant brocade'.[12] In his attempts to be kind to this shy figure, Yeats nevertheless tended to talk down to him, mistakenly addressing him as 'Casey'. Among his other guests was a group of young writers whom Yeats helped to found an iconoclastic review called *Tomorrow*.

Senior members of the government were also frequent visitors to his house. Prominent among these was the 31-year-old Minister of Justice Kevin O'Higgins, who after the deaths of Michael Collins and Arthur Griffith had emerged as the man who more than any other brought backbone, strength and stability to the seemingly shaky Cosgrave government. O'Higgins was an impressive young man, 'the one pillar of strength left', in the opinion of the successful and perceptive Irish artist John Lavery who had painted his portrait.[13] Lavery's good friend, the amateur painter Winston Churchill, was also an admirer of O'Higgins. Churchill, who had come to know the young man during the Anglo-Irish negotiations, called

him 'a figure out of the antique cast in bronze'.[14] O'Higgins had great presence; he had a very high brow and piercing eyes, and was both down to earth
and utterly uncompromising. His father had been murdered by the
Republican Irregulars and O'Higgins, with his single-minded commitment
to the Free State, would allow no concessions to them. He had a very pretty
wife and Yeats was always pleased to see the young couple at his drawing-
room gatherings, though he was made a little uneasy by O'Higgins' wilfulness and truculence. He and some of the other government ministers who
came to his house in Merrion Square were, Yeats told Olivia Shakespear,
not scintillating conversationalists but yet were able and courageous.[15]

One of the political initiatives with which O'Higgins was associated was
the revival of the Tailteann Games, an ancient sporting festival from
Ireland's Celtic past. The Games were held in August 1924 straight after
Dublin's Horse Show week. The celebrations, which also took place on the
race-course, included a literary festival inspired by Yeats in which certain
talented writers were crowned with laurel leaves. These included G.K.
Chesterton and Yeats's friend Oliver St John Gogarty. The chief prize, a
gold medal, was awarded to Synge's friend Stephen MacKenna for his
translation of the third-century Neo-Platonic philosopher, Plotinus. This
was a work that had a strong influence upon Yeats's poetry. But at the
Tailteann Games Yeats looked less the philosopher and more a man of the
turf. He wore a top hat, carried binoculars and amazed G.K. Chesterton
with his knowledge of horseflesh and racing, picked up from Uncle George
when, as a penniless young man, he had lived with him in Sligo thirty years
before.

This same summer John Quinn died of cancer in New York City. This
great blow to Yeats was all the worse for coming at a time when his own
health was starting markedly to deteriorate. In his sixtieth year Yeats was
putting on weight and was often painfully short of breath; his doctor diagnosed high blood pressure. George decided that her husband needed a
break from Dublin and all his commitments there, and insisted that they
spend some of their newly acquired money on an extended holiday abroad
in a warm climate. She had her way and in November 1924 they arrived in
Sicily, at the start of a long and leisurely journey through Italy. They would
not return to Ireland until the spring of the following year.

In Sicily there came a resurgence of Yeats's interest in things Italian, particularly in the mosaics of the Byzantine period, an interest that had begun on his first visit with Lady Gregory in 1907. He and George stayed for some time in Palermo and spent hours in the Palatine Chapel built by the Normans. The twelfth-century chapel has a fascinating mass of mosaics on its upper walls, apses and dome, of a quality matching that of those at Ravenna and Constantinople. Five miles south-west of Palermo in the richly, brightly marbled cathedral of Monreale there was another fine collection of mosaics, representing the entire cycle of the Old and New Testaments. For Yeats they were a stimulating example of an art free of the illusionism created by Renaissance perspective, an art that compelled the viewer by its self-sufficiency and its conspicuous artifice. These were notions of art that would inform the poems about Byzantium that he would soon write.

Ezra Pound was also in Italy at this time. He had abandoned Paris and was about to establish himself in a new home in the northern coastal resort of Rapallo. In early January 1925 the two poets and their wives met in Palermo. To Yeats it was once more a pleasure and stimulus to see his energetic old friend again after five years. Ezra, now coming up to his fortieth birthday, was his usual hectic self, full of plans and literary initiatives. In 1925 the Three Mountains Press in Paris published his *Draft of XVI Cantos*, a sequence which presented images of major occasions in the history of Western consciousness from Homer through to the First World War. Also in this year his lover Olga Rudge bore him a daughter, Mary. His wife, George's friend Dorothy, also became pregnant and was to bear him a son in the following year. In Sicily Ezra was restless. He considered Taormina nothing but a British suburb and in Palermo he could not find a cheap place to play tennis. Suddenly he was gone. He reached Rapallo the following month and would be based there for nearly twenty years. In Rapallo, from the start, he attracted new talents to him, and it was here that he would initiate a new phase, a new 'ism' in the development of modernist poetics known as objectivism. A strong supporter of the Mussolini government, he was arrested by anti-Fascist partisans in 1945, and later would stand trial in Washington DC for treason.

Yeats and George headed north from Sicily to Capri, where Yeats com-

cf.

pleted *A Vision* in February 1925 and wrote out a dedication 'To Vestigia', by which name he alluded to Moina, the widow of his old friend and spiritual teacher, the leader of the Golden Dawn, MacGregor Mathers. When he settled himself in Rome, visionary philosophy continued to pre-occupy him. Italy was in its third year of Fascist rule under Mussolini and there was a great deal of discussion of Facist thought and ideology. The young Irish writer Joseph Hone, who would later write the first biography of Yeats, was in Rome at this time and one day in conversation with Yeats referred to the work of Giovanni Gentile. A professor of philosophy at Rome University, Gentile was a Hegelian who had developed the German philosopher's notions of the state in such a way as to justify Fascist assumptions and policies. Yeats was interested to know more of Gentile, who had become Mussolini's Minister of Education. Unfortunately Yeats could not read Italian, so George had to make summaries for him of Gentile's arguments in *La riforma dell'educazione*. Later he read an English translation of Gentile's major work, *A General Theory of the Spirit as Pure Act*. He was impressed by both works. During these weeks in Rome Yeats also read the work of the anti-Fascist philosopher, Benedetto Croce. Yeats knew his *Aesthetics* and annotated his *Philosophy of Vico*, a work with much to contribute to that central, characterizing concern of modernist writers, the nature and principles of the processes of history.

Yeats also gave a good deal of attention to the great art in Rome. He went to the Vatican to examine the two large frescoes by Raphael representing Theology and Philosophy and known, respectively, as *The Disputation Concerning the Blessed Sacrament* and *The School of Athens*. He went many times to contemplate those two other climactic achievements of the High Renaissance, Michelangelo's *Last Judgement* and his ceiling in the Sistine Chapel. In order to study them further, Yeats bought photographs of the ceiling and its various sections, its scenes from *Genesis*, Prophets, Sibyls and nude young men.

On his return to Ireland in the spring Yeats tried to use these photographs to resist the puritanism of the censorship that was establishing itself in the new Irish state. In particular he wanted to lift the ban which the censors had placed on George Bernard Shaw's *The Black Girl in Search of God*. The ban, he assumed, was due to the nakedness represented in the illustrations. In front of his lively young friend, the Minister of Justice Kevin O'Higgins, Yeats laid out the photographs he had brought from the headquarters of Catholic Christianity. But even the forceful O'Higgins could do nothing. It was the portrayal of God on the cover of Shaw's book that was the chief reason for its banning. Yeats's discomfort with the intensifying Catholic ethos which he encountered on his return to Dublin became still more acute when the government introduced a resolution that, in effect, prevented divorce. Yeats's opposition to this proposal, inspired by the Catholic Church, was so intense that it produced the most memorable and powerful speech that he ever delivered in the Senate of Ireland.

Yeats opened the debate on 11 June 1925 with his carefully prepared speech. He began by saying that he spoke for that non-Catholic minority in the Free State that found the proposed legislation 'grossly oppressive'. As he gave further expression to this radical opposition to the bill, Catholic Senators started to become angry. Some shouted interruptions; some walked out of the chamber. But Senator Yeats was undeterred. He criticized both the Catholic Church and the Church of Ireland; he argued against institutional controls over any person's conscience; he spoke of individual liberty. In a mocking parenthesis he made a point that he would repeat in his poem 'The Three Monuments'. Three great figures from history, Parnell, Nelson and O'Connell, all had monuments on the main street of Dublin. And all three were known to have been involved in what the Church would consider gross sexual improprieties. Therefore, Yeats wanted to know, should the three monuments be removed from O'Connell Street? His fellow Senators were pained rather than amused. But as his speech drew to an end Yeats grew more serious and emphatic. He spoke up proudly for the minority in Ireland to which he belonged. Of the Protestant Anglo-Irish he declared ringingly, 'We against whom you have done this thing are no petty people. We are one of the great stocks of Europe. We are the people of Burke; we are the people of Grattan; we are the people of Swift, the people of Parnell. We have created most of the modern literature in this country. We have created the best of its political intelligence.'

The social and political feeling that throbs here, together with some of the very same phrases, appear again in the major poem 'The Tower' to

which Yeats put the finishing touches in the late autumn of this year. This
poem, which gives its title to what many regard as Yeats's finest collection,
is a substantial piece of 195 lines divided into three prosodically very different sections. It begins with an explosion of exasperation at the shocking
realization that old age has suddenly 'been tied to me'. In the more mea-
sured stanzas of the second section the poet, pacing the battlements at
Ballylee, speculates on how others have dealt with the tension between the
calendrical, numerical actuality of old age and the reality of still feeling
young, excited, passionate. As he brings to mind a succession of persons
associated with the area surrounding Ballylee, the painful discrepancy
shows itself in other ways, in the tension between art and reality, between
aspiration and fact. The person he questions at greatest length is Red
Hanrahan, the figure of the Irish artist whom he had created when he was
young. To the great poet who had lost his beloved Mary Lavel, Yeats puts
a question that is another version of the question: calendar or feeling? He
asks Hanrahan, 'Does the imagination dwell the most / Upon a woman
won or woman lost?' In the dialogue that Yeats imagines continuing with
Hanrahan, remembering and feeling are the only conditions that are finally
allowed consideration.

The third and final section of 'The Tower' marks a great shift in subject
and prosody. Short, decisive lines show the poet turning away from the
instances and answers supplied by others and making up his own mind. In
unhappiness one can look at others as a measure of one's own condition but
at the last the individual must come to terms with unhappiness in isolation.
For the remainder of the poem Yeats faces old age and death entirely on his
own. He faces his ending by writing, forthrightly, his will. It is an intellectual, cultural and psychological testament in which he lists the qualities
which as a poet he wishes to bequeath to those who live after him. The first
is his pride, a pride which is carefully defined by a vital, fast-moving quartet
of metaphors but is first described in social and historical terms and in
words reminiscent of the Senate speech as 'The pride of people that were
/ Bound neither to Cause nor to State . . . The people of Burke and of
Grattan / That gave though free to refuse –' The second quality in this
testament which the poet (in two senses) wills for those who live on is his
faith. It is a faith in a life after death and in a continuity between this world

and a hereafter. The final fifteen lines of this poem are a memorable literary achievement, conveying the calm, still transition from a deteriorating life to a good death. The last few lines with their slow heavy sibilants leave the reader with a sense of a final equanimity and peace, after the agonized sounds of the tormented animal in the opening lines of the poem.

Such peace, the middle parts of 'The Tower' show, had to be worked for and earned. Yeats describes one of his methods for so doing when he writes, 'I have prepared my peace / With learned Italian things'. And to Italy Yeats had gone again in the autumn of 1925, some two months after delivering his speech in the Senate. Sir Henry Lunn, a famous travel agent of the day who specialized in cultural excursions, had been very pleased to pay the Nobel Laureate to lecture to his vacationers assembled at Mürren in Switzerland. From there Yeats and George, accompanied by Lennox Robinson of the Abbey Theatre, went south to Milan. Joseph Hone saw him again there and remembered Yeats being irritated with the city and calling its vast, white Gothic cathedral 'Nottingham Lace'.[16] But for Yeats there was more to Milan than the shimmering marble cathedral; there was also the twelfth-century basilica of Sant'Ambrogio with its elegant Romanesque arches and its beautiful spacious calm. In a later edition of *A Vision*, the work that was much on his mind towards the end of 1925, he remembered his first visit to the basilica with Lady Gregory and his sensing within it something that transcended Christianity.

The first version of *A Vision*, the book which he later said was to 'proclaim a new divinity',[17] was published in London in January 1926. In March Yeats reported sadly to Olivia Shakespear that his ambitious book on which he had worked so long and hard had attracted scarcely any attention in the press. Only AE had written a review. Otherwise total silence. He had, however, received a letter about it from his old correspondent, Dr Frank Pearce Sturm, who practised medicine at Southport in England and who since the days of the Golden Dawn had sent Yeats extracts from ancient philosophies on the subject of gyres (circles and spirals). But this did little to console Yeats for the failure of the newspaper reviewers to respond. Were they silent for reasons of indifference or of incomprehension?

Dublin literary and political life was far from quiet. In February Sean O'Casey's new play *The Plough and the Stars*, which gives a detached and by no means eulogistic account of the Easter Rising, was staged at the Abbey Theatre. Republicans were enraged by the play's sceptical, ambivalent attitude to the uprising and on the opening night it became clear that a riot was imminent. On the day it came Yeats was ready. As uproar mounted in the theatre pit he strode on stage and, as on a similar occasion years before, berated the audience. The noise was such that he could not be heard. But that did not concern him. Along with his many other talents Yeats was skilled at managing the media. Just before he went on to the stage, he had gone round to the offices of the *Irish Times* and given Bertie Smyllie, the editor, a copy of his speech. The newspaper was therefore in a position to 'report' what nobody in the theatre could hear. Yeats told the rioters, 'You have disgraced yourselves again. Is this to be an ever-recurring celebration of the arrival of Irish genius? Synge first, and then O'Casey! The news of the happenings of the past few minutes will go from country to country. Dublin has once more rocked the cradle of genius. From such a scene in this theatre went forth the fame of Synge. Equally the fame of O'Casey is born here tonight. This is his apotheosis.'[18] One hostile onlooker wrote in the Republican weekly *An Poblacht*, 'Mr Yeats struck an attitude – legs wide apart – hand well raised over the head – result pandemonium.'[19] Nevertheless the riot did finally subside and the play went on to complete its run. When, three months later, *The Plough and the Stars* was to be performed again at the Abbey, Yeats received a tip-off from one of the Republicans that their response would be to blow up the theatre. Yeats and his fellow directors had to seek protection from Kevin O'Higgins.

As a controversial figure at the centre of so much that was going on in Dublin Yeats was irritated with himself when his health started to let him down. He was dismayed to find that he had a hernia, then he found he had measles. He thought it all rather ridiculous, but he was in a very run-down state when the family set off for Ballylee in the early summer. Here he had ample time to mull over a new political responsibility which he had agreed to accept, that of chairing the committee that would recommend designs for the new coinage of the Free State. At the tower this summer he also read Spengler's recently translated account of the historical process, *The*

Decline of the West. Yeats was amazed to see the similarities between the breakdown of periods of history in this work and those in *A Vision*. The many resemblances supplied a striking validation of the concept of *Zeitgeist*, the spirit of the time. Yeats remarked to Olivia that he was glad that Spengler had not been translated till after his own book was published or he would have been deterred from writing.[20] Before he left Dublin for Ballylee Yeats had also been struck by the similarity between his own world view and that of Alfred North Whitehead, who had become Professor of Philosophy at Harvard about eighteen months before. He read Whitehead's *Science in the Modern World* and saw the relationship between Whitehead's thought and his own work as being like that between the rules of chess and the playing of an actual game. Whitehead, he thought, had written the theory of the game that Yeats had actually played. Though he doubted that Whitehead would recognize this if he read *A Vision*.[21]

At Ballylee Yeats enjoyed the country quiet; he enjoyed talking to a country beggar who passed by; he had Baudelaire and MacKenna's *Plotinus* to read; he watched the herons; and he wrote poems. In early June he worked upon 'Among Schoolchildren', one of his masterpieces, a work which has been much written about, frequently analyzed and long recognized as one of the finest poems in English this century. The poem had its origins in his experience, a few months earlier, of visiting a Montessori school in Waterford in his capacity as a Senator of Ireland concerned with education. It begins very simply, with the description of a kind old nun showing the distinguished, white-haired visitor around the school and explaining what and how the children are taught. As he smiles down at the children an involuntary memory leads him to think of a story Maud had told him of some unhappy incident in her childhood. This quickly monopolizes his consciousness as he goes on in a series of swift images to review the course of her life and his own. Yeats draws a parallel between the two life histories and the evolution of Europe since the Greeks. At the end of the fourth stanza, exactly half-way through the poem, Yeats turns from the personal experience of process to the question of how process may be known and understood. The solutions of Plato, Aristotle, Pythagoras and Christianity are quickly sketched in, and dismissed. The poem concludes with a rhetorical question that implies the futility of asking the question.

Like other major modernist texts, 'Among Schoolchildren' commends an ontological rather than epistemological response to the life process. Being is to be prized over knowing. D.H. Lawrence, whom Yeats would come greatly to admire, was another prophet of this new emphasis within the modernist *Zeitgeist*. What Lawrence, twelve years before, had written about the duality of being and knowing in human life bears very much on 'Among Schoolchildren'. Lawrence, himself a poet of history, defined the antithesis in this rich, intricate, single sentence:

> *So, facing both ways, like Janus, face forward, in the quivering, glimmering fringe of the unresolved, facing the unknown, and looking backwards over the vast rolling tract of life which follows and represents the initial movement, man is given up to his dual business of being, in blindness and wonder and pure godliness, the living stuff of life itself, unrevealed; and of knowing with unwearying labour and unceasing success, the manner of that which has been, which is revealed.*[22]

The final stanza of 'Among Schoolchildren' takes up the notion of the labour of 'knowing' and endorses it only insofar as it does not detract from being. Knowledge derived from 'reading-books and history' such as is imparted to the schoolchildren is, by the end of the poem, called in question, and the famous epistemologies of the great age of Greek philosophy are set aside. Like T.S. Eliot in the *Four Quartets* Yeats here moves to an emphasis on being rather than knowing, an ontological emphasis recalling the Greek Pre-Socratics, and Martin Heidegger's *Time and Being* – one of the major philosophical works published in this decade.

Greek thought and art were still very much on Yeats's mind when he returned to Dublin at the end of the summer. The final months of 1926 were in great part taken up by the completion and production of his version of a Sophocles play, *King Oedipus*. It was staged at the Abbey at the end of the first week in December and Yeats was greatly concerned about how the Catholics in the audience would receive it. Watching rehearsals, Yeats was himself much moved by the production.[23] In the event the first night passed off without complaint: '*Oedipus* great success.' Yeats happily reported to Olivia in London that both critics and audience had been enthusiastic.[24] Olivia herself had dramatic news to send. Her daughter

Dorothy had given birth to a son, Omar, but Ezra and Dorothy felt that their lifestyle precluded the raising of children, so Omar was to be sent to Olivia to be brought up in England. Likewise Ezra's daughter by his mistress Olga Rudge had been sent to be fostered in the little town of Gais in the Tyrol. Having to pursue her career as a musician in order to support herself, Olga felt unable to bring up Mary alone.

The success of *King Oedipus* encouraged Yeats to do another version from Sophocles, *Oedipus at Colonus*. He worked at this during the early months of 1927. At this time he also made what he called 'a long impassioned speech' in the Senate against a proposed copyright bill which would allow Irish copyright only to Free State citizens who published their work in Ireland. For Yeats, whose works were published in Britain and the United States, this was an intolerable prospect. He succeeded in getting what he wanted. The Senate dropped the bill. Political activity and literary activity both came hard to Yeats during this winter preceding his sixty-second birthday. He found himself suffering badly from arthritis and then he had a serious bout of flu. He was greatly relieved when the summer came and, following his usual pattern, he could return to Ballylee. Here he wrote, and read Hegel. The place was wonderfully quiet, their only visitor a large white dog which, Yeats said, had a face like Queen Victoria's husband's, a face that showed him 'capable of error but not of sin'. But the condition of urbane, mellow contentment was not to last.

$[1927-1932]$

O N A FINE SUMMER MORNING IN JULY 1927 YEATS'S YOUNG FRIEND, the spirited and determined Kevin O'Higgins, Cosgrave's Minister for Justice, prepared to set off for midday mass in Booterstown, on the Bay just south of Dublin. He kissed his young wife and his three-year-old daughter Maeve and the tiny Una asleep in her pram. O'Higgins, in a carefree mood, didn't bother to summon his bodyguard and set off briskly in the bright sunshine. At a turn in the road he came upon a parked car from which a man got out and fired at him at point-blank range. O'Higgins staggered and tried to run, but his attacker followed him, continuing to fire. When he finally fell on to the roadside path two other men appeared from the car and shot him as he lay there. Blood poured from the many wounds in his body; one of the bullets had smashed into his skull behind the ear. His attackers drove off at great speed.

O'Higgins writhed in agony as local residents slowly and nervously emerged from their homes. A priest was fetched and he administered the Last Sacraments there by the roadside. An ambulance came and took the blood-drenched figure back to his house. During the afternoon his wife looked on as doctors struggled to save his life. Despite the intense pain O'Higgins remained cheerful. He joked about 'having to go upstairs and play a harp sitting on a damp cloud with Mick' (Michael Collins). But steadily his strength left him. He said, 'I forgive my murderers', and by five o'clock he was dead. Though de Valera, the leader of the Republican opposition to the Free State, swiftly condemned the shooting, it emerged some years later that the gunman in charge of the carefully planned operation was a member of Fianna Fail, the political party that was de Valera's creation. The especially brutal assassination was yet one more horrific illustration of the division within the new Irish state. The government reacted angrily and a number of suspects were quickly arrested, including Maud Gonne's son, Sean MacBride, now twenty-three and recently married. A staunch Republican who had served as de Valera's international secretary, Sean had returned to Ireland after working as a journalist and IRA propagandist in Europe.

Like all supporters of the Cosgrave government Yeats was appalled by the killing. For him and for George it was a personal as well as a public misery. He wrote to a friend of his grief for the loss of O'Higgins and his concern for the bereaved wife. He saw the death of this man as depriving Ireland of a strong intellect.[1] Yeats and George heard the news just as they were entering the Gresham Hotel in evening dress for Sunday dinner. They turned about and wandered the streets of Dublin instead. The murder was a bitter blow that shocked and scandalized a whole society, much as the killing of John F. Kennedy did thirty-six years later. At the time of the burial of Kevin O'Higgins AE wrote of him, 'It was as the chief moral architect of the Free State that he was recognized by the hundreds of thousands who followed or watched his funeral with a deeper emotion we think than was felt for any Irish leader since the death of Parnell.'[2]

In poems such as 'Blood and Moon', 'Death' and Parnell's Funeral' Yeats would pay tribute to the bravery, the dignity and the statesmanship of O'Higgins. But this most recent horror in Irish political life stayed with him and contributed to his growing weariness with his country. The assassination and the resulting imprisonment of Sean MacBride provoked a flurry of letters between Yeats and Maud Gonne which showed their political differences to be irreconcilable. Between them, as within Irish society generally, there was a wearying deadlock. Yeats tried to use his political influence with the government to arrange a meeting between Maud and her son, but his efforts were fruitless.

In the autumn what began as something Yeats called 'an exhausting cold' developed quickly into a dangerous congestion of the lungs and then into what he later called 'my first nervous illness'. He was in a state of exhaustion. He had not realized how his many activities in Dublin during the last five years had tired and depleted him. George was advised to remove her husband to a warm climate where he could rest and restore his health. She took him first to Algeciras, a town marked by its Moorish architecture, on the Spanish coast not far from Gibraltar. This was the beginning of the moving to and fro between Dublin and the Mediterranean which would be the pattern of Yeats's life for most of his remaining years.

From his window in the Hotel Reina Christina at Algeciras Yeats could watch the great flocks of white herons flying over from Moroccan shores to rest in the branches of the garden trees immediately outside his room. The birds became the leading image in 'At Algeciras – A Meditation Upon Death', a concise pondering of the life process and its sundry forms and of the extent to which he could give answers about them at this time of sensing, keenly, his own mortality. A far less sombre prospect was the city of Seville on the day of the Feast of the Immaculate Conception. In the cathedral Yeats and his wife watched sixteen boys perform a dance of celebration in front of the high altar. This, wrote Yeats, in one of his many retorts to the convert Maud Gonne during that year, was 'a ceremony of your church I do not hate'. He also told her that though his lung had not yet healed, he was enjoying his life in the warm Spanish sunshine.

But George began to doubt the quality of the medical attention available at Algeciras, so the couple decided to move to a larger, more modern city. They travelled up the Mediterranean coast to the French Riviera and settled into the Hôtel-Chateau Saint-Georges in Cannes. Here Yeats was attended by a doctor who was very strict with him, declaring that he must move no further than from the bed to the couch except to go downstairs to lunch.[3] When George set off for Ireland to bring the two children over for Christmas, the doctor would telephone her to report any undue exertion on Yeats's part. The patient fretted at the prospect of the long inaction on which the doctor insisted and wrote to Maud that 'having to turn my mind from any too exciting thought bores me beyond words'. He simply could not let his mind idle. During the Christmas holiday he read closely, and admiringly, Wyndham Lewis's *Time and Western Man*, a radical criticism of modernist aesthetics as evidenced in the work of a group of writers which included James Joyce and Ezra Pound.

After Christmas Yeats became uneasy with life in the hotel. There had been an unpleasant incident. A woman claiming to be from the Russian Embassy in Paris, who was prone to denounce fellow guests in the dining-room and to create dreadful scenes, decided one day to turn on Yeats. She put it about that Yeats had tuberculosis. He was highly infectious, she maintained, a danger to everyone else in the hotel. The manager unhesitatingly dismissed her malicious rumour-mongering and, through a succession of kindly acts, made it clear that he wished Yeats and George to stay. But the disturbing episode was one of the reasons they decided to move on. A more positive motive was provided by the enthusiastic urging from Ezra and Dorothy Pound that they join them in the attractive resort town of Rappallo some miles further east on the Italian Riviera.

Ezra and Dorothy had an apartment overlooking the long, curving promenade with its palm trees and the bright blue Mediterranean beyond. Ever the modernist impresario, Ezra attracted to Rapallo a succession of writers who in later years would create some of the major modernist poems. From New York City came Louis Zukofsky, whose long poem *A* would not be completed until the 1970s. And from England, or from Northumbria as he always insisted, came Basil Bunting who nearly forty years on, in 1965, would publish *Briggflatts*, undoubtedly the greatest long poem written in Britain since T.S. Eliot's *Four Quartets*. Basil Bunting was in his late twenties when Yeats first met him at Rapallo. A Quaker, the young man had been imprisoned during the First World War for being a conscientious objector. As the young Pound had modelled his appearance on that of Whistler, so Bunting modelled his on that of Pound. In Paris in the early 1920s Pound had helped Bunting when the young man had been held in prison after a drunken affray. And whilst Pound wrote an opera about François Villon, the medieval French poet, Bunting wrote his first major long poem on the same subject. Pound assisted him with 'Villon' as he had assisted T.S. Eliot with the editing of *The Waste Land*.

In Rapallo Pound continued his interest in music. With his lover, the violinist Olga Rudge, he organized concerts and did research on Vivaldi. Musicians came to Rapallo to work with him, including George Antheil, the boyish-looking pianist who in Paris in the early 1920s played his highly advanced compositions with a loaded revolver on the piano to intimidate conservative critics of his work. A little improbably the 62-year-old Yeats quickly established an excellent relationship with this wild young protégé of Ezra's. The move from Cannes to Rapallo meant for Yeats and for George inclusion in a new group of friends. They were no longer tourists and outsiders; they were joining a vital and creative artistic community. Above all for Yeats the move meant a renewal of that important friendship with Ezra Pound begun nearly twenty years before – sometimes collaborative, sometimes argumentative, sometimes highly stimulating, sometimes extremely irritating for both men. For Yeats, life in the 'Rapallo group' meant a quickening after the illness and demoralization he had experienced in recent times in Ireland. Within days of arriving in the little resort town Yeats and George took an important decision and excitedly set about looking for a flat that would be their home in the coming winters. With Yeats's Senate term now approaching its end, they would sell the Merrion Square house and with the proceeds take on two other homes – a flat in Rapallo and a flat in Dublin for use during the summers. But Rapallo and the beautiful Gulf of Tigullio was their great enthusiasm. Immediately after their arrival there in February 1928 Yeats told Lady Gregory that it was beautiful beyond description; it made him think of the little Greek town evoked by Keats in 'Ode on a Grecian Urn'.[5] George also was happy to be in Rapallo in the company of Ezra and Dorothy, who were close to her own age. To renew her old friendship with Dorothy was an especial pleasure for her.

For Yeats and for George the association with Rapallo and the Pound circle there would last, on and off, for more than four years. The Rapallo era would be a distinctive period in Yeats's life as the Senator of Ireland set a distance between himself and his native country to become primarily an artist again. Among these radical modernists, all younger, some very much younger than he, his thought and art developed a new dynamic.

All the pleasures promised by Rapallo had to be deferred for a few months, however, because Yeats and George had responsibilities in Dublin. They travelled back to Ireland through Villars-sur-Bex in Switzerland where nine-year-old Anne and six-year-old Michael were at boarding school. Then they took the train across France to Cherbourg from where they set out on the long sea voyage to Cork. Back in Dublin, Yeats almost immediately found himself caught up in yet one more literary controversy.

Sean O'Casey had submitted his most recent script *The Silver Tassie* to the Abbey Theatre. Given the success the earlier O'Casey plays had brought to the theatre, Yeats was dismayed to discover that he did not like the new piece. It dealt with the First World War of which, as Yeats pointed out, O'Casey had no direct experience. Yeats thought the play contained too many ideas and opinions and lacked dramatic action and force. The criticism was founded on Yeats's long-standing insistence on the pre-eminence of image over idea in literary art. But O'Casey could not accept the criticism and he was wounded and angered by the rejection of his play. He sent Yeats's letter and some comments of his own to the *Observer* and thus began an estrangement between the two men that was to last until close to Yeats's death. However, at the same time as this literary quarrel developed, Yeats's latest volume of poems, *The Tower*, was having a great success. The reviews were excellent, and so, his publishers Macmillan reported, were his sales figures. In the first month alone he sold two thousand copies. Never in his career to date had he done so well with a volume of poems. The news was a boost to him in those early summer days in Dublin when his health had again become so poor that he had to stay in bed until lunchtime. When he steeled himself to make his last brief speech in the Senate, it was brought to an end by an excruciating minute of pain that convinced him he had been right not to seek a second term. Nevertheless he felt uneasy about giving up the annual £360 that his membership of the Senate brought in.

As George and Yeats had planned, the big house in Merrion Square was sold and they now leased a flat in a house in that still perfectly preserved and elegant piece of Georgian townscaping, Fitzwilliam Square. The flat would be their Dublin base for the next four years. Yeats was relieved that his study was nearly as large as the one in Merrion Square. It had a fine view out on to the square, blue walls and gold curtains. The moment he took up residence, he resumed his writing, despite his uncertain health. He worked on some notes for the Coinage Committee and began writing about that fascinating, brash, complex, provocative personality, Ezra Pound.

His mind was very much taken up with Pound and his attitudes and also
with Rapallo and the new life which he and George so eagerly anticipated
enjoying there. But he had to help with the Abbey revival of *The Player
Queen* for which the theatre's director of ballet, Ninette de Valois, had
choreographed extended dances in the middle and at the end of the play.
As he helped with this, Yeats became increasingly depressed by the
Catholic intolerance which he considered to be on the rise in Dublin. He
was pained as well as amused when the widow of Kevin O'Higgins reported
to him that a Mother Superior had told her that there were two men in
Dublin who should in no circumstances be acknowledged or greeted on the
street: Lennox Robinson and W.B. Yeats.

So he was glad and relieved when in mid-October he could consider his
duties in Dublin complete and at last return to Rapallo. He went first to
London for a while, staying at the Savile Club and seeing friends. Then
George joined him and they travelled to the Italian Riviera. They found
their flat in Rapallo fascinating because of all the electrical gadgets it contained – very unlike a Dublin flat. It was bright, airy and quite high up,
with a climb of eighty-two steps to the front door, and a balcony from
which they could look out over the sea. Michael was not allowed to use the
little elevator because of his strong temptation to monopolize it by constantly going up and down.

For Yeats the literary and intellectual relationship which he renewed
with Ezra Pound continued to be both intense and ambivalent. By the end
of 1928 it had stimulated the older man to complete the three-part prose
work which described and sought to come to terms with it, *A Packet for
Ezra Pound,* first published by Cuala early in the following year. The parts
are written in three very different kinds of prose, each offering a different
perspective on Pound. The first is somewhat Poundian in its discontinu-
ous observations upon Rapallo, the difficulty of grasping the structure of
Pound's *Cantos*, and the two men's excursions into night-time Rapallo to
feed the cats. Yeats is especially interested in his friend's compassion for
these outcast creatures. It prompts Yeats to 'examine his criticism in this
new light'.[6] And he concludes that Pound's pity for the oppressed is similar
to that of Maud Gonne and is questionable because it contains 'some drop
of hysteria'.[7] The attitude to Pound in the first item in *A Packet* is often a

negative one. Ezra Pound's art is 'the opposite of mine'. 'His criticism commends what I most condemn.' If they were 'not united by affection' Yeats would quarrel with Pound 'more than with anyone else'.

The second part of *A Packet*, however, shows Pound as a beneficent literary presence in Yeats's life. This is an autobiographical essay in which Yeats relates the history of George's automatic writing and the subsequent composition of *A Vision*, a work which in Rapallo he was now revising. Yeats recalls that one of the Communicators had told him that a village described in a certain Chinese poem, in which old men could devote themselves to the study of the classics, was the kind of place where a person might escape the 'knots' of passion that prevent Unity of Being. Yeats, who would use *A Packet for Ezra Pound* as an introduction to the new edition of *A Vision*, asks himself, 'Have I not found such a village here in Rapallo? for, though Ezra Pound is not old, we discuss Guido Cavalcanti and only quarrel a little.' In this second essay Pound figures as the creator of an intellectual community, the partner in abstruse but necessary aesthetic talk.

The final piece in *A Packet* adopts yet another attitude to Pound, both in formal literary terms and in its informing feeling. It is a letter to Pound, in which Yeats sets out gently to caution the younger man, the enthusiastic Fascist, for the oversimplifications that drive his political opinions. Yeats recalls his own sense of apartness from the other members of the Irish Senate during his years of service there. You and I, Ezra, he insists, are 'as much out of place' in practical politics 'as would be the first composers of sea-shanties in an age of steam'. But then Yeats goes on to say what is their true function. It is sometimes extremely ambitious and something which they share. It is the crafting of language, not for political rhetoric, but for the realization and evocation of the divine in the world. They share a belief in, and an artistic service to, divinities. *A Vision*, to which Yeats is now sending Pound the introduction, will 'proclaim a new divinity'. And divinity is what Yeats identifies as the subject of Pound's art, beginning with the early poem 'The Return'. Pound himself, as a critic, has spoken of this poem merely as an early example of *vers libre*, as a stage in the technical evolution of his art. But for Yeats, in the post-Wagnerian world following the *Götterdämmerung*, the poem is important as a prospect of the return of divinities.

See, they return; ah, see the tentative
Movements, and the slow feet,
The trouble in the pace and the uncertain
Wavering!

Yeats was entirely right. Despite their many differences of literary practice (Yeats, for instance, would never use this kind of free verse), they
shared the same intense ambition for their art. The sharing is, above all,
what drew them together as artists and what in literary history dis-
tinguishes and keeps them together. Their techniques differed; their particular form of high seriousness was the same.

The protracted discussions of issues of poetic technique focusing on the
example of the master craftsman Guido Cavalcanti continued throughout
the final months of 1928 and on into the New Year. At this time they were
joined in Rapallo by Pound's follower Basil Bunting, who was deeply committed to the idea of poetry as a matter of the careful, lapidary crafting of
each line, phrase, image, sound and counter-sound. At first Yeats was a
little wary of this nomadic Bohemian from Newcastle-upon-Tyne who had
such explosive passions. Bunting was, Yeats told Olivia Shakespear, one of
Ezra's wilder disciples who had gone to jail as a pacifist and then been
arrested for assaulting the police and carrying a weapon.[8] At this moment
in Rapallo, Yeats added, Bunting, who was also a music critic, was writing
articles promoting the compositions of George Antheil, who had also
recently rejoined the Pound circle. Yeats continued to get on well with this
young and rather rough Polish American from Trenton, New Jersey. The
two of them talked a good deal together about that favourite Rapallo topic,
the relationship between poetry and music. Antheil, whose highly experi-
mental music, featuring doorbells, aeroplane propellers and car horns, had
caused a riot in America, now set about writing musical scores for Yeats's
plays. The texts he chose were *At the Hawk's Well*, *On Baile's Strand* and a
new version of *The Only Jealousy of Emer* entitled *Fighting the Waves*. With
some difficulty Yeats managed to persuade Antheil to keep the costs of his
settings within the Abbey budget. (When Antheil set Yeats's *Oedipus at
Colonus* his scores for the fight scene had called for twelve pianos playing
simultaneously.) Antheil now showed great restraint, however, and when,

in the summer, his setting of *Fighting the Waves* formed part of the Abbey production in Dublin, the show was an immense success. Antheil's score was subsequently published with the play in the collection which Yeats entitled *Wheels and Butterflies.*

Sitting out at the streetside cafés of Rapallo, Yeats and Antheil spent a good deal of time together considering the incidental music. Yeats was not above joshing Ezra's would-be outrageous protégé, who was sometimes disconcerted by this older man who was 'a veritable expert on seeing ghosts in broad daylight' and who 'was always getting messages from spirits'. Antheil later remembered:

> We would sit together discussing our project, when suddenly he'd say: 'Hello. William,' and he'd tip his soft felt sombrero.
>
> I'd follow his look and, seeing nobody within fifty feet of our table, I'd ask him, not without astonishment, where William was.
>
> 'Right in the chair alongside of you; he's the ghost of my indigestion,' Yeats would say.
>
> Yeats would sometimes talk quite a bit to William, and also other Irish spirits who had been kind enough to come all the way from Dublin to see him.[9]

Antheil, like Yeats and Pound, was a keen reader of detective stories. When the group had exhausted all those available in English in Rapallo, Antheil set about writing one for them which Yeats and Pound then annotated, footnoted and improved. Pound later prevailed on his friend T.S. Eliot, now working for Faber & Faber, to publish it. Eliot also marked up the manuscript which, with its marginalia from such distinguished men, Antheil was to regret losing. The book was published with the title *Death in the Dark* and Antheil employed the pseudonym Stacey Bishop.

Yeats was not the only figure of maturity and eminence to join the group of predominantly young, radical talents that gathered about Ezra Pound in Rapallo. Another was Yeats's fellow Nobel Laureate and near contemporary Gerhart Hauptmann. He, like Yeats, made annotations to Antheil's detective novel. Just a little older than Yeats, Hauptmann had gained a world-wide reputation as a writer of poetic drama. He received his Nobel Prize eleven years earlier than Yeats, and had been awarded an honorary degree by Oxford as early as 1905, not long after the time, as Yeats told Pound, that the young James Joyce was translating Hauptmann's plays into English. When Pound, the compulsive promoter, heard this, he immediately wrote to Joyce urging him to dig out the translations and 'cash in on 'em' by submitting them to the Abbey Theatre which he thought might be relaxing its policy of doing 'nowt but 100% green or Erse plays'.[10]

Yeats met Hauptmann at a formal dinner given by Ezra and Dorothy Pound, and was much impressed by his German colleague, finding him handsome in the manner of William Morris.[11] The two men shared a profound love of Rapallo and the Gulf of Tigullio, which for both was a place of romance become real. Hauptmann arrived there in November 1928, around the same time as Yeats. Released from the cold and the dark of Germany, he settled into his hillside villa, and was immediately moved to write a prose poem about the place in his diary.

> *I sit on the tiered terrace of the Villa Carlevaro. At seven o'clock this morning I heard the subdued sounds of the birds as they awakened in the secret places of the plane trees, the palms and olive trees, in the twigs of the orange bushes and the laurel and the camelia. Now the sun warms me while the vibrantly blossoming bougainvillea surround me with their draperies. Yesterday when I walked in the garden in the soft warm rain, the numbing scents, the exquisite aromas were already quickening. They carry delightful suggestions of the sweetness of unknown worlds . . . Butterflies like yellow humming birds with long antennae whizz from blossom to blossom, compelling my eye which at this moment is the innocent marvelling eye of a child . . . Below, beside the rocks on the shore, the ocean roars . . . Here you experience the power of beauty in simplicity.*[12]

As the summer of 1929 approached both men had to leave the place they thought of as paradise. Yeats, gaining strength, was writing poems again (some of which would help to make up the important sequence *Words for Music Perhaps*) but he could not live all the time in this beautiful Italian place. Like Hauptmann he had theatrical responsibilities in the north. The general meeting of the Abbey Theatre was due to take place in Dublin in late May and Yeats had to be there. He was in London by early May seeing old friends such as Sturge Moore, Charles Ricketts and Lady Ottoline Morrell. He also visited one of the well-loved places of his childhood, the Round Pond in Kensington Gardens, in order to discover what sort of model sailing-boat would be best to buy for Michael. Then he was back in Dublin for his meetings. One pleasure there was the success of Antheil's music at the Abbey, 'the only dramatic music I ever heard', Yeats told Lady Gregory. Later in the summer he went to stay with her and finished his poem 'Coole Park 1929'. This was also the last summer in which he and his family spent time at Ballylee. The damp was bad for his health. George, with a ten-year-old and an eight-year-old to take care of, had grown tired of the four-mile cycle ride into Gort to do the shopping. The living out of the famous vision of life close to nature in the remote tower now came to an end. Rapallo provided the new vision.

In July Yeats received an offer of a year's professorship at a Japanese university. He said he was both 'relieved and disappointed' when George decided that Michael's poor health would not allow them to go. But soon Yeats's own health again gave cause for anxiety. In mid-August he went to see a performance at the Abbey of his *Fighting the Waves*, which was on a double bill with Shaw's *The Apple Cart*. The following morning he awoke in the apartment in Fitzwilliam Square to discover that he had a bad cold. It quickly got worse. His lungs again became congested and there was haemorrhaging. The long-anticipated return to Rapallo had to be postponed; it was October before he began to recover. Looking back on his most recent illness he noted that it had probably begun whilst he was watching *The Apple Cart*. He hated Shaw's play, seeing it as a superficial skit designed to please English conservatives.

Though far from well, Yeats set off in the last week of October on the first stage of his return to Rapallo. In England he met some people interested in spiritualism and mysticism but these conversations overtired him. He began spitting blood again, and had to retire for some days to his hotel. George came over to join him and on the night before they set off for Italy they gave a dinner for Edmund Dulac and his wife at the Grosvenor Hotel. Belatedly they arrived back in Rapallo in the last week in November. Sadly this third stay did not bring restoration, stimulus and renewal. Not long after they were re-established in their flat, Yeats started to cough up blood again and within days he came down with what he later referred to as 'some sort of nervous collapse'. Gerhart Hauptmann had also returned and become ill; his doctor told him he had very high blood pressure. Yeats in his sickroom was amused and envious when he heard of Hauptmann defying his doctor with the words, 'Why should he say I drink too much champagne? I only drink two or three bottles a day and there are men who drink four.'

As Christmas approached Yeats's near-breakdown continued. George was sufficiently anxious to feel unable to leave him in order to go and fetch the children from their Swiss boarding school, as she usually did at holiday times. Ezra Pound, very busy himself as usual, suggested that Basil Bunting be sent to bring them, and George agreed. Anne Yeats remembered the supposedly wild young man as being painfully shy with them as they took the train across the Alps together; very shy but very kind. When they had to change trains at Milan the bearded young poet took them out of the station to visit a splendid toyshop decked out for Christmas.

Bunting had a baby daughter of his own and was touched and grateful when Yeats and George gave her a Wendy house their children had grown out of. Yeats, he remembered, could be 'kind and thoughtful of other people'. Yeats was attentive to Basil Bunting's widowed mother who, like Pound's parents, had come to live in Rapallo. This ample-bosomed lady, close to Yeats in age, was a voracious reader of books on astrology and Yeats was pleased and intrigued when she cast his horoscope. Bunting felt less comfortable with Yeats's insatiable hunger for gossip and 'his pleasure in scandals which must have been terrible to the people concerned'. But in later life he felt grateful for the tolerance Yeats showed to the younger men around Ezra Pound: 'he put up with the presence of Antheil or myself at times when he must have found us intrusive, merely because the young learn from the old and the old must let them.'[13]

Yeats's illness this year in Rapallo was painful to watch. 'He had the disease which was called in those days Malta fever (the Maltese were said to catch it from the goats whose milk they drank); it was also called relapsing fever, since patients are continually getting better and then suddenly showing all the symptoms again as badly as ever or even worse. At one time he would be strolling about the town – a little town still in those days – and the next he would be what is now called "serious". This went on so long that he began to think he had been bewitched, so that the doctors were helpless: what he needed was a powerful and well-disposed wizard.'[14]

By Christmas Yeats felt so ill that he thought he was likely to die within hours. In great distress and alarm he sent for Ezra Pound and Basil Bunting to come to his room where he managed to draft a one-sentence will. It was dated Christmas Eve 1929 and in it Yeats bequeathed everything he had to George to be used by her for the well-being of his two children, Anne and Michael. He managed to sign his name and the two younger poets added their signatures as witnesses.

Yeats did not die, nor did his state of health change with the new decade. He had night after night of delirium; he could do little for himself; he grew a beard, entirely white, which George trimmed for him. It was a struggle to read even the American detective stories and cowboy novels he enjoyed. Only very slowly, as the spring began, did he start to show signs of getting better. By March he was able to sit outside and talk to Ezra Pound who, terrified of infection, had not visited for weeks. Their literary and philosophical disputes soon began again. Pound enthusiastically pro-claimed the importance and contemporary relevance of Confucius, but Yeats regarded the conservative Chinese sage as no more than a dull ration-alist from the pre-Romantic age.[15] When Ezra and Dorothy set off on a trip in May, Yeats found Rapallo rather dull without him. There was one moment of excitement when Anne, a spirited eleven-year-old, ran away from home briefly. But otherwise the place was not as exciting as it once had been. Yeats was able to write a little again but his ill health obliged him to remain in Italy far longer than he had expected. From Dublin Lennox Robinson, manager of the Abbey, wrote dispiritedly about the state of the theatre. A recent development in motion pictures, the talkies, was now well established in Ireland and was, he believed, causing serious reductions in Abbey audiences and revenue.[16]

It was the second half of July when Yeats arrived back in Dublin to catch up on his responsibilities there. He had an idea for a new play for the Abbey. In Rapallo he had been reading Swift, and at the end of the summer when, still weak, he was resting at Coole, he wrote a play about him. *The*

Words Upon the Window-Pane is, unusually for Yeats, a realist prose work
set in a sitting-room in a contemporary Dublin lodging-house, a house
which in the eighteenth century had belonged to a member of Swift's
circle. The play is about spiritualism and also about Swift who, with the
two women, he loved, first Stella then Vanessa, intrudes into a séance,
much to the discomfort of the medium. The words cut into a window-pane
of the house are from a poem by Stella to Swift recalling how he taught her
about the power of inner, spiritual qualities. Yeats, remembering Lady
Gregory's neighbour, Edward Martyn of Tillyra Castle, who admired the
ascetic St John Chrysostom and his ideas of the spiritual life, has his Swift
character say that once he had accepted the teachings of this saint but now
'There are moments when I think Chrysostom may have been wrong.' The
sceptical young man present at the séance who is writing a doctoral thesis
about Swift speculates on this crisis of belief and of the resulting torment.
'Swift was the chief representative of the intellect of his epoch, that arrogant intellect free at last from superstition. He foresaw its collapse. He
foresaw Democracy, he must have dreaded the future. Did he refuse to
beget children because of that dread? Was Swift mad? Or was it the intellect itself that was mad?'

But though he is ready to question the limitations of 'intellect', the aspiring young scholar also wishes to prove that 'in Swift's day men of intellect
reached the height of power . . . that everything great in Ireland and in our
character, in what remains of our architecture comes from that
day . . .' Yeats's view of Swift in this play is much blacker than the young
scholar's. It reveals something of his own bleak state of mind in the aftermath of serious and extended illness. The conclusion of the piece shows us
a Swift whose mind is giving way and who ends the play with a bitter, agonized cry, 'Perish the day on which I was born!'

Another figure from the intellectual life of Georgian Ireland came to
interest Yeats after his return from Rapallo. This was the philosopher
Bishop George Berkeley, a friend of Swift's. Yeats agreed to contribute an
introduction to a book on Berkeley written by the Dublin author and publisher Joseph Hone in collaboration with a young Italian philosopher,
Mario Rossi. Yeats also continued to develop his own 'philosophy' as he
worked away on his new edition of *A Vision*. Integral to this and to its

theory of historical turning-points was another play, *The Resurrection*, which Yeats finished over Christmas. Six weeks later, in early February 1931, he could at last claim that his philosophy was complete. Triumphantly he declared in a letter to Olivia Shakespear that he had at last finished *A Vision*.[17]

Yeats wrote this from Coole Park to which during 1931 he felt increasingly compelled to return, since Lady Gregory's health was clearly deteriorating. Still a convalescent himself, Yeats felt he must give special attention to his friend and it was one of the reasons he did not return to Rapallo that winter as he had planned. There were other claims on him. In May he had to help Cuala industries out of new financial difficulties. He was also working hard to complete the Edition de Luxe of his works which Macmillan long ago had agreed to bring out. His editor was the Tory MP and future prime minister, Harold Macmillan. By early summer Yeats was ready to deliver the manuscript and went over to England for a few weeks. In Oxford he received, as his Rapallo friend Gerhart Hauptmann had before him, an honorary doctorate.

Forty-three years before, shabby and unknown, he had first come to Oxford struggling, with his bad eyesight, to earn a few precious pounds as a copyist. Now the university was to bestow high honour upon him. One of those present in the Sheldonian Theatre on that bright May morning in 1931 was a young Fellow of All Souls, A.L. Rowse, who wrote a keenly observant description of Yeats as, just as few days before his sixty-sixth birthday, he proceeded to the platform to receive his degree.

> *As he advances up the gangway an expression of confused diffidence mingles with one of ingenuous pleasure. I am surprised to see so large, so noble a figure; the hulking shoulders, well balanced though somewhat rounded by age, and the shock of grey hair, lifted back in two swathes from the wide brow. While the Public Orator's eunuchoid chaffering goes on, the poet looks lost in embarrassment, then advances with slow considered steps up to the Vice-Chancellor and takes his seat as a doctor. I hadn't expected so masculine a figure; yet how feminine is the expression of the face. The eyes are weak behind the huge spectacles, giving the face an owl-like appearance.*

At first a bit dazed, he looks uncomprehendingly around. The head
settles into its regular habit of repose (or is it the mask long arranged with
which to greet the world?) I observe the conflicting characters of the
expression: drooping corners of the mouth; melancholy and petulance; the
thick loose lips, sensual and self-indulgent; a puckered look of a small child;
weak eyes, visionary and estranged from the world.[18]

When Yeats returned from Oxford to London, his old friend Sturge
Moore gave a lunch in his honour at his Hampstead home at 40 Well Walk,
an attractive house in which the painter Constable had lived, now a well-
known gathering place for artists and intellectuals from all over the world,
especially from India and China. Here Yeats met someone who was to
supply his most important new spiritual relationship for the next few years.
This was Shri Purohit Swami, an Indian monk in white robes and a vivid
orange turban, about fifty years of age and handsome, who had been sent
to Europe as a missionary by his spiritual director to explain the sacred
scriptures of Hinduism. In London the Swami soon became involved in
several problematical relationships with Englishwomen which led to
recriminations about matters of money, but at that summer lunch Yeats
knew none of this. He was impressed and charmed by the Swami; a friendship was quickly struck up. Yeats later said that the Swami had great spiritual sophistication; he made 'one think of some Catholic theologian who
has lived in the best society, confessed people out of Henry James's novels,
had some position at Court where he could engage the most absorbed
attention without raising his voice'. At the same time the Swami was
'something much simpler, more childlike and ancient'. His 'care for the
spontaneity of the soul', continued Yeats who remembered Mohini
Chatterjee as his teacher almost half a century ago, 'seems to me Asia at its
finest and where it is most different from Europe.'[19]

As Yeats came to know more of the Swami and his spiritual history he
urged him to write the story of his life. The Swami readily accepted the
idea, sending sections of his manuscript first to Sturge Moore for correction. When Yeats read the complete work just after the end of the year, he
declared that it was 'something I have waited for since I was seventeen years
old'. It had 'the homely precisions' about the spiritual life such as the

theosophists could only dream of. Yeats recommended that the auto-biography be submitted to his own publishers, Macmillan. It was accepted and published under the title *An Indian Monk*, with an introduction by Yeats. While writing this in Fitzwilliam Square in the spring of 1932 Yeats also wrote to Olivia Shakespear in London, asking her to go and hear the Swami sing the little poems he had sung throughout India when living by his begging bowl. Yeats wanted her opinion as a musician, but his own admiration for the Swami was clearly strong. Sturge Moore in Hampstead might have lost confidence in the Swami, seeing him as 'incapable of consistency'[20] but Yeats still identified strongly with one who, like himself, was philosopher, poet and performer.

As he was gaining a friend, Yeats was also losing one. Lady Gregory's condition continued to worsen as the year 1931 drew to an end. Yeats became virtually a resident at Coole Park, supplying her with company and comfort, though he did go occasionally to Dublin to help with Abbey business and once to Northern Ireland to broadcast poetry for the BBC from Belfast. But by the beginning of 1932 it was becoming clear that Lady Gregory had not long to live. She could no longer go up and down stairs and, stoic though she was, she finally and reluctantly agreed, in March, that Yeats should bring some pain-killing drugs from Dublin. However, she still insisted that these should contain no morphine which would deprive her of her mental consciousness in her last days. Distraught at the prospect of her death, Yeats put all his time and energies into trying to console and divert her.

In the middle of May the Abbey's manager, Lennox Robinson, returned to Dublin after an American tour. Yeats had to see him about a backlog of decisions that needed to be made concerning the theatre. After he had taken the train eastwards across Ireland, Lady Gregory's condition rapidly grew worse. Her solicitor tried to phone Yeats at various locations in Dublin but could not reach him. Lady Gregory rallied slightly, summoned the servants and insisted that they help her down the great staircase. Slowly, with their assistance, she moved through each of the principal rooms of the great house. She studied the many paintings and portraits and the beautifully bound volumes in the library. It seemed, one of the servants later said, as if she were 'saying goodbye' to the house. The solicitor at last contacted Yeats who set off westwards on the first available train. Lady Gregory had herself taken back to her room and shortly afterwards she died. Yeats arrived at Coole a few hours later. To Mario Rossi, who had recently come to Coole with him, he wrote in simple stark misery saying that he had lost the woman who for nearly forty years had given him strength and acted as his conscience.[21] The woman who more than any other human being had sustained him physically, financially, socially and intellectually, was now gone from him. And the house that was part of her importance to him now ceased to figure in his life. All the beautiful pictures and heirlooms were taken from it and sent to the home of Lady Gregory's heirs in County Dublin. Coole Park, which had been the one stable reference point for the rootless Yeats in his life of incessant wandering, was no longer a place to which he could go.

Coole was not the only home Yeats lost that summer. After four years the lease on the apartment at 42 Fitzwilliam Square came to an end and the family had to move on. George, as on earlier occasions, did all the work of moving. Whilst she packed up the apartment, including the many books in his study, Yeats removed himself to the Royal Hotel at Glendalough, the little town with many monastic ruins some miles southwest of Dublin. Relaxing and enjoying the prestigious resort hotel, Yeats remained there on his own for about a week until his new home was made ready for him. He looked forward to a new phase in his life, hoping to 'recreate in some measure the routine that was my life at Coole, the only place where I have ever had unbroken health'. But the last phase of his life in his new and last home would be different from what he envisioned in the quiet of Glendalough. His remaining six and a half years would be marked by a frenzied quest for more and different sexual experience, by discontent with home and domestic comfort, by frequent escape from Ireland, wife and family, by manic pursuit of women, by debauch and resulting illness.

They were also years which produced a massive crescendo of achievement.

VII

Forays from Rathfarnham: The Last Years

'Because I am mad about women
I am mad about the hills'
Said that wild old wicked man
Who travels where God wills.
'Not to die on the straw at home,
Those hands to close these eyes,
That is all I ask, my dear,
From the old man in the skies.'

W.B. Yeats, 1937

IN JULY 1932, A FEW WEEKS AFTER HIS SIXTY-SEVENTH BIRTHDAY, Yeats and his family moved into Riversdale, a renovated farmhouse in the Willowbrook area of Rathfarnham, in the countryside on the then southernmost edge of Dublin. He and George had taken a thirteen-year lease on this attractive, creeper-covered house which was set in several acres of land and had stables and outhouses. There were lawns where the family and their guests would play croquet, a game at which Yeats was very skilful. There was a fruit garden, a lily pond, tennis lawns and a bowling green, and Yeats had a fine study which George had decorated for him, the walls lemon and the doors green and black. The view to the south was of the beautiful skyline created by the Wicklow Mountains. Socially and geographically this secluded home in the wealthiest of suburbs was far removed from the cheap lodging-houses in inner Dublin where Yeats had lived forty years before.

But Yeats was not to be left in peace to enjoy this farm converted into a place for 1930s gracious living. Earlier in the year there had been an election in Ireland and the party with which Yeats was closely associated, Fine Gael, led by William Cosgrave, had been defeated. Eamon de Valera and his Fianna Fail party now ruled Ireland. The changeover in power had been a great test of the democratic principles of the ten-year-old Irish Free State. The two sides that had fought each other in a bitter civil war now had to conduct themselves as constitutional parties carrying out the verdict of an electorate. Around polling time there was talk that some in the Cosgrave government would not accept a de Valera takeover. Eoin O'Duffy, an engineer who was once a close associate of Michael Collins and now Cosgrave's commissioner for the Gardai, or police force, was rumoured to be lobbying to organize a *coup d'état*. But in defeat Cosgrave insisted on ceding power gracefully to the victorious de Valera. When the new Taoiseach soon dismissed Eoin O'Duffy from his position as chief of the Gardai, this charismatic figure quickly reappeared as leader of the Army Comrades Association, begun to aid the veterans of the Free State Army. But under the leadership of this most right-wing figure in right-wing Fine Gael, this organization engaged in violent clashes with the Irish Republican Army and soon precipitated a major crisis for Ireland, and for Yeats personally. It renamed itself the National Guard, but came to be known as the Blueshirts, after its uniforms.

Whilst these political tensions were developing in the first year of de Valera's government, Yeats set off on a speaking tour of America, sailing from Southampton in October 1932 and spending three months in North America. Yet one more successful and lucrative tour would help to finance the expensive new home at Rathfarnham. A month or so after he disembarked in New York, Lolly using the Cuala handpress, now established in its new home on Lower Baggot Street, brought out his next volume of poems, *Words for Music Perhaps*. The title alluded to Yeats's continuing concern with the relationship between poetry and song, a relationship which he had once sought to effect through the 'chanting' which he had worked on with Florence Farr, and which he returned to in conversations with Ezra Pound and Basil Bunting at Rapallo. One talking point at that time was evidently an essay by Basil Bunting, the typescript of which was found among Yeats's papers after his death. Called 'Notes on Spoken Music and Schoenberg', it is a consideration of how the Austrian composer, who went on to become the great pioneer of atonality in music, set the 'Songs of Gurre', a series of poems by the Danish poet J.P. Jacobsen. Bunting essentially is writing about the tension present in the phrase 'Spoken Music',[1] and the interaction of song and statement is likewise an important part of this new work by Yeats, which had its beginnings in Rapallo.

Since drawing close to Ezra Pound whose major works were in the sequence form ('Hugh Selwyn Mauberley', *Homage to Sextus Propertius* and, on a very much larger scale, *The Cantos*) Yeats had also created sequence poems such as 'Upon a Dying Lady', 'Meditations in Time of Civil War' and 'A Man Young and Old'. But *Words for Music Perhaps* is a longer and more intricate sequence than its predecessors. Made up of twenty-five short stanzaic poems, some of them dramatic monologues, some of them lyrics, the work is a small, taut masterpiece which presents Yeats's view and sense of life as a man and artist in his mid-sixties. It begins with seven poems expressing the memories and opinions of Crazy Jane, a character based on an old woman known as 'Cracked Mary' who lived near Gort in County Galway and who was 'the local satirist and a really terrible one'. Her earthy views on the interrelation of fair and foul in life at the beginning of the sequence are balanced by those of another wise fool at the end, Tom the Lunatic. And Tom's views are made to contain within them the one Christian statement in the sequence, the monologue of St Cellach.

Youth and old age, love and lovelessness, hatred within love, body and spirit are some of the subjects figuring within this tight, frugal verbal architecture. The physical, down-to-earth language of Crazy Jane at the beginning transmutes into other sorts of language. There are simple Lieder-like songs, lullabies, dreams, dialogues. And the final constituent poem is a brief, restrained, and thus all the more powerful passage of grand vision. This evokes Plotinus fighting his way 'through the roaring tumult of the fleshy life' along what, in Stephen MacKenna's translation of *Porphyry's Life of Plotinus* (a translation which Yeats knew), is called 'the straightgoing way to the celestial spheres'. The sequence ends in a place far removed from the Ireland of Crazy Jane, a Yeatsian Paradiso 'where all is unison and winning tenderness and guileless joy and the place is lavish of nectar streams the unfailing Gods bestow', a place where

> Scattered on the level grass
> Or winding through the grove
> Plato there and Minos pass,
> There stately Pythagoras
> And all the choir of love.

This brief, concise divine comedy quickly found admirers. When he returned from America Yeats was greatly pleased to learn how well the work had been received. Fellow poets such as Masefield and Gordon Bottomley sent letters 'full of praise'.

His tour of the United States had also been a success. Just before he returned home he wrote to Olivia Shakespear from the Waldorf Astoria in New York City reporting that he had made about £600 for himself and had collected the same amount of money for the newly created Irish Academy of Letters. This was an institution that Yeats had recently founded in association with his old acquaintance from Kelmscott days, George Bernard Shaw. An important motive behind it was a fear of the censorship which, they feared, could only get worse under de Valera. In their joint letter to prospective members Yeats and Shaw observed, 'There is in Ireland an official censorship possessing, actively exercising, powers of suppression which may at any moment confine an Irish author to the British and American market, and thereby make it impossible for him to live by distinctive Irish literature.' Yeats wished that he were younger and could spare the time to fight the new government, 'and force de Valera's Ministers . . . to repudiate the ignorance that has in part put them into power'.

In fact, a fight with the Fianna Fail government was forced upon him just two months after his return from the United States. Shortly before Yeats sailed out of New York City, a Fianna Fail group there had passed a motion deploring the Abbey Theatre's American tour of the previous year, 1932. The objections were familiar ones. It was resolved

that plays such as The Playboy of the Western World, Juno and the Paycock, The Shadow in the Glen and others are anything but elevating to the Irish character . . . that the money of the Irish taxpayers be not spent to subsidise the Abbey Theatre in Dublin, which is responsible for presenting these plays, with their filthy language, their drunkenness, murder and prostitution, and holding up the Irish character generally to be scoffed at and ridiculed by people of other races.[2]

De Valera in Dublin, ever mindful of Irish American opinion, immediately requested his Minister of Finance, who was responsible for paying the Abbey's subsidy of £1,000 a year, to act on this. The Minister in turn instructed a civil servant to write to the directors of the theatre warning them that if their repertoire were not made more acceptable, their grant might no longer be forthcoming. Yeats preferred to risk the future of the Abbey rather than submit and wrote back stating that the chief work of Synge and O'Casey would not be dropped: 'We refuse such a demand; your Minister may have it in his power to bring our theatre to an end, but as long as it exists it will retain its freedom.' To make it clear that there was absolutely no room for compromise on the issue Yeats declared, 'My Directors empower me to say in their name and in my own that we refuse further financial assistance from your Government.'[3]

This was Yeats the fighter at his most intransigent. De Valera grew concerned, uneasy about the political costs of endangering or closing down the theatre, so he decided to arrange a meeting in his office with Yeats to try to resolve the conflict. So in the grand, turn-of-the-century baroque buildings on Merrion Row two of the great figures of the new Ireland came face to face. And how different and irreconcilable they were: the tall, gaunt Catholic zealot and the plump, white-haired mystic of Anglican origins whose life had been dedicated to spiritual unorthodoxies; the insistently logical mathematics teacher and the poet of the passions and the irrational; the one brought up amidst the poverty of peasant life in rural Ireland, the other remembering always his many connections with the gentry and aristocracy; the inexorably single-minded politician and the poet of profound interrogatives; the immensely shrewd leader of Fianna Fail confronting the chief intellectual ornament and sometime placeman of Fine Gael.

A month after their hour-long interview Yeats wrote the poem 'Parnell's Funeral' which concludes with lines in which he suggests de Valera's deficiencies in comparison with the great hero of the 1880s. An image from the act of communion is used to characterize the political tradition that had been debased:

> *Had de Valera eaten Parnell's heart*
> *No loose-lipped demagogue had won the day*
> *No civil rancour torn the land apart.*

But Yeats's assessment of his adversary was by no means harsh. He was 'impressed by his simplicity and honesty'; they disagreed absolutely and yet 'each recognised the other's point of view so completely'. No solution of the

Abbey Theatre problem was agreed upon. The conflict continued through 1933 and on into the following year when, finally, the Fianna Fail government neglected to pursue the matter.

It was a triumph for Yeats. So too was his visit to Cambridge during the summer to have an honorary degree conferred upon him. During his stay in England he celebrated his sixty-eighth birthday with a grand formal dinner at the Savile Club. But when he returned to Ireland he found himself drawn into another political crisis. Hostility to de Valera was growing fast. Yeats, like Eoin O'Duffy and his Blueshirts, saw definite dangers in the new government and he thought that the O'Duffy organization on the extreme right of Fine Gael might function as a saving force. He told Olivia Shakespear that a Fascist opposition was forming behind the scenes to be ready should a tragic situation develop. In his next sentence he went on to declare his own political position, saying that he found himself constantly urging the despotic rule of the educated classes as the only end to the troubles.

So began what has sometimes been regarded as Yeats's involvement with Fascism. Certainly Yeats met O'Duffy, telling Olivia Shakespear about the man who had been 'head of the Irish police for twelve years', 'I did not think him a great man though a pleasant one, but one never knows, his face and mind may harden or clarify.' But his sympathy for O'Duffy and his movement was sufficiently keen for him to set about writing what were highly inflammatory lyrics for the Blueshirts to sing. 'For the first time in my life,' wrote the poet of high culture, just a few months later, 'I wanted to write what some crowd in the street might understand and sing.' The songs are full of extreme right-wing sentiment and make a rabble-rousing appeal for street action.

> *What's equality? Muck in the yard;*
> *Historic Nations grow*
> *From above to below.*
>
> . . .
>
> *When Nations are empty up there at the top,*
> *When order has weakened or faction is strong,*
> *Time for us all boys, to hit on a tune boys,*
> *Take to the roads and go marching along.*[4]

But to say that Yeats was a Fascist at this point in the 1930s is to overstate. Rather he was a conservative after the style of Edmund Burke. It is true that there is a fine line between the Fascist imagination and that of extreme right-wing conservatism, but Yeats never crossed it. His short-lived support of O'Duffy was an expression of hostility to de Valera and the new Fianna Fáil government rather than an espousal of the ideology of Hitler and Mussolini. And as was the case with the Irish people generally, his hopes of the Blueshirt movement did not last long. The marching songs were soon regretted and rewritten.

What had looked like a possible Blueshirt *coup* in July seemed like comedy and anti-climax by September. The critical moment came when O'Duffy announced a very provocative march of his Blueshirts past the government buildings on Merrion Row in late August. The de Valera government denied the necessary authorization and for some days the political atmosphere in Dublin was extremely tense, until O'Duffy finally cancelled his march. After this his influence upon Irish politics steadily diminished. A couple of years later when the Civil War broke out in Spain O'Duffy led a force of Irish Blueshirts to fight with the Spanish Fascists under General Franco.

George Yeats hated Blueshirts but close neighbours in Rathfarnham who supported O'Duffy's movement put her in a predicament. The neighbours had a collie dog which George one day discovered in the Yeats hen-house. A white hen that was an especially good layer was missing. When she wrote to the neighbours to protest, George received an apology and the news that Blueshirt sympathizers with their fervent belief in law and order had had the thieving collie put down. Yeats was startled by the 'Hitler touch', and then amused when the white hen turned up safe and sound.

Yeats's life in his last decade was marked by a number of impulses and even infatuations. In the early 1930s there was much talk of the 'monkey gland' operation which, it was claimed, could restore the sexual energies of the elderly. Pioneered by Dr Steinach in Germany, the operation was promoted and performed in England by the celebrated Australian sexologist Norman Haire, the author of a book entitled *Rejuvenation*. This outspoken prophet of sexual freedom, fat, gluttonous and homosexual, had a consulting room in Harley Street decorated in flamboyant Chinese style with a silver ceiling and walls hung with exquisite embroideries on silk. Here he treated the rich and the famous, shocking his patients by discussing their problems in earthy, Anglo-Saxon language. Yeats, who was as attracted to Haire as he had been to other unorthodox systemizers such as MacGregor Mathers of the Golden Dawn and Madame Blavatsky, for some years had been concerned about his sexual potency, so made up his mind to ask Haire to perform the operation upon him, travelling to London in the spring of 1934 to undergo the expensive treatment. Haire also interested him in eugenics, the study of racial purification and enhancement through selective breeding; eugenics was a subject that interested many in the 1930s, not merely Adolf Hitler.

After his return to Rathfarnham in May he reported to Olivia Shakespear that the first consequences were that his blood pressure was down and that 'I am not irritable and that is a new event.' By June he could tell her that he felt 'marvellously strong, with a strong sense of the future', and, he added flirtatiously, in some ways better than he had felt at Woburn Buildings more than twenty years before. The past was also brought to mind by the writing of a further volume of autobiography, *Dramatis Personae*, dealing with the years 1896–1902. He was outspoken about the friends of his youth Edward Martyn and George Moore, both now dead, and regarded his critical, mocking chapters about them as exciting and sensational. He was sure George would be able to make a good deal of 'household money' out of them when she sent them out to English and American magazines.

He and George set off for Italy in June to dismantle their former home in Rapallo, ensuring that Ezra Pound's parents could retain the use of their furniture. Then after returning to Rathfarnham for a summer of work Yeats and his wife were back in Italy in October for a conference on drama organized by the Royal Academy of Italy in Rome, at which Yeats was to speak. He was greatly concerned about what kind of hat to wear to such a grand, international occasion. Should it be a top hat or his poet's broad-brimmed soft felt hat? A fellow visitor to the conference, the theatre producer Ashley Dukes, recalled that 'He was himself rather concerned as a Senator for the prestige of Ireland, where hats are as important as anywhere else and even more varied; but Mrs Yeats settled the question by declaring that "Willie never really looks his best in a top hat," and he was persuaded to agree.'[5]

The subject of his speech was 'The Dramatic Theatre'. He was gratified to see in his audience people from the world of theatre who had long been important to him: Pirandello; Maeterlinck, the author of *Pelléas and Mélisande*; and the stage designer whom Yeats had admired since the turn of the century, Edward Gordon Craig. When, later on, Marinetti the Futurist and supporter of Fascism delivered a violent speech denouncing decadent peoples and decadent art, Yeats and Craig, who had enjoyed a vinous lunch, slept soundly in their seats. The climax of the conference was a gala performance of *La figlia di Iovio* by Gabriele d'Annunzio, one of the heroes of Italian Fascism and of its leader Benito Mussolini, il Duce, who hosted the gala occasion.

On his way back to Ireland Yeats spent some time in London where there was renewed interest in poetic drama. The recently founded Group Theatre was presenting *The Dance of Death*, a play by the 27-year-old left-wing poet W.H. Auden. Ashley Dukes was doing well with his small Mercury Theatre in Notting Hill Gate and in the coming year would have a great success when he staged T.S. Eliot's *Murder in the Cathedral*. Yeats talked to those organizing these theatres about the possibilities of having his own plays produced by them. Others who joined in the discussions were Edmund Dulac, Eliot himself, E. Martin Browne who had directed Eliot's first play *The Rock*, and Frederick Ashton who had studied with Massine and Marie Rambert and who in 1935 in his early thirties would shortly become choreographer at the Sadler's Wells Ballet. Yeats, who had pioneered a drama of poetry and dance more than a quarter of a century before, now sought to have his work accepted by a new generation.

At one of his meetings Yeats was introduced to a young actress who became the last of the several actress lovers of his life – the 27-year-old Margot Collis, who performed under the stage name Margaret Ruddock. She was slim and attractive with dark luxuriant hair, a melodious, resonant voice and beautiful large eyes. It was her eyes Yeats dwelled upon in the poem 'Margot' which he sent her a few weeks after their first meeting.

All famine struck sat I, and then
Those generous eyes on mine were cast,
Sat like other aged men
Dumbfounded, gazing on the past
That appeared constructed of
Lost opportunities to love.

The two following stanzas lead up to an appeal for her to love him 'as though still young', concluding with the argument that when his 'brief final years are gone,' she will 'have time to turn away / And cram those open eyes with day'. The soft-eyed Margot, now married to her second husband, was also an aspiring poet, and Yeats was eager to offer his services as adviser and editor of her work. He took a service flat in Seymour Street, near Portman Square, where on subsequent visits to London he was able to receive her.

During October 1934 Yeats and Margot had some intense, memorable assignations. In letters she addressed him as 'Darling Yeats' and he called her 'My Dearest'. When he had to return to Dublin she wrote to him at the Kildare Street Club. But he also urged her to write occasionally to him at Riversdale, Rathfarnham, Dublin. He told her that his wife would expect this, knowing they were working together on a theatre project.[6] How physically robust their relationship was is in doubt. There is much to suggest that he was enchanted and content just to see her take her clothes off and to look upon her beautiful nakedness. But in one letter he insists that he must not be tired on his next visit.[7] Certainly by November thoughts and memories of her obsessed him: she was an image of kindliness and beauty always before him.[8] He pondered their sudden love, wondering how they had chosen each other, and concluded that it had been fate.[9] Writing that first poem to her created such excitement that he could not sleep.

Years later Yeats wrote that Margot Ruddock had that rare quality in an actress, 'intellectual passion'. He also saw her as 'a frustrated tragic genius'. But Margot, for all her beauty, sensibility and responsiveness, was to prove mentally unstable. She enjoyed getting drunk on beer, was prone to depression and feared madness. Once when she lost patience with her second husband, an out-of-work actor, and spent an evening with her first husband, she was upset that he did not resume sexual advances to her. She complained to Yeats, 'What's the use of having a nice body and wanting to give people happiness if no one will take it?'[10] She tried many ventures in the theatre but with little success. She finally found herself living with her baby in a shabby one-room flat in Ladbroke Grove on the edge of Notting Hill.

At the end of this same year, 1934, in one of his forays out of the rural domesticity of Rathfarnham and into London life, Yeats also began a relationship with another younger woman, the 34-year-old Ethel Mannin. A great friend of the sexologist Norman Haire, Ethel Mannin came from a lower-class background in Clapham in south London. She left school at fifteen, got a job as a shorthand typist in a publisher's office and went on to achieve fame and fortune as a journalist and a writer of romantic novels. She also had more serious literary aspirations. She held strong opinions which were very much opposed to those of her elderly Irish admirer. Philosophically a materialist and politically left-wing, along with prominent writers of the day such as Herbert Read, Rebecca West and John Cowper Powys she was a leading figure in the British branch of the International Anti-Fascist Solidarity Committee. Oak Cottage, her large and beautiful house in Kent, was the meeting-place of the local Communist party. Well-off, unattached and a free spirit, she could have been a model for one of the leftish women satirized by Wyndham Lewis in his 1930s novel *The Revenge for Love*. An attractive blonde of Irish descent, talkative and extremely vivacious, she loved to argue about politics and philosophy and liked to drink Burgundy while she did so. Wine was one of the means, she thought, by which she and Yeats could set aside 'the wide disparity in our ideas, Yeats with his innate mysticism, and I with my inveterate materialism . . . Yeats full of Burgundy and racy reminiscence was Yeats released from the Celtic Twilight and treading the antic hay with abundant zest.' Towards the end of their more than four year relationship illness curtailed his drinking but not their fun. 'In the latter years of his life because of his health he took only a little white wine and weak whiskey and was less racy, but his tremendous Irish wit remained unimpaired.'[11]

In her concluding volume of autobiography Ethel Mannin, remembering a succession of memorable visitors to Oak Cottage, notes simply and
with discreet ellipses, 'W.B. Yeats came for the weekend . . .'[12]

That theirs was a sexual relationship both intense and tender, there can
be little doubt. In her letters to Yeats, he is soon 'My Dear' and she herself
is 'Ever devotedly, E'. He, for his part, writes to her freely about himself
and his concerns; he is sometimes teasing, always affectionate. He worries
greatly that a day might come when their deep differences of belief might
jeopardize their relationship. And indeed such a crisis would come. But as
1935 began the bond was a joy to them both. Ethel Mannin had become an
important figure in his life, a distinctive, if unlikely member of the length-
ening list of women to whom Yeats could refer for love, company and
hospitality on his trips to England.

Frequently Yeats's sorties from his home and family would end with
exhaustion and relapse into illness. Then George would either have to go
and retrieve him or nurse him when he returned to Ireland, depleted and
in need of attention and rest. George, the evidence indicates, encouraged
her husband in his excursions and liaisons. The novelist Sean O'Faolain,
who had been made a founder member of the Irish Academy of Letters
by Yeats, even spoke of George as 'almost his procuress'.[13] O'Faolain
remembered bringing the novelist Elizabeth Bowen to tea at the
Rathfarnham house and Yeats immediately taking a fancy to this young
woman from a landed gentry family in County Cork. 'She made such a hit
with him that George, his wife, kept imploring me in whispers every time
I rose to go not to take her away. "He likes her! He likes her!"' O'Faolain
observed that 'George was mother and wife to him . . . she was understanding about what she sympathetically called his "girls": as when for
example she once advised him when they were discussing the logistics of
one of his romantic excursions not to ignore his mistress on the railway
platform and occupy a distant carriage until the train moved out, as he was
proposing to do, but rather to go forward to her and greet her joyfully
before the world.'

Despite his dissipation of energy on love affairs, carried on simultaneously and increasing in number, the great crescendo of poetic activity and
high achievement which marked Yeats's last years continued. In September

1933, shortly after the fiasco of the Blueshirts, there had appeared from
Macmillan in London *The Winding Stair and Other Poems*. Its contents,
which include *Words for Music Perhaps*, extend over a wide range of forms
and material. There is 'For Anne Gregory', one of the most perfect short
lyrics of the twentieth century in English. There are the meditations on the
great houses of Ireland whose families he had known: 'In Memory of Eva
Gore-Booth and Con Markievicz', 'Coole Park, 1929' and 'Coole and
Ballylee, 1931'. And then there are the profound and intricate philosophical
poems, 'Vacillation' and 'A Dialogue of Self and Soul'. When Yeats sent his
old friend AE a copy of the book, he responded 'Your mastery of the craft
of writing would be the despair of the envious.' In his congratulations to
Yeats he spoke for other readers when he wrote, 'I reread with increasing
admiration for the way in which you make words work your will. I can
think of no poet since the Elizabethans who can be so rich and so simple,
who can make an intricate density and again be bare without being empty.'
Then comes a more personal touch as this friend of nearly half a century
asks Yeats, now the great poet of old age, 'Why do you growl about your
age when you never were so vital in youth?'[14]

As he approached his seventieth birthday Yeats's literary energy and
creativity lost none of their power. A little more than a year after *The
Winding Stair* was published he was assembling his next collection, *A Full
Moon in March*, which was published in late 1935. These poems constitute
a lesser achievement than those in the preceding or in the two later
volumes, *New Poems* and *Last Poems*, which show Yeats's literary life concluding in a spectacular climax of creativity. This 1935 collection has as its
principal pieces the political poem 'Parnell's Funeral', the revised versions
of the marching songs originally done for O'Duffy and a twelve-poem
sequence entitled 'Supernatural Songs'. These express the thoughts of
Ribh, yet another character and persona by Yeats, an old hermit who is a
'critic of St Patrick'. Yeats noted that Ribh's Christianity, coming 'perhaps
from Egypt, like much earlier Irish Christianity, echoes pre-Christian
thought'. At the time he was working on this sequence Yeats was also
writing his 'Introduction' to Shri Purohit Swami's translation of *The Holy
Mountain*, and the influences of this work are evident in the Ribh poems.
The interest of the sequence is its philosophical and religious insights; it is

far more abbreviated in verbal range and texture than the earlier sequence *Words for Music Perhaps.*

Not long after T.S. Eliot of Faber & Faber had published *The Holy Mountain*, Yeats suffered a serious congestion of the lungs. During the early months of 1935 he was confined to bed where he struggled to read books of modern poetry in order to compile an anthology of modern verse which he had contracted to do for Oxford University Press. But George could be a stern nurse, and she allowed him only so many hours of attention to serious literature before sweeping in to make sure that he read only 'Wild West' novels. Her motherly strictness worked; towards the end of March he was well enough to set off for London on various enterprises including further discussions with the people at the Group Theatre and the Mercury Theatre. And of course he looked forward to seeing Margot and Ethel. But after a few weeks of living on his own in the Seymour Street flat, his lungs became badly congested once again. He was so ill that Edmund Dulac feared for him and sent a telegram to George. She came immediately to London to take care of him.

Again she helped him to recover, and as he did, he returned to work on the anthology, which now led to a wonderful discovery. He had found himself unresponsive to most of the work by younger poets: 'It was perhaps my illness that made me hard to please, for almost all seemed clay-cold, clay-heavy; I thought at my worst moments, "I have read too much abstract philosophy; I can no longer understand the poetry of other men." Then in an anthology edited by Sir John Squire, I found poems signed Dorothy Wellesley.' The impact of these poems was immediate and powerful. 'My eyes filled with tears. I read in excitement that was the more delightful because it showed I had not lost my understanding of poetry.'[15] Yeats was curious to know who this writer was. 'I asked a visitor to find out who was called, or called herself "Dorothy Wellesley"; was it name or pseudonym? – learnt to my surprise that she was neither harassed journalist nor teacher.' No, Dorothy Wellesley was by no means in the dire position of most apprentice poets; she was an aristocrat, immensely rich, and the future Duchess of Wellington. When Yeats finally managed to be introduced to her (through the good offices of Lady Ottoline Morrell) he was entranced by her in every way.

Not everyone was as impressed by Lady Wellesley as Yeats was. Virginia Woolf who knew her well was made uneasy by 'Dottie's passion for property'. After a visit to her wealthy friend at her grand house Penns in the Rocks in the village of Withyham in Sussex, a few miles south-west of Tunbridge Wells, Virginia Woolf wondered in her journal: 'Can one really **Yes!** be in love with a house? Is there not something sterile in these passions? She is too anxious for other people to praise it. And I don't want possessions . . . I feel on the verge of the world, about to take flight. Dottie on the other hand feels "I have at least, in spite of every other grudge of fate, ten or fifteen thousand a year; and it is only fair that I should get from my money what I can."'[16] One of Dottie's grudges against fate was her unhappy marriage to Gerald Wellesley. After having two children Dottie had separated from her flamboyantly homosexual husband, though they never divorced, and when he inherited the dukedom she duly became the Duchess of Wellington. Sexually Dorothy was as drawn to women as to men. The break-up of her marriage was connected with her relationship with another aristocratic woman, her near neighbour Vita Sackville-West, who had grown up in the magnificent Tudor mansion of Knole and whose closest friends included several other bisexual women; Vita had also been in love with Virginia Woolf. When Lady Dorothy invited her new admirer Yeats to stay at Penns in the Rocks the physical relationship that quickly developed allowed, as will become clear, for her bisexuality. She encouraged him to enjoy thoughts, sensations, feelings and experiences of androgyny.

Their first days together at Penns in June were an immense success and two months later Yeats returned for another stay. On this occasion George insisted that Anne accompany her father to look after him, but immediately upon arrival at Penns sixteen-year-old Anne was sent off to the schoolroom to join the Wellesley children and she saw hardly anything of the adults during her visit. It was the practice of the British aristocracy to keep children in the schoolroom until it was time for them to 'come out' and enter the marriage market. On the train journey down to Sussex Yeats lectured his daughter on the high culture she should expect to encounter, but in the Wellesley schoolroom Anne did not find any. Lady Dorothy's children were frivolous and happily ignorant: when the Mona Lisa was mentioned they thought it referred to a current hit song.

Meanwhile in the drawing-room Yeats conferred with his hostess about the poems to be included in his *Oxford Book of Modern Verse*. The anthology was to be a great publishing success despite the outrageous omission of the great First World War poet Wilfred Owen and the disproportionate amount of space given to Yeats's cronies and friends such as Lady Dorothy. Yeats was deeply gratified to be received into the family of the Duke of Wellington. He had long felt that he belonged with aristocrats. He was also captivated by Lady Dorothy with her long, beautiful face and intense blue eyes, her heavy sensuous lips, her elegant and expensive clothes, lingerie and jewels, and her chic haircut. With her casual unassuming manner and her occasional pleasure in behaving and being treated like a young man, she was very different from Ethel and from Margot.

Dorothy, for her part, was happy to show off her elderly literary lion. Vita Sackville-West, who like Dorothy was now in her early forties, said she would 'rather like to meet the old man' and came over to Penns. Vita reported to her husband Harold Nicolson that Yeats is 'the sort of person who has no small talk at all, but who either remains silent or else plunges straight into the things that matter to him. So little small talk that he doesn't even say "How do you do?" when shaking hands on arrival. He just sits down on the sofa, looks at his nails for two minutes silence, and then tells stories about Manley Hopkins or Lady Gregory or Gogarty, or else expounds his views on T.S. Eliot and *les jeunes*.'[17] He also read aloud to the ladies a section of the introduction to his Oxford anthology. In her journal that night Vita made one last note about him. 'A handsome man with a fine head but also unfortunately a fine tummy.'

Certainly weight was a continual problem for Yeats at this time. As he shuttled between calm and convalescence in rural Rathfarnham and hectic sexual adventures in London his weight, like his health, oscillated greatly. During convalescence his weight could rise to sixteen stone and more, or well over two hundred and twenty pounds. Anne remembered how hard it sometimes was to push him about Rathfarnham in the wheeled chair he was now forced to use. But dieting and abstinence carefully controlled by George would enable him to lose weight and get up his strength, so that he might once again set forth.

URING THIS TIME THE VERY LARGE YEATS (HIS DOCTORS diagnosed obesity) was often seen in London with a very thin, birdlike little man. This new admirer and friend was W.J. Turner, an Australian with a thick accent who talked incessantly except for occa-sional, strangled hesitations. Turner, who was in his mid-forties at this time, was a poet and novelist and the music critic for the *New Statesman*. Yeats was intrigued by his 'strange philosophical poems' and was flattered and grateful when Turner wrote an admiring review of the *Broadsides* which Yeats and Cuala, in a spirit of Irish patriotism, had recently resumed pub-lishing. (Each *Broadside* sheet had a poem by a living Irish poet, a tradi-tional ballad, the music for both and a hand-coloured picture. Yeats was still more pleased when Turner wrote to him to say, 'They will some day be grateful for your discovery of Lady Dorothy.' But some observers, Lady Ottoline Morrell for example, saw the relationship as an instance of Yeats's need for cronies. In her eccentrically punctuated English she wrote to a friend:

> *I was very angry with W.B. Yeats who edited the New Oxford Anthology, and . . . omitted many . . . He did it under the influence of Lady Gerald Wellesley, whose Poetry he admires very much. Indeed, I introduced them to each other, and little foresaw it would have such bad results!! He praises up the poetry of that Shoddy fellow WJ Turner, which is the same Type as*

a 'Medium'. He absorbs what WBY talks to him about, in the Savile Club, and hurries off and writes it down as a Poem, and hands it to WB who of course thinks it Perfect![1]

Lady Ottoline Morrell, however, also had personal reasons for disliking Yeats's new friend. Like D.H. Lawrence in *Women in Love* and Aldous Huxley in *Those Barren Leaves*, Turner, to whom she had in the past shown much hospitality, satirized her in a novel. This was *The Aesthetes* in which he mocked her affectation, her countless flamboyant hats, her heavy make-up, her horselike face, her dottiness and her snobbery. When Yeats wrote an admiring introduction to a volume of Turner's poems, he made the mistake of making favourable remarks about this novel. Lady Ottoline, Yeats's friend of some thirty years, was outraged; she wrote him a letter of bitter, angry reproach. Over in Rathfarnham Yeats was upset by his own tactlessness and by the trouble it had caused. He wrote back trying to make a joke of the matter, but this did not work. When Lady Ottoline received his last letter in her house in Gower Street, she took her pen and under his signature wrote 'Yeats fini'.[2] The two, who had first come to know each other in Bloomsbury in Edwardian times, never met again.

In November 1935 Yeats left Ireland on another major expedition without George. He and Shri Purohit Swami were to travel to Majorca to winter in the warmth of the Mediterranean and to work on a translation of the *Upanishads* together. Yeats would also continue with a new play, *The Herne's Egg*. As the day of their departure approached, Yeats wrote to Lady Dorothy, 'I await Friday with longing, on that day a curtain blots out all my public life, theatre, Academy, Cuala. My work on the anthology is finished – the rest, the business arrangements are my wife's task . . . Why do you not own a coral island? My public life I will pare down to almost nothing. My imagination is on fire again.' Indeed a little earlier Yeats had turned down a very remunerative offer from Harvard University in return for a small number of lectures and a few weeks' residence on campus.

George accompanied her husband and the Swami as far as Liverpool. She was uneasy. She did not care for the Swami, and her suspicions about him were confirmed later when he returned to India leaving behind numerous debts, some to Yeats and more still to fashionable women whom he had counselled in spiritual matters. George also thought that the Swami lured her husband into abstract and abstruse issues of philosophy to the detriment of his poetry.

Nevertheless Yeats was eager for his company and they set off in high spirits. They were accompanied by Mrs Gwyneth Foden, a 53-year-old would-be novelist who was the Swami's follower and lover and also a great fan of Yeats. Olivia Shakespear thought her 'silly and very egotistical and rather a poseuse'. On the voyage out Mrs Foden astonished the ship's crew by appearing in the dress of an Indian temple dancer. A pugnacious lady, she also quarrelled a good deal with the stewards on behalf of her two charges. But on Majorca she showed her more vulnerable side. One evening Yeats had too much to drink and slighted her writing. To be thus criticized by the man she so admired devastated her and she shut herself in a darkened room for two days.[3] Not long after, she had a bitter quarrel with the Swami, ended the affair and stormed off to London. Yet despite such upheavals the two men worked happily together for their first two months or so on Majorca and their projects developed well.

They had settled into large, sunny, white-walled rooms in a clean new hotel on the outskirts of the town of Palma. Just before Christmas 1935 Yeats wrote, 'I am delighted with my life here,' but in little more than a month he fell seriously ill again. The doctor diagnosed problems with both his kidneys and his heart. Once again an urgent message was sent to George, who arrived by plane on 2 February 1936. The children followed: Michael, because he was a boy, was allowed to travel by train; but George insisted that for reasons of safety her daughter travel by sea.

George had her husband removed from the Hotel Terramar to a hillside villa, the Casa Pastor, a substantial house with tall marble pillars and a wide balcony with a view of the wooded coast by the bright blue Mediterranean. Very slowly over the next two and a half months George nursed her husband back from seemingly fatal illness to near recovery. But Yeats fretted again at being under George's orders, and grumbled to Olivia Shakespear about George's decision that he must never again go away without Anne or her. This, he declared, did not suit him at all: as he grew older he needed more not less freedom.[4] Then a figure from one of his recent periods of freedom suddenly appeared on Majorca, plunging him into distress. This was Margot Ruddock, who arrived quite unexpectedly at the Casa Pastor one day, unkempt and obviously insane.

She was hungry, had very little luggage, and her dress was badly torn. She talked wildly of killing herself; she also wanted Yeats's opinion on some poems. A heavy rainstorm had begun and she abruptly rushed out into it saying she was going to throw herself into the Mediterranean. But then she had second thoughts and stayed on the rainswept seashore dancing and singing. When at last she tired, she set off for the lodging-house where the Swami was now staying. She had come to know him in London through Yeats, and greatly admired him. The Swami lent her dry clothes; he also gave her some money from the sum she had formerly lent him. The next morning she decided she would take the ferry back to Barcelona, and there she completely lost control. As she herself later wrote, she wandered about the city: 'men by the shore jeered at me; many eyes followed me, I was suddenly filled with strong sexual passion.' She sat down on a seat to try to control herself. Her sexual feelings were further kindled when she became aware of a voice commanding her: 'Make yourself a prostitute for me as I did for you.'[5] She hurried off to the home of some friends who told her bluntly that she was mad. She assured herself, 'If I can get back to Majorca Yeats will know I'm not insane.' Her friends had sent for the police and Margot was desperate to escape from the flat, which was on the upper floor. She climbed out of a window, jumped, and fell through the glass roof of a bakery, severely injuring her kneecap so that she had to go to hospital. As she grew better she sang her poems aloud, then suffered a relapse, then finally recovered her sanity. When the Spanish police referred the matter to the British Consul, he did not know what to do. He got in touch with Yeats who with George's help went to Barcelona to deal with the problem of his lover. Together they decided that they would have to bear the costs of having her escorted back to England.

'The mad poetess', as George always called her, was both a sadness and an embarrassment for Yeats. The episode had been reported in the newspapers. When he returned to London he hid himself from the now limping, dishevelled Margot even though he knew she was recovered and eager to see him. But in the long run he did his best to stand by her, attempting to boost her career as a poet. He got the *London Mercury* to publish 'Poems by Margot Ruddock with Prefatory Notes on the Author by W.B. Yeats'. He told her that she had 'an intensity no writer of this time can show in the expression of spiritual suffering'. And when, in the following year, he presented his poetry on the fashionable new medium of radio and himself helped to organize some programmes, he found work for Margot as a reader. Unfortunately the BBC broadcasting was too much of a strain on her and brought about another collapse. She was sent to a mental hospital and never left. The once startingly beautiful Margot remained in the asylum until she died at the age of forty-four in 1951. But defiantly Yeats continued to stand up for the insane woman whom he had loved. In his poem about her, 'A Crazed Girl', he declares that Margot, 'Her soul in division from itself' is 'A beautiful lofty thing, or a thing/Heroically lost, heroically found'. In *New Poems* published by Cuala in 1938 Yeats gives this poem a special position, placing it immediately after the poem 'Beautiful Lofty Things' in which Yeats dramatically recalls 'the Olympians', people who were major creative influences in his life: his father, John O'Leary, Standish O'Grady, Lady Gregory and Maud Gonne. The phrase 'A beautiful lofty thing' applied to Margot in her poem and the collocating of the two poems serve to associate the mad, unhappy lover of his late years with those who were the great presences in his earlier life.

When Yeats returned to Barcelona, he told Lady Dorothy that 'After this wild week . . . I long for your intellect and sanity.' He went on to hint that he was beginning to think of Lady Dorothy with her fine house as a replacement Lady Gregory. Such intellect and sanity as Lady Dorothy's he had never previously found anywhere 'but at Coole'. However, as the year wore on his relationship with Lady Dorothy deepened in an entirely different way, becoming highly sexual and complicatedly so; it catered to that turbulence of the senses and the emotions that marked the last few years of his life.

In the summer, after seeing Shri Purohit Swami off on his return voyage to India, Yeats sailed from Barcelona to London and went to stay with Lady Dorothy at Penns in the Rocks. On this visit he grew increasingly intrigued by her masculine aspect and her bisexuality. They brought out in him his own feelings of femininity. Remembering an occasion during the visit he later wrote, 'My dear, my dear – when you crossed the room with that boyish movement, it was no man who looked at you, it was the woman in me.' Not long after, when commenting on her poetry, he tells her that her lines reminded him of the movement of her boyish body. He wished that he could be a nineteen-year-old girl on occasion to enjoy the sensation more strongly.[6] His poem 'To Dorothy Wellesley', which follows immediately after that to Margot in *New Poems*, is full of sexual suspense and complex possibility.

At the same time that he was writing with intricate flirtatiousness to, and of, Lady Dorothy he was engaged in an intense and emotionally more direct correspondence with Ethel Mannin, highly personal but also political. A little earlier there had come a rift between them as a result of their differing political views. One evening in London Ethel Mannin had arranged a meeting of Yeats, Ernst Toller and herself in the bar at Claridge's Hotel in Mayfair. She and the well-known German expressionist playwright wanted Yeats to help them campaign for the Nobel Prize for the German pacifist writer Karl von Ossietzky, whom the Nazis had sent to a concentration camp in 1933 for an article he had written about secret rearmament in Germany. Ossietzky's candidacy for the prize would be greatly strengthened if Yeats, as a Nobel Laureate, would support him. Passionately the two left-wing writers urged on Yeats their belief that such international attention would compel the Nazis to release the political prisoner. Yeats sipped uneasily at his drink as his two younger companions begged for his support. In that expensive art deco bar the stout old man with the white hair stood out all the more conspicuously because of the large black opera cloak he wore. He fiddled with his 'pop up' black top hat; he looked at Ethel uncomfortably; he grew ever more embarrassed. When they paused for a reply from him, he unhesitatingly refused to help them as 'He never meddled in political matters, he said; he never had . . . His interest was Ireland, and Ireland had nothing to do with Europe politically; it was outside, apart. He was sorry but this had always been his attitude.'[7] Ethel Mannin was greatly disappointed in him and months later as he recovered his health at the Casa Pastor on Majorca, he felt it necessary to continue to justify himself to her. He writes, 'Do not try to make a politician of me, even in Ireland I shall never I think be that again . . . If I did what you want, I would seem to hold one form of government more responsible than any other, and that would betray my convictions. Communist, Fascist, nationalist, clerical, anti-clerical, are all responsible according to the number of their victims.' Yeats also tried another way of justifying himself, this time on the grounds of practicality rather then principle. 'If Germans are like my own countrymen the antagonism so roused would doom the prisoner you want to help, either to death or to long imprisonment.' The letter ends with an emotional plea: for her to forgive him and to remain affectionate.[8]

Good-natured and tolerant, Ethel Mannin did not drop him. The relationship survived, though it is uncertain how virile a lover the ailing seventy-year-old Yeats was able to be to her. When back in London after staying at Penns in the Rocks, he writes to Ethel a little sadly about their last encounter, explaining that he had been ill when they met.[9] It was just a week or so later on his return home to Rathfarnham that he wrote the poem about sexual inadequacy entitled 'The Chambermaid's Second Song', lines which he sent to Ethel in a letter.

> *From pleasure of the bed*
> *Dull as a worm,*
> *His rod and its butting head*
> *Limp as a worm,*
> *His spirit that has fled*
> *Blind as a worm*

That same month he told Ethel that all his poetry came out of rage and lust. However questionable the latter was between them, his rage was for her paradoxical: though Yeats claimed to be above politics, his rage was chiefly a response to political matters. There were two 'rouser' poems honouring Roger Casement as a hero of the Irish cause and attacking the Englishmen who had sought to vilify him as a homosexual. Ethel Mannin was quick to spot a political inconsistency here. She asked him how he could reconcile the anti-British feeling in these rhetorical poems and in others such as 'The Curse of Cromwell' and 'Come Gather Round Me, Parnellites' with his status as a pensioner of the British crown. How could he as a citizen and former Senator of the Irish Free State continue in the pay of the government in London? As in the Ossietzky case Yeats took a lot of trouble justifying himself. He wrote a long and careful paragraph explaining his position to her. The pension had been granted when Ireland was a part of Britain. Giving it up now would not leave a vacancy for anybody else. Yeats also maintained that he had earned his pension by services for the people rather than the government and he had accepted it from the people. As he ends his letter he is startled to see how much space he has devoted to explaining himself to her. He asks her forgiveness for the unusual length of his self-defence.[10]

This letter was mailed on the day after King Edward VIII had abdicated because of his love for the divorced American Wallis Simpson. Yeats was very much on the King's side and thought that his speech of abdication, broadcast on the radio, was moving in its restraint and dignity.[11] Two months later, in February 1937, he was still justifying his attitude towards the King, insisting to Ethel Mannin that, as in his ballads about Casement, he would defend a noble-natured man but that he would not defend a cause. He had evidently forgotten that for Ethel Mannin the anti-Fascist Ossietzky was just such a man. Yeats then turned to the Civil War in Spain and, as he so often did with this politically minded young woman, tried to have his cake and eat it. Yeats told her that if he were pressed, he would have to side with the Fascists but this was just a feeling he had. It would not lead to any real action on his part. Though a pensioner of the British government, he was also 'an old Fenian', and that the old Fenian in him would rejoice if a Fascist nation or government controlled Spain. He thought that would weaken the British empire, perhaps force England to be civil to Indians and even to set them free. But, he told her, this was an instinct and he would never act on it. He declared that he had a horror of modern politics, seeing them as nothing but false news manipulating popular enthusiasm.[12]

The new medium of radio came to have an important place in Yeats's life. His daughter long remembered how after one of his sorties to London he brought home to Riversdale the first radio set the family owned. When he first 'listened in' Yeats would sometimes fail to catch what the announcer said and would turn to the bulky wooden set and say, 'I beg your pardon. What did you say?' Like Ezra Pound in Italy who also first acquired a radio set around this time, Yeats became a broadcaster on this ever more popular medium as well as a listener. But Yeats's use of radio did not have the dramatic consequence his old friend's did; Pound's broadcasts on Radio Rome during the Second World War in support of Mussolini's Fascist government would lead to his indictment for treason by a grand jury in the United States and his arrest and imprisonment at the end of the war. Yeats's radio programmes were always essentially literary. Early in 1937 he was involved in a broadcast reading of some of his poems from the stage of the Abbey Theatre for Radio Eireann. Yeats was horrified by the poor quality of the sound on the recording that was made for transmission. All the robust singing and handclapping that accompanied 'Come Gather Round Me, Parnellites' and that sounded so stirring on the stage sounded insignificant on the wireless, Yeats said.[13]

Nevertheless Yeats persisted with the unfamiliar medium. Two months later, in early April, he organized a poetry programme for the BBC with the title 'In the Poet's Pub' and then, three weeks later, another one entitled 'In the Poet's Parlour'. In July he was involved in yet another broadcast about 'My Own Poetry'. Yeats designed this programme in such a way as to contrast 'the tragic real Ireland' with the Ireland of the dream. The first section was made up of the four poems: 'September 1913', 'The Rose Tree', 'The Curse of Cromwell' and 'An Irish Airman'. The second part of the programme dealing with the dream Ireland comprised 'Running to Paradise', 'The Happy Townland' and 'The Song of Wandering Aengus'. Some of the poems were spoken and some were sung. Accompanying music was composed by Edmund Dulac.

Ever mindful of his finances Yeats was pleased to have the fees these broadcasts brought in. He was still more pleased to learn in June that a Testimonial Committee had been formed in the United States with the prime aim of ensuring that he should be free from financial anxieties for the rest of his life. Irish America assisted his career yet again, and he was presented with a cheque for £600. In August two prominent members of the committee arrived in Ireland and dined and sang songs with Yeats and his bawdy young protegé and friend, the poet Fred Higgins. One of the visitors was James A. Farrell, head of the American Steel Trust, and the other Patrick McCartan, formerly an Irish revolutionary and now a prosperous doctor in America. In the middle of the month Yeats's Irish Academy (and as Sean O'Faolain once observed it was very much *his*) held a convivial banquet at which Yeats announced the gift and expressed his thanks for what these American benefactors had done. On that same occasion he also spoke of a major new poem that was forming in his head and which he would like to send to each one of his fifty Irish American supporters who had contributed to his gift. The poem finally came to completion under the title 'The Municipal Gallery Revisited'. It is a ringing piece which records an emotional occasion on which Yeats comtemplated the portraits of the dead who had been his companions in the Irish literary revival and the Irish revolution: Augusta Gregory, Arthur Griffith, Kevin O'Higgins and John Synge. The poem testifies to his deep, living involvement with them and the milieu they created. The conclusion is forceful, declaiming an unashamed pride in creative fellowship.

> *You that would judge me, do not judge alone*
> *This book or that, come to this hallowed place*
> *Where my friends' portraits hang and look thereon;*
> *Ireland's history in their lineaments trace;*
> *Think where man's glory most begins and ends,*
> *And say my glory was I had such friends.*

In December Yeats sent copies of this substantial seven-stanza poem, printed with two smaller items, to each of the fifty subscribers in America. The composition of the piece had been time-consuming and laborious. He first made prose notes and then slowly crafted them into rhyming, or sometimes significantly half-rhyming eight-line stanzas. Each of the seven stanzas took a whole day to complete.

Yeats described this process in a letter to a woman who had become the most recent member of his circle of lovers in England. This was Edith Shackleton Heald with whom he had fallen deeply in love in the spring of 1937. Fifty-two years old and a successful London journalist, Edith lived with her elder sister Nora, who was the editor of the genteel magazine *The Lady*. Their home was the Chantry House in Steyning in Sussex, a building dating back to the sixteenth century, when it had been the lodging of the choral priests at Steyning church. It had been enlarged and given

cf. Yeats reading
p. 238
Keith Aldritt

Georgian features in the early eighteenth century but had become almost derelict by the time the Shackleton Healds decided to buy it. The two unmarried, middle-aged sisters devoted much time and money to a painstaking and architecturally sensitive restoration of the old house. Edith and Nora then furnished it with rare carpets, their painting collection, expensive tableware and much antique furniture. Into this gracious home Edith invited Yeats when he became her lover and here he would compose some of the last, great poems of his life. ∠ ✱

Edith, who had Irish family connections and owned a cottage in Rosapenna in Donegal, had been a lively, provocative journalist for thirty years. As a special correspondent for the London *Evening Standard* owned by the wealthy Canadian imperialist Lord Beaverbrook, she had covered events in Paris during the First World War and the political crisis in Ireland as it developed in and after 1919. She subsequently became the *Evening Standard's* book critic for a while. Edith had long been a supporter of votes for women and had a feminist wit. She was dark and attractive with a wide, vulnerable mouth and liquid, intelligent eyes. When her friend Edmund Dulac, who brought her together with Yeats, did a drawing of her, he subtitled it 'the little kitten'. Edith, like Dorothy Wellesley, was bisexual and though at times she could be the worldly, hard-bitten journalist, she was also extremely impressionable and sensitive. She was susceptible to the dominance of others too, as is shown by her near thirty-year relationship with the tyrannical heiress and artist Hannah Gluckstein which began a few years after Yeats's death when Edith was still grieving for him.

Her involvement with Yeats began in April 1937 when he was in London working with Dulac and others on his BBC poetry broadcast. Later he went to stay at the Chantry House, which was just thirty miles from Lady Dorothy Wellesley's home. The visit to Edith at Steyning was a restorative for Yeats. Now approaching seventy-two, he was about the same age that his hero Goethe had been when he experienced the last great passion of his life, for the nineteen-year-old Ulrike von Levetzow at Marienbad. When the time came for Yeats to return to London to do his broadcasts he wrote to Edith that she brought him 'that kind of understanding or sympathy ⩹ which is peace'. He took a pleasure in the maturity of their relationship. Only a week or two before his birthday he told Edith, some twenty years younger than he, that 'Were you younger a true intimacy would be impossible . . I think the finest bond is possible when we have outlived our first rough silver – and that it may be very sweet to the old and the half old.'[14]

In early autumn Yeats returned from entertaining his Irish American benefactors in Dublin and went again to Steyning. His erotic experiences with Edith during this stay fired his emotions and stayed with him when he returned to Rathfarnham for the necessary reorganization of Cuala. Sensing his life approaching its end, Yeats did not wish to leave Cuala in financial disarray. He restored the firm to solvency and set up a board of directors which included George and the young poet Fred Higgins. At first Lolly accepted the reorganization, but soon came to resent Higgins.

Before escaping to the French Riviera for the first two winter months of 1938 Yeats also worked on articles for a periodical called *On the Boiler*, modelled on Ruskin's *Fors Clavigera*. Yeats's title recalled the old ranter 'the great McCoy', a mad ship's carpenter whom Yeats remembered from his childhood climbing up on to a large, rusty ship's boiler on the Sligo quays and from that height proceeding 'to read the Scriptures and denounce his neighbours'.[15] The title suggests that Yeats retained some irony about himself as he delivered his crotchety opinions on such fashionable right-wing topics as eugenics.

In France he stayed first at Menton and then at the Hôtel Idéal Séjour on Cap Martin a little closer to Nice. From here, though in uncertain health and mithered in his sleep by horrific dream apparitions, he wrote regularly to Edith and also, indeed, to the other women he called on in England. In March, with the promise of spring, he wrote asking Edith if he might stay with her again. She agreed and he lived and worked at his poetry at Steyning for several weeks. George, left behind in Rathfarnham, while recognizing that she could not supply the mental excitement created by her husband's lovers in England, worried continually about his cardiac condition and his health generally. She wrote, appealing to Edith, 'Do please extract from him his prescriptions for digitalis and make him take it twice a day while he is still with you. He needs so much intellectual stimulus that you and others can give, but he unfortunately also needs that heart stimulus. And nobody can feel more passionately than I that he has to return to this desolate place.'[16]

After Yeats had to leave the beautiful Chantry House and return to 'this desolate place' on Abbey Theatre business and also for more work on the Cuala reorganization, involving violent arguments with Lolly over Higgins's role, his letters to Edith became ever more passionate. 'I have great need of you, needing you as earth needs Spring . . . I begin to hold you, gently, timidly at the top of your head and then – having got so far, my dear it is best to close this letter.'[17] A week later he bursts out, 'I am longing for you in body and soul . . . O my dear – I want to say all those foolish things which we sometimes read out in breach of promise cases. I know what it is to think what transcends speech and what speech gloriously transcends, that is perhaps what savage tom toms are for.'[18]

Just over three weeks after that letter to Edith, Yeats had, with deep sadness, to report the death of Olivia Shakespear. The event marked an important, an almost unbearable ending in his life. A few weeks later there occurred for him another ending, though he cannot have known it at the time. Maud Gonne went to Riversdale to have tea with him. It was their last meeting. He had previously offered glamorous, expensive ways in which they might meet, such as paying for a car to fetch her or entertaining her at Jammet's, Dublin's most exclusive restaurant. It was surely a way of indicating to her that the once poor poet who had lacked the money to follow her to Paris now had the means to entertain her in the most opulent fashion. In any event she simply came over to see him. She was seventy-two, and looked a little haggard. When she entered the drawing-room, he found it difficult to rise from his chair to greet her. Their conversation was gentle and kindly. As it drew to an end Yeats murmured, 'Maud, we should have gone on with our Castle of heroes, we might still do it.'[19]

At the end of October he sailed for England for the last time. Though he did not know it, he would never see Ireland again, nor the house at Rathfarnham that had been his home for the last six years. After a few weeks in London he and George continued their journey, to winter again in the warmth of the Mediterranean. They once more settled into the Hôtel Idéal Séjour on Cap Martin; high above them was Roquebrune, the picturesque hill-top town overlooking the cape. With less than two months to live Yeats retained his creative energy. With his thoughts on imminent death the crescendo of literary achievement did not falter. 'I do nothing but write verse,' he told Dorothy Wellesley at the beginning of December. He wrote his substantial valedictory poem 'Under Ben Bulben' and also worked at a second edition of the socio-literary miscellany *On the Boiler*. As with the first edition, the royalties were intended to support Cuala. He also completed the last of his plays, *The Death of Cuchulain*, which led him on to compose a related lyric entitled 'Cuchulain Comforted', an intricately managed, delicately half-rhyming *terza rima*. In his life, as in this poem, the prospect of death was vivid. The kidney trouble, which of his several illnesses was the one now affecting him most, grew worse. Nevertheless Christmas that year by the Mediterranean was a lively time. Michael, now a teenager, came for the holidays and played a great deal of chess with his father when Yeats was well enough. On Christmas Day the family went over to Beaulieu on the coast near Nice where Dorothy Wellesley was staying with her friend, the musician and BBC producer Hilda Matheson. To these two visitors he managed to read aloud his very last poem, 'The Black Tower', which alludes to King Arthur, the once and future king awaiting his return from death to life. The poem has a strong refrain and Yeats asked Hilda Matheson to compose a tune for it. Lady Dorothy Wellesley remembered that 'she and I went out of the hotel, walking up and down in the rain and darkness trying the tune. When we came back she sang him the air. He seemed pleased. His last projective thought seems to me to have been this wish for "words for melody".'[20]

The little Australian W.J. Turner and his jealous wife were also staying with Lady Dorothy at Beaulieu. Down the road at the Hôtel Eden on the Cap d'Ail in Monaco were Dermod and Mabel O'Brien, Dubliners who were well known to Yeats and his wife. Dermod, a painter who was exactly Yeats's age and had served with him on the Coinage Committee, had taught drawing and painting to Anne Yeats in Dublin. Within a couple of years he would be President of the Academy there. So there was plenty of congenial company for the holidays and Yeats, when well, enjoyed the toing and froing and the socializing. But he also found that it quickly tired him. In the early days of January, though he could occasionally have periods of vitality, he grew weaker. Mabel and Dermod O'Brien went over one day not long before he died expecting to visit a very sick man, only to find him sitting up in bed, happy and eager to talk and still writing poetry. Mabel's

last memory of him living was that he was such an entertaining host that
he did not seem like an invalid. Yet despite such occasions he was gradually losing his hold on life. When Edith Shackleton Heald arrived at
Roquebrune towards the end of January she found him extremely weak.

During the morning of Saturday 28 January he had bouts of intense pain
and breathlessness. The French doctor gave him morphia. He lost
consciousness never to regain it, and at two o'clock in the afternoon he was
pronounced dead. Distraught, George telephoned the O'Briens to tell
them the news and to ask Dermod to help with the funeral arrangements.[21]
She asked Mabel to write to Lily in Dublin. On the night of his death she
and Edith Shackleton Heald took it in turn to hold a vigil beside his body.
Nearly thirty years later Edith still remembered, 'I watched over him until
4 a.m. His features had become even more noble and beautiful than I had
known them. It was a wonderful southern night of stars and I remembered
that "the heavens themselves blaze forth the deaths of princes".[22] On the
Monday morning the coffin was carried up the steep narrow road to
Roqueburne. It lay in the little chapel in the hill town until three o'clock
when it was taken to the local cemetery where George and the friends
staying in the locality attended the simple, Protestant graveside service.

I found this very moving C. L. Y.

YEATS WAS DEAD AND BURIED BUT HIS STORY WAS NOT ENDED. Even in his last days he had been working on his image as an Irishman. No matter that he knew he was likely to die in Europe, where he had spent much of his life; he was intent on writing a poem which included an epitaph for a gravestone for himself in Sligo. 'Under Ben Bulben' makes a statement of his belief in the afterlife before defining his view of the role of the artist and enjoining Irish poets to 'learn your trade'. At the end of the 95-line poem comes the concise and peremptory epitaph which Yeats commanded should be carved on his tombstone in Drumcliffe churchyard under the shadow of Ben Bulben.

> *Cast a cold eye*
> *On life, on death.*
> *Horseman, pass by!*

It is an imperative to the living, a command to be calm, confident, stoical, indifferent to life and death alike, since both form the continuum for spirit. It was, of course, an epitaph which George could not use when she buried her husband in Roquebrune. But, almost as if Yeats were exerting his will from beyond the grave, there were forces at work in Ireland to ensure that the poet returned to Sligo. For some years Maud Gonne approached members of the government, including Eamon de Valera, agitating for the national poet's reinterment in Ireland where she considered he rightly belonged. Yeats's friend F.R. Higgins had been sympathetic to her idea and had promised his help. Nine years after Yeats's burial in Roquebrune and three years after the end of the Second World War, the wishes Yeats had expressed in his valedictory poem were at last honoured.

Ironically it was Sean MacBride, Maud's son by the hated John MacBride, who played a prominent part in arranging for the return of Yeats's remains. In 1948 this purposeful and energetic politician had helped to end the government of Yeats's old antagonist Eamon de Valera. In the same year he set about organizing a ceremonious occasion such as would have delighted the poet. An Irish naval corvette, *Macha*, brought the coffin containing Yeats's remains from the South of France to Galway. Here it was met by Yeats's fellow poet and former director of Cuala, Frank O'Connor. Yeats's family was also present. George had not remarried or returned to England. She had taken a house in Adelaide Road in Dublin where she would continue to live until her death. She had done her part to perpetuate her husband's reputation by publishing many poems posthumously through the Cuala Press, which she had operated for some years after Lolly's death in 1940. Anne, now in her thirtieth year, had begun her career as a set designer for the Abbey Theatre but, with the encouragement of Jack Yeats, was devoting herself to painting. Michael had received a legal training and, unlike his grandfather John Butler Yeats, had a successful career in the law. Later in life he would become a Senator like his father and subsequently a member of the European Parliament.

From Galway Yeats's coffin was taken to Sligo where the hearse, preceded by pipes and muffled drums, made its way slowly through streets long familiar to the poet. The coffin rested for a while in front of the Town Hall before being taken, on that day of misty weather so typical of Sligo, to the nearby village of Drumcliffe. Past the ruined tower and the Celtic cross the coffin was borne to the church where Yeats's great-grandfather, Parson John, had once officiated. Sean MacBride, representing the government of the Republic of Ireland, which was proclaimed this same year as successor to the Irish Free State, met the coffin of his mother's famous lover. There was a service in the little church and then Yeats was laid to rest in a grave close to the west door. The final act in his transformation into an icon was completed.

Led by Lennox Robinson, a number of those attending the reburial returned to Sligo for a vinous wake. These were people who had known Yeats in his lifetime: they had been his milieu and they remembered him as man as well as poet. They had enjoyed many a convivial occasion in his company and so, after the solemnity of the ceremonies celebrating Yeats the poet, they now celebrated the vigorous life of Yeats the man.

Feb., 2014
June 28, 2014
Aug. 14, 2014

I: An Irish Childhood, An English Education, 1865–1880

1. William M. Murphy, *Family Secrets: William Butler Yeats and His Relatives*, p.6
2. Lolly Yeats to John Butler Yeats, 16 August 1912, Yeats Collection, National Library of Ireland, manuscript 31113 (2)
3. Joan Hardwick, *The Yeats Sisters*, p.16
4. Ibid, p.18
5. Idem

II: The Young Nationalist 1880–1890

I 1880–1885

1. Winston Churchill, 'Charles Stewart Parnell', *Great Contemporaries*, p.273
2. Ibid, p.272
3. Ibid, p.271
4. Ibid, p.273
5. Joseph Hone (ed.), *John Butler Yeats: Letters to his Son W.B. Yeats and Others*, p.210
6. W.B. Yeats, *Mythologies*, p.15
7. W.B. Yeats, *Reveries over Childhood and Youth*, p.40
8. Ibid, p.43
9. Ibid, p.36
10. W.B. Yeats, *Autobiographies*, p.37
11. Ibid, p.36
12. Ibid, p.37
13. Ibid, p.38

14. John Eglinton (W.K. Magee), 'Yeats at the High School' in *The Erasmian: The Magazine of the High School*, Dublin, June 1939, pp.11–12
15. Reverend Dr F.R. Montgomery Hitchcock, cited in Murphy, p.568, n.15
16. 'W.B. Yeats at School: Interesting Reminiscences of the Irish Poet's Schooldays', by a Classmate, *T.P.'s Weekly*, 7 June 1912, p.709
17. George Bernard Shaw. Cited in Michael Holroyd, *Bernard Shaw*, Volume 1, *1856–1898, The Search for Love*, p.352
18. Murphy, p.132
19. *Autobiographies*, p.39
20. Ibid, p.41
21. Idem
22. Idem
23. Ibid, p.42
24. Idem
25. Ibid, p.43
26. W.B. Yeats, *Memoirs*, pp.71–2
27. Ibid, pp.40–1
28. *Autobiographies*, p.42
29. Ibid, p.50
30. John Kelly and Eric Domville (eds.), *The Collected Letters of W.B. Yeats*, 1, p.155. Yeats here misremembers the title of the first play. He actually called it 'Vivien and Time'. 'Time and the Witch Vivien' is a poem taken from the play, which appeared in Yeats's first published volume of poems, *The Wanderings of Oisin*
31. Unpublished letter in the New York Public Library, JBY to John Quinn, 3 December 1917
32. *Letters*, 1, p.155, n.2
33. *Autobiographies*, p.55. The house now has as its address 418 Harold's Cross Road
34. Murphy, p.139
35. W.B. Yeats, 'How I Began to Write'. Manuscript prepared for the BBC and now number 30790 in the Yeats Collection, National Library of Ireland
36. John Turpin, 'The South Kensington System and the Dublin Metropolitan School of Art', *Dublin Historical Record*, 36, 1982–3, p.62
37. *Autobiographies*, p.54
38. *Letters*, 1, p.18, n.8
39. *Autobiographies*, p.53
40. *Letters*, 1, p.155, n.2
41. Murphy, p.137

2 1885–1887

1. John O'Leary, *Young Ireland: The Old and the New*, 1885, p.4
2. Ibid, p.7
3. Ibid, p.13
4. The copy is in the possession of the National Library of Ireland

5. *Memoirs*, p.56
6. *Dublin University Review*, Volume I, no. 1, February 1885
7. 'How I Began to Write' (see n.35 above)
8. *Dublin University Review*, Volume I, no. 7, August 1885, p.46
9. *Autobiographies*, pp.25–6
10. Charles Johnston, 'Esoteric Buddhism', *Dublin University Review*, Volume I, no. 6, July 1885, p.114
11. Ibid, p.163
12. 'How I Began to Write'
13. Roger McHugh (ed.), *W.B. Yeats: Letters to Katharine Tynan*, p.11
14. Claude Colleer Abbott (ed.), *Further Letters of Gerard Manley Hopkins*, p.373
15. *Memoirs*, p.51
16. Ibid, p.118
17. *Autobiographies*, p.65
18. *Memoirs*, p.195
19. Ibid, p.66
20. Ibid, p.196
21. *Autobiographies*, p.64
22. Ibid, p.66
23. In declining to take the oath, Yeats was availing himself of a precedent established by John O'Leary. For Yeats's involvement with the IRB, see John Unterecker, *Yeats and Patrick McCartan: A Fenian Friendship*, Dolmen, Dublin, 1967
24. Yeats remembered this exchange in his preface to Lady Gregory's *Cuchulain of Muirthemne*
25. A short summary of this article did in fact appear in print a month earlier in the *Irish Fireside*, a middlebrow magazine to whose editors Yeats had been recommended by John O'Leary
26. A. Norman Jeffares and Warwick Gould (eds.), *Yeats's Poems*, p.362
27. *Autobiographies*, p.63
28. *Memoirs*, p.82
29. Ibid, p.63
30. *Further Letters of Gerard Manley Hopkins*, p.374
31. W.B. Yeats, 'The Poetry of Sir Samuel Ferguson', *Dublin University Review*, November 1886, p.924
32. *Letters*, I, p.8
33. 'The Poetry of Sir Samuel Ferguson', p.931
34. *Dublin University Review*, December 1886, p.1047

3 1887–1889

1. *Letters*, I, p.15
2. Ibid, p.24
3. Ibid, p.14

4. Ibid, p.52
5. Ibid, p.12, n.1
6. *Autobiographies*, pp.139–40
7. *Letters*, I, p.22
8. Ibid, p.22, n.2
9. Ibid, p.59
10. *Letters*, I, p.22
11. *Memoirs*, p.34
12. Ernest Rhys, *Wales England Wed: An Autobiography*, pp.91–3
13. Ibid, p.92
14. Idem
15. *Letters*, I, p.33
16. Idem
17. Ibid, p.35
18. Ibid, p.38
19. Ibid, p.41
20. The work was not completed and performed until 1896, long after Sibelius had completed another work deriving from the *Kalevala*. Similarities and connections between Ireland and Finland are alluded to in the title of James Joyce's final work and referred to within its text
21. *Letters*, I, p.141
22. Ibid, p.98
23. A.P. Sinnett, *Esoteric Buddhism*, p.50
24. Jeffares and Gould (eds.), *Yeats's Poems*, p.629
25. Even such a strong believer in Yeats's literary gifts as John O'Leary was put off by this kind of rhyming: 'Her hair was of a citron tincture/And gathered in a silver cincture'.
26. *Letters*, I, p.53
27. Ibid, p.54
28. Ibid, p.56
29. *Autobiographies*, pp.117–18
30. Ibid, p.32
31. *Memoirs*, p.38
32. Idem
33. *Autobiographies*, p.83
34. *Memoirs*, p.39
35. *Autobiographies*, p.84
36. Angus Wilson, *The Strange Ride of Rudyard Kipling: His Life and Works*, p.143
37. *Autobiographies*, p.83
38. *Memoirs*, p.38
39. *Autobiographies*, p.85
40. Idem
41. *Letters*, I, p.50

42. Ibid, p.64, n.5
43. Ibid, p.64, n.3
44. Ibid, p.74
45. Ibid, p.99
46. Ibid, pp.45–6
47. Ibid, p.70
48. Ibid, p.82
49. Ibid, p.88
50. Idem
51. Years later Yeats would learn that the story had been taken from a French work *Les Matineés de Timothé Trimm*. In a letter to the press, the adapter of the story remarked, 'To my small share in the work Mr Yeats is heartily welcome . . . but I question if a story concocted as a pot-boiler by a student in an attic from the French of Timothé Trimm, of the *Petit Journal* can be labelled as genuine, unsophisticated Irish folklore': *Letters*, I, p.165
52. W.B. Yeats (ed.), *Fairy and Folk Tales of the Irish Peasantry*, p.213
53. *Letters*, I, p.88
54. *Fairy and Folk Tales*, p.7
55. *Memoirs*, pp.21–2
56. Idem

4 1889–1890

1. Janet Egleson Dunleavy and Gareth W. Dunleavy, *Douglas Hyde: A Maker of Modern Ireland*, p.133
2. *Autobiographies*, p.82
3. Idem. Apple blossom seems improbable at the end of January in London. Perhaps Yeats, writing more than a quarter of a century later, here employs a later image of her beauty to evoke the Maud he first saw. The anachronism does not detract from the memorability of the experience
4. *Memoirs*, p.40
5. Idem
6. Ibid, p.42
7. *Letters*, I, p.137
8. *Autobiographies*, p.82
9. *Letters*, I, pp.140–1
10. *Memoirs*, p.43
11. The review is reprinted in A. Norman Jeffares (ed.), *W.B. Yeats: The Critical Heritage*, p.73
12. 'William Carleton', in John P. Frayne (ed.), *Uncollected Prose of W.B. Yeats*, I, p.145
13. *Letters*, I, p.183
14. Ibid, pp.198–9
15. *Representative Irish Tales*, p.25

16. Ibid, p.28
17. Ibid, p.31
18. Ibid, p.27
19. *Letters*, I, p.151, n.3
20. Idem
21. Ibid, p.171
22. Ibid, pp.201–2
23. Ibid, p.163
24. Ibid, p.164
25. Idem
26. Ibid, p.182, n.2
27. Ibid, p.172
28. Ibid, p.170
29. 'A Sicilian Idyll', in Horace Reynolds (ed.), *Letters to the New Island*, p.114
30. Ibid, p.76
31. Idem
32. Ibid, p.74
33. *Letters*, I, pp.202–3
34. Ibid, p.209

III: The Calculating Dreamer 1890–1901

1 1890

1. 'The Rhymers Club' in *Letters to the New Island*, p.143
2. Ibid, p.144
3. *Autobiographies*, p.113
4. *Memoirs*, p.35
5. Idem
6. *Memoirs*, p.97
7. Ibid, p.35
8. Idem
9. *Letters*, I, p.239, n.3
10. Ibid, p.217
11. Arthur Ransome, *Bohemia in London*, pp.161–2
12. *Letters*, I, p.255
13. *Autobiographies*, p.113
14. *Memoirs*, p.92
15. Lionel Johnson, 'Poetry and Patriotism in Ireland', *Post Liminium: Essays and Critical Papers*, p.173
16. *Memoirs*, p.35
17. Francis King, *Modern Ritual Magic: The Rise of Western Occultism*, p.47
18. *Autobiographies*, p.123

19. *Memoirs*, p.27
20. Idem
21. Idem
22. *Memoirs*, p.29
23. Ibid, p.30
24. *Letters*, I, p.233
25. Ibid, p.235
26. Idem

━ 2 1890–1894

 1. *Letters*, I, p.241
 2. Idem
 3. John Edwin Ellis and William Butler Yeats (eds.), *The Works of William Blake, Poetic, Symbolic and Critical*, Vol. I, pp.243–4
 4. *Mythologies*, pp.107–8
 5. *John Sherman and Dhoya* by Ganconagh, p.31
 6. Ibid
 7. Ibid, p.31
 8. Ibid, p.2
 9. *Letters*, I, p.248
10. *Memoirs*, p.45
11. Idem
12. Idem
13. *Letters*, I, p.260
14. *Memoirs*, p.46
15. Ibid, p.47
16. Ibid, p.48
17. Idem
18. Idem
19. *Memoirs*, p.49
20. Idem
21. *Letters*, I, p.327, n.3
22. 'Maud Gonne' in *Letters to the New Island*, pp.149–50
23. *Freeman's Journal*, 7 September 1892
24. *Freeman's Journal*, 9 September 1892
25. *Memoirs*, p.63
26. Ibid, p.66
27. *United Ireland*, 28 August 1892
28. Ibid, p.404
29. Ibid, p.321
30. Ibid, p.339
31. Ibid, p.347
32. Ibid, p.357
33. *Memoirs*, p.54

34. Quoted in Michael Holroyd, *Bernard Shaw*, Volume 1, *1856–1898 The Search for Love*, p.247
35. *Memoirs*, pp.72–3
36. *Autobiographies*, p.213

3 1894

1. *Letters*, I, p.379
2. *Memoirs*, p.73
3. *Autobiographies*, p.229
4. *Letters*, I, p.460
5. Idem
6. 'Accepter, désormais, de vivre, ne serait plus qu'un sacrilège envers nous-mêmes. Vivre? Les serviteurs feront cela pour nous.' *Œuvres Complètes de Villiers de l'Isle-Adam*, p.261
7. John P. Frayne (ed.), *Uncollected Prose by W.B. Yeats*, I, pp.324–5
8. Idem
9. *Memoirs*, p.72
10. Frayne, pp.332–4
11. *Letters*, I, p.396
12. Ibid, p.416
13. Ibid, p.415
14. *Memoirs*, p.85
15. Hilary Pyle, *Jack B. Yeats: A Biography*, p.39
16. *Letters*, I, p.393
17. Ibid, p.418
18. *Memoirs*, p.78
19. *Letters*, I, p.418
20. *Memoirs*, p.79

4 1894–1895

1. *Letters*, I, p.438
2. Ibid, p.434
3. Idem
4. *Letters*, I, p.409
5. Ibid, p.459
6. *Memoirs*, p.86
7. Ibid, p.87
8. Idem
9. *Autobiographies*, pp.210–20
10. *Letters*, I, p.475, n.1

5 1896

1. John Harwood, *Olivia Shakespear and W.B. Yeats: After Long Silence*, p.55
2. *Memoirs*, p.88

3. Allan Wade (ed.), *The Letters of W.B. Yeats*, p.264
4. *Autobiographies*, p.211
5. Anne Chisholm, *Nancy Cunard*, pp.15–17
6. Arthur Symons, 'A Causerie from a Castle in Ireland', *The Savoy*, No. 6, October 1896, p.94
7. Arthur Symons, 'The Isles of Aran', *The Savoy*, No. 8, December 1896, p.76
8. Ibid, p.79
9. *Memoirs*, p.102
10. Idem
11. Anna MacBride White and A. Norman Jeffares (eds.), *The Gonne–Yeats Letters 1893–1938*, p.61
12. Ibid, p.62
13. Idem
14. *Memoirs*, p.89

6 1897–1899

1. In *The Tragic Generation* Yeats misremembers the name of the theatre, saying that it was the Théâtre de l'Œuvre. In the same year of 1896 this theatre saw the production of one of the great works of late nineteenth-century poetic drama, Ibsen's early play *Peer Gynt* with incidental music by Grieg and the set designed by Munch
2. *Autobiographies*, p.234
3. Idem
4. *Gonne–Yeats Letters*, p.79
5. *Autobiographies*, p.231
6. Wade, p.279
7. Ibid, p.280
8. *Autobiographies*, p.235
9. Wade, p.284
10. *Gonne–Yeats Letters*, p.73
11. *Mythologies*, p.271
12. Ibid, p.306
13. Ibid, p.1
14. Idem
15. Wade, p.288
16. *Gonne–Yeats Letters*, p.97
17. *Memoirs*, p.132
18. Ibid, pp.133–4
19. Deidre Toomey, 'Labyrinths: Yeats and Maud Gonne', *Yeats and Women, Yeats Annual*, no. 9, 1992
20. Ibid, p.125
21. Cited in Mary Lou Kohfeldt, *Lady Gregory: The Woman Behind the Irish Renaissance*, p.130

15. *New Freewoman*, 15 December 1913, quoted in *Ezra Pound and Dorothy Shakespear*, p.282
16. *Ezra Pound and Dorothy Shakespear*, p.280
17. Ibid, p.301

2 1914–1917

1. Wade, p.589
2. Ibid, p.590
3. Ibid, p.611
4. *Gonne–Yeats Letters*, p.369
5. Ibid, p.375
6. Wade, p.626
7. *Mythologies*, p.328
8. Ibid, p.345
9. Arthur Symons to John Quinn, 11 November 1917, Quinn Papers, New York Public Library
10. Wade, p.633
11. George Mills Harper, 'Introduction', *Yeats's Vision Papers*, Vol. 1, p.10

3 1918–1922

1. Hardwick, p.206
2. Wade, p.651
3. *Gonne–Yeats Letters*, p.393
4. Douglas Goldring, *The Nineteen Twenties*, p.118
5. Wade, p.659
6. L.A.G. Strong, *Green Memories*, p.243
7. Ibid, p.244
8. Wade, p.661
9. Quoted in Joseph Hone, *W.B. Yeats 1865–1939*, p.323
10. *Gonne–Yeats Letters*, p.417
11. L.A.G. Strong, p.259
12. *Autobiographies*, p.193
13. Ibid, p.129
14. Idem
15. Hone, p.336
16. Quoted in Lord Birkenhead, *Rudyard Kipling*, pp.294–5

VI: MEDITERRANEAN DAYS 1922–1932

1 1922–1927

1. Wade, p.678
2. Idem

3. Ibid, p.684
4. Ibid, p.693
5. Valerie Eliot (ed.), *The Letters of T.S. Eliot*, Volume 1, *1898–1922*, p.611
6. Jeffrey Meyers, *Joseph Conrad: A Biography*, p.355
7. 'The Bounty of Sweden', *Autobiographies*, p.362
8. Ibid, p.374
9. Ibid, p.364
10. Ibid, pp.371–2
11. Ibid, p.376
12. Sean O'Casey, *Autobiographies* II, p.232
13. John Lavery, *The Life of a Painter*, p.219
14. Terence de Vere White, *Kevin O'Higgins*, p.131
15. Wade, p.705
16. Hone, p.371
17. Ibid, p.27
18. Quoted in Garry O'Connor, *Sean O'Casey: A Life*, p.199
19. Idem
20. Wade, p.716
21. Ibid, p.712
22. D.H. Lawrence, 'Study of Thomas Hardy', *Phoenix*, p.430
23. Wade, p.720
24. Idem

2 1927–1932

1. Wade, pp.726–7
2. De Vere White, p.233
3. Wade, p.733
4. *Gonne–Yeats Letters*, p.444
5. Wade, p.738
6. *A Packet for Ezra Pound*, p.6
7. Ibid, p.3
8. Wade, p.759
9. George Antheil, *Bad Boy of Music*, p.228
10. Forrest Read (ed.), *The Letters of Ezra Pound to James Joyce*, pp.234–5
11. Wade, p.758
12. Translated by the author from Gerhart Hauptmann, *Diarium 1917 bis 1933*, pp.116–17
13. Basil Bunting, 'Yeats Recollected', *Agenda*, Vol. 12, no. 2, Summer 1974, p.42
14. Ibid, p.38
15. Wade, p.774
16. *Letters to W.B. Yeats*, II, p.504
17. Wade, p.781
18. A.L. Rowse, *A Man of the Thirties*, pp.125–6

19. W.B. Yeats, 'An Indian Monk', in *Essays and Introductions*, pp.426–7
20. *Letters to W.B. Yeats*, II, p.534
21. Wade, p.796

VII: Forays from Rathfarnham: The Last Years 1932–1939

1 1932–1935

1. Basil Bunting's typescript is now part of the Yeats Collection, National Library of Ireland
2. Cited in Tim Pat Coogan, *De Valera: Long Fellow, Long Shadow*, p.501
3. Ibid, p.502
4. *Spectator*, no. 5513, 23 February 1934
5. Ashley Dukes, *The Scene is Changed*, p.190
6. *Ah Sweet Dancer*, p.26
7. Ibid, p.24
8. ibid, p.30
9. Ibid, p.26
10. Ibid, p.77
11. Ethel Mannin, *Privileged Spectator*, p.80
12. Ethel Mannin, *Sunset Over Dartmoor*, p.18
13. Sean O'Faolain, *Vive Moi! An Autobiography*, p.308
14. *Letters to W.B. Yeats*, p.559
15. W.B. Yeats, 'Introduction', Dorothy Wellesley, *Selected Poems*, pp.vii–viii
16. Virginia Woolf, *A Moment's Liberty: The Shorter Diary*, ed. Anne Olivier Bell, p.247
17. Quoted in Victoria Glendinning, *Vita: The Life of V. Sackville-West*, p.279

2 1935–1939

1. Helen Shaw (ed.), *Dear Lady Ginger: An Exchange of Letters between Lady Ottoline Morrell and D'Arcy Cresswell*, p.102
2. Sandra Jobson Darroch, *Ottoline: The Life of Lady Ottoline Morrell*, p.287
3. Harwood, pp.174–6
4. Wade, p.852
5. Margot Ruddock, *The Lemon Tree*, pp.4–5
6. Wade, p.875
7. *Privileged Spectator*, p.83
8. Wade, p.851
9. Ibid, p.864
10. Ibid, p.873
11. Ibid, p.874
12. Ibid, p.881
13. Ibid, p.879

14. Quoted in Diana Souhami, *Gluck: Her Biography*, p.216
15. In 'The Name', *On the Boiler*, p.9
16. Souhami, p.217
17. Idem
18. Idem
19. *Gonne–Yeats Letters*, p.48
20. Dorothy Wellesley (ed.), *Letters on Poetry from W.B. Yeats to Dorothy Wellesley*, p.213
21. Letter from Mabel O'Brien to Lily Yeats, 29 January 1939. Yeats Collection, National Library of Ireland, 30732
22. Souhami, p.217

[Bibliography]

Abbott, Claude Colleer (ed.). *Further Letters of Gerard Manley Hopkins*, London, Oxford University Press, 1956

Adams, Steven. *The Arts and Crafts Movement*, London, Apple Press, 1987

Allt, Peter and Alspach, Russell K. (eds.). *The Variorum Edition of the Poems of W.B. Yeats*, London, Macmillan, 1957

Alspach, Russell K. (ed.). *The Variorum Edition of the Plays of W.B. Yeats*, New York, Macmillan, 1966

Anon. 'W.B. Yeats at School: Interesting Reminiscences of the Irish Poet's Schooldays', *T.P.'s Weekly*, 7 June 1912

Antheil, George. *Bad Boy of Music*, New York, Doubleday, Doran & Co., 1945

Archibald, Douglas N. *John Butler Yeats*, Lewisburg, Bucknell University Press, 1974

Bax, Arnold. *Farewell, My Youth*, Westport, Connecticut, Greenwood Press, 1970

Bax, Clifford (ed.). *Florence Farr, Bernard Shaw, W.B. Yeats: Letters*, London, Hone & Van Thal, 1946

Beckson, Karl. *Arthur Symons: A Life*, Oxford, Clarendon Press 1987

Bell, Anne Olivier (ed.). *Virginia Woolf: A Moment's Liberty, The Shorter Diary*, London, The Hogarth Press, 1990

Birkenhead, Lord. *Rudyard Kipling*, London, Weidenfeld & Nicolson, 1978

Bloom, Harold. *Yeats*, New York, Oxford University Press, 1970

Bolsterli, Margaret Jones. *The Early Community of Bedford Park*, Ohio, Ohio University Press, 1977

Bridge, Ursula (ed.). *W.B. Yeats and T. Sturge Moore: Their Correspondence 1901–1937*, London, Routledge & Kegan Paul, 1953

Bunting, Basil. 'Yeats Recollected', *Agenda*, Vol. 12, no. 2, Summer 1974

Cain, Richard. *Susan L. Mitchell*, Lewisburg, Bucknell University Press, 1972

Cardozo, Nancy. *Lucky Eyes and a High Heart: The Life of Maud Gonne*, New York, The Bobbs-Merrill Company, 1978

Carswell, Catherine & Fay, W.G. *The Fays of the Abbey Theatre*, New York, Harcourt Brace, 1935

Chisholm, Anne. *Nancy Cunard*, London, Sidgwick & Jackson, 1979

Churchill, Winston S. *Great Contemporaries*, London, Odhams, 1947

Colum, Mary. 'Memories of Yeats', *The Saturday Review of Literature*, Vol. XIX, 25 February 1939

Coogan, Tim Pat. *De Valera: Long Fellow, Long Shadow*, London, Hutchinson, 1993

Cowell, John. *Sligo, Land of Yeats' Desire*, Dublin, O'Brien Press, 1990

Cullingford, Elizabeth. *Yeats, Ireland and Fascism*, Dublin, Gill & Macmillan, 1981

Darroch, Sandra Jobson. *Ottoline: The Life of Lady Ottoline Morrell*, New York, Coward, McCann & Geoghegan, 1975

Donoghue, Dennis. *Yeats*, London, Fontana Collins, 1971

Dukes, Ashley. *The Scene is Changed*, London, 1942

Dunleavy, Janet Eagleson and Dunleavy, Gareth W. *Douglas Hyde: A Maker of Modern Ireland*, Berkeley, University of California Press, 1991

Egan, Maurice. *Recollections of a Happy Life*, New York, Harcourt Brace, 1924

Eglinton, John. *A Memoir of AE*, London, Macmillan, 1937

——. 'Yeats at the High School', *The Erasmian: Dublin, The Magazine of the High School*, June 1939

Eliot, Valerie, ed. *The Letters of T.S. Eliot*. Volume I, *1989–1922*, London, Faber & Faber, 1988

Ellis, John Edwin and Yeats, W.B. (eds.). *The Works of William Blake, Poetic, Symbolic and Critical*, London, Bernard Quaritch, 1893

Ellmann, Richard. *James Joyce*, London, Oxford University Press, 1966

——. *Golden Codgers: Biographical Speculations*, London, Oxford University Press, 1973

——. *Yeats: The Man and the Masks*, Harmondsworth, Penguin, 1988

——. *The Identity of Yeats*, New York, Oxford University Press, 1964

Fahy, Catherine. *W.B. Yeats and his Circle*, Dublin, National Library of Ireland, 1989

Fallon, Ann Connerton. *Katharine Tynan*, Boston, Twayne Books, 1979

Fay, Garard. *The Abbey Theatre*, London, Hollis & Carter, 1958

Fingall, Elizabeth Countess of. *Seventy Years Young*, London, Collins, 1937

Finneran, Richard J.; Harper, George Mills; Murphy, William M. (eds.). *Letters to W.B. Yeats*, London, Macmillan, 1977

Finneran, Richard J. (ed.). *The Correspondence of Robert Bridges and W.B. Yeats*, London, Macmillan, 1977

—— (ed.). *W.B. Yeats: The Poems: A New Edition*, London, Macmillan, 1984

Foster, R.F. *Paddy and Mr Punch: Connections in Irish and English History*, London, Allen Lane, 1993

Fraser, Grace Lovat. *In the Days of My Youth*, London, n.d.

Frayne, John P. (ed.). *Uncollected Prose of W.B. Yeats*, London, Macmillan, 1970

Glenavy, Lady Beatrice. *Today We Will Only Gossip*, London, Constable, 1964

Glendinning, Victoria. *Vita: The Life of V. Sackville-West*, London, Weidenfeld & Nicolson, 1983

Goldring, Douglas. *South Lodge*, London, Constable, 1943

——. *The Nineteen Twenties*, London, Nicholson & Watson, 1945

Greene, David H. and Stephens, Edward. *J.M. Synge 1871–1909*, New York, New York University Press, 1989

Gregory, Lady Augusta. *Seventy Years*, Gerrards Cross, Colin Smythe, 1974

——. *Fifty Years After*, ed. Ann Saddlemyer and Colin Smythe, Gerrards Cross, Colin Smythe, 1987

Hardwick, Joan. *The Yeats Sisters*, London and San Francisco, Pandora, 1996

Harper, George Mills and Hood, Walter Kelly (eds.). *Critical Edition of Yeats's A Vision 1925*, London, Macmillan, 1978

Harper, George Mills. (ed.). *Yeats's Vision Papers*, Iowa, Iowa University Press, 1992

——. *Yeats's Golden Dawn*, New York, Barnes & Noble, 1974

——. *W.B. Yeats and W.T. Horton: a Record of an Occult Friendship*, London, Macmillan, 1980

Harwood, John. *Olivia Shakespear and W.B. Yeats: After Long Silence*, New York, St Martin's Press, 1989

Hauptmann, Gerhart. *Diarium 1917 bis 1933*, Herausgegeben von Martin Machatzhe, Frankfurt am Main, Propyläen, 1980

Himber, Alan (ed.). *The Letters of John Quinn to William Butler Yeats*, Ann Arbor, UMI Research Press, 1983

Holroyd, Michael. *Bernard Shaw*, Volume I, *1856–1898, The Search for Love*, London, Chatto & Windus, 1988

Hone, Joseph. *W.B. Yeats 1865–1939*, London, Macmillan, 1962

——. *The Life of George Moore*, London, Gollancz, 1936

—— (ed.). *John Butler Yeats: Letters to his Son W.B. Yeats and Others*, London, Secker & Warburg, 1983

Jeffares, A. Norman and Gould, Warwick (eds.). *Yeats's Poems*, London, Macmillan, 1989

Jeffares, A. Norman. *W.B. Yeats: The Critical Heritage*, London, Routledge & Kegan Paul, 1977

——. *W.B. Yeats: A New Biography*, London, Arena, 1990

—— (ed.). *Yeats the European*, Savage, Maryland, Barnes and Noble, 1989

—— (ed.). *Yeats, Sligo and Ireland*, Gerrards Cross, Colin Smythe, 1980

Johnson, Harold E. *Jean Sibelius*, New York, Knopf, 1959

Johnson, Josephine. *Florence Farr: Bernard Shaw's New Woman*, Gerrards Cross, Colin Smythe, 1975

Johnson, Lionel. *Post Liminium: Essays and Critical Papers*, London, Elkin Mathews, 1912

Jullian, Philippe. *Oscar Wilde*, trans. Violet Wyndham, New York, Viking, 1968

Kee, Robert. *Ireland: A History*, London, Sphere Books, 1982

Kelly, John and Domville, Eric (eds.). *The Collected Letters of W.B. Yeats*, Volume 1, Oxford, Oxford University Press, 1986

Kelly, John and Schuchard, Ronald (eds.). *The Collected Letters of W.B. Yeats*, Volume 3, *1901–1904*, Oxford, Oxford University Press, 1994

Kenny, Michael. *The Fenians*, Dublin, National Museum of Ireland, 1994

Kilroy, James. *The Playboy Riots*, Dublin, Dolmen Press, 1971

King, Francis. *Modern Ritual Magic: The Rise of Western Occultism*, Bridport, Dorset, Prism Press, 1989

Kirby, Sheelah. *The Yeats Country*, Sligo, Dolmen Press, 1985

Kohfeldt, Mary Lou. *Lady Gregory: The Woman Behind the Irish Renaissance*, New York, Atheneum, 1985

Kuch, Peter. *Yeats and AE: The Antagonism that unites Dear Friends*, Gerrards Cross, Colin Smythe, 1986

Lavery, John. *The Life of a Painter*, London, Cassell, 1940

Lawrence, D.H. 'Study of Thomas Hardy', *Phoenix*, London, Heinemann, 1936

Levenson, Samuel. *Maud Gonne*, New York, Reader's Digest, 1976

Lewis, Giffard. *The Yeats Sisters and the Cuala*, Dublin, Irish Academic Press, 1994

Longenbach, James. *Stone Cottage: Pound, Yeats, and Modernism*, New York, Oxford University Press, 1988

MacBride, Maud Gonne. *A Servant of the Queen*, London, Gollancz, 1938

McHugh, Roger (ed.). *W.B. Yeats: Letters to Katharine Tynan*, Dublin, Clonmore & Reynolds, 1953

—— (ed.). *Ah Sweet Dancer. W.B. Yeats–Margaret Ruddock. A Correspondence*, London, Macmillan, 1970

Mannin, Ethel. *Privileged Spectator*, London, Jarrolds, 1939

——. *Sunset Over Dartmoor*, London, Hutchinson, 1977

Marcus, Phillip L.; Gould, Warwick; Siddell, Michael J. (eds.). *The Secret Rose: Stories by W.B. Yeats: A Variorum Edition*, Ithaca, NY, Cornell University Press, 1981

Martin, Augustine. *W.B. Yeats*, Gerrards Cross, Colin Smythe, 1990

Masefield, John. *So Long to Learn: Chapters of an Autobiography*, London, Heinemann, 1952

——. *Some Memories of W.B. Yeats*, New York, Macmillan, 1940

Masters, Brian. *Now Barrabas was a Rotter: The Extraordinary Life of Marie Corelli*, London, Hamish Hamilton, 1928

Meyers, Jeffrey. *Joseph Conrad: A Biography*, London, John Murray, 1991

Miller, Liam. *The Dun Emer Press, Later the Cuala Press*, Dublin, Dolmen Press, 1973

Moore, Virginia. *The Unicorn*, New York, Macmillan, 1954

Murphy, William M. *Family Secrets: William Butler Yeats and His Relatives*, Syracuse, Syracuse University Press, 1995

——. *Prodigal Father: The Life of John Butler Yeats 1839–1922*, Ithaca, Cornell University Press, 1978

Maddox, Betty. [ret. in Harold Bloom as good biographer of Yeats]

Nelson, James G. *Elkin Mathews: Publisher to Yeats, Joyce, Pound*, Wisconsin, University of Wisconsin Press, 1989

O'Casey, Sean. *Autobiographies II*, London, Macmillan, 1963

O'Connor, Garry. *Sean O'Casey: A Life*, London, Hodder & Stoughton, 1988

O'Donnell, William H. (ed.). *The Speckled Bird by William Butler Yeats*, Toronto, McClelland & Stewart, 1976

O'Faolain, Sean. *Vive Moi! An Autobiography*, London, Sinclair Stevenson, 1993

O'Leary, John. *Young Ireland. The Old and the New*, Dublin, Young Ireland Society, 1885

Pearce, Donald R. (ed.). *The Senate Speeches of W.B. Yeats*, London, Faber & Faber, 1960

Pound, Ezra (ed.). *Passages from the Letters of John Butler Yeats*, Churchtown, Cuala Press, 1917

Pound, Omar and Litz, A. Walton (eds.). *Ezra Pound and Dorothy Shakespear: Their Letters 1909–1914*, London, Faber & Faber, 1985

Pound, Omar and Spoo, Robert (eds.). *Ezra Pound and Margaret Cravens: A Tragic Friendship 1910–1912*, Durham and London, Duke University Press, 1988

Pyle, Hilary. *Jack B. Yeats: A Biography*, London, André Deutsch, 1989

Ransome, Arthur. *Bohemia in London*, London, 1907, reprinted by Oxford University Press, 1984

Read, Forrest (ed.). *The Letters of Ezra Pound to James Joyce*, London, Faber, 1968

Reid, B.L. *The Man from New York: John Quinn and his Friends*, New York, Oxford University Press, 1968

Rhys, Ernest. *Wales England Wed: An Autobiography*, London, J.M. Dent, 1940

Rowse, A.L. *A Man of the Thirties*, London, Weidenfeld & Nicolson, 1979

Ruddock, Margaret. *The Lemon Tree*, London, J.M. Dent & Sons Ltd, 1937

Saddlemeyer, Ann, *Theatre Business: The Correspondence of the First Abbey Theatre Directors, W.B. Yeats, Lady Gregory and J.M. Synge*, Gerrards Cross, Colin Smythe, 1982

Shaw, Helen (ed.). *Dear Lady Ginger: An Exchange of Letters between Lady Ottoline Morrell and D'Arcy Cresswell*, London, Century, 1984

Shiubhlaigh, Maire nic. *The Splendid Years*, Dublin, Duffy, 1955

Sinnett, A.P. *Esoteric Buddhism*, London, Trübner & Co., 1883

Smith, Constance Babington. *John Masefield*, London, Oxford University Press, 1978

Smyllie, R.M. *Irish Literary Portraits*, 1972

Somerset Fry, Peter and Fiona. *A History of Ireland*, London, Routledge, 1991

Souhami, Diana. *Gluck: Her Biography*, London, Pandora, 1988

Strong, L.A.G. *Green Memories*, London, Methuen, 1961

Summerfield, Henry. *That Myriad Minded Man: A Biography of G.W. Russell – AE*, Gerrards Cross, Colin Smythe, 1975

Torchiana, Donald. *Yeats and Georgian Ireland*, London, Oxford University Press, 1966

Tuohy, Frank. *Yeats*, Dublin, Gill & Macmillan, 1976

Tynan, Katharine. *Twenty-five Years: Reminiscences*, London, Smith Elder, 1913

——. *The Middle Years*, London, Constable, 1916

Unterecker, John. *Yeats and Patrick McCartan: A Fenian Friendship*, Dublin, Dolmen, 1967

Van Voris, Jacqueline. *Constance Markievicz: In the Cause of Ireland*, Amherst, University of Massachusetts Press, 1967

Vendler, Helen Hennessy. *Yeats's Vision and the Later Plays*, Cambridge Massachusetts, Harvard University Press, 1963

Wade, Allan (ed.). *The Letters of W.B. Yeats*, London, Rupert Hart Davis, 1954

Ward, Margaret. *Maud Gonne: Ireland's Joan of Arc*, London, Pandora Press, 1990

Webster, Brenda. *Yeats: A Psychoanalytic Study*, London, Macmillan, 1973

Wellesley, Dorothy. *Selected Poems*, London, Williams & Norgate, 1949

——. (ed.) *Letters on Poetry from W.B. Yeats to Dorothy Wellesley*, London, Oxford University Press, 1964

White, Anna MacBride and Jeffares, A. Norman. *The Gonne–Yeats Letters 1893–1939*, London, Hutchinson, 1992

White, Colin. *Edmund Dulac*, London, Studio Vista, 1976

White, Terence de Vere. *Kevin O'Higgins*, London, Methuen, 1948

——. *The Anglo-Irish*, London, Gollancz, 1972

Wilhelm, J.J. *Ezra Pound in London and Paris 1908–1925*, Pennsylvania State University Press, 1990

Wilson, Angus. *The Strange Ride of Rudyard Kipling: His Life and Works*, London, Secker & Warburg, 1977

Woolf, Virginia, *A Moment's Liberty: The Shorter Diary*, London, Hogarth Press, 1990

Yeats, John B. *Essays Irish and American*, New York, Books for Libraries Press, 1969

Yeats, William Butler. *Letters to the New Island*, Cambridge, Harvard University Press, 1934

——. *Explorations*, London, Macmillan, 1962

——. *A Vision*, London, Macmillan, 1961

——. *Collected Poems*, London, Macmillan, 1961 and 1950

——. *John Sherman and Dhoya* by Ganconagh, London, T. Fisher Unwin, 1891

——. *Fairy and Folk Tales of the Irish Peasantry*, Gerrards Cross, Colin Smythe, 1977

——. *Memoirs*, transcribed and edited by Denis Donoghue, London, Papermac, 1988

——. *Essays and Introductions*, London, Macmillan, 1989

——. *On the Boiler*, Dublin, Cuala Press, 1939

——. *Mythologies*, London, Macmillan, 1992

——. *Autobiographies*, London, Macmillan, 1955

——. *Representative Irish Tales*, Atlantic Highlands, N.J., Humanities Press, 1979

[Index]